Geoffrey Robertson QC is recognised as human rights advocates, whose work as has been a key inspiration for the glo and educated in Sydney, and then at Oxford as a Rhodes Scholar, Mr Robertson has had a distinguished career at the English bar, as a Queen's Counsel and as founder and head of Doughty Street Chambers, Europe's largest human rights practice. He has appeared in many celebrated cases, prosecuting Hastings Banda and General Pinochet and defending Salman Rushdie and Julian Assange.

He served as first President of the Special War Crimes Court in Sierra Leone and in 2008 was appointed by Ban ki-Moon as a 'distinguished jurist' member of the UN's Internal Justice Council. In 2011 he was awarded the New York Bar Association's prize for achievement in international law and affairs.

Mr Robertson is a Master of the Middle Temple and visiting professor in Human Rights Law at the New College of Humanities. His books include *The Tyrannicide Brief*, which led to a re-evaluation of English civil war history; *Does Dracula Have Aids?*; *Mullahs Without Mercy: Human Rights and Nuclear Weapons*; *The Case of the Pope*; an acclaimed memoir (*The Justice Game*); and the influential text *Crimes Against Humanity – the Struggle for Global Justice*.

Mr Robertson lives in London with his wife, the author Kathy Lette, and their two children. He returns to Australia regularly to visit family and conduct his trademark *Hypothetical*.

Praise for *Dreaming Too Loud*

'As ever from Robertson, wonderful insights and great writing' Peter FitzSimons

'A superb, illuminating and powerful book written by a great Australian with a true passion for Australia and its history. Challenging, humorous and informative. And most important of all, a riveting read' David Hill

'Geoffrey Robertson is one of the most opinionated Australians living. I would thank God for that fact, except that this book reveals that he recently addressed the Global Atheists' Convention. Here are wonderful essays on the Queen, Dr Haneef, Lady Chatterley, Doc Evatt, successive popes, Christopher Hitchens, Julian Assange and a great parade of larger than life Antipodean characters. No icon connected with Down Under is safe from his withering gaze. Which is why he is so loved – and listened to – in Australia. A great read. Bound to upset. A tonic to be taken once a day to ward off latent conservative tendencies' Hon Michael Kirby AC CMG

Also by Geoffrey Robertson

Reluctant Judas
Obscenity
Freedom, the Individual and the Law
Geoffrey Robertson's Hypotheticals (Vols 1 & 2)
Does Dracula Have AIDS?
Robertson & Nicol on Media Law
The Justice Game
Crimes Against Humanity
The Tyrannicide Brief
The Levellers: The Putney Debates
The Statute of Liberty
The Case of the Pope
Mullahs Without Mercy: Human Rights and Nuclear Weapons

DREAMING TOO LOUD

Reflections on a race apart

GEOFFREY ROBERTSON

VINTAGE BOOKS
Australia

A Vintage book
Published by Random House Australia Pty Ltd
Level 3, 100 Pacific Highway, North Sydney NSW 2060
www.randomhouse.com.au

First published by Vintage in 2013

Addresses for companies within the Random House Group can be found at
www.randomhouse.com.au/offices

National Library of Australia
Cataloguing-in-Publication entry

Robertson, Geoffrey, author
Dreaming too loud/Geoffrey Robertson

ISBN 978 0 85798 189 9 (paperback)

Robertson, Geoffrey – Anecdotes
Human rights
Australia – History – Anecdotes
Australia – Social life and customs – Anecdotes
Australia – Social conditions – Anecdotes
Australia – Biography – Anecdotes

919.404

Front cover image and design: Design by Committee
Inside front cover image: *Geoffrey Robertson QC*, 1999, oil on board by David Boyd;
donated by Mr Frank Robertson through the Australian Government's Cultural Gifts
Program 2010 to the University Art Collection, University of Sydney. Licensed by
Viscopy, 2013. Image photographed by Eva Breuer Art Dealer, Sydney, representing the
late David Boyd and works in the Estate of the artist.
Map on p. 120 © Ice Cold Publishing
Typeset in Sabon 11.5pt on 14 by Midland Typesetters, Australia
Printed in Australia by Griffin Press, an accredited ISO AS/NZS 14001:2004
Environmental Management System printer

Random House Australia uses papers that are natural, renewable and recyclable
products and made from wood grown in sustainable forests. The logging and
manufacturing processes are expected to conform to the environmental regulations of
the country of origin.

CONTENTS

In loving memory of

Harold and Florence Robertson and Henry and Bernice Beattie

Time present and time past
Are both perhaps present in time future
And time future contained in time past
If all time is eternally present
All time is unredeemable.

T. S. Eliot, *Four Quartets*

'Ned Kelly told Tom Curnow that he and his family were free to go, suggesting that they go directly home and then straight to bed, warning Tom, "Don't dream too loud." He then casually suggested that if he did, he would probably be shot.'

Ian W. Shaw, *Glenrowan*

PRELUDE: QUIZINE

Once upon a time, I devised a program for the national broad-caster called Hypotheticals. *As soon as it began to rate in the top ten, ABC executives in their wisdom decided that it was 'a bit dated', and asked me instead to host a quiz show. I declined the opportunity to master this groundbreaking format, but a few years ago I was asked by the Australia Council to devise a new kind of entertainment for leaders of Sydney's artistic and business communities, who would sit in teams on tables at the Art Gallery of New South Wales, contribute to a good cause, and try to win a crate of Penfolds Grange. The competition comprised questions to which I thought well-rounded Austra-lians should know the answers, plus references to the gallery art and particularly to the cuisine that was being experienced on the night. Here are the questions. Answers can be found by reading this book or (to save time) by turning to page 419. The exercise was called 'Quizine', in honour of the flavours and bouquets of Bill Granger's banquet, which cannot, alas, be reproduced in print.*

ROUND 1: AUSTRALIAN HISTORY

1. Who named Australia? Bonus point if you can name his cat.
2. From which island did Captain Cook descry the break in the Great Barrier Reef through which he sailed the *Endeavour* back to Britain?

3. Where is white Australia's founding father, Vice Admiral Arthur Phillip, buried?

4. The only armed revolt by Aborigines against white settler power was led by a police tracker known as Pigeon. Where did he and his army make their last stand?

5. When did Australia become independent?

6. What was the name of the schoolteacher at Glenrowan who fooled the Kelly Gang and prevented a terrorist atrocity?

7. In 1916 the family name of the Australian head of state was changed to 'Windsor' in order to avoid association with Germany. What was their original name?

8. John Howard's Gallipoli hero was Simpson, the man with the donkey. Where did Simpson hail from?

9. Eleanor Roosevelt handed the *Universal Declaration of Human Rights* to the President of the UN General Assembly on 10 December 1948, proclaiming it 'the *Magna Carta* of mankind'. The president's name?

10. Which prominent New South Wales politician terminated a debate in the Upper House by crossing the floor and urinating in his opponent's ear?

ROUND 2: FLORA, FAUNA & FORA

1. What shared characteristic makes the kangaroo and emu appropriate symbols for the emblem of a progressive nation?

2. Which marsupial has the largest brain and the most deadly bottom?

3. What animal other than the big red kangaroo can kill you with its back legs?

4. What African animal brought down a New South Wales Labor government when its speaker, Ray Maher, dropped his trousers and imitated its facial features to his secretary, Miss Shepherd?

5. How did Blinky Bill's father meet his fate?

6. The emu and the cassowary are flightless birds belonging to what species?

7. Baby koalas are fed on their mother's what?

8. What flower adorned Sir Robert Menzies' chest?

9. Where was the picnic at Hanging Rock?

10. The Beaumont children went missing from what beach?

ROUND 3: BUSINESS

1. For what purported financial institution did Christopher Skase work before moving on to Qintex? Bonus point for journalists: how much older was Pixie?

2. Where did BHP begin operations? For a bonus point, when did they begin?

3. The Aboriginal word for message stick was chosen by the late Gordon Barton as his corporate vehicle – what was it?

4. In what city was the first stock exchange, and when was it established?

5. Of which Sydney business identity did Neville Wran say 'I wouldn't hang a dog on his evidence'? Bonus point, which well-connected woman did that person get away with murdering?

6. What nationality was Tirath Khemlani?

7. In 1986 then Treasurer Paul Keating remarked to John Laws that Australia was in danger of becoming a 'Banana Republic' because of the size of our debt to GDP. Where was the original Banana Republic?

8. In the 1950s, an Australian working in Melbourne invented a piece of equipment now used in every aircraft. What is it? For a bonus two points, what was his name?

9. The High Court case of *Finn v Commissioner of Taxation* is beloved of all Australian professionals because it allows them to deduct the cost of overseas travel to attend

'conferences' in London, Paris, Acapulco etc. Finn was a member of which profession?

10. Sir Richard Branson was prosecuted in England in 1977 for publishing an indecent record cover. What was its title?

ROUND 4: ART AND MUSIC

1. The painting *The Golden Fleece* hangs in the Art Gallery of New South Wales. What was its original title?
   a. *Men at Work*
   b. *Shearing at Newstead*
   c. *Click Go the Shears*
   d. *Heidelberg Exhibition No. 23*

2. *On the Wallaby Track* was painted in the 1890s and hangs in the Art Gallery of New South Wales. What is the artist's name?

3. 'Buy a Kodak and win the Archibald' was the protest against the painting that won the 1943 prize and became the subject of a celebrated court case.
   a. Who painted it?
   b. Of whom is it painted?
   c. Which young KC made his name by representing the plaintiff?

4. What was Dame Nellie Melba's real name? Was she born:
   a. Isobel Marion Mackellar?
   b. Grace Ethel Dorrington?
   c. Helen Porter Mitchell?
   d. Maria Anna Schicklgruber?

5. Which creative Australian describes his mental state thus: 'I walk around with a bunch of violets in my hand and a sledgehammer and grain of sand in my head. I am happy'?
   a. Robert Hughes
   b. Michael Hutchence

   c. Albert Namatjira

   d. Brett Whiteley

   e. Percy Grainger

6. In *Turandot*, Calaf must answer this riddle: 'What flickers red and warm like a flame and is not a fire?' What is his answer?

7. In 1956, Sydney Symphony Orchestra conductor Sir Eugene Goossens was arrested at Sydney Airport on his return from London with over a thousand pornographic pictures hidden inside his score of *Salome*. Some of them featured a well-known Kings Cross identity dabbling in what she termed 'Sex Magic'. What was her name? A bonus point if you can name the magical act.

8. In *The Pirates of Penzance*, the modern major-general is momentarily stumped over a rhyme for the word 'strategy'.

   a. What does he come up with?

   b. For a bonus point, can you do better?

9. When Eddie McGuire said he would like to 'bone' Jessica Rowe, did he mean he would like to:

   a. fillet her?

   b. fire her?

   c. fornicate with her?

   d. all of the above?

10. Set out the second verse of our national anthem (bonus points for every two lines that are correct).

ROUND 5: SPORT

1. What sporting hero is unwittingly celebrated by the ABC's PO Box 9994 ('triple nine four in your capital city').

2. Who played the last rubber to clinch Australia's victory in the 1953 Davis Cup?

3. Where was golf invented?

4. Who said words to the effect of 'Waiting for the Cronulla

Sharks to win the premiership was like leaving the porch light on for Harold Holt'?

   a. Alan Jones

   b. Jack Gibson

   c. Rex Mossop

5. In the notorious 1936 Olympics in Hitler's Berlin, Australia won only one medal. Jack Metcalfe took bronze in what event?

6. What was originally the name of the team that became the Sydney Swans?

7. In the 'Fine Cotton Affair', what was the name of the substitute horse?

8. Who was the first Australian to run the four-minute mile?

9. Compose a seemingly authentic Shane Warne text message.

10. Which prime minister's wife represented Australia in the third Empire Games in 1938?

ROUND 6: LITERATURE AND FILM

1. Who were the co-stars of the 1959 film of the novel *On the Beach* by Nevil Shute?

2. Australian-born writer and Booker Prize winner Peter Finlay is better known as DBC Pierre. What does DBC stand for?

3. Patrick White won the Nobel Prize for Literature in 1973, but refused to travel to Stockholm to accept the award from the king of Sweden. Who did he send to accept it on his behalf?

   a. Manoly Lascaris

   b. Sidney Nolan

   c. Robert Helpmann

   d. The young David Marr

4. *The Fortunes of Richard Mahoney* was written by the pseudonymous male Henry Handel Richardson. What was the author's real name?

5. 'Such is life' are allegedly Ned Kelly's last words but they were also the title of an early Australian novel by Joseph Furphy. What pseudonym did he use?

6. In 1969 the New South Wales government banned the rock musical *Hair* but relented when which important person danced on stage at its London production?

7. What is the meaning of Life, the Universe and Everything – according to Douglas Adams in *The Hitchhiker's Guide to the Galaxy*?

8. Which published Australian poet attempted to assassinate a leader of the ALP under the delusion that he had to kill an important world figure, and who did he try to kill?

9. Who was it that said of Charlie Chaplin, 'He's not dead, he's just touring Australia'?
   a. Barry Humphries
   b. Spike Milligan
   c. Peter Ustinov

10. Which touring and towering literary figure described the kookaburra's laugh as 'like a maniac consumed with humorous scorn over a cheap and degraded pun'?
    a. D. H. Lawrence
    b. Mark Twain
    c. Bill Bryson
    d. Kathy Lette

11. Classic Australian humour: why is a can of Fosters like sex on the beach?

And so it went, into the night, with further rounds on art and music, and the food and drink set out on the table. I can't remember who won, but I do recall Philip Ruddock's embarrassment when the media subsequently revealed that none of the movers and shakers in the room could answer the final question: 'On the way home tonight, you encounter Jihad Jack with a bag of agricultural chemicals and a box of matches. To dial the terrorist hotline, what number do you ring?'

So much for the government's multi-million-dollar advertising campaign for 1800 1234 00, and all those fridge magnets.

PREFACE

The View from Lizard Island

The perspectives on Australian history, politics and people reflected in this book are those of an Australian who is now a dual citizen of the UK: one who lives and works in both countries, who has his prostate checked in Harley Street and his teeth maintained in Macquarie Street (look at an English smile and you will understand why). Australians abroad are not necessarily appreciated: just before I was to cross-examine the late Princess Diana, I found myself described in *The Times* as 'anti-establishment, republican and Australian' – presumably in ascending order of horror. We are all victims of the image we have allowed Fosters to foster.

Although an expatriate, I am not an ex-patriot: I remain an often proud, sometimes appalled, member of what can by now be called the Australian race. ('Race: a group of persons connected by common descent or origin,' *Oxford English Dictionary*.) For critical race theorists, who reject biology and ethnicity as criteria, the truly defining character of a race is how its members' history has contributed to a distinctive moral outlook that they wish to preserve and carry into their future. What might our 'distinctive moral outlook' be? Other races teach national solidarity through patriotic songs and preambles to their constitutions, but we have given our children nothing they can recite with pride. We have a national anthem, the second verse of which we seem to have a mental block about singing, for fear its words

> For those who've come across the sea
> We've boundless plains to share

might encourage asylum seekers. It was a failure of nerve, not of moral vision, when Australians voted to foist the doggerel of 'Advance Australia Fair' on children at school assemblies and on medal-winning Olympians. The astonishing, beautiful and different 'Waltzing Matilda', with its haunting story of a homeless man who takes his life rather than lose his liberty, would have made the world's most interesting (and most tuneful) anthem, appropriate for a race apart, separated by sea and the kindness of distance from the rest of the world.

When I commenced to travel that world, in the 1970s, carrying an Australian passport was the easiest way of crossing borders, avoiding arguments and not being taken hostage. That has changed: we want to be connected with other countries in more ways than on the internet, so our alliances (especially with America) attract terrorist attention and our currency – propped up by Chinese demand for our resources – makes overseas travel so much cheaper. Irritatingly, we are still edged out of the G8 by a country as colourless as Canada, and our fabled post-war sporting prowess, to which my generation contributed, now seems to be fast fading. Expatriates notice these things. We perceive the ironies, too, when a multi-lingual prime minister (Kevin Rudd) can teach an English yob (Gordon Ramsay) how to be polite to Tracy Grimshaw. It took a female prime minister, however, to provoke that deep-vein sex hate that infects some inadequate Australian males. We watch with pleasure as wine sales increase and surveys announce that Australians are reading more books and attending more cultural events than the people of any other nation. Of course, there was the 'children overboard' disgrace, the barbed wire over the Woomera refugee camp, the refusal to contemplate gay marriage, the increase in obesity (all the fine wine and nibbles at those cultural events) and, always and irremediably, Aboriginal disadvantage. But when the news is of natural disasters – fires or floods in the sunburnt country – we grieve as sincerely as if we were there. We are lassoed by a psychological umbilical cord, drawn back in imagination to the warm beaches and cold beer of our mother country. And distance, if it sometimes lends too much enchantment to the view, may also provide perspective.

The perspective from which I write or speak about Australia is, I like to think, the view from Lizard Island – a place without which Australia would not have become Australia. It might instead be a French municipal colony once discovered by La Perouse or a part of the Portuguese-speaking, badly governed and impoverished global south. Lizard is several kilometres offshore from Cooktown in Northern Queensland, with a small mountain that overlooks the distant ribbon of the Barrier Reef. When, in 1770, HMS *Endeavour* smashed on the reef and laid up on the mainland for repairs, its crew despaired of ever getting back to England. James Cook took the longboat and rowed to Lizard. He clambered up to the top of its hill twice (the first time the view was too foggy) and in full naval uniform (it takes me three hours in running gear, up a cleared track). From the headland, he could faintly discern a tiny break in the reef that had imprisoned his ship. He took *Endeavour* to it and through it, to bring back to London the tidings and maps of the Great South Land that convinced the Admiralty to settle convicts in Sydney. To look from Lizard Island is to glimpse both a means of escape and the promise of return. Every Australian schoolboy and schoolgirl should be taken there, made to climb that hill and look for the opening in the reef, and think on the whirligigs of time. What should be one of Australia's most sacred places is now just another up-market tourist resort, which bans children.

Turn Cook's telescope around, however, and extend its focus two thousand kilometres across the continent to a gorge in the Western Kimberleys named Windjana. This is an eerie, silent place, the high ochre rocks casting their silhouette over its limpid green pools studded with black logs that turn out to be crocodiles. Poke around in the sand and you may find an old musket bullet, or a shard of bone, because this is Australia's only civil war battleground. It was here that a small Aboriginal army was massacred one hundred and fifty years ago. It was led by Jandamarra, a charismatic police black tracker nicknamed Pigeon, who turned rebel. He stole police guns and quickly recruited and trained other Aborigines incensed at the white settlers who had invaded their spirit sites, polluted their water with cattle and scared away their game. Take a four-wheel drive along the track that diverts from the highway between Derby and Fitzroy Crossing and you pass a few burnt-out police stations before you reach the site of the massacre. Although early settlers suffered isolated incidents of reprisal spearings and counter-attacks, this is the only armed resistance in Australian history that could be termed a battle, where Aboriginals fought the colonists with their own weapons in a doomed attempt to liberate their stolen land.

The essays and speeches collected in this book peer through Cook's telescope to find white heroes in our history – Arthur Phillip, Tom Curnow, John Jackson, 'Doc' Evatt, Michael Kirby – but it swivels to see the beaten people that Windjana symbol- ises. The bog at Cunnamulla, spreading the disease that took Nancy Young's child; the stolen children; all the false promises once made to a people whose 'degenerate' traits we now respect – they have taught us to dream, to be easy-going, to suffer adver- sity nobly and to find our way through the bush. I said that in a Bicentennial oration (Chapter 1) and I can see no reason to update the sentiments: a quarter of a century on, perhaps most people would agree.

Other speeches and articles strike more provocative notes. They mainly bear on Australia – a reinterpretation of its past or a hope for its future. Some of my dreaming is a politician's nightmare – a charter, for example, or a republic or even a preamble to the constitution, but I persist in thinking that these are not lost causes. The book includes some reflections on worldwide problems that resonate here, such as torture and terrorism and the Catholic Church, added as examples of what I care about in my professional life. For an old friend, Christopher Hitchens, there is a reprint of the lecture dedicated to his memory at the 2012 Global Atheists Convention. There are stories as well, from both World Wars, updated by articles on Guantanamo Bay and targeted killings with drones. In the final section, I have tried to answer the question most often asked of me in recent years, namely what I think about Julian Assange.

My gratitude for assisting this publication goes to Nikki Christer and Catherine Hill at Random House, to Judy Rollinson and Toby Collis at Doughty Street, to Kathy Lette, Julius and Georgina at home; and to friends who have kept me abreast of events in Australia – especially Lesley Holden, Jen Robinson, Julian Disney, David and Kristen Williamson, Richard Neville, Tim Robertson, Patrick Cook, Dick and Pip Smith, Jane Mills, Giampaulo Pertosi, Patrick George, and Jim and Alice Spigelman. I am utterly indebted to my parents for their love and longevity. To the organisations that invited me to give the lectures and the newspapers and journals that published the articles here collected, thanks for giving me the opportunity to dream so loudly.

Doughty Street Chambers
September 2013

AUSTRALIANA

Chapter 1

BEYOND THE BICENTENNIAL

The dawn of 1988 found me freezing on the Portsmouth dock, surrounded by horses and carts with amateur actors dressed up as the convicts, marines, whores and villains of Georgian England. By what seemed then a miracle of modern commun- ications, my two-minute 'grab' describing the scene at the departure of Captain Arthur Phillip's floating prison would be downloaded from the ether by Phillip Adams and thrown to Ernie Dingo, spear in hand, warily watching from the shore of Botany Bay as the tall ships moved into view a few seconds (a.k.a. nine months) later. Australians were awed, if not awe- inspired, by Australia Live – *the Bicentennial telecast. (A more recent poll has revealed that most of them do not know what they are celebrating on 26 January, other than a holiday.)*

On this day in 1988, at the invitation of the city of Launces- ton in Tasmania, I ventured my explanation of 1788 and all that by delivering an oration to celebrate the two-hundredth anniversary of white settlement in Australia.

On this historic day, it's a privilege to share with you some thoughts about our past and our future as citizens of Australia, and as Australian citizens of the world. Two days ago I slipped the surly bonds of earth at Heathrow Airport and climbed to cruising altitude above the fogbound fields of Surrey, which were left in 1816 by my first Australian ancestor, a young lieutenant of marines on convict escort duty. We hit turbulence over Turkey, where a grand-uncle fell like a Trojan on that Gallipoli beach, not far from Homer's 'windy city' of Troy. On Sunday we descended over Singapore Harbour, where an uncle I never knew lies drowned in *The Perth* – an Australian warship sunk when that city fell to the Japanese. These images of death and of distance, of curious connection with countries and legends that have shaped our modern world, haunted me as QF2 homed in on this Bicentennial beacon. I can only think of this event in the way that airline pilots think of radio beacons; they call them 'way-points' – an aid to work out how far we have come, and how far we have yet to go.

Those whose epic and dangerous voyage we celebrate today took over eight months to sail from Portsmouth to Sydney Cove. My weekend journey from London took twenty-two hours, with no greater hazard than Qantas food. Yet in that insignificant tick of time, I covered a distance which has not been our tyranny, but our protection. Distance has been the making of us, and it has made us different. Australia has made what criminologists call 'a fresh start' – without the burden of expectations created by long social evolution or violent revolution. Invasion, plague and rebellion have not troubled us, we have acquired no special ideological fervour or savage class divisions, no view of ourselves as saints or missionaries ramming capitalism or communism, or Protestantism or Catholicism, down others' throats. We have inherited the best thing about Britain – its institutions. We have been joined, over two centuries, by people from Europe, America, Asia and the Middle East, coming to Australia for refuge or adventure, bringing us vivid memories of what they have most valued in their culture and in their family life and their traditions. We have taken a hard but yielding land, richer than most for primary industry and astonishing in its grave and shimmering beauty. A land we have taken the liberty of sharing with an ancient, noble and comparatively gentle people who occupied it for thousands of years before the fall of Troy. Our very distance has lent us enchantment; we are, in world terms, a unique social experiment.

I don't intend to measure our achievements in terms of gross national product or physical comfort or gold medals at games, but in terms of whether we have acquired any sort of distinctive moral visions that we can be proud to call Australian. We are, after all, celebrating today what was a squalid and pitiless project to relieve overcrowding in British prisons by establishing a 'colony of thieves'; two hundred years on, we are in a position to give rather than to take. In developing any distinctively Australian moral vision, how far have we come, and how far have we yet to go?

To answer that question we have to cerebrate before we can celebrate, and apply our minds to that most deceptive of disciplines, national history. It's easy to re-write history: as Josef Stalin demonstrated, you begin by eliminating those who made it. That's what our forebears almost did when they killed Aborigines as though they were wild animals that threatened the crops. When I was down in Portsmouth on New Year's Day, trying to summarise the story of the First Fleet in two minutes and in a howling gale for *Australia Live*, I was taken over Lord Nelson's flagship the *Victory*. I was given a lump of grapeshot to hold: nine cannonballs the size of cricket balls, tightly wrapped in canvas, which unravel in the air and kill dozens in a crowd. It was British grapeshot that terrified the French and won the Battle of Trafalgar in 1805. A few months before, at Risdon Cove, a cannon loaded with grapeshot was fired at a large party of Aborigines happily hunting game. This was the first of many massacres in Australian history, and for that reason Risdon Cove should be stamped on our mental map just as clearly as Eureka and Gallipoli. It symbolises an inhumanity, extending even into the twentieth century, which we must never forget and which can never be forgiven.

Perhaps the most perverse man in our history is Dr Jacob Mountgarret, Launceston's first magistrate. He was the man who ordered the cannon to be fired at Risdon Cove, and who later recovered many Aboriginal bodies, melted them down and crammed the bones into casks which he sent, for anthropological amusement, to his colleagues in Sydney. If we look back on that horror today, and write it off as past history, we are wrong. It remains a potent part of the inheritance of those who are demonstrating against the Bicentennial. But the demonstrators are equally mistaken if they think we can somehow compensate for lost tribes by offering money or cancelling Bicentennial celebrations: that doesn't bring back the dead or the children they never had or the grandchildren that those children never begot. We cannot right historical wrongs: they are there, they are part of our history. What we can do is make them a living part of our imagination, and a part of the moral vision that animates our future. We can find out what was missing in the minds of those soldiers and surgeons that they could not recognise the humanity of fellow beings, and we can ask how different our minds are from theirs, whether the tolerance and compassion they never felt are now abundantly in evidence, two hundred years down the track, in this social experiment that is Australia.

Two hundred years is such a short space of time that we can almost talk across it. The music that Mozart was composing on the day the First Fleet landed still moves us, Tom Paine's *Rights of Man* (which a few of our republican forebears were transported for selling) remains a basic testament for civil liberties; whenever I address a jury in the Old Bailey I mentally thank their predecessors for sparing the lives of so many of our founding fathers and mothers. It was jury compassion that was instrumental in getting this show on the road. Britain in the days of George III was run by an undemocratic oligarchy, a bit like Queensland under Bjelke-Petersen. The electorates were all gerrymandered, power was in the hands of corrupt politicians and court favourites, sodomy was punished by death and there were 50,000 prostitutes living among the million people in London, not to mention such colourful characters as mudlarks, scufflehunters, bludgeon men, Morocco men, flash coachmen, grubbers, bear baiters and strolling minstrels. Wealth, of course, was all inherited; there were no dole bludgers because there was no dole for them to bludge. It was a time, eighteenth-century novelist Oliver Goldsmith tells us, where:

> Each wanton judge new penal statutes draw,
> Laws grind the poor, and rich men rule the law.

You were born into a certain rank and station in life, and you were expected to stay in it. Hence the old nursery rhyme: 'Tinker, tailor, soldier, sailor, rich man, poor man, beggar man, thief.' Their lives were costume dramas, for which the costumes were handed out at birth. The greatest offence against property was to have none. So when born in poverty – and millions were – you stayed in poverty, making ends meet by snapping up the gentry's unconsidered trifles. If you stole more than forty shillings' worth, you went to the gallows – if less, your sentence was transportation beyond the seas. And it was the jury that did the valuing. When you read the criminal records of these First Fleet convicts, it strikes you how many of them were convicted of stealing goods to the value of thirty-nine shillings. That's because the jury, in common humanity, time and again brought back verdicts that placed a price of thirty-nine shillings on goods estimated by their indignant owners as worth hundreds of pounds.

It was the jury's sense of mercy, their bargain with the barbarity of the law, which filled the prisons with people the government had wanted to hang, and forced that government, when the American colonies rebelled, to look for another dumping ground for the human debris of Georgian England. So while the First Fleet was, in one sense, a sailing garbage can, full of the bludgers of Britain – East End villains out of some eighteenth-century series of *Minder* – remember what they were up against. It comes down to us now in the paintings of Hogarth and in the poetry of William Blake, who had the moral vision to see the tears of the chimney sweeps and to hear the curses of the London harlots and to feel the cruelty done to the children in the poorhouse. While the First Fleet was sailing to Australia, Blake was writing his 'Songs of Innocence': those simple rhymes that sum up the hypocrisy and inhumanity of the age. Listen to him describe the starving workhouse children forced by the beadles to sing in St Paul's on Holy Thursday, 1788:

Is this holy thing to see
In a rich and fruitful land,
Babes reduc'd to misery,
Fed with cold and usorous hand?
Is that trembling cry a song?
Can it be a song of joy?
And so many children poor?
It is a land of poverty!

Britain's idle rich needed to get rid of Britain's idle poor. They were going to send them to Das Voltas Bay, in Namibia, until they discovered that its soil was barren and its lions were restless. Then they remembered that Banks and Cook had written of a bay called 'Botany', where meadows were lush and anchorages were deep, and the climate was just like San Tropez. Exactly why our English discoverers had this happy lapse of concentration is not quite clear: perhaps the *Endeavour*'s rum had gone to their heads, or they partook of some hallucinatory plant then growing around Kurnell. But for the British government, it was an ideal dumping ground. It was out of sight and out of mind, and the natives were not reckoned to be restless. They knew, of course, that there were 'Indians', but in the terminology of the time these were nomads, who had staked no claim: they had no greater rights to the country than the kangaroos. They were expected to blend back into the scenery – the First Fleet, unlike other colonising voyages, carried few trinkets to bribe or to buy the inheritance of the original occupiers. That's why it is fair to say that Australia, planned as a colony of thieves, began by an act of theft.

But it's not fair to say that there was any intention to subjugate or oppress the native people. Read those old Home Office reports now, couched in the language of the British civil servant through the ages, and what comes through is a kind of live-and-let-live philosophy: the Great South Land is big enough for us all – except, of course, for the French. The prime minister, that workaholic bachelor William Pitt, had ordered that no wives should accompany the convicts – as one wag put it, 'he did not intend to allow felons a luxury he denied himself.' Men outnumbered women by seven to one so Phillip was ordered by the Home Office to procure brides for them from among the natives and the women of the South Sea Islands. So our little penal colony was planned as a multicultural society from the outset. Of course, things didn't work out that way. Governor Phillip didn't have the heart to bring wives from New Caledonia to share the misery of those first years, and Aboriginal women had the dignity to turn down such attentions as were not forced upon them by rape. Indeed, Phillip became so worried about an outbreak of sodomy that he threatened the suspects with the most devastating fate that could befall anyone, then or now: a one-way ticket to New Zealand.

Of course, there were blacks among the First Fleet – nine of them, West Indian convicts and cooks. It was a Noah's Ark of nationalities – there were prisoners from Europe and America and lots from Ireland, and many, including Governor Phillip himself, had Jewish ancestry. Phillip appears to us now, out of all that gang of cynical marines and squabbling villains who peopled our settlements in the early years, as something very close to a saint. His wisdom, his patience, his humanity, his moral vision shine down over the years as a beacon: his very first law on landing – 'there can be no slavery in a free land, and hence no slaves' – makes him truly our Thomas Jefferson. His overwhelming belief that he was founding a new nation (a belief derided by everyone else at the time) is like the dream that came true and that we celebrate today. It is Arthur Phillip's dream. His sense of fairness was extraordinary for the age and for the place. Only six months after the landing, he wrote perceptively:

> Living with the natives – to the officers they were an amusement, to the convicts they were people inferior even to themselves. They all tried to take their own wrongs out on the blackman or to make what profit they could out of him.

When two convicts were speared, cutting rushes at a place called in consequence Rushcutters Bay, Phillip personally investigated and decided that the Aborigines had good reason to be provoked. When some convicts who had been harassing natives were reported to him, he ordered those convicts to be flogged in front of the tribe. But even Phillip was outdone in humanity on that occasion: the Aborigines, appalled at the calculated brutality of what they were witnessing, began to whimper and weep and beg for the punishment to stop. We should not, incidentally, idealise their lives – some tribal rituals were barbaric even by the standards of the British navy, although Phillip realised how culturally anachronistic it would be to make the comparison. What he showed in his own actions, and recognised in theirs, was a common bond of humanity that distance and time and spiritual beliefs could not disguise.

The very first gesture that Phillip made towards the curious Aborigines he met – on 22 January 1788, when he stopped at Botany Bay – was extraordinarily symbolic: he ordered his party of marines to pull down their trousers. To show they were men, not gods. That they shared, in their nakedness, the same mortal organs of human reproduction. I suppose that if you are a feminist, you might interpret this historical moment differently: as the first limp assertion of dominance by the new Australian male. I don't know what the Aborigines thought at the time as they were vouchsafed a sight of those white and wrinkled scrota: their own would, in years to come, be cut off and dried and used by early settlers as pouches for tobacco.

Phillip's moral vision did not long survive in the colony after his departure in 1792, but it's there, in our history, a standard of decency and justice briefly set, for which we should express gratitude on this day.

Phillip was the first and the finest white Australian. His own selection was a miracle: an act of coincidence and mateship. He had been a courageous naval captain, retired at forty-nine, farming land in Hampshire adjacent to the estate of the Colonel Secretary. When other choices fell through – nobody with a career in the navy wanted to go off as a prison governor – his neighbour prevailed upon him to emerge from retirement. Phillip proved a Caesar in so many ways. It was he who kept the convicts alive throughout that eight-month voyage by ordering daily exercise and daily oranges. His practicality, his optimism, and his courage kept that wretched settlement going in its first desperate years. As a nation, we probably owe more to him than to any other single person. Yet where is he now? Lying in a little village cemetery outside Bath. He fell, perhaps he jumped, out of a high window at his home in Bath. The city records curiously list no record of his death – one of several clues that he might have left this life by his own hand. An old war wound aggravated by his harsh years here, an unhappy second marriage, anxiety about the colony he had founded and fears for the natives he had sworn would never be slaves: the very improbability that his dreams would ever be realised may have driven him to suicide, nineteen thousand kilometres from the land he had tried to love and whose future as a nation he alone believed in.

The great races of this world, from the Greeks at Troy to the Irish in their cups, have one thing in common: they bring home their dead heroes. Nelson's body was brought back from Trafalgar, pickled in a barrel of the fleet's finest brandy, to Westminster Abbey. The Irish sent their navy to bring home the coffin of their poet Yeats, who had been interred in France, and one of their first acts as a nation was to demand that Britain give them back the body of Sir Roger Casement, their patriot buried in an English prison cemetery. If the Bicentennial fairy could grant me one wish, it would be to see the remains of Australia's founding father lifted from that obscure grave in that inconsequential English village, and brought back to where he will always belong. We should give him a state funeral and re-bury him in the Botanic Gardens overlooking Sydney Cove, beneath a headstone inscribed with that first law he laid down for Australia: 'there can be no slavery in a free land, and consequently no slaves.'

But enough of history – what will life be like after the Bicentennial? When the tumult and the shouting dies, the tall ships and the prince depart, we'll still have plenty of prawns left to throw on the barbie. Australia, our social experiment, will enter upon its third century with 31,000 millionaires and about two million of its people – most of them single mothers and children – living below the poverty line. Amongst the advanced nations of the world, our figures for child poverty, that social failing that so appalled William Blake, and our figures for youth unemployment are among the worst. To improve them, to give *all* our children a present and a future, is the great challenge which lies ahead. Mind you, we have notched up one curious achievement – we have more politicians per head of cattle than any other country in the world. Politicians who sometimes seem to create problems rather than solve them. If I have one hope for Australian governance by the tercentennial, it is that we shall have had the sense to abolish all state governments. They are unnecessary, dangerous and prone to corruption. Let us think like Australians, on the one hand, and let us bring more power back to our local communities, on the other. Distribute some state power to the top, and the rest to local districts. Be citizens of Launceston and citizens of Australia: let jokes about 'Tasmanians' be heard no more in the land.

You may think I am starting to whinge. But, in spite of all temptations to belong to other nations, I remain an Australian abroad. When I surprise people in London or New York by revealing that my ersatz English vowels were nurtured not at Eton but at state schools in lesser Sydney suburbs, it's interesting how they start making assumptions about my possession of 'Australian' characteristics: the innocence of Hogan and the cunning of Murdoch, a facility at sports or at one-line verbal put-downs. They have bought our stereotypes, you see. They think of us in our own image – or at least in the downmarket image we suffer others to project. We never seem to boast about how we pioneered universal suffrage and votes for women and maternity allowances, how we invented the secret ballot and the basic wage, how our miners at Broken Hill achieved the thirty-five-hour week for workers in dangerous jobs fifty years before that idea caught on overseas. Indeed, Australia elected the world's first Labour government – an achievement of some sort when you remember it was elected in Queensland. We were the first Commonwealth parliament to introduce a *Freedom of Information Act* and a comprehensive court system for reviewing the actions of bureaucrats. We produced, in Doc Evatt, the most influential architect of the United Nations and in Sir Owen Dixon the greatest common lawyer in the twentieth century. These, our true visionaries and their visions, are worth celebrating, because what is distinctive about them is their effort to achieve fairness, to reflect a society that has developed with a commitment to giving its people a 'fair go'. Mind you, one problem now is how to develop a commitment towards the 'fair stop': those who go fairly towards buying up sixty per cent of our newspapers or 'developing' in concrete large areas of natural wonder should be stopped fairly in their tracks.

There will be life after the Bicentennial, and I think it will be more confident and more challenging than the life we have lived before. We read the records of World War I, and are haunted by the protests made by Australian commanders at Gallipoli and Passchendaele and Pozieres against the mindless, murderous stupidity of the orders given by blimpish British generals to lead their men to slaughter. These criminally reckless commanders were responsible for more loss of Australian lives than the Turks and the Germans put together. But that sort of experience does not mean we should shrink from foreign engagement or fail to challenge the cruelty and oppression and truly appalling poverty that is today being visited upon so many fellow human beings. I find it depressing that our foreign-aid budget has now sunk to half the minimum standard set by the United Nations, that we have no equivalent of the Peace Corps or the Voluntary Services Organisation, that our schools teach so little of the languages and the cultures of other nations, that Australia, a country built by refugees, can sometimes be reluctant to give refuge to those who need it now.

Perhaps it's because our history and mythology are so obsessed with overcoming the physical hardships of the outback that we shrink from problems of a more mental or emotional kind. 'No worries', 'she'll be right' and 'I've got no problems with that' are our stock phrases. But problems, by the very challenges they create, make life more inspiring and more fulfilling. In the last few years I have been privileged to spend some time with dissidents in Czechoslovakia and South Africa, people under constant threat of persecution, who when they hear the early-morning knock on the door know that it will not be the milkman. I have been amazed at the intensity of their lives, at their capacity for love and laughter and human commitment, indeed for a sort of happiness that carefree comfort can make so elusive. I've always thought that our most distinctive and certainly most attractive quality was that demonstrated by the small boy who pointed out that the Emperor wore no clothes. He was, I suspect, an Australian tourist, full of restless curiosity about the way the world works and a lack of inhibition in pointing out when it doesn't. As my grandmother would say, 'He had a hide.' In our third century, let's show more of the heart that beats beneath our hide.

There are two statistics we cannot, as a nation, escape. Comparatively speaking, we put more of our indigenous inhabitants in prison than any other country in the world. And there are more black deaths in custody in Australia than in South Africa. That's mathematical proof of our failure, after two hundred years, to measure up to Arthur Phillip's ideal of living

and letting live, and it's a failure that can be seen more dramat-
ically in the squalor and poverty of Aboriginal settlements on
the outskirts of many of our country towns. This failure is
starting to rankle, starting to get under our white skins because,
quite frankly, it is spoiling the Bicentennial party. At dinners in
London, Australians are starting to sound like South Africans.
You hear the same phrases: 'After all we've done for them';
'It's the outside agitators'; 'They're exploiting our Bicentennial
to give us the worst publicity we've ever had.' That may all be
true, but it's really beside the point. A nation that venerates the
opportunist can scarcely criticise the Aborigines for taking an
opportunity when it's offered. We – white Australians – have
done a lot for them: at least since 1967, we've thrown a lot of
money at their problems, allowed them land in the Northern
Territory to call their own, and done what we always do when
we can't think of anything else – set up a Royal Commission.
But we have not given them back what we have taken over the
past two hundred years – the right to decide their own destiny.

Self-determination is the right of every race. The white
Australian race has emerged, distinctively and creditably, from
a polyglot mixture of nationalities, with the help of some
Aborigines who have opted or been co-opted in. But the utterly
distinctive Aboriginal race has been dispossessed and largely
destroyed. I spoke earlier of Risdon Cove and the massacres that
came after – unforgettable, unforgivable wrongs that are there
in our history and cannot be 'put right'. We can offer apologies
today, but only in the knowledge that these apologies will not
be accepted. Not yet, anyway. In time, perhaps, but at a time
of their choosing, not ours. And that truly historic time, when
they decide to join our celebrations, will be hastened by negoti-
ating – not imposing – a treaty that will give them legal rights
of co-existence, which allow them the pride that we feel today.
I don't mean a treaty setting up a separate Aboriginal state –
on a *Hypothetical* I offered Tasmania to Aboriginal lawyer
Michael Mansell and he wouldn't take it. I am not even sure
that Aborigines are ready to negotiate. They are the remnants of

over three hundred tribes – the leadership structures are weak, they have no certain consensus about what they want. A treaty at least would recognise their uniqueness. It would recognise the Aboriginal contribution to multinational Australia – they have, after all, taught us to dream, to be easy-going, to enjoy ourselves, to suffer adversity nobly, and to find our way through the bush. But above all, it would show that we have, after two hundred years, acquired the confidence to be humble, the strength to give as well as to take, the moral vision to see the simple logic in Phillip's first law: 'There can be no slavery in a free land, and consequently no slaves.'

Chapter 2

LOSING THE PLOT

The Bicentennial oration lauded the enlightened genius of Arthur Phillip, whose humanity, egalitarianism and moral vision (not to mention his seamanship) provided history with the best example, in a country that began as a convict colony, of the possibility of reforming the human spirit. I had been struck by his miserable resting place in a small church by the motorway outside Bath, and by the failure of the British state to recognise his achievements and move him to lie with its other heroes in Westminster Abbey or even with the local worthies at Bath Abbey. It seemed only right that he should find a proper resting place in Sydney, and I once encouraged a team of Australian Rhodes Scholars to dig him up and smuggle him home aboard a Qantas jet – plans that received a tentative (if post-prandial) approval from the then High Commissioner, Doug McClelland.

Fortunately a legal solution became possible when a Church of England Consistory Court ruling permitted 'national heroes' buried in Britain to be returned to the nation that benefited from their heroics. My secret plans to uplift Phillip and Yemmerrawannie, the nineteen-year-old Aborigine he had brought to Britain, began then to take the shape described in 'Losing the Plot', an article published in The Bulletin *in 2007.*

Sadly, Yemmerrawannie's tombstone is still being pissed on by English racists, and Arthur Phillip (as 60 Minutes discovered when I participated in a segment with them in 2007) is nowhere to be found. His home in Bath has been turned into family flats, and the mistake on the blue plaque outside it has not been corrected.

In a small room in the British Admiralty in 1787, during the delay caused by his insistence that the First Fleet be properly provisioned, Captain Arthur Phillip devised the first law for a colony that only he believed would ever amount to more than a dumping ground for criminals. 'There can be no slavery in a free land,' he wrote, 'and consequently no slaves.'

Given that slavery was not abolished in British colonies for another twenty years, Phillip's first law for the colony that was to become Australia shows a prescient humanity in which we should all take pride. He was, quite literally, our founding father: his egalitarian consideration for the convicts brought them safely through the First Fleet's perilous voyage and later his concern for Aborigines was such that, even when speared through the shoulder at Manly, he urged reconciliation. When forced by ill-health to return to England, he took two Aborigines, Bennelong and Yemmerrawannie, to meet King George III.

Yemmerrawannie stayed, becoming the first Australian expatriate, but he died of pneumonia and was buried in a church in Eltham, South London. Phillip paid for his medical care, and had a tombstone erected above his grave in the churchyard. Then Phillip moved to Bath for reasons of his health, later fighting under Lord Nelson and then commanding a 'Dad's Navy' reserve. When he died, the British establishment did not give him his rightful place in Westminster Abbey and even refused him a grave in Bath Abbey. It was, perhaps, because his father was Jewish. His work in New South Wales may not have seemed very important when he died in 1814, but never since have the British shown the slightest inclination to honour him.

Phillip was buried in an insignificant church, now beside a motorway in the village of Bathampton. No notice was taken of his grave until 1906, when a visiting Australian delegation alerted the locals to its value. A ledger stone was duly laid inside the church door, where it remains today to inform the occasional Australian tourist that 'underneath lie the remains of ARTHUR PHILLIP Esq – Admiral of the Blue'.

Some years ago, it occurred to me that both Phillip and Yemmerrawannie would be better remembered if brought back and laid to rest in Sydney's Royal Botanic Gardens, overlooking what Phillip was first to describe as the world's finest harbour. They might be given a state funeral and, their coffins respectively and respectfully draped in the Australian and Aboriginal flags, buried beneath a monument inscribed with Phillip's first law for this country. It might serve as a symbol for reconciliation, as a source of pride in the governor's idealism, and as a means of stimulating interest in Australian history.

I canvassed a few political acquaintances: the federal member for Bennelong (John Howard) was not interested, but former New South Wales premier Nick Greiner was, and so a few years later was another premier, Bob Carr, and his adviser Evan Williams. What made it suddenly achievable was a landmark decision by the Church of England's Consistory Court, in a test case brought by Brazil, that national heroes buried in Britain could be exhumed and sent for reburial in the state they had served so well. If Brazil could get a hero back from a country churchyard, why not Australia?

I was duly appointed by the New South Wales government, in necessary secrecy and (at my insistence) *pro bono,* to negotiate the legalities. The bishops for Bath and South London could not have been more helpful. It seemed a simple matter to uplift Yemmerrawannie, whose headstone stood in Eltham. But then, to his almighty embarrassment, the bishop discovered that the grave was empty: the plot had been needed for more important white parishioners and the Aborigine's bones had been thrown away.

Of course, the bishop confided, if it was bones we wanted,

there were some lying around ... I resisted the temptation. DNA testing exposes historical frauds. When the Irish brought Sir Roger Casement back to Dublin from Pentonville Prison, the quicklime burial meant that part of the patriot's remains were of another executed man – reportedly the poisoner Dr Crippen. Yemmerrawannie was irretrievable and the reconciliation project could not proceed.

But we could still bring back Arthur Phillip, who must surely lie where the church ledger stone says. But then came another bombshell. A report prepared by the Church of England's own expert for the proposed exhumation concluded that 'the statement on the ledger stone is untrue'. Phillip's coffin is not where it is said to be. It may be beneath the floorboards or in the churchyard, but only 'archaeological research' will find him. The Church of England has, quite literally, lost the plot.

And so has the Australian government, despite John Howard's often-stated concern for our history. Phillip's home, which still stands near the Royal Crescent in Bath, has much of its original wallpaper and kitchen furnishings. It was offered for sale very cheaply a few years ago but the Australian government declined to buy it. It is now a dump, used by squatters. The ignorance of those who represent our history is on display on the blue plaque outside, which mis-describes Phillip as 'The first Governor of Australia'.

Yemmerrawannie's headstone still stands against the church wall in Eltham, just opposite the bus shelter where a black youth named Stephen Lawrence was infamously murdered by local racists. Alongside the wall is a path that runs from the local pub. When I visited in April 2007 with *60 Minutes* we watched as lunchtime drinkers stumbled out to use the tombstone as a urinal. The Australian High Commission has asked that it be taken inside the church, but the parish council has refused the request. So the headstone is desecrated every day.

Australia needs to look after its own history because other countries certainly will not. Thus far, other than in respect for our war dead, Australia's overseas efforts have been abject – although judging from the cesspool that is Kurnell (first landing place of both Cook and Phillip) perhaps we really do not care.

Chapter 3

AS GAME AS TOM CURNOW

That my fellow countrypersons should idolise – or at least iconise – a cruel murderer such as Ned Kelly has always been a source of irritation, especially after I discovered in the embers of that siege at the Glenrowan Hotel a man of true moral distinction. He was a young country schoolteacher, Tom Curnow, whose courageous actions saved many lives that would otherwise have been doomed in Kelly's planned terrorist atrocity. Our mental block about celebrating Curnow's heroism does say something about the immaturity of our national vision. Recent studies have not improved the case for 'Jihad Ned' – with his morose hatred of police, his racist paranoia over their black trackers, his evil wish for civilian casualties from the planned train crash. He lacks the cunning of other countries' picaresque villains: his moronic decision to remain at the hotel cost the lives of his gang (for which he did not care, although they included his younger brother) and resulted in his own capture.

When invited to contribute to a book on 'Australian Greats' – short essays on national treasures ranging from Vegemite to Dawn Fraser – I took the opportunity to stake a claim for Tom Curnow, using the Hypothetical *method to challenge readers to decide which man was the real hero of Glenrowan.*

Imagine yourself a young country schoolteacher, taking your pregnant wife and her sister for a Sunday drive. Outside the local pub you are bailed up by a gang of terrorists, and held captive while they plan an atrocity. They are going to derail a train and then shoot any survivors of the crash. You make the terrorists believe that you sympathise with their cause, so they allow you to leave with your family whom they threaten to kill if you do anything to foil their dastardly plot. As darkness falls, you hear the train whistle in the distance. You could leave your home to warn the driver, but your hysterical wife and her weeping sister beg you to stay put, and not to risk their lives, your life and that of your unborn child by trying to save the lives of the passengers. What do you do?

True heroism must pass two tests – of historical time (will the nobility of the cause still be recognised in the future?) and of actual time: was there long enough for reflection and for a genuine choice of the heroic course of action? The dividing line between greatness and foolhardiness may be a nano-second, with the outcome decided by luck. But people worth celebrating as exemplars always make choices that are informed by a clear-eyed appreciation of the consequences. They are prepared to risk the sacrifice of themselves, and/or their loved ones, to serve a greater human good, and unlike self-regarding jihadists and other martyrs, expect nothing in return, in this life or after it.

A nation that does not honour its heroes condemns itself to an undistinguished future. So how come Australians have never heard of Tom Curnow?

He was that young schoolteacher, in Glenrowan in 1880, who risked his life when 'Jihad Ned' Kelly rode into town with the blood of three policemen and a police informer (Aaron Sherritt, murdered the previous night) fresh upon him. At gunpoint, the Kelly gang forced railway workers to pull up the rail tracks and the stationmaster to give information about the special train, with police and black trackers aboard as well as journalists and women and children, that had been sent from Melbourne and that would run off the broken rails and careen into a gully just beyond the town.

Of all the townsfolk held hostage at the pub, only the clever, calculating and utterly courageous schoolteacher proved capable of doing the right thing. He pretended sympathy with the gang, giving them advice and even dancing a jig with the disgusting Dan Kelly, while the outlaws boasted of how they would shoot any passengers as well as police if they survived the train crash. Curnow tricked them into allowing him to take his family home after dark. His pregnant wife and her sister huddled in the buggy as Ned Kelly waved his pistol at Curnow: 'You are free to go, but drive straight to your home and go to bed. And don't dream too loud, or you are a dead man.' With a further threat to send an outlaw to check on obedience to this order, Kelly turned his horse back towards the hotel, leaving the schoolteacher to head for his home.

That was where the real showdown took place. When Tom explained that he had a duty to stop the train to avoid the massacre the gang was planning, his wife became hysterical and both women begged him not to put everyone's life – including that of his unborn child – in danger from the kind of murderous reprisal Aaron Sherritt had just suffered for informing on these gangsters. But Curnow had been told by both Kellys how they intended to shoot survivors of the train wreck, and the station-master had whispered to him back at the pub that Ned had refused his request to repair the track after the police train ran off it, to protect the next day's passenger train from crashing. His wife's tearful entreaties gave Curnow pause, along with the memory of Kelly's threats, but a train whistle in the distance forced an immediate decision.

Grabbing his sister-in-law's bright red shawl, a candle and a box of matches, he left the house and walked jerkily (he had a congenital hip deformity) to the nearby railway line. Then, lighting the candle and holding it aloft behind the red shawl, he limped along the railway track towards the sound of the train. The red glare from the makeshift signal warned the driver of the pilot engine to stop, and the train behind it screeched to a halt amid the terrified braying of the police horses. Curnow told the driver of the murderous trap that lay a short distance down the line. Ned Kelly – waiting in his armour for the sound of the crash – suddenly realised what had happened: 'By God,' witnesses at the hotel heard him shout, 'that bastard Curnow has deceived us.'

Curnow rushed back to comfort his wife, holding her tightly in the bed in fear that Kelly might kill them before escaping from the police.

The rest is history – Australian history, at least.

Thomas Curnow had every reason to expect vengeance – the Kellys repeatedly threatened to kill anyone who helped the police. Perhaps if he *had* been gunned down, as these murderous thugs had gunned down Aaron Sherritt, he might have been noticed and even applauded by the later generations who were to idealise and iconise Ned Kelly. Instead, Curnow has disappeared down history's memory hole, no more than a trivia-quiz question that nobody (not even Barry Jones, who once flunked the question on a *Hypothetical*) answers correctly. In fleeting appearances in films and plays about the siege at Glenrowan, Curnow is depicted as an ugly, elderly pedant, a caricature dobber-inner of these likeable, misunderstood Irish larrikins.

The real Tom Curnow was handsome – only twenty-five at the time – although he walked with that limp from his dislocated hip. After his heroic action at Glenrowan he had to be posted to Gippsland to avoid reprisals from the extended Kelly family and their thuggish friends – a measure of how bushranging had morally corrupted the bush. Curnow's later life was useful and uneventful – he taught until retirement at sixty, fathering two sons who came to grief at Gallipoli (one killed, the other severely wounded), and two daughters, one of whom served as a nurse in combat zones throughout the First World War.

Tom Curnow was an ordinary, decent person who did the right thing at the right time, preventing the mass murder of strangers at the risk of his own life. None of the other townspeople at

Glenrowan dared to lift a finger, while the railway workers and the stationmaster, albeit at gunpoint, became accomplices to the attempted atrocity. No doubt the Kellys had grievances – some police were corrupt and the jail sentence on Kelly's mother for attacking one such constable was overly harsh – but this cannot begin to excuse her son's bloodthirsty rampage. There is no excuse, either, for Kelly hagiography. At least Nolan's bushrangers inhabit a morally primitive landscape, although Peter Carey wrings a kind of maudlin sympathy for Ned. But the transcript of his trial reveals nothing out of the ordinary about this vicious, reckless criminal. The Jerilderie letter, which inspired Carey, was written by Joe Byrne. Ned's wheedling, lying petition to the governor for mercy, like his other reported utterances – 'Such is life' is a pretty stupid remark to make to your executioners – is banal.

Tom Curnow was an ordinary person every day of his life except that momentous Sunday night when his moral sense impelled him to extraordinary action. His bravery may be more capable of recognition today, when every news bulletin reports some terrorist outrage and even fridge magnets urge us to turn police informer, albeit through the safety of an anonymous hotline.

Ned Kelly is absurd as a national figure. Some day, when Australians come to recognise the cruelty of the man with the upturned bucket on his head, they may allow a fresh hero to emerge from the ashes of the Glenrowan Hotel. A man whom children will compare to others they admiringly describe as being 'as game as Tom Curnow'.

Chapter 4

DOC EVATT AND THE TOLPUDDLE MARTYRS

'Doc' Evatt is the archetype of the prophet who has gone without honour in his own land. He is the Australian who has had most influence on human progress, through his work in establishing the United Nations and promulgating the Universal Declaration of Human Rights. *It has always irked me that the nation has never paid proper tribute to Evatt and his team – the cantankerous Colonel Hodgson, the quick-witted Alan Watt, the early feminist Jessie Street and others whose names, recorded on the first UN committee transcripts, we seem to have lost long ago. We persist in the disingenuous belief that it was Gallipoli that 'put Australia on the map' and speak proudly of the rantings of Billy Hughes at Versailles. In fact it was Evatt's performance at the post-war Peace Conferences in 1945–6 and in the first years of the UN that demonstrated how a small country (the population was just seven million) could emerge as intellectual leader of most of the nations then in the world.*

The injustice done to the labourers from Tolpuddle in Dorset in the south-west of England, transported for forming a trade union and who became Australia's most famous political prisoners, had so fired Evatt's imagination that in 1937, despite his heavy workload on the High Court bench, he wrote a book about their case. As Bishop Burgmann (another great thinker of the 1930s) said in his original foreword:

Neither churches nor courts rise much above the prevail-
ing opinion of the time, and that is why the spirit of
truth and justice must whisper in the ear of individuals
who will listen and respond and suffer, if need be, 'til the
consciences of the majority begin to awaken.

Evatt's post-war pursuit of human rights on the world stage
stemmed from his realisation, through analysing the Tolpuddle
case, that no state could be trusted not to make life miserable
for those of its citizens who lacked any lever of power. By insist-
ing that international legal instruments guaranteed the right to
join trade unions, he hoped to ensure that workers' legitimate
aspirations would never again be destroyed by unjust laws. As
Evatt's international importance is being belatedly recognised,
Sydney University Press in 2009 produced a new edition of his
book on the Tolpuddle martyrs, with this introduction.

Herbert Vere Evatt was an architect of the world's most important institution. His genius is present in the Charter of the United
Nations and his influence is reflected in the post-war human
rights triptych – the Genocide and Geneva Conventions and the
Universal Declaration of Human Rights. He was the progenitor
of the European Court of Human Rights and the International
Criminal Court, both of which he proposed at the Paris Peace
Conference. His international renown led to his election as President of the General Assembly of the United Nations in 1948.
Why did this intellectual giant concern himself with six Dorsetshire labourers, convicted in 1834 of administering an unlawful
oath, and sentenced to transportation to Australia, whose sad
story he recounted in a short book: *The Tolpuddle Martyrs –*
Injustice within the Law?

Evatt wrote this work in 1937 while he was a judge of the
High Court of Australia, appointed by a Labor government
in 1930 at the astonishingly young age of thirty-six. By then
the case of the Dorsetshire labourers was already celebrated

in Britain. The legend of working men who were victims of a miscarriage of justice was inspiring for the union movement in the 1930s, and today it has acquired a mythic quality: Tony Benn claims that the campaign to free them 'was the turning point from feudalism to capitalism and socialism'. But 'Doc' Evatt (as he was affectionately known by a Labor party in which few politicians had doctorates) realised that the case of the Dorsetshire labourers stood for something very different, and something more frightening. He wrote:

> The Dorsetshire case illustrates the fact that oppression and cruelty do not always fail. Indeed, they sometimes succeed beyond the hopes of the oppressors. Unless trade unionists throughout the world are always ready to sacrifice their personal interests, their safety, or even their lives for the amelioration of the lot of the poor, their elaborate organisation may perish overnight either in a holocaust of terror and force or in the slower process of legal repression.

This early example of a workingman's combination was utterly crushed, by use rather than by misuse of the law. The government achieved exactly what it wanted – the suppression of a nascent trade union movement – through the fear and terror engendered by the savage sentences, emphasised by the desperate campaign begging mercy for the men. Although the judge and jury were biased and the sentences were brutal, the men were nonetheless guilty as charged: Evatt found no violence in the Dorsetshire case 'save the extreme and horrible violence of the law itself'.

This revelation of injustice *within* the law came as a shock to Evatt: it moved him to write a book (an unusual exercise for a sitting High Court judge) and it inspired him to think about the necessity for incorporating into the law a set of basic guarantees of human rights that would make 'injustice within the law' much less likely. Two years later, when H. G. Wells published his Penguin special *A New World Order*, arguing for a universal declaration of human rights, Evatt saw how such a charter, introduced into domestic law, could provide the necessary inbuilt protection against the kind of cruelty that had been so evident in the case of the Tolpuddle Martyrs.

That cruelty comes through to us today, in reading the proceedings against these good, simple, hardworking men. They laboured for rich landowners for a few shillings a week, in a stratified society that allocated rank and station at birth and which allowed, even after the 1832 *Reform Act*, only about five per cent of the population to vote at elections. The hopes engendered by the repeal of the *Combination Acts*, which made trade unionism legal at least in theory, imbued intelligent men like George Loveless, a Methodist lay-preacher, with the idea of setting up a 'friendly society' that might seek through collective bargaining an increase in their meagre wages. They feared victimisation – hence their rather pathetic ritual of kneeling with a copy of the Bible before the picture of a skeleton, and swearing to keep the union's secrets, while the sepulchral injunction to 'remember thy end' was intoned. The rules of their society were hardly revolutionary: 'that no person should be admitted to their meetings when drunk; that no obscene songs or toasts should be allowed; that they should not countenance any violence or violation of the laws of the realm.'

But 1834 was the year when the Grand National Consolidated Trade Union was established in London, extending even to women workers such as the bonnet makers, and the Tolpuddle society belonged to it. William IV, a king who despised his lesser subjects, demanded 'some checks to the progress of this evil' (i.e. trade unionism). And Home Secretary Lord Melbourne, a Whig (i.e. a liberal) who ruled in the interests of the upper class, boasted in private correspondence with the king of 'the mortal blow which it [the sentence of transportation] strikes at the root of their whole proceedings' (i.e. of national trade unionism).

When a vicious Dorchester landowner and magistrate, George Frampton, wrote to Melbourne to complain about this little Tolpuddle 'friendly society', the government decided to make it a scapegoat whose fate would destroy the union movement. The six men were arrested under the *Illegal Oaths Act*. This statute had been passed in 1797 as a result of mutinies in the navy and was intended to combat seditious conspiracies in the armed forces, but its words were wide enough to catch oaths taken by members of friendly societies (and Masonic and Orange lodges, whose members were, of course, never threatened with prosecution). A lickspittle judge, Baron Williams, was despatched to Dorchester to ensure their conviction – a certain thing before a jury of landowners in any event – and to pass an unconscionably brutal maximum sentence of seven years' transportation in order to discourage other would-be friendly societies. The local magistrate and landowners were improperly encouraged to prosecute by Melbourne and the attorney-general (and by clergymen of the Church of England, always supportive of the upper classes in this period). Melbourne himself selected the charge and arranged for a speedy trial: his brother-in-law became the foreman of the grand jury that indicted the men! They could – and should – have been prosecuted summarily (i.e. before magistrates, not a judge and jury) for their pathetic oath-taking ceremony, but this would carry a maximum sentence of three months, and the government wanted them put away for much longer. So its law officers opted for the more serious charge, a felony carrying transportation for up to seven years. Evatt describes the imposition of this maximum sentence as 'cruelly unjust and disproportionate', and demonstrates that it was a political decision, since a few months later members of a much more active trade union branch who swore a similar oath were merely discharged on a good-behaviour bond. The Tolpuddle sentences were designed to destroy the trade union movement – so these men were 'martyrs' to that cause in the true sense of the word.

George Loveless and his five comrades were transported twelve thousand miles to 'Botany Bay' (in fact, of course, to Port Jackson, the harbour of Sydney), shackled to the debauched and violent villains for whom transportation meant a reprieve from the death sentence. For two years they toiled as convicts, while a protest movement – fuelled by a reaction to the savagery of the sentences rather than sympathy for trade unionism – gathered apace in London. A quarter of a million people signed a pardon petition, and tens of thousands turned out at street rallies demanding that the men be brought back home.

Lord Melbourne remained hostile, as did Pitt, his brief Tory replacement as prime minister, but the fact that the sentences had been effective in smashing the trade union movement allowed the next Melbourne government to be more generous. The six were pardoned, and they returned to a hero's welcome in London in 1837.

But nothing had changed for the better: as Evatt emphasises, society remained as class ridden as ever, the Grand National Consolidation Union had collapsed, and the privileged few showed no interest in sharing political power or economic wealth with 'those they contemptuously termed the lower orders'. Further proof of Evatt's thesis is provided by the men themselves, who were set up with land in Dorchester purchased from the proceeds of a tribute fund. They were ostracised by neighbours, and George Loveless saw no future for the working class in England. Five of the six set sail for Canada, where today they are buried in modest graves in an Ontario cemetery. Neither the Labour Party nor the trade union movement, which now hails them as martyrs, has ever thought to bring them back for burial in Westminster Abbey, resting place of British heroes, although the Trade Union Congress does hold an annual festival in their honour in Tolpuddle.

Evatt was writing in 1937, as war clouds gathered over Europe and as Japan's militant nationalism had begun to threaten Australia. Laws in Germany and Italy had already turned trade unions into instruments of the fascist state, and Evatt was prescient in his perception that workers' rights would 'perish overnight . . . in a holocaust of terror and force' unless they were defended by the sacrifice of lives. He recognised that obedience to such laws – the Tolpuddle Martyrs had accepted their fate with resignation – was no example for this time, and that movements protesting only for merciful sentences were not a satisfactory response. The true lesson of 1834, that tyranny will triumph unless workers are prepared to stand and fight, was a lesson that he drew for 1937. Evatt's thinking in this book soon inspired him to resign from the High Court and win a seat for Labor in the federal parliament. When Labor took office in 1941, he became both attorney-general and Minister for External (i.e. foreign) Affairs – posts he held for the next eight years.

Evatt made his – and Australia's – first international mark in 1945 at the San Francisco Conference that founded the United Nations. My friend the late Michael Foot, then a young journalist (he would go on to lead the UK Labour Party), always remembered his sense of awe at this gravel-voiced Australian who emerged to dominate it. Evatt became the *de facto* leader of the small and medium-sized nations who sought to build an institution that would assist their development as well as their security. He led the fight against the Soviets in an attempt to limit the 'great power' veto, and the fight against the United States to secure a pledge of full employment in the UN Charter, a document which benefited in many ways from his drafting suggestions. At the end of the conference Edward Stettinius, Jr, the American Secretary of State, publicly declared that 'no one had contributed more to the conference than Mr Evatt' and the Peruvian delegation even moved a resolution by small powers to 'pay homage to their great champion, Mr Evatt'. In the words of the *New York Times*, the conference had seen the exercise of two kinds of political power, the first packed with heavy national muscle and coercion and the other purveyed by force of ideas, argument and intellectual effort – and the paper hailed Herbert Vere Evatt as the epitome of the latter.

Evatt's far-sighted vision for the enforcement of human rights was on display the following year at the Paris Peace Conference, when he was first to propose the establishment of a European

Court of Human Rights, which would have the power to admit individual complaints and make binding determinations for that war-ravaged continent. He argued that even democratic governments could not be trusted to protect the rights of individual citizens, as they could be ridden over roughshod by prejudiced majorities: 'State declarations, standing alone, are not sufficient to guarantee the inalienable rights of the individuals and behind them it is essential that some sufficient sanction be established.' Only a court could give legal remedies that would deter other states from abusing their powers. The European Court of Human Rights was established in 1959 in Strasbourg, and is the most influential human rights court in the world today.

As a result of Evatt's pre-eminence in San Francisco and Paris, Australia was elected to the first UN Commission on Human Rights and presented that body with a statute for an international human rights court. To arguments from nervous delegations that such a court would impinge upon national sovereignty, Australia's delegation, instructed by cablegram from 'the Doc' in Canberra, feistily replied that sovereignty was 'an outmoded conception, a fetishist survival whose worship should be anathema in the face of economic and human inter-relationship of our one atomic world'. Non-aligned countries were mightily impressed and the UK and US were forced to concede the strength of the argument, although, of course, the Soviets opposed it from the outset and the Cold War made it unsustainable. It was later reversed by Robert Menzies, whose government opposed international cooperation in respect of human rights for fear that it would come to target the White Australia policy and the treatment of Aborigines. But it is a remarkable fact – upon which Australians rarely remark – that Evatt and his delegates were the first to beat the drum for policies that Amnesty International and other human rights organisations were to take up again in the 1990s, and which today are beginning to come to pass.

On Evatt's instructions, the Australian delegation played an important part in many debates over particular articles of

the *Universal Declaration of Human Rights*. It called the bluff
of the Soviet Union and its highly strung puppet states when
they wanted to change the right to 'independent and impartial'
courts merely to a right to 'open' courts. (Stalin's rigged trials
were always open, but were never independent or impartial.)
It stood up for minorities, against the opposition of the great
powers (especially the US with its 'Jim Crow' segregation laws,
and the Soviets with their subjugated peoples). The Australian
delegation explained that human rights were all about protecting minorities from oppression, including the oppression of the
majority in a democracy.

Australia had, by this time, a fifty-year history of flourishing
trade unions and Evatt was appalled to find these two words
unmentioned in the first draft of the *Universal Declaration of
Human Rights*, so he insisted on inserting them in Article 23(4):
'Everyone has the right to form and to join trade unions for
the protection of his interests.' Evatt's greatest achievement was
to ensure the *Universal Declaration of Human Rights* included
social and economic rights – for example, to minimum standards of health and housing. Eleanor Roosevelt, who chaired the
drafting committee, remarked that rights needed to be universal and not just 'for a progressive state like Australia', but she
accepted that economic and social rights should at least feature
in Article 22 of the declaration. And so it was that the man who
had been so concerned by the fate of the Tolpuddle Martyrs that
he wrote a book about their case later came to ensure that the
rights for which they had been sacrificed were written into
the *Universal Declaration*, including:

> Article 23: the right to work; to equal pay for equal work;
> to just remuneration; and the right to join trade unions;
>
> Article 24: the right to reasonable working hours and
> periodic holidays with pay;
>
> Article 25: the right to an adequate standard of living,
> including food, clothing, housing and medical care and

benefits in the event of unemployment, sickness, disability, widowhood or old age.

Evatt's Presidency of the UN General Assembly was a tribute to his international standing. On 10 December 1948 he received the *Universal Declaration of Human Rights* from Eleanor Roosevelt, who described it as 'the *Magna Carta* for mankind'. The previous day he had unveiled the Genocide Convention, the brainchild of Raphael Lemkin, a Polish lawyer. Evatt had taken Lemkin under his wing as soon as he recognised (and he was one of the first to do so) the importance of forging an international criminal law that would require state intervention against any regime that embarked upon the mass murder of its own people for racial or religious reasons. This too was a historic moment. Evatt declared:

> Today we are establishing international collective safeguards for the very existence of such human groups ... whoever will act in the name of the United Nations will do it on behalf of universal conscience as embodied in this great organisation. Intervention of the United Nations and other organs which will have to supervise application of the Convention will be made according to international law and not according to unilateral political considerations. In this field relating to the sacred right of existence of human groups we are proclaiming today the supremacy of international law once and forever.

A few months later came the Geneva Conventions, requiring humane treatment of prisoners of war and laying down rules to protect civilians in wartime. These three instruments now form a great human rights triptych and Evatt had played a crucial part in their design and in their acceptance as the basis for a new international human rights law. Séan MacBride, the Irish Minister for External Affairs of the time, once told me that he regarded Evatt as the statesman who most contributed to this crucible period for modern history.

But prophets are not honoured in their own country. In today's Australia, 'Doc' Evatt is perceived as a political failure: his leadership of the Labor party between 1950 and 1958 was marked by bitter in-fighting and by repeated electoral defeats at the hands of the conservatives led by Sir Robert Menzies. Evatt is, however, favourably recalled for his lonely, utterly courageous and ultimately successful battle, at the height of McCarthyism, against Menzies' attempt to abolish the Communist party. In 1951 'the Doc' put on his legal harness of wig and gown and had the *Communist Party Dissolution Bill* declared unconstitutional by the High Court. Then, when Menzies put the question to a national referendum, Evatt led the campaign that had the proposal narrowly defeated. But his mind began to crack and to falter as he reached his sixties. I will always remember the look of sadness in my Labor-supporting grandfather's eyes when, as a precocious ten-year-old, I taunted him about how much better Mr Menzies sounded on radio broadcasts than Doctor Evatt. 'If only you had heard the Doc at the height of his powers.' If only . . . but I hear it now, unmistakably on those old newsreels of the first UN meetings and read his name in books of UN history or international law. Ironically, there is seldom any reference to Menzies – only an occasional footnote about his failed Suez mission. Evatt, whom he so often taunted and outclassed on the national political stage, was the man who contributed so much more to the building of a better world.

It was as a law student that I was first impressed with 'the Doc', when I came across a judgment he delivered shortly after he wrote about the Tolpuddle Martyrs. *Chester v Waverley Municipal Council* concerned a mother who had suffered permanent mental damage on seeing the drowned body of her young son recovered from a roadwork trench, seven feet deep, which the council had negligently failed to guard or to fence after it filled with rainwater and attracted local children. The other judges cavalierly dismissed her claim for damages for nervous shock, despite the gross negligence of the council, because in their Anglo-centric male minds she should have shown a stiff upper lip: 'death is not an infrequent event . . . it is not the common experience of mankind that the spectacle even of the sudden and distressing death of a child produces any consequences of more than a temporary nature.' (Decoded, this meant that the plaintiff was a working-class immigrant from Poland, who had to learn to be less emotional.)

Evatt, in a passionate yet scholarly dissent, pointed out 'the notorious fact that children of working people are frequently compelled to play on the streets' and that the council should have foreseen the trauma for parents of a missing child as they waited 'in an agony of hope and fear with hope gradually decreasing'. To assist his unfeeling and unimaginative brethren, he quoted from William Blake 'The Little Boy Lost' and from Tom Collins (*Such is Life*) and proceeded to refashion the law of negligence to permit recovery in such circumstances.

It was a masterly piece of jurisprudence, infused with humanity, which came in time to be recognised as correct in law as well as in morality. It was an example of Evatt's profound belief that humanitarian principles could be deployed by judges to develop a common law that would meet the needs and challenges of a changing world.

The world has benefited from his passion for human rights in ways that his own country has overlooked. When Eleanor Roosevelt presented him with the *Universal Declaration of Human Rights*, he replied, 'Millions of men, women and children, all over the world, will turn for help, guidance and inspiration to this document.' They have – but not in Australia, where its promises have never been translated into law. This is despite the fact that the *Universal Declaration of Human Rights* was hailed by the General Assembly as 'a common standard of achievement for all peoples and all nations', to be promoted by education and in particular by 'progressive measures, national and international, for their universal and effective recognition and observance'.

Australia, unlike all other progressive democratic nations, has taken no national measures to secure the effective recognition of these universal rights by passing them into law – in other words by legislating a bill of rights. Frank Brennan's report, released in October 2009, demonstrates convincingly that the rights of the poor and vulnerable would be measurably improved by adopting such a charter. That is the simple reason why 'the Doc', at the height of his powers, wanted Australia to adopt a bill of rights; how he would have deprecated Labor politicians such as Bob Carr who have spent so much time bullishly campaigning against a measure that would help the disadvantaged. Those who truly wish to benefit both workers and those who, in Brennan's words, 'fall through the cracks', should insist on its adoption as a means of preventing the kind of 'injustice within the law' exemplified by the case of the Dorsetshire labourers.

Chapter 5

1901

*If I am a refugee from anything, it is from the Australian consti-
tution, or at least from having to spend my time in court in
arid arguments over a constitutional law that is mainly about
allocation of power between federal and state governments.
Australians – or at least the Australian – react with mindless
patriotism whenever 'our' constitution is said to need updating.
It is necessary to remind them, in this case in a* Bulletin *edition
celebrating in 2001 the centenary of Federation, of the virulence of the racism of the time, which ensured that human
rights were absent from a document agreed at a referendum
from which women, blacks and territorians were excluded.
It is anachronistic to see the Australian constitution in any
true sense as the work of Australians: it was the work, more
accurately, of unevolved Australians who were hooked intra-
venously to British blood. And in the class-calcified Britain of
Queen Victoria, where small children were put up chimneys
and down mines, there was no talk of human rights.*

Pauline Hanson is the modern politician who most closely resembles the founding fathers of our constitution. Federation was forged not from any belief in human dignity or liberty, but from an obsession with racial purity: the felt need was for a common barrier to stop Chinese immigration and the importing of Kanakas by Queensland planters. Perhaps it's time for a nation which has recently saved the credibility both of the United Nations (over East Timor) and of the Olympic Games to turn its genius to redressing the most fundamental failure of its founders: their opposition to human rights.

That a bill of rights did not feature on the agenda of the 1890s Conventions is hardly surprising – the federation movement was not a struggle against tyranny but a matter of economic and strategic sense encouraged by the British Colonial Office. Indeed, the mother country was a mother that had to push its reluctant young out of the nest. Earl Grey (of tea fame) had greatly upset nervous Australians as early as 1850, when as Colonial Secretary he had suggested that they federate. In 1890 the Colonial Office became more insistent that the Australian states grow up and develop a national defence capacity which might balance the French and German settlements in the Pacific. Australian statesmen of the time were avowedly British to their bootstraps (or, as old photographs show, from their bowler hats to their brogue shoes) and had willingly agreed to the Colonial Office's main condition, that Australia's appeal court should be the Privy Council, because British investors would feel more secure if friendly law lords in London could ultimately decide any claim against an Australian.

So Federation came about, not after a struggle against brutal colonial governors, but from a struggle by Sir Henry Parkes (supported by the Colonial Governor) to convince Australians in different states that there was a 'crimson thread of kinship' running through them all. Embarrassing for next of kin today, the crimson thread uniting them in 1901 was not a belief in human dignity but a fervent desire for racial purity. An attempt at the 1898 Melbourne Convention to inject into the draft of the

Australian constitution those great US guarantees of equality and due process was rejected after Isaac Isaacs (much later the first Australian-born governor-general) warned of the 'danger' of ending discrimination against Chinese workers, while Sir John Forrest openly spoke of the 'great feeling' Australians had against 'coloured peoples'. Henry Higgins, later a High Court judge, assured Sir John that by rejecting the US equal rights clause he could ban Asiatics wherever he liked, or confine them to specific areas or jobs, or deport them: discrimination that was 'simply based on colour and race' would be unchallengeable. Aborigines were mentioned at Federation only as a part of the fauna, a sub-human species denied the most basic right of being counted in the census.

What should distress modern Australians is not so much the virulence of the racism which infected these founding fathers as the fact that it blinded them to the advantage of adopting, like the US, a code of universal human values, a bedrock of principles upon which Australian law could develop logically and humanely. Instead, at the insistence of the British government, they kept the English law lords (sitting in the Privy Council in Downing Street) as Australia's final Court of Appeal. This meant blind adherence to English common law, made up of rulings given by its judges down the centuries: the only 'rights' that common law fully protected were to property and its continued possession by the upper classes.

In the result, Australia was endowed with a supreme law – its constitution – which lacked any systemic protection for citizen liberties. Australian constitutional law is mainly about demarcation of state and federal power – a matter of no relevance to anyone outside Australia and largely incomprehensible to anyone within it (other than to constitutional lawyers). The dominance of the Privy Council (incredibly, its role as the final Court of Appeal for Australia was not finally abolished until 1986) meant adherence to the common law tradition, which develops by painstaking and obsequious regard for previous court rulings, treated as precedents that control subsequent decisions.

That a system based on precedent delivers much less justice than a system based on principle has recently been acknowledged by Britain, which has adopted the *European Convention of Human Rights* to provide its constitutional bedrock. Canada, South Africa and even New Zealand have already adopted similar legislation. Australia is now left behind, as the only advanced democracy in the world which offers no constitutional protection for the rights of its citizens.

The reason this matters is that without an organising system based on universally recognised values, Australian law is becoming inaccessible and incomprehensible. It's a jumble of state and federal statutory rules and precedents extrapolated from a forest of loose-leaf casebooks or (increasingly) from torrential computer print-outs. The essential quality of law – citizen understanding, leading to citizen trust – is being lost.

On a sociological level, this means that the law makes inadequate contribution to culture and to national identity. There is nothing about human liberty in our constitution that we can point to with pride, or happily invite our children to recite.

Moreover, human rights jurisprudence is of increasing international importance as a measure of a country's commitment and freedom. The courts of advanced democracies vie to elucidate the common principles of justice contained in their constitutions. In these legal Olympics, the dominance of the US Supreme Court is currently challenged by the South African Constitutional Court and by the newly empowered British Supreme Court judges. Without a bill of rights as their starting block, Australian judges – although intellectually among the world's best – cannot begin to compete.

Politicians jealously guard their own power and so oppose the idea of granting legal rights to citizens. Bob Carr has warned that a bill of rights would be 'rorted by lawyers' – ignoring the fact that a rights-based system affords the best protection against sharks and pettifoggers. As Tony Blair has pointed out, the idea of giving courts more power to do justice should be threatening only to those politicians and governments who fail to deliver it.

One hundred years have passed since Federation: do we still have no statesmen or stateswomen farsighted enough to vouch-safe constitutional human rights to all Australians?

Chapter 6

INDEPENDENCE DAY?

When 'Quizine' was posed to Sydney's business and artistic communities, two questions nobody could answer were the name of the schoolteacher who stopped the train at Glenrowan and the telephone number of the terrorist hotline that Attorney-General Ruddock had spent millions of dollars advertising. There was also a trick question – what was the date of Australian independence? – to which there are at least seven answers. Australia is one of the few nations that lacks an 'independence day' – a matter of pride in other countries, but here a matter of indifference, other than to constitutional lawyers, to whom it is a matter of confusion. In my 2009 book The Statute of Liberty *I pondered seven of the arguably correct answers to the question 'when did Australia become independent?'*

- **1901: The year of Federation**

  But this was an act of the British parliament, which could have repealed Australia the very next day, since it could still impose its legislation. Australian law remained under the control of British judges, sitting in the Privy Council. Every state parliament remained subject to the British Crown. The governor-general of Australia was to be appointed directly by the British government, without consultation with the Australian government, and state governors were appointed on the advice of the British Colonial Office, not of the state premier.

- **1931: The *Statute of Westminster***

  This was an act of the British parliament, sitting as parliament for the dominions and adopting a resolution from an imperial conference in 1926 (the Balfour Declaration), which permitted the federal parliament to amend or repeal British legislation applying to Australia. But the statute did not give state parliaments this power. The common law rule giving supremacy to British statutes still applied: Australia's final Court of Appeal remained the British law lords sitting in the Privy Council in London. In any event, Australia did not adopt the statute until 1942, although in 1931 the Australian government was finally and graciously allowed to advise the monarch about whom he (in other words, the British government) should appoint as governor-general, though not as state governors.

- **1939: The *Statute of Westminster Adoption Act***

  This was passed in 1942 but it was backdated to 3 September 1939, which thus becomes a possible date for Australian independence. But on this very day the Australian government believed itself legally bound by the British declaration of war on Germany, as Robert Menzies KC, its then prime minister, made clear in his radio broadcast immediately afterward, declaring that because Britain was at war so was Australia. Since the power to declare war is fundamental to an independent nation, Australia did not have independence.

- **1941: Declaration of War on Japan**

  The Curtin government acted on its own initiative to declare this war. But the legal bonds to Britain remained, notwithstanding the fall of Singapore.

- **1942: The *Statute of Westminster Adoption Act***

  This was passed by the Australian parliament to remove doubts about the validity of Australian laws that might previously have been struck down as repugnant to British law, and to remove the right of the British parliament to pass laws affecting Australia, other than at the request of the federal government. This did not apply to the states and did not remove the Privy Council as our final Court of Appeal. The *Adoption Act* was passed in October 1942, but was made retrospective to 3 September 1939, when Britain took Australia to war.

- **The *Australia Acts*, 1986**

  Seven laws enacted by the states, the British government and finally by the Commonwealth government severed the constitutional tie to Britain. No longer could the queen exercise her powers on the advice of the British Foreign and Commonwealth Office rather than the state governments, and the power of the British parliament to legislate for Australia was finally abolished. With it went the absurdity of having Australia's highest court manned by British law lords, who were often intellectually inferior to our High Court judges and out of touch with the nation whose legal disputes they were deciding from their chamber in Downing Street. However, the British monarch remained as Australia's head of state, the 'Queen of Australia'.

- **Not Yet**

An obscure seventeenth-century German princess, Sophia of Hanover, has had her genes enshrined in the Australian constitution's pride of place. Those of Princess Sophia's descendants who mount the British throne automatically become head of state in Australia. The constitution remains part of British law – the British parliament's *Commonwealth of Australia Constitution Act 1900* (the original is lodged in a public records office in London), although the source of federal power is now the Australian constitution, which can pursuant to section 128 be amended or replaced by the Australian people voting in a referendum. So the source of federal power in Australia remains the UK parliament, until Australia decides to adopt a brand new constitution, or at least amends the present document to establish a republic. As constitutional amendments are fiendishly difficult to pass – thanks to provisions in the constitution itself – we are likely to be reigned over by the Saxe-Coburg Gotha family for many years to come.

Chapter 7

IN A TASMANIAN FERRY, ON THE THAMES

There must be a little bit of Sir Les Patterson in us all. I do not quite know how I was persuaded, by Neal Blewett when he was High Commissioner in London, to launch yet another campaign for recognition of Australian excellence. This one was called 'New Images', and was designed to send the message that Australia was a very clever, technologically advanced country, with a vast potential trading relationship with the UK.

It was 1996: republicanism was so much in the air that John Howard had been forced to call a 'People's Convention' to work out how to de-monarchise, which most thought inevitable. How wrong they were.

In Britain, at the fag end of seventeen years of harsh Conservative governance, Home Secretary Michael Howard was running out of prison space: his latest wheeze was to call for criminals to be housed in hulks on the Thames. That was where I stood to launch 'New Images' in the stateroom of the Holyman Express, a reputed wonder of Tasmanian technology built to ply the English Channel – shortly before the opening of the Channel tunnel made it obsolete. There is a nostalgic anachronism about this speech – one of the last before Australia was transformed by the Chinese grab for its resources. Some of the jokes are still topical, however – the biggest being on me. I actually said all of this free of charge.

Private Eye describes me simply as 'an Australian who's had a voice transplant'. I lost my irritable Australian vowels very early in my career of bowing and scraping in the English courts. In my first appearance at the Old Bailey I had to tell a very prim and proper judge that I appeared on behalf of a company that manufactured T-shirts emblazoned with the 'F' word. I nervously mustered up the courage to tell him that the offending logo read 'Fuck Art, let's Dance'. His eyebrows shot up in horror. 'Fuck Art, let's WHAT, Mr Robertson?' 'Let's dance, my lord.' 'Oh I see. You're an *Australian*. What you mean to say is 'Fuck Art, let's *Dãnce*.'

Linguistic antipathy is no longer one-sided. When the exquisitely spoken Alexander Downer briefly became leader of the opposition, he was deemed to require the services of a voice coach to change his pronunciation from BBC English to Channel 9 Australian, to teach him to say 'dance' instead of 'dãnce', and to learn how to amputate the endings of words of more than one syllable (well, it's just too hot in Australia to say all of a long word).

But at least it's one measure of our common cultural heritage that we pronounce our swear-words in exactly the same way.

It's a terrific privilege to stand on the deck of the good ship *Holyman Express*, and to celebrate the newly discovered Australian creative gene for manufacturing and technology, and the future this holds for trade with Britain. It says a lot for Holyman as a company that it's had the confidence to make such a major commitment of £200 million to design and build these vessels in Tasmania, which, despite occasional appearances to the contrary, *is* part of Australia. You can see at a glance it's from Tasmania, from the words on its stern: 'Holyman Express – Nassau.' Nassau is that big port just below Launceston. I guess it's registered there because Nassau is an offshore tax haven and Tasmania isn't, although Tony Randle is working on it. It will be a change from Tasmania being known as the world's largest golf course. That's an old image; Tasmania's new image, at least outside of Australia, is as the epitome of sophistication.

The other day I was taken to a fashionable London bistro by the editor of the *New Statesman*, who said, 'You must try this Tasmanian wine. It's actually quite sophisticated.' 'Not a word I associate with Tasmania,' I replied, but I was soon drinking my words.

I've only found one design fault in the *Holyman Express* – have you noticed, there's nowhere for passengers to feed seagulls? Given the toxicity of any droppings from birds that have been in the North Sea, that's probably just as well. Instead, however, the passengers will get seagull cries piped over the intercom, and I'm assured that the high-grade aluminium alloys on the window frames will be strong enough to withstand dive-bombing birds frantic for a taste of the emu-meat leftovers. The catamaran will take 670 passengers and 180 crew, crossing the Channel at twice the speed of conventional ferries. It will also be safe. Unlike those of other companies which I could name but won't because some are our guests.

So here's to the *Holyman Express* and its commercial success. Even if the bottom does drop out of the ferry market, or the GEC engines drop out of the aluminium hull, the company will have noticed that Mr Michael Howard's new prison policy has created a big demand for hulks. Tenders are shortly to be called for prison ships, to be moored right here on the Thames. Just as they were two hundred years ago, when their overcrowded state caused the Tory government of William Pitt to transfer so many prisoners of Her Majesty to Botany Bay and Van Diemen's Land. How piquant, then, if Tasmanian technology should return with a vengeance to incarcerate the modern British criminal. Holyman Catamarans would be sure to win the tender, since the cry of 'Bring back the cat' is one which Mr Howard would find utterly irresistible.

For Australians, prison ships have a particular resonance. They brought out my ancestors, who were in the Marines, escorting the convicts (my wife's ancestors) and many herds of merino sheep. The convicts and their guards were mainly men, hence the definition of 'shearing' as the Australian version of foreplay. My forebears stayed on, to farm a 500-acre grant of virgin forest on which stands today the industrial city of Wollongong. They sold about a century too soon.

But the old image of Australians as farmers, in a rural country that rose to prosperity on the sheep's back (if not its flanks), is one that dies hard. At school in the fifties, we were indoctrinated to believe we lived in a lucky and lazy country that would continue to live high on the hog so long as we kept out the teeming yellow hordes to the north and concentrated on plundering the fertile and mineral-rich earth that fringed our coast. We were happy to be perceived as a raw people with raw materials for sale: almost everything we made was made on license from abroad.

There was one important exception. Since Australians think sex drive means doing it in a car, the Holdens we learned to make love in we kidded ourselves were Australian made. We overlooked the fact that they were made by General Motors, to a design that Americans wouldn't be seen dead in.

But Australians in those days despaired of indigenous industry. My contemporaries who wanted to go into medical research or design engineering were told to go to Europe or America. We just weren't interested in being clever. The classic example was the work carried out by David Warren at the Aeronautical Research Laboratory in Melbourne, after the British comet airliner crashes. In 1958, incredibly, brilliantly, he hit upon the design of, and he actually produced, the very first 'black box' flight recorder. The government was asked to support its manufacture. 'Nah,' said the Department of Transport, 'it will never catch on – wholly unnecessary.' Fortunately for the history of airline safety, a British company picked up Warren's design a few years later and the rest is history – but Australia just wasn't interested. In those days, the idea we might design and build ferries to ply the straits of the world was beyond our wildest dreams. And beyond our aspirations.

I guess that self-deprecating image really changed when Ben Lexcen designed the keel that won the America's Cup. And when some ex-veterinary surgeons in Melbourne realised that the reproductive apparatus of Australian cows was on all fours with the reproductive apparatus of Australian women, and went on to create human life from frozen embryos. Barry Jones and Neal Blewett and some of their colleagues in Canberra decided it might be more interesting to run a clever country than a lucky country, and this idea slowly caught on. Just to what extent can be seen from the fact that twenty-seven per cent of our total exports now fall into the category of 'elaborately transformed manufactures': computer software, aircraft components, internal combustion engines, gas pumps, medical supplies and the like.

What is also interesting, in analysing the export statistics, is that almost half of these high-tech goods go to the UK. British companies, far more than those from America or Japan, have had faith in Australia's new self-image, and have put in the investment to make its realisation possible. Britain is the biggest investor in our manufacturing sector, to the tune of £42 billion, and its companies have, more than any other, chosen Australia for their regional headquarters. The view of Australia as a really interesting country, and of Australians as really interesting people, is a view from Britain much more than it is a view from anywhere else. Cynics might think that's because Britain is further away, and distance lends enchantment to the view, but it takes more than enchantment to invest £42 billion.

There's another story the trade statistics tell, about the real Australian attitudes to Britain. I need hardly remind you of the popular myths. What do cold beer and a warm welcome have in common? You can't get either of them in London. Where does an Englishman hide his money? Under the soap. These prejudices are belied by the business facts. Where do Australians put their money? Under the Union Jack. We are the third largest investor in the UK, well ahead of Germany and Japan and the so-called tiger economies of Southeast Asia. Over eighty Australian computer software companies have set up offices here. We have fought and won almost ten per cent of the British wine market. And so on. Beneath the surface prejudices which the 'New Images' campaign seeks to redress, there lies a great wedge of mutual trade and mutual trust.

Mutual affection? Perish the thought. And yet . . . I went back to Australia just before Christmas to find the whole country in a paroxysm of rage about some stupid lost frog yachtsman, who expected the taxpayer to foot the bill for saving his miserable Gallic life. But on the way to haul this idiot out of the Indian Ocean, one of our destroyers discovered a jovial Brit named Tony Bullimore marooned beneath his boat. Well, that changes everything. The nation just went berserk with happiness. They didn't mind all the bankruptcies he was sailing away from, they forgave his attempts to con the chocolate companies, they didn't even mind that his wife was black – and that's another real change from the fifties. They loved him because he was British, so British that the first thing he said was that he couldn't believe anyone would send a destroyer to save him because he was only lower middle class. That, actually, is why I think they loved him: because we share the same sense of humour.

That, when you come to think of it, is what we really have in common. You can't share a joke with a New Zealander, they are the joke. You can't share a joke with a Canadian, they wouldn't get it. Americans have an irony deficiency, Germans have no sense of humour, Malaysians always take offence and South Africans are still very sensitive. We are probably the only two countries in the world that can actually enjoy each other, if we really try.

For that to happen, to make Bullimore syndrome a permanent state of mind, we have to staunch the bad blood that spatters each country's image of the other. The arrogant, condescending 'Pom', the bitter Aussie with the chip – make that now the microchip – on the shoulder. It stems not from a trading bloc, but from a psychological block, created by an artificial and slightly ridiculous constitutional arrangement. If 'New Images' has a message, it's the message that appearances do matter. And the £5 million that the UK government is spending on it will be money squandered, so long as most Australians feel, in some arcane and legalistic way, that they are still subjects of Her Majesty. 'Reigned over', in some irrelevant but apparently meaningful sense, by the heirs of Princess Sophia of Hanover, that well-favoured Anglican line established by the *Act of Settlement 1701* to provide the head of state of Great Britain, eight smallish islands, Newfoundland and the Falklands and Australia. It is this largely theoretical sovereignty that fuels the old antagonism, and becomes for Australians a royal scapegoat for its failure to find a real identity in Asia. As for British arrogance and condescension, well, perhaps they are entitled to be condescending to a people so constitutionally backward that they can't even rule themselves in their own name.

Only yesterday, our prime minister announced a 'People's Convention' to consider how and when Australia might become a republic. Mention the queen to most Aussie kids and they think you are talking about Elton John. Mr John Howard is usually described as a monarchist, although a more appropriate description of him is a politician – one who will not, for example, stand in the royal shadow at the opening of the Sydney Olympics. It's one of the ironies of politics that it's easier for Conservatives to achieve revolutionary change, just as it's easier for Labour parties to dismantle socialism. So the Republic of Australia should be the really new image on the design board. Its declaration, far from damaging relationships between the two countries, will lead to a much clearer recognition of the culture and the comedy and the trading ties that really do bind us. It will make Australians value the British genius, what Lord Scarman describes as the invention of institutions that work: the common law, the civil service, the whole democratic inheritance that provides the surest foundation for Australia's role in Asia.

With this constitutional adjustment, the future is assured. Australia is the number-one holiday destination for young people in Britain; the United Kingdom remains the place young Australians would most like to visit. Australians want to marvel at a country where you can leave butter out of the fridge, and where, when you step on someone on the tube, it's *they* who apologise to *you*. They want to see with their own eyes the only country in the world that had a revolution – and then invited the monarchy back.

They want to leave it here. But may I suggest a farewell present, Mr High Commissioner? What could be more fitting, as a way of saying goodbye, than to present Her Majesty with *Britannia II*; the new royal yacht. A catamaran designed and built by Holyman. Commission it now, Mr Commissioner, as a farewell gift from the Republic of Australia.

FIRST AUSTRALIANS

Chapter 8

BRINGING BACK THE BONES

This was a case that starkly pitted scientific curiosity against cultural identity. Britain's Natural History Museum, renowned repository of Darwin's enlightened legacy, had acquired over the years the skulls and bones of early Tasmanian Aborigines. This tribe, cut off from the mainland, may have genetically developed in a unique way. Not that the museum's scientists had been interested – for half a century they had kept these relics in cardboard boxes, stored away and forgotten, until the Australian government backed a demand by the Tasmanian Aboriginal Centre (TAC) for their return. Museum scientists insisted that the human remains should be first subjected to 'destructive testing': they planned to cut teeth and bone sections from the skulls in DNA laboratories and dissolve them in acid. This mutilation of their forebears outraged the TAC, as it breached cultural taboos and was yet another form of desecration and disrespect.

In law, there is no property in a dead body and the museum had possession (which is nine-tenths of the law). Could they be stopped? That was the question TAC leader Michael Mansell put to me in an urgent phone call on a Thursday night, before the testing was to begin on the following Monday. The museum had ignored Britain's Human Rights Act, *which required some* respect for religion and for family. On Sunday, we obtained an injunction – ironically, from Britain's only black High Court judge – but on Monday, the museum rushed into court to try to discharge it. Their counsel proclaimed that the skulls were museum property and they were only going to 'cut them about a bit' in the interests of science. What they were going to do, I responded, was to experiment on the bones of victims of genocide. We held the injunction, and the battle began.

There were endless points of legal interest as the case developed. Hundreds of pages of erudite submissions were made on both sides, involving the Genocide Convention and international treaties, the European Convention on Human Rights, the old English common law relating to property in human remains and abandoned corpses, and whether 'destructive testing' would amount to trespass and assault. The UK Commission on Racial Equality intervened in our support, arguing that the museum would be in breach of the Race Relations Act. The genocide argument certainly rattled its trustees: for all the legal niceties this case really involved a question of morality, and they soon capitulated to the TAC's demand that the case go to mediation, before the former Chief Justice of England (Lord Woolf) and the former Chief Justice of New South Wales (Sir Laurence Street).

After several days locked in anxious ethical wrangling, the museum was forced to concede all the TAC demands, made in this 'skeleton argument' I drafted on behalf of the skeletons. It was not the easiest of submissions in the sense that the museum had made a rationalist case for acquisition of scientific knowledge, but I do believe that there are moral limits to this quest.

The remains of the lost tribe now rest in peace, safe from the carving knives of scientists, unless their descendants agree at some time in the future that further knowledge about them is really worth acquiring.

Submissions on Behalf of the Tasmanian Aboriginal Centre

> It appears that not a single native now remains upon Van Diemen's Land. Thus nearly has the event (the extinction of the race) been accomplished which was thus predicted and deprecated by Sir Gilbert Murray: 'It is impossible not to contemplate such a result of our occupation of the island as one very difficult to be reconciled with feelings of humanity, or even with principles of justice and sound policy; and the adoption of any line of conduct, having for its avowed or secret object the extinction of the native race, could not fail to leave an indelible stain upon the British Government.'
>
> House of Commons, Report from the Select
> Committee on Aborigines
> 5 August 1836

Introduction

Over a century after this parliamentary committee owned up to the appalling barbarities that British governance had inflicted upon Tasmanian Aborigines, the 'indelible stain' was forever identified in the word coined by Raphael Lemkin: 'genocide'. That was, precisely, the crime perpetrated by colonial Britain against Tasmanian Aboriginals, some thirteen of whom still have their remains – unlawfully looted from graves, grotesquely snatched from death beds to serve as mantelpiece curios, or boiled down after massacres – detained in cardboard boxes by the Trustees of the National History Museum. On them, these Trustees propose to inflict further indignities before they perform their grudgingly acknowledged ethical duty to hand them back: they intend to dispatch them to some unnamed and unsupervised private laboratories to be deliberately mutilated. Sections will be carved off the bones and teeth of these genocide victims and will then be destroyed, by vaporisation, pulverisation or dissolution.

This is said to be 'in the interests of science', although in fact it is in the interests of the scientists at the National History Museum (NHM), who hope by this exercise in genetic pros-pecting to profit by obtaining some – any – further information about Tasmanian Aborigines, irrespective of whether it is of any value and utterly heedless of whether the Aboriginal community consents to its extraction in this way or at all. The NHM has, in effect, shown the same disrespect for Aborigines and contempt for their rights that caused the 'indelible stain' to run in the first place.

There can be no dispute that the processes to which the NHM proposes to subject the remains are contrary to Aborig-inal law, custom and religious belief in relation to treatment of the dead. They obviously interfere with the community's rights to manifest its religious beliefs, which envisage the souls of the departed in torment unless and until laid to rest with customary ceremony in traditional lands. The experiments that the NHM proposes to carry out will torture these thirteen souls, and their descendants have a spiritual duty not merely to grieve for that suffering but a binding obligation to bring it to an end.

Tasmanian Aboriginals are a minority group under inter-national law, which means that protection of their rights of identity, culture and religion must be given special status. There is an emerging principle of free, prior and informed consent of indigenous peoples to policies affecting their rights and welfare 'where a sufficient connection with the relevant indigenous people is capable of being established' and that relevant connec-tion has been established in the case of the TAC. Article 13 of the draft *United Nations Declaration on the Rights of Indig-enous Peoples* specifically grants 'the right to repatriation of human remains' and stresses the importance of the right to manifest cultural traditions and religious beliefs and to obtain restitution of spiritual property 'taken without their free and informed consent or in violation of their laws, traditions and customs'.

The TAC renewed its request that the museum repatriate

the remains and was promised by the museum director that its request would be considered in a 'fair, open and ethically sound way' with provision for 'independent advice'. However, the six-person advisory panel set up by the museum included a museum trustee and the museum's own Director of Science, with the museum's Science Policy Co-ordinator as its secretary – a composition that precluded meaningful 'independence' from the museum, whose scientific staff have always been contemptuous of the concerns of indigenous people. The procedure adopted was obviously unfair. The TAC was not permitted to comment upon, or even see, the museum staff's own submission to the advisory panel, a document which came to sway the panel with exaggerated and bogus claims about the benefits of future research. The advisory panel's advice was given, and the subsequent Trustees' decision to conduct experiments was taken, without any consultation with the TAC or the Australian government.

The NHM must now recognise, as a condition of any mediated settlement, the need to respect both these human remains and their descendant community. The museum must acknowledge the barbaric historical circumstances in which the deaths occurred, and the unlawful way in which the remains were brought to the UK, ultimately to come wrongfully into their possession. They must rectify their past lack of interest in Tasmanian Aborigines – there is no reference to them in any public exhibition ever held at the museum, or in any of its publications. Against that background, it must be prepared to apologise for its disrespectful conduct in the past, and be genuinely prepared to accept the best ethical practice for the future. That means it must begin, albeit belatedly and retrospectively, by asking TAC consent to every aspect of its treatment program begun in secret last December.

The Thirteen Aborigines

Until the pressure mounted for repatriating these remains, the NHM did not care at all about the people from whom they were taken. So let us ask: who are – or were – these thirteen human beings? How did they meet their deaths? How were the skulls and skeletons made available to British museums in the first place? All the museum knows about them is in its records produced in the litigation, and it has never bothered to find out more. What is clear from its scrappy, inconclusive and hearsay records is that the museum has no idea at all *when* they died or in most cases *where* they died, and has had no interest in *how* they died. It can be said with confidence that the remains were acquired either by coercion or by theft and looting – i.e. both immorally and unlawfully.

The individuals include:

*PA HR 343 An adult female skull which was 'picked up' (a euphemism for grave-robbed) on the north coast of the island. This woman seems to have been the victim of a massacre: it was a spot where 'a white man had fired into an encampment and wounded a woman. Her head was chopped off and she was buried in the sand.' It was later 'picked up' together with another female massacre victim, by Dr Joseph Milligan, one of the notorious 'protectors' of Aborigines – in this case the official that supervised the transportation of gulag survivors from Flinders Island to Oyster Bay in 1847. Milligan is said to have 'collected' on the north and east coasts of Tasmania – again, a euphemism for robbing graves and in fact cutting off the skulls of newly deceased Aborigines whom he was meant to be 'protecting'. He was, by so doing, guilty of breach of trust and of actions recognised as criminal by the common law of the time. (There is some seemliness in the fact that the TAC plans to bury these poor women at Oyster Bay, the place where Milligan probably 'collected' their skulls.)

*PA HR 590 This is interesting, because it is avowedly 'dug up from a grave on Flinders Island by Morton Allport'. He was the curator of the Hobart Museum who robbed Aboriginal graves and betrayed his trust by selling his museum's contents to anthropologists in Britain. This skeleton he sold to the Anthropological Society of London in 1873, when he was still curator. The remains were purchased by the defendant in 1898 for £195. It was clearly a valuable skeleton, and the defendant must have known, at the time it was purchased, of its unlawful origins.

*PA HR 593 These remains are associated with Lady Franklin, wife of the colonial governor, who unlawfully ordered officials to obtain skulls for her to display as curios. It was probably the skull obtained for her by the governor's private secretary, who with Robinson (another notorious 'protector' of Aborigines) arranged for a corpse to be decapitated by a surgeon and then packed up for transport to the governor's wife. The museum is fully aware of these unlawful origins since it notes that both Lady Franklin and the governor's private secretary requested Robinson to find skulls for them when they visited Flinders Island.

The above facts severely undermine the museum's claim that experimenting with these remains would yield information of significant public interest. It is essential to know the context and history before data extracted from the remains can be sensibly claimed to be of significant use. Otherwise, such data can be misleading. Some of these individuals may not even be Tasmanian Aborigines – the museum itself is not sure. They are all probably post-colonisation, so will not provide examples of a geographically isolated island race: they could well have had

various associations with white colonists, mainland Aboriginals, sealers and sailors, and will have imbibed diets and alcohol
and will have contracted white men's diseases.

Without a proper context (and of course the lack of information may well be attributable to the clandestinity of the trade
in skulls) it is difficult to understand how any data from these
remains could be reliably interpreted. However, even if some
data of significance could be extracted, the museum has no
right to extract it without consent. Although its scientists hold
to the belief (as did Dr Mengele) that the pursuit of knowledge
is an overriding good in itself, it is necessarily constrained by
three facts:

1. these are remains of human beings killed in British genocide,
    and

2. these remains were unlawfully and immorally brought into
    the UK, and

3. the experiments are to measure racial characteristics.

The Consequences of Genocide

These remains were unlawfully acquired by coercion, theft and
looting of graves. These crimes were committed in the course of
what was genocide, namely by Britain's 'attempt to destroy, in
whole or in part, an ethnic/ racial group' by killing its members
or inflicting upon them debilitating conditions of life designed
to bring about their destruction in whole or part. British atrocities in Tasmania were so appalling that in 1836 they provoked
a special inquiry by a Select Committee of the House of
Commons, which describes how British soldiers, convicts and
settlers occupied the island from 1803 and British policies led to
the destruction of almost all of some five to eight thousand indigenous Tasmanians. The genocide commenced with massacres,
with rape of indigenous women and enslavement of Aboriginal children and destruction of crops and hunting areas and
grave sites. When Aborigines in 1828 resisted, martial law was
declared and search-and-destroy parties within twelve months

'destroyed more than two-thirds of these wild peoples'. (See *Patterns of Frontier Genocide* by Benjamin Madley.) Robinson, the 'protector' of Aborigines to whom some remains in the NHM are attributed, was responsible in 1829 for removing all the survivors to a gulag on Flinders Island, where most died of malnutrition or from diseases introduced by the settlers.

This was during the regime of Governor Franklin, whose wife obtained several of the museum's skulls as curios. It is noteworthy that Plomley, the accepted authority upon whom the defendant's collection repeatedly relies for its notes, tells how colonists seized Aboriginal children and dashed out their brains and lined their parents up for musket practice, considering them less than human. Robinson himself described the treatment of Aboriginal women as 'the African slave trade in miniature' with routine rape, kidnapping and murder. The proclamation of martial law 'gave every white a license to kill Aborigines'. Robinson recognised that his actions would cause the extinction of the race: when the reserve was closed only forty-six survivors remained. Like 'blood diamonds' imbued with the deaths caused in their quest, these human remains carry the moral horror of the crime against humanity once perpetrated against them.

Genocide is a crime against humanity and as such is subject to no time bar. (Imagine the ethical outrage throughout the world if similar experiments were proposed on Holocaust victims in a recently discovered mass grave.) The remains were unlawfully taken in the course of the genocide, in actions that may be considered in furtherance of it. This illegality taints the original taking and acquisition of the remains, whether direct (in a few cases) or accepted from other collectors, and it taints any institution that detains or deals with the remains, other than repatriating them for burial.

Scientific Racism

It is noteworthy that this data is being collected to reveal racial characteristics – this is what the museum is looking for. Body structure, physiognomy, muscles and heart size, the shape of the brain, and particularly (through genetic analysis) what is termed 'abnormality'. Racial characteristics ('natural abnormalities') are to be the focus of these experiments in what is termed 'human diversity': the aim is to put Tasmanian Aborigines on an evolutionary ladder of diverse humanity, and it is not difficult to imagine they will be placed on a lower rung. Is this of any real or abiding value, other than to those who wish to denigrate them? Australian Aborigines have been condemned to a century of stigmatic denigration by racist British scientists who portrayed them as 'primitives' with small brains, heavy brows and flat heads.

As recently as 1974, Oxford University Press could publish vicious denigration by John R. Baker, who likened them to pongids, or apes, 'who serve as a reminder of a stage of more advanced forms.' It is little wonder that the TAC does not trust British scientists capable of making such racist judgments, even after Claude Lévi-Strauss established that Aborigines were 'so far ahead of the rest of mankind' in matters touching on the organisation of harmonious family life and community relations.

No doubt the NHM scientists will claim that their experiments will be 'neutral', but they admit they have no idea of the results they will get, if any. But what are they looking for? 'Diversity' at the lower end of the spectrum? If they produce a little knowledge, how then can they prevent it becoming a dangerous thing in the hands of racists (and there are plenty in Australia as well as Britain) who will use some non-contextual and incomplete data as evidence of small brains, thick heads, kinship with apes, etc.

This is the danger of experimentation controlled by scientists who believe Aborigines to be an inferior race (or at least behave as though they believe this, by totally ignoring the TAC protests and by testing these remains without condescending to tell them).

Indigenous Rights

Tasmanian Aboriginals are a minority according to international law, which means that protection of their rights of identity, culture and religion must be given special status. There is an emerging principle of free, prior and informed consent of indigenous peoples to policies affecting their rights and welfare. The NHM must be prepared to follow the majority advice of the Working Group on Human Remains in Museum Collections, since that majority comprised ten experts as against the NHM's then director, who was in a minority of one. In any event, there was unanimous agreement (at paragraph 340) that 'the wishes of the deceased person are paramount and should transcend the interests of science' provided:

- lack of consent is known to the museum;
- there is a group claiming the return of the remains; and
- that group satisfies the test of closeness of relationship.

The guidance on research and sampling requires that sampling, including destructive sampling, should only be undertaken after scientific justifications are placed on file and fully recorded. The questions asked must include:

- Can the research questions be addressed using non-destructive techniques? Destructive sampling should only be contemplated if this is not so.
- Any program of destructive analysis on human remains should take place within a planned research program and should have a realistic prospect of producing useful knowledge.

Amongst the litigation material, statements of Professor Webb and of Sir Peter Morris and the second statement of Michael Mansell address the failure of the defendant to ask these questions. There was no planned research program, just a fishing expedition hastily put forward because the skulls had to be repatriated, by scientists who had never shown any interest in such a testing program before.

The exercise was one of 'genetic prospecting'. Whether the information would be useful in any meaningful sense was not addressed by the museum scientists, who regard any information as useful. They make the most general reference to 'understanding the environment in which the Tasmanian Aborigines lived' and producing information about 'diet, climate and lifestyle'.

But we already understand the Tasmanian environment of the nineteenth century, and its climate, and we know their diet (of which the British deprived them by confiscating their hunting grounds) and their lifestyle, which the British disrupted by ending their lives, and the diseases that the British spread among them.

The Position Today

In all the circumstances, the museum should hand all the remaining remains over to the TAC for decent burial forthwith and abandon its program of experimentation. That program comprises seven stages, namely:

1. Measuring and observing;
2. High resolution photography;
3. CT scanning, lasers and X-rays;
4. Casting;
5. Histology, involving cutting off pieces of bone and teeth ('sectioning');
6. Isotopes, involving the vaporisation of extracted bone and tooth;
7. Genetic analysis (DNA) in the process of which, to be done in laboratories outside the museum, cellular material taken from the bones will be destroyed.

There can be no dispute over the fact that all seven processes are contrary to Aboriginal law, custom and religious belief in relation to treatment of the dead and interfere with the claimants' rights to manifest their religious beliefs. The museum as a 'public body' for the purposes of the *Human Rights Act* has a duty to give full faith and credit to these indigenous religious beliefs. They are after-life beliefs and are all-pervasive in Aboriginal lore and life, in their custom and rituals, which require constant solicitude for the departed. It is a belief that particularly connects ancestors with the land – a land that became in the case of Tasmania, a killing field when they were extirpated from their hunting grounds by a British invasion of the island. The continuing attachment of Aboriginals to their dead, and to the location of their graves, was one of the first features of their life noted by early European observers. There is no question but that those who looted these graves and wrongfully sent skeletons to England were well aware that this was desecrating Aboriginal religious beliefs about the treatment of the dead.

Conclusion

An acceptable mediated result might be as follows:

1. That the trustees of the NHM say 'sorry' to the TAC, and extend that apology to the Indigenous peoples of Australia, for the past disrespect they have shown to the remains of Aboriginal victims of genocide, unlawfully brought to and detained in the UK.

2. The trustees undertake to cease all testing on these remains forthwith, and to hand them over to representatives of the TAC at an appropriate ceremony in order that they may be repatriated and buried in accordance with Aboriginal custom and tradition.

3. The trustees will humbly ask the TAC for retrospective consent for the collection of data by the techniques used between December 2006 and February 2007, and for permission to collate and make such data available for *bona fide* researchers, subject at all time to the permission of the TAC.

4. The TAC will publicly accept the apology of the trustees, and welcome the NHM's acceptance for the future of ethical best practice in relation to human remains.

5. The TAC will participate in the ceremonial hand-over of the remaining remains, and would consider inviting a representative of the NHM to attend the interment at Oyster Cove.

Chapter 9

RABBIT-PROOF FENCE AND THE
GREAT SOCIALIST SHAME

The ignorance of Australia's conservative commentariat was on ironic display in their hostility to the film Rabbit-Proof Fence, *based on a moving story by Doris Pilkington of how she and other 'stolen' Aboriginal girls escaped and managed to walk 1500 miles home to their mothers. The fact, confirmed by a Royal Commission, that Aboriginal children had been 'stolen' by the state so incensed one government minister, Eric Abetz, that he squandered federal funds to fight Phillip Noyce, the film's director, while refusing – along with the rest of the Howard government – to apologise to the Stolen Generation.*

The critics knew nothing about social history, because the real villains of Rabbit-Proof Fence *were English socialists. The genocidal notion that Aboriginality was a feeble trait that should be 'bred out' over the generations was just one consequence of a eugenics movement between the wars that was taken up not only by fascists, but by the best and brightest of the left-wing intellectuals. I find it fascinating how many of my boyhood political and literary heroes – Shaw and the Webbs, D. H. Lawrence and Virginia Woolf – could go so morally wrong, unable to recognise the hideous inhumanity to which their intellectual snobbery had led them. Kenneth Branagh finely portrayed the enthusiastic eugenicist A. O. Neville in the film, and my chambers organised its British premiere in November 2001. Kylie Minogue came as our guest, which led to some snarkiness from the over-defensive peanut gallery back home. It took the New Statesman to understand the point, publishing the following article under the heading 'The Great Socialist Shame – left-wing thinkers backed policies that tore Aboriginal girls from their mothers'.*

The impact of the film in Australia contributed to the overwhelming support for the formal apology to the Stolen Generation, given by Prime Minister Rudd in 2008 after the less sensitive John Howard was given a mighty electoral boot. The British press reported the apology as if it were an entirely local matter, a confession to some kind of racism bred in Australian bones, so once again I thought it necessary to point out, because no one else had, that the British should say sorry, too. The Guardian *headlined my comment 'Australia's apology does not absolve Britain of its role in the degradation of the Aboriginal race'. Exactly.*

Rabbit-Proof Fence is guaranteed to jerk tears from cinema audiences. It's the life-affirming story of a great escape by three Aboriginal girls, torn from their mothers by a state bent on stripping them of their culture and their dignity. Headlines such as 'Australia's shameful secret exposed' have already appeared in the British press. But thanks to Kenneth Branagh's performance, what it also exposes is the most shameful secret of British intellectual life between the wars: its love affair with eugenics.

Branagh plays A. O. Neville, the English administrator who served from 1915 to 1940 as 'Chief Protector of Aborigines' in Western Australia. This position, ironically, had been created by the UK parliament in response to atrocities committed against the native population in the late nineteenth century. Under the *Aborigines Act* of 1905, the Chief Protector was given almost absolute power over the destinies of indigenous peoples of both full and mixed descent. Neville would use this power, in his own words, 'to merge the blacks into our white community' so that 'we could eventually forget that there ever were any Aborigines in Australia'. His belief that eugenics principles could be applied to produce a 'superior' society was typical of English public servants and Fabian socialists of the time.

Aborigines were to them inferior; like (as they thought) the mentally handicapped. They were a 'degenerate' element capable of scientific removal from society. The first thing to be done, Neville proclaimed, was to 'eliminate the full blood'. This would be accomplished by a process of natural selection: the diseases and drink brought by white settlers were decimating the tribes. The problem, as a ministerial adviser in Western Australia bluntly put it in 1930, was that 'the full bloods were dying out, but the half castes were breeding like rabbits'.

In fact, they were breeding because of the casual rape of Aboriginal women and the fathering of 'half-caste' children by pastoralists who made no attempt to educate or support them. Neville's eugenic solution, since Aboriginality was regarded as a valueless trait, was to 'breed it out' by progressive miscegenation, to produce generations with skins light enough to permit their 'absorption' into white society. In practice, this meant forcible removal of girls from their indigenous families, then training them to work as domestics for white families where they would mate with whites and produce whiter children, who would be unaware of their part-Aboriginal identity.

'To achieve this end, we must have charge of the children at the age of six years,' Neville insisted. 'In Western Australia,' he boasted, 'we have power under the Act to take away any child from its mother at any stage of its life' and 'until the children are taken . . . and trained apart from their parents no real progress towards assimilation is to be expected'. The children were to be kept apart from their families and their culture, educated at settlement schools and turned into 'useful workers', by which he meant poorly paid servants for white families. By thus entering the white community in the lowest social strata, marrying (with state approval) whites and lighter 'castes', Aboriginal physical and genetic features would gradually be bred out. As Anna Haebich in her book *Broken Circles* concludes: 'essentially Neville's vision was a program of racial and social engineering designed to erase all Aboriginal characteristics from a desired white Australia . . . it was predicated on the removal and institutionalisation of "mixed race" children.'

Rabbit-Proof Fence is at one level a simple tale about the human consequences of A. O. Neville's policy. In 1931, three girls were taken from their mothers in the north and transported 1500 miles south – to Neville's joyless training camp at Moore River, just north of Perth (which even a Royal Commission sympathetic to his policies described as a 'woeful spectacle'). Led by fourteen-year-old Molly Craig, the girls escaped and eventually reached the world's longest fence – built from top to bottom of the continent to protect western pastures from eastern rabbits – and followed it to find their way home to their mothers. Neville pursued them with an Inspector Javert-like determination to prevent their 'recontamination' by their mothers' Aboriginal culture. His agent in the film is a police black tracker, equivocally played by David Gulpilil (the mystical boy in *Walkabout*, the comic native in *Crocodile Dundee*, now the compromised tribal conscience of the 'black set to catch a black'). Phillip Noyce, the director, coaxed astonishing performances from the children, aged from eight to eleven, who play the runaways. Neville is presented as fairly as possible by Branagh, speaking lines mainly culled from the Chief Protector's own writings.

Neville was not, in ordinary terms, a racist: he genuinely cared for his charges, some of whom did need protection from tribal abuse and hostility. Indeed, his encouragement of miscegenation (mixed marriages) outraged the socially conservative local establishment. The most significant thing about his 'absorption' policy was that it applied the warped biological principles of the English eugenics movement, which were being enthusiastically promoted by socialist thinkers (the Webbs and other Fabians,

Keynes and Bertrand Russell), left-wing literary giants (Shaw, Lawrence and Huxley), and some of the UK's most distinguished doctors and civil servants. In 1934, a Department of Health report, by a committee chaired by Sir Lawrence Brock, praised Nazi legislation and recommended adoption in the UK of compulsory sterilisation of the 'feeble-minded', a class comprising 'a quarter of a million mental defectives and a far larger number of the mentally subnormal'.

Neville's policy of 'cutting off the worst' (as Brock put it) sought to eliminate the 'degeneracy' and 'feeble-mindedness' of the biologically inferior Aborigine. It could have been challenged before the English judges who, in this period, sat as Australia's highest court (the Privy Council), but they would doubtless have approved the US Supreme Court decision of *Buck v Bell* in 1927, which upheld eugenics-based forcible sterilisation of 'degenerates' (i.e. of the poor, and especially of poor blacks). The liberal jurist Oliver Wendell Holmes dismissed the court challenge with the comment that 'three generations of imbeciles are enough'. In the same year, after lobbying from the Eugenics Society, the British government updated the UK's *Mental Deficiency Act*, which provided for the detention of the 'feeble-minded', including 'moral imbeciles' such as single mothers on benefits.

The love affair with eugenics is the secret shame of between-the-wars British socialism. Shaw was irresponsibly arguing for humane extermination of 'the sort of people who do not fit in', Huxley was seeking to 'prevent the sub-normal from having any families at all', Marie Stopes publicly pleaded for sterilisation of 'the hopelessly rotten and racially diseased'. Both Virginia Woolf and D. H. Lawrence privately urged that the state should exterminate 'imbeciles'.

This moral blindness cannot be explained away by the seductive, seemingly scientific logic of Darwinism or the acceptance of heredity studies which later proved to be flawed. Professor Desmond King has in a recent book concluded that their 'desire to improve the lower orders was invariably well-intentioned but commonly revealed notions of social superiority'. This is over-kind: these arrogant intellectuals were perfectly capable of imagining the inhumanity that their policies entailed. Their main objective – compulsory sterilisation of the unfit – did not get up in Britain because of opposition from the Catholics (thank God, in this respect, for G. K. Chesterton) and from Labour MPs (who rightly feared that the working class would be the real victims of the Fabian intelligentsia). But in Australia, Neville's 'absorption' policy, with its explicit eugenicist basis, was formally adopted by Commonwealth and state officials in 1937.

It was, of course, a form of genocide.

The crime of genocide did not crystallise as an offence against the law of nations until the Nuremberg trial exposed the horrors of the concentration camps. The 1948 Genocide Convention, which came into force in 1951, covers acts committed 'with intent to destroy, in whole or in part, a national, ethnical or racial group as such'. Those acts are defined to include 'forcibly transferring children of the group to another group' – the corner-stone of Neville's absorption policy. The author of the concept of genocide, Raphael Lemkin, regarded it as typically involving 'the destruction of the cultural and social life' of the group followed by the imposition upon its members of the lifestyle of the dominant society.

'A principle aim (of Neville's absorption policy) was to eliminate indigenous cultures as distinct entities', an Australian Royal Commission Report, 'Bringing Them Home', concluded in 1997. It recorded that in 1952, Neville's successor finally renounced his policy: 'We have helped to destroy [in half-caste Aborigines] a pride of origin which should have been our Christian duty to protect and preserve.' With that awareness, the policy should have been immediately abrogated, but the Royal Commission concluded that 'the Australian practice of indigenous child removal continued to be practised as official policy long after being clearly prohibited by treaties to which Australia had subscribed.' It is the continuation of that practice after 1951 until as late as 1970 that requires, at the very least, an official apology.

Rabbit-Proof Fence is based on a book by Molly Craig's daughter, Doris Pilkington, who suffered like her mother the experience of separation and removal. Let Australia's present political leaders beware: being cruel to be kind is no longer an option. Today, their cruelty takes the form of forcibly imprisoning all asylum seekers, including hundreds of children. Perhaps the child of an Iraqi refugee, currently behind barbed wire in the 100-degree heat of Woomera detention centre, will in years to come make a film as moving as *Rabbit-Proof Fence*, which will depict these leaders, like A. O. Neville, as the well-intentioned architects of evil.

Chapter 10

THE TRIALS OF NANCY YOUNG

Australians who grew up in cities in the 1950s did not much notice Aborigines. They were mythologised as 'the watcher on the headland' – a noble savage, spear in hand and kerchief on brow, gazing into the middle distance. It was a come-down to be taken to visit the sad black men with painted faces at La Perouse, who would for a few pence toss a boomerang and catch it when it came back. But in 1959, a death sentence was passed in Adelaide on Rupert Max Stuart, an itinerant carnival worker. His conviction for the rape and murder of a young girl was based on prejudice rather than evidence, and it began a debate on the law's treatment of Aborigines.

While an undergraduate, in the late 1960s, I contributed this study of the wrongful conviction of an Aboriginal mother for the manslaughter of her baby. It was written with a fellow student, John Carrick, and became part of a campaign that forced the Queensland legal establishment to reconsider the case. The Court of Appeal quashed her sentence on a technicality, without any apology or any misgivings, as if the next time it happened they would ensure that nobody noticed. It provided my first inkling of how justice often only gets done when someone notices its absence.

This article, published by the Australian Quarterly *in 1970, describes the kind of society we as students thought the law could help to change. Our 'freedom rides' to outback towns had exposed the colour bars that were everywhere, from pubs to swimming pools – a petty apartheid unsanctioned by law, but almost as entrenched as it was in South Africa. I had been brought by Faith Bandler on to the Board of the Foundation for the Advancement of Aborigines and Torres Strait Islanders, and began to act for blacks, usually arrested on minor criminal charges. There was a problem in bringing them to the otherwise enlightened firm to which I was articled: as the senior partner explained, 'We just couldn't have criminals sitting beside our commercial clients in our waiting rooms.'*

Nancy Young's case is a reminder of a time when law was thought to have no business helping the poor. It brought in its wake the establishment of the Redfern Legal Centre and then the Aboriginal Legal Service, so her trials – and the publicity they generated – had some significance.

The death of an Aboriginal child is by no means a newsworthy event in a society where the incidence of Aboriginal infant mortality is six times higher than that of white infants. But the departure from this world of Evelyn Young, four-and-a-half months old, from causes unknown and highly disputed, has already inspired two television documentaries, a large protest meeting, two irreconcilable judgments of the Queensland Supreme Court, and a lively medical controversy which is yet unresolved. The written and cinematic material produced in the fight to free Nancy Young has exposed the black tragedy of the Aboriginal fringe-dweller, played out in this instance against a background of legal and medical inadequacy and small-town racism.

Evelyn died in Cunnamulla Hospital on 9 July 1968. Four months later her mother Nancy was charged with manslaughter on the grounds of an alleged failure to provide her with adequate food or to seek medical attention. After three months spent in jail for failure to raise bail, Nancy was found guilty by an all-white, all-male jury and sentenced to three years' hard labour. Her appeal was heard and dismissed by the full Queensland Supreme Court which, two months and a public outcry later, reversed itself on the grounds of fresh evidence, and freed Nancy one month before she was due to be released on parole.

The Queen v Nancy Young is a classic example of the familiar process that has been described by Jim Spigelman as 'expiation by cause célèbre'. An obvious injustice is located, spotlighted by the media, publicly protested and finally remedied by an establishment device, such as a Royal Commission, or re-appeal with 'fresh evidence', which fails to come to grips with the real cause of the original injustice. Nancy Young *was* set free. But the manner of her liberation left unsolved, even untouched, the intractable social problems that brought about her prosecution. Still to be remedied are the problems any Aboriginal faces when enmeshed in a legal machine not programmed to take account of his or her particular cultural handicaps. Still to be researched are those medical theories advanced in her case that hold out some hope of breakthrough in the disastrous cycle of Aboriginal infant mortality. Still the filthy, insanitary conditions of outback reserves denigrate and depress the potential for Aboriginal advancement.

On the Cunnamulla Fringe

Cunnamulla, set in the midst of Queensland's richest beef and cattle country, is a prosperous, self-satisfied south-west Queensland township, replete with brand-new Civic Centre and Bowling Club, a theatre and three large hotels. Bowling club membership, like the theatre's best seats, is 'out of bounds' to the town's black population, and two of the hotels are well entrenched behind the colour bar. The local squattocracy, recent hosts to Princess Anne, not surprisingly failed to show the Royal visitor the example of genuine Australiana that squats uncomfortably on the fringe of their town. For just beyond the well-kept cemetery, and flush against the town's sewerage outlet, lies 'the reserve'. Here, between the devil and the deep brown sea, the township's two hundred Aborigines subsist.

'Mary McCarthy's' is one of the eighteen tin shanties that dot the reserve. Constructed of corrugated iron, this ten-by-twenty shack was home to Nancy, three other adults and ten children, all of whom slept on flax mattresses laid out on its dirt floor. The nearest supply of water (artesian bore water, which requires boiling before it can be safely consumed) is from a tap forty yards distant, and further still is the block of unsewered earth closets that provides the communal lavatory. Empty bottles and dumped rubbish swim in the stagnant water, which even in summer carpets large portions of the camp. Add to this the plagues of flies and mosquitoes caused by the neighbouring sewerage outlet and the incidence of disease among the reserve's inhabitants, particularly the children, comes as no surprise. Eye, nose and ear infections, and intestinal diseases such as gastroenteritis and non-specific diarrhoea are rampant, while the more serious illnesses such as tuberculosis and pneumonia produce an Aboriginal death rate that could be as much as three times higher than the Cunnamulla average. Even the local council's own health inspector, a Vietnam veteran, admitted to a *Four Corners* team that 'the conditions here are in many respects worse than the conditions which exist in refugee villages in Vietnam'.

Cunnamulla's attitude to its poor relation is disturbingly ambiguous. Aboriginal labour is utilised for menial jobs at low wages – for the men, the town offers station employment or council labouring; for the women, laundry or kitchen work. Yet reaction to the reserve from white power centres in the town varies from lethargic (the local hospital, aware that its post-natal clinic is not used effectively by Aboriginal mothers, has no apparent plans to improve the situation), to aggressive (the Shire chairman claimed to *Four Corners* that the only alternative to the status quo is to 'put these people on the run'). The chairman's answer to charges of parochial neglect is simple – the Aborigines do not pay rates, so they are entitled to very little consideration.

This explains why more council money is spent on the upkeep of the cemetery than on improving the reserve – ex-rate-payers have a 'right' to enjoy in their decomposing years a better water supply than their freeloading Aboriginal neighbours. When taxed with their insensitivity to Aboriginal problems, townspeople will usually dodge the issue by inveighing bitterly against the endemic ignorance, disease, drunkenness and prom-iscuity of the reserve, for which they hold its inhabitants solely responsible. They find it impossible to comprehend the concept of a 'duty' owed by them to 'shiftless blacks', much less a causal connection between their own apathy and the squalor of the reserve. They tend to be angered more by the occasional drunk-enness and de facto sex relations of the fringe-dwellers than by the abysmal failure of the state or local governmental authori-ties to provide minimum standards of welfare.

The World of Nancy Young

Nancy Kate Florence Young has lived in the Cunnamulla reserve since she was five, brought thence by a mother who was later to die in Brisbane jail while serving life for a crime of passion. Her father, an incorrigible if incompetent petty thief, Nancy never knew. The odds stacked against her by these antecedents were not improved when she left school at the age of thirteen, having attained Grade Three (a standard reached by most Queensland nine-year-olds) to work as a housemaid for a white Cunnamulla couple.

Ironically this very first job involved caring for children, and lasted until she had one of her own at the tender age of fifteen. During the next twelve years she was to mother nine more, most, like Evelyn, springing from a de facto relationship with three-quarter-caste- Aboriginal Walter Turnbull, who was wont to squander his irregular pay cheques leaving Nancy to provide for herself and her children by child welfare payments and part-time waitressing, which together during Evelyn's lifetime averaged six dollars per week. This was the amount with which the law was to insist that she 'adequately' feed herself and her children. At the time of Evelyn's death, poverty had forced five offspring into child welfare institutions, another had long since died, one was living with relatives, and two (aged three and five) were with her in Mary McCarthy's crowded shanty.

Nancy Young is now twenty-nine – but looks well over forty. She admits to 'drinking a bit', which is probably responsible for the sole entry on her police record – a five-dollar fine for using obscene language in 1965. Otherwise her demeanour is somewhat cynical, if resigned. Looking at reserve conditions and speaking to inmates like Nancy, one is surprised not by apathy but by group fortitude. Their general attitude is resilient, and a kind of wry humour survives. When we asked what she thought of her manslaughter charge Nancy replied laconically: 'I don't think much of it, really.'

The Life and Death of Evelyn Young

Evelyn was born on 23 February 1968, and weighed eight pounds two ounces when, as an apparently healthy infant, she was taken home by her mother to Mary McCarthy's on the Cunnamulla reserve. Five weeks later, Evelyn weighed only ten pounds – an abnormally low weight gain average of two ounces per week. As the child had at this time contracted gastro-enteritis, Nancy carried her to the local hospital for treatment. There Evelyn remained for eight days, during which time her weight increased at the same abnormally low rate. No notice was apparently taken of her failure to thrive.

No tests were made, no special treatment given, and the child was discharged as soon as she 'looked much better' to the local nurses. There was no special advice for Nancy on how to feed her, no instructions to bring her back for check-ups, no supply of vitamins or medicine. Nancy could be (but was not) forgiven for assuming that Evelyn's low weight gave no cause for alarm.

For the next two months Evelyn was fed five or six bottles of Sunshine milk daily, augmented with custard and Farex when Nancy could afford them. But on Saturday 6 July Evelyn fell seriously ill, vomiting all her food. So at midnight Nancy wrapped her daughter in a blanket and set off in the cold to walk the mile and a half from the reserve to Cunnamulla Hospital.

The duty nurse, a Cunnamulla housewife, gave Nancy a reception several degrees lower than the night air, and later complained of the 'offensive odour' of the blanket. Her contribution to the child's welfare was to give her a bottle of glucose and water and put her to bed, where she stayed for nine hours until the local doctor arrived in the normal course of his Sunday-morning rounds.

Dr Thomas Osborne had been on call all night, but his nurses had not called him to the sickbed of the Aboriginal child who, on their own evidence at the trial, was badly dehydrated and looked seriously ill on admission. Dr Osborne began feeding by stomach tube and subcutaneous drip. Neither method, according to specialist evidence at subsequent appeals, was 'indicated' by the circumstances.

By the time normal intravenous feeding was commenced, Evelyn's life was probably beyond repair. Broncho-pneumonia set in and she died on Tuesday morning, two days after her admission to hospital, and weighing seven pounds five ounces – six ounces less than her admission weight. A post-mortem was held on that same day – 9 July. Even before he conducted it, Dr Osborne had a conversation with the local CIB detective, as a result of which that officer sought out Nancy for questioning as to her responsibility for the child's death for what he termed 'gross malnutrition and neglect' (this at 10.50 am – six hours before the post-mortem). Three weeks later he interviewed her again.

By the end of July, the Crown had all the evidence it would ever gather against Nancy. For three-and-a-half months, nothing happened. Then her four-year-old daughter was admitted to Cunnamulla Hospital suffering from gastroenteritis, and the very next day Nancy was arrested for manslaughter. This circumstance, and the inexplicable delay, supports those local Aborigines who view the prosecution as some sort of 'reprisal' – a manifestation of white Cunnamulla's desire to 'punish' the reserve for its standing reproach to the town's complacency. There were too many diseased children littering the hospital, too many illegitimates roaming the streets in rags, too many claims being made on the town's grudging spirit. Nancy Young's crime was not to neglect her child – her real mistake was to be coloured, poor and occasionally tipsy, to breed without benefit of clergy a swarm of children who brought the 'offensive odour' of the reserve into the local hospital once too often.

Hence to charge her with manslaughter, to set bail at $1000 (surely unnecessary in the light of the nature of her offence and her six-dollar weekly earnings), to jail her for three months, including Christmas, without trial – was all part of the working out of this primitive desire to reprimand 'the reserve' for flaunting its untaxed poverty and promiscuity in the faces of the sober citizenry of Cunnamulla.

The Trial

On 14 April 1969, Nancy boarded the train – incredibly, at her own expense – for Roma, three hundred miles distant, where her trial for Evelyn's manslaughter commenced the following day.

One of the first witnesses called against Nancy was her own 'husband', Walter Turnbull, a three-quarter-caste Aboriginal. He swore that he had never seen Nancy ill-treat the child, and freely admitted to dissipating his occasional pay cheque. Turnbull was followed by three nurses, only one of whom was qualified, who confirmed the hospital's failure to give special treatment to Evelyn in April. They told of Evelyn's 'pitifully thin', dehydrated and discoloured body on admission, as though her life had been ebbing away before their eyes. This was meant to be damning evidence against Nancy (the inference being that a reasonable mother would have sought medical attention much sooner) but was difficult to reconcile with their failure to call the hospital doctor.

The chief witness for the prosecution was Dr Osborne. He admitted that Evelyn should have received tests in April to establish why she was not coping efficiently with her food. But he committed himself, the Crown and ultimately the Court to the proposition that Evelyn's perilous condition and the consequent necessity for medical assistance should have been obvious for several weeks before her death. He firmly ruled out any possibility of a sudden and rapid weight loss in the few days before death, and denied the possibility of scurvy.

Nancy's defence began with Aboriginal Mary McCarthy, who swore that she had seen Evelyn fed regularly, with five or six bottles of Sunshine milk daily, and Farex and mashed potatoes when they could be afforded. Only on the Saturday before her death did Evelyn look sufficiently ill to warrant treatment. Nancy's other witness was Dr Archivides Kalokerinos, medical superintendent of the District Hospital at Collarenebri since 1957. He explained his own research in this area suggests that Aboriginal children are born with an inbuilt vitamin C deficiency, which if not remedied will lead to scurvy, severe weight loss, dehydration and death. As weight loss is the most dramatic manifestation of both scurvy and starvation, it would be impossible, he claimed, from Dr Osborne's superficial examination, to differentiate between malnutrition from lack of food and malnutrition from deficiency of vitamin C. He argued that the failure of the hospital to administer or recommend vitamin C, and Nancy's inability to buy fresh fruit at inflated Cunnamulla prices, made the onset of scurvy inevitable. This would cause a sudden and traumatic loss of weight, 'as if a tap was turned on, and weight drained out of the infant'. In his view, the child would have looked normal two days prior to admission, yet have suffered catastrophic weight loss from the combined effects of scurvy and pneumonia over the next few days.

Nancy's counsel decided not to put her in the witness box. The tendency of uneducated Aboriginal defendants to say what they believe white 'authority figures' expect of them, to acquiesce readily in a line of questioning, would here have been disastrous in cross-examination. He was afraid that her psychological make-up was such that if badgered by the Prosecutor she would simply shrug her shoulders and 'admit' anything put to her.

The judge instructed the jury to ignore the two Aboriginal witnesses – Turnbull because he could have been out to protect himself, McCarthy because the jury might conclude (on what grounds it is difficult to understand) that she was 'quite a smart woman'. He seized in particular upon Nancy's 'failure' to give evidence as a circumstance likely to be confirmatory of her guilt. His penultimate paragraph, which must have stuck in the jurors' minds, was virtually an invitation to convict:

> The accused has not given any evidence at all. She has not gone into the box – you heard her invited to do so if she wished to do so – she has not gone into the box and said, 'I fed this child properly. I gave it the necessaries.' She has given no explanation as to why she did not take it to the doctor. Or say she did take it to another doctor, or anything like that. She just allowed all this evidence to be given without denying it. I am giving you this direction . . . that it is legitimate for you to take this failure into account as a consideration which makes it less unsafe to infer guilt than it otherwise would have been.

The jury did what the judge apparently expected of them. Nancy Kate Florence Young was found guilty of manslaughter.

Aftermath

A ten-minute television report on the trial was aired on *This Day Tonight* on the evening of the verdict. A large meeting at Sydney University Law School condemned legal aspects of the prosecution and trial, in particular the high bail figure, the judicial comments on Nancy's non-appearance in the witness box, and the failure to obtain a specialist medical opinion to resolve the crucial conflict between the two general practitioners. The public defender appealed to the full Queensland Supreme Court, on the ground, *inter alia,* of fresh evidence from Dr Felix

Arden, a senior physician and specialist in paediatrics at the Royal Brisbane Children's Hospital. Dr Arden affirmed that it was 'reasonably possible' that Evelyn was born with an abnormality of body chemistry, which was responsible for her failure to thrive. Her treatment on arrival at the hospital on 7 July was unusual and incorrect. Had she been treated 'in accordance with normal medical procedure' (intravenous feedings and antibiotics) there was a 'reasonable possibility' that her life would have been saved, he said.

After delaying for two months, the court unanimously rejected all the grounds of appeal. Dr Arden's affidavit was almost contemptuously dismissed on the grounds that ending litigation is better than doing justice. The Queensland Council for Civil Liberties launched an appeal to the High Court while simultaneously a petition for pardon was despatched to the Governor. But the real turning point in Nancy's case came when *Four Corners* screened its documentary 'Out of sight, out of mind' – a study of the Cunnamulla reserve, written around Nancy's trial and punishment.

The report highlighted the local hospital's failure to provide prompt treatment for Evelyn, exposed the town's racism in a series of interviews, pictured the abject squalor at the reserve with devastating effect, and concluded with a table of Aboriginal infant mortality, superimposed on a close-up of Evelyn's rough grave. So ugly was the impression it gave of Australian treatment of Aborigines that the sale of a copy of the film to the BBC was prohibited.

Before the High Court could hear the case, the governor referred the pardon petition back to a Queensland Supreme Court of three different judges. This bench unanimously decided to quash Nancy's conviction and sentence (which had only one month to run in any case!), on the grounds of fresh evidence. Just how much 'fresher' the evidence was than that rejected at the first appeal is open to doubt. It consisted of one further affidavit, made jointly by Dr Arden and by Dr David Gilbert Jose, who concluded that Evelyn's dehydration had occurred suddenly, within the forty-eight hours before she was admitted to hospital on 7 July. Prior to this, they claimed, the child would not have appeared in urgent need of medical attention to a medical practitioner, let alone to an uneducated Aborigine lulled into a sense of false security by the child's premature discharge in April.

The doctors agreed that it was 'probable', not just 'reasonably possible' that her failure to thrive was due to a disorder of body chemistry, or, Dr Jose added, supporting Dr Kalokerinos, because the foodstuffs fed to her did not contain sufficient vitamin C. The Court decided that the child died 'more probably than not' from a disorder of body chemistry. On 5 November, having spent ten months in jail since her arrest, Nancy was released.

Who Killed Evelyn Young?

Nancy and Evelyn, and the social and medical conditions that determined their lives, were caught up in a legal machinery that had to be politically tampered with before a 'just' outcome could be secured. The failure of traditional legal procedures to produce a satisfactory resolution of the issues involved in her trial – indeed the very process which allowed her to be put on trial in the first place – suggests that an inbuilt discrimination exists whenever common law rules are applied to indigent and ignorant fringe-dwellers.

The majority of fringe-dwelling Aborigines have never been more than marginally integrated into the mainstream of white society. Their former identity, customs and culture are often forgotten, but they have progressed almost nowhere towards the attainment of a new role and identity. They are thus in a worse position as regards the law than tribal Aborigines. Denied the benefits of white society, they are nevertheless punished by its standards. All these standards are applied to them by judges, jurors and policemen whose law enforcement roles are insufficiently flexible to take much account of the cultural clash, even when its existence is recognised. In consequence, it is possible to pinpoint the following stages at which our legal machinery signally failed to provide fair treatment for Nancy, although it would probably have assisted a wealthier, more sophisticated defendant in the same circumstances.

1. Police discretion to prosecute was abused by the three-and-a-half-month delay in charging Nancy. Local detectives apparently exercised their discretion only when another of Nancy's children was admitted to hospital.

2. Fixing bail at $1000 is little short of scandalous in the circumstances. Nancy had lived in the town with relatives since childhood, and the possibility of her absconding was remote. She had no police record of any consequence. Her average earnings of $6 per week should have alerted the magistrate to the impossibility of her funding such an amount. Her three-month pre-trial stretch in Cunnamulla Gaol is impossible to justify on legal or moral grounds.

3. It transpired that specialist evidence was available in Brisbane that would almost certainly have decided the issue in Nancy's favour. This could and should have been sought by both prosecution and defence, as failure to do so vitiated the whole trial. This absence of adequate pre-trial preparation is reminiscent of the Rupert Stuart case, in which fresh evidence favourable to the Aboriginal defendant unfolded only when the case became a public issue. The ideal of 'equal justice' makes it imperative that sufficient funds and resources be provided to public solicitors to give each indigent defendant access to all evidence that could work for his acquittal, irrespective of the cost of collecting it.

4. Another echo of the Stuart case was present in the inference of guilt from Nancy's failure to give evidence. Stuart's counsel believed his client was not sufficiently articulate to stand up to cross-examination. Nancy was kept out of the box by her counsel in deference to the well-known Aboriginal habit of acquiescing in statements by authority figures that they do not understand. As Professor Elkin concludes, 'Their fundamental aim is to satisfy the questioner, to tell him what they think he wants to be told.' In these circumstances

it is unjust and artificial to accuse the defendant of having something to hide when her 'failure' to give evidence is in reality her counsel's decision to avoid a cross-examination that his client's 'psychological make-up renders useless as a means of eliciting truth'.

Most of the above points are of general application to the failure to secure minimal standards of justice for the poor. But it is nevertheless significant to view the Young case within a general pattern of failure to do justice to Aborigines.

All relevant studies show a pattern of high arrest rate, almost invariable 'guilty' pleas, lack of legal representation, and general acceptance of the inevitable. They conclude that Aborigines suffer more legal deprivation than poor whites specifically because of the added factors of racial discrimination, conspicuousness and consequent police attention.

Finally, the Young case is a significant illustration of the proposition that in our courts Aborigines are always defendants and never plaintiffs. This fact should trouble those lawyers who still believe that their professional services are open to all. The evidence suggests that Nancy Young may have a case of civil negligence against Cunnamulla Hospital, its servants and agents. A wealthier or more sophisticated white mother whose child had died after receiving treatment not indicated by her condition, after lying seriously ill in hospital for nine hours without an 'on call' doctor being summoned, after being prematurely discharged previously by the same hospital, would normally have her lawyer investigate a civil action to recover damages she had suffered from the child's consequent death.

In the United States, Nancy would no doubt have such a case enthusiastically pressed by the top-line lawyers who now staff federally funded 'Neighborhood Law Offices' for the Office of Economic Opportunity. But the case in *Young v Cunnamulla District Hospital* is inconceivable in this country. That it is provides a sad reflection on the limited and defensive operation of our legal aid schemes.

Conclusion

Nancy's 'life situation' remains unaltered, for all the publicity that surrounded her trials. Her special vulnerability to the processes of white man's law, like her children's vulnerability to disease from the reserve, has in no way been alleviated. Predominant attitudes of local whites, presumably reflected by circuit judges and small-town juries, remain suspicious rather than sympathetic.

This life situation is shared by the great majority of Aborigines dwelling on the fringes of country towns who are equally locked in a vicious cycle of under-privilege and discrimination. White townspeople come to believe that the Aborigine lives like this simply *because* he is an Aborigine. They talk of 'good' Aborigines – i.e. those who adopt white manners, attitudes and habits, and are allowed the status of honorary (if inferior) whites. As a result of this prejudiced situation the black 'out' group is stereotyped by the white 'in' group as dirty, lazy, inferior, sexually immoral, and so on. Aborigines are seen as 'that way' *because* they are Aborigines, not because of their history of subjection. Thus there is a strong feeling among some Cunnumullans that Nancy was a 'bad' Aborigine and should have been punished.

The State Department of Native Affairs appointed a welfare officer to Cunnamulla the week after the *Four Corners* program. He has now bought seven houses and has plans to move selected families from the reserve into the town. The local council responded by installing one extra tap – thereby giving the reserve a water supply equal to that of the cemetery next door.

The negative side is more striking. The reserve, like many Aboriginal shanty towns, remains an appalling health hazard, spawning diseases that promote an abnormally high Aboriginal infant mortality rate. Whites in the town resented the publicity, and this had led to a hardening of attitudes, with Nancy Young singled out as an object of blame and resentment. When it was rumoured that a particular house had been set aside for her, three petrol bombs were lobbed at it by white 'vigilantes', some of whom have apparently armed themselves with shotguns. Thus blame and resentment are projected onto a scapegoat instead of being directed to sources of trouble and to solutions.

The attitudes that conspired in Nancy's charge should be seen as part of a total pattern of attitudes in the town, mirroring other outback towns with Aboriginal enclaves. The contradictions abound. The reserve is dangerously unhealthy, so you charge Nancy Young with neglect but don't improve health conditions there. The medical authorities in the town agree that the reserve is a source of too many of their clients, but no program of health education for Aborigines is felt to be appropriate. Had Nancy been instructed to feed her child on a proper diet she would just have been able to afford the fruit and vegetables recommended. Regret, often of a sentimental sort, is expressed about the child's death, but this regret becomes almost a desire for revenge upon Nancy rather than any attack on the vicious conditions that produced the death. Meanwhile both Shire council and state government sanctimoniously disclaim financial responsibility for the living conditions on the reserve, each claiming that this is within the other's province and in consequence nothing is done.

What is lacking is any attempt at understanding or reme-dying such a situation. Instead, old attitudes and roles harden. As C. D. Rowley puts it, 'Aborigines are reacting in their caste system situation precisely as would any group of human beings, similarly placed by their history in contact with the whites, and by the continued existence of a racial barrier to upward social mobility in the predominant society. Such reactions confirm the stereotype Aborigine of the white "in" group, and are explained as something inherently "Aboriginal".'

In other words – those of Jack Tonkin, Chairman of the local Council 'responsible' for the reserve, on national television – 'They get together in their little groups, they play their cards in the sun and have their gambling, and it's their way of life. They're quite different to the white people in that respect ... "Something for nothing" I think is their motto. They don't get very much for nothing, I'll admit that too. I think you'll find if you poke down there they are pretty happy in their environment.'

Chapter 11

GIVE ADELAIDE BACK
(GROTIUS ON THE TORRENS)

*It is said that South Australians regard themselves as cultur-
ally superior because they had no convict forebears – Adelaide
was settled by nice English middle classes anxious to turn the
Torrens into something like the Thames at Maidenhead. In fact,
it was acquired in 1836 by a rapacious joint stock company,
under a royal patent requiring it to respect Aboriginal land
rights – a requirement that the company, the state and the judiciary have studiously ignored.*

*Adelaide may have been an act of theft, but, unlike most
colonial acquisitions, it might one day be returned – if lawyers
in the future can work out how to enforce the patent as the king
of England and his Whig ministers, back in 1836, intended.
This would provide an example of how, in the law, time past
is present in time future. Grotius (a prescient sixteenth-
century Dutch jurist whom international lawyers refer to as
if he were still alive) would be able to explain this, and perhaps
already has.*

*Shaun Berg is an Adelaide lawyer much exercised by the
illegal commercial capture of the land on which his city is built.
In 2007 I contributed this foreword to* Coming to Terms, *his
book on Aboriginal title in South Australia.*

International legal scholars talk of 'Grotian moments' in history, referring to times that give birth to a value or a proclaimed principle that is quickly discarded, but in due course re-emerges, freighted with acceptable meaning for a later generation. Similarly, there are events that resonate in a nation's history – actions, deals or documents – that mean more today than they did at the time, precisely because they express values we have learnt, the hard way, to cherish. Exactly what 'meaning' they should be accorded in law may be a matter of debate: *Magna Carta*'s promise of justice is now entrenched (although it had no effect at all for 400 years until it was taken up in Coke's 1628 *Petition of Right*). Other prescient or inspirational utterances remain merely aspirational, viewed by courts as historical curiosities from a past that is passed.

Grotian moments are few and far between in the Australian colonial period: among them I would number Arthur Phillip's first law against slavery (for a country that at the time only he thought would ever amount to more than an open prison); Governor Macquarie's refusal to discriminate against emancipists; the shearer's strike of 1891 (which led to the formation of the ALP and inspired both 'Waltzing Matilda' and Henry Lawson's warning against 'blood on the wattle'). It is now time to argue into contemporary significance an obscure proclamation by William IV, the king of England in 1836, which placed an all-important condition upon the settlement of South Australia, the only state free of convicts:

> Provided always that nothing in these Letters Patent contained shall affect or be construed to affect the rights of any Aboriginal Natives of the said Province to the actual occupation or enjoyment in their own Persons or in the Persons of their Descendants of any Land therein now actually occupied or enjoyed by such Natives.

For any contemporary reader, and indeed for the king and the Colonial Office in 1836, this meant what it plainly says:

that the South Australian Company and all who settled there must acknowledge and respect indigenous land rights. Modern judges, however, faced with the possible consequences of that plain meaning, have contrived to interpret the proviso as 'not intended to be more than the affirmation of a principle of benevolence inserted in the Letters Patent in order to bestow upon it a suitably dignified status' – the verdict in the Gove land rights case of 1971.

But this construction cannot stand: the proviso in fact embodies the position of a parliment imbued with a muscular humanitarianism that had stopped the trade in slaves and was now determined to end the degradation and destruction of Aborigines in British colonies. It is a resolve that should not be brushed aside as the hypocritical window dressing of perfidious Albion – notwithstanding the failure to enforce its terms by curbing the greed of settlers and investors who ignored its injunction against extirpating the tribes in actual occupation and enjoyment of the land of South Australia.

So what meaning can the proviso have now, for the 'descendants' (to which it specifically refers) of tribes who were dispossessed by a joint stock company?

The architects of the British empire in this period had an overweening sense that God was an Englishman, but that imbued them with a civilising mission and a belief that natives, however 'primitive', were nonetheless fellow humans, entitled to education, healthcare, religious instruction, and the right to keep their land or be compensated for its loss. The proclamation was influenced by despair at the treatment of indigenous inhabitants in Australia: the Select Committee on Aborigines (British settlements), which heard evidence in 1836, was appalled by the massacres in Van Diemen's Land, which had left not a single Aboriginal alive on the mainland. It endorsed the conclusion of Sir Gilbert Murray that 'the adoption of any line of conduct, having as its avowed or secret object the extinction of the native race, could not fail but to leave an indelible stain upon the British government'. The 'indelible stain' (which was, a century

later, to be described as 'genocide') shocked this committee of
MPs to its moral core. The evidence of Presbyterian minister,
and later radical MP in the New South Wales parliament, John
Dunmore Lang, told them all too truly of the treatment of the
natives in Australia thus far:

> Their hunting grounds have been seized by Europeans
> and the kangaroos have accordingly disappeared from
> their wonted fields and the opossums from the fallen trees
> of their ancient forests. But what compensation have they
> received for their loss of all things that are held valuable by
> savage man? What equivalent has been afforded them in
> exchange for their fields and their forests? Why, the very
> worst features of English civilisation have re-appeared in
> their territory. They have been transformed into a race
> of paupers and taught to beg their bread where they
> formerly earned it. Their native habits of temperance
> have been succeeded by scenes of beastly intoxication.
> Their tongues have been taught to frame horrid impreca-
> tions in a language which they imperfectly understand.
> Their bodies have been wasted by strange and incurable
> diseases. Their impatience of injuries has been tried with
> the most wanton and brutal aggressions, and in moments
> of frenzy they have sometimes been stimulated to deeds
> of indiscriminate and murderous revenge.

The Select Committee was determined to uphold what they
repeatedly described as 'the rights of the natives', and were in
no doubt that these included rights to land. 'The land has been
taken from them without the assertion of any other title than
that of superior force' and it followed that the state had a duty
to establish official 'Protectors of Aborigines' who should ensure
legal aid for them and look after their welfare: 'especially they
should claim for the maintenance of the aborigines such lands
as may be necessary for their support'. The Select Committee
had been exercised by the profiteering already rampant over the
sale of South Australia:

Although it be true that the land in our colonies has derived the greater part of its exchangeable value from the capital and the labour employed in the cultivation of it, yet, even in its most rude and wild state, that land is demonstrably worth a very large amount of money. Thus parliament has fixed a minimum price of 12 shillings per acre for the lands of South Australia, at which rate they appear to have been sold in London for the amount of some hundred thousand pounds sterling, before a single European had landed on the spot; yet for this important acquisition the ancient occupiers of the soil have not received so much as a nominal equivalent . . . It requires no argument to show that we thus owe to the natives a debt, which will be but imperfectly paid by charging the Land Revenue of each of these Provinces with whatever expenditure is necessary for the instruction of the adults, the education of their youth, and the protection of them all.

It did not work out this way, of course. The Colonisation Commissioners for South Australia initially planned to provide for Aborigines to make 'voluntary transfers' of some lands (in return for welfare subsidies) and to remain in 'undisturbed enjoyment' of country they declined to cede to the settlers. But no deals were ever done and no treaties or bargains were ever made. Neither South Australia's first governor, John Hindmarsh, nor resident Commissioner Fisher nor Surveyor General William Light ever bothered with tribal transactions. Under pressure from greedy investors, the land was simply stolen: the proviso to the Letters Patent was ignored.

In Adelaide, land initially bought for twelve shillings an acre sold for £2000 and after three years 300,000 acres had been sold to support fifteen thousand white settlers brought over by the South Australian Company. Not a penny was paid to the Aborigines, many of whom died or were reduced to beggary within five years.

King William, followed by Queen Victoria, gave no thought to these dispossessed subjects, and parliament failed to monitor the company of whose initial land sales its Select Committee had been so critical. The preamble to the *South Australian Act* had declared that the area 'consists of waste and unoccupied lands which are supposed to be fit for the purpose of colonisation' and it was readily assumed that this 'covered the field' and included land that was occupied by Aborigines. Colonel Torrens, with breathtaking ignorance (masking, perhaps, a racist determination that native rights should not stand in the way of profit) declared his belief that Aborigines had no such land.

In due course, all the land that could be claimed and sold by the corporation or the Crown was designated as 'waste' and the Protectors of Aborigines did not protect Aborigines in the way the Select Committee proposed they should – and indeed, barely protected them at all. The complex social and cultural relationship between tribes and the lands they had accounted theirs, centuries before the birth of Christ, was regarded as irrelevant: the common law position was, at least so far as the colonists were concerned, that 'indigenous people as barbarians had no rights'.

There is no need to rely on the decision a century and a half later in *Mabo* to refute this proposition: the Letters Patent show their rights were recognised by the king and the government of the time. The founders of the state of South Australia behaved unlawfully in disregarding them.

So what can happen now?

Lawyers might argue that the mistaken characterisation of the proviso to the Letters Patent provides a basis for reconsidering the assumptions of land law, at least in South Australia, or for exacting belated compensation, but litigation can be arid, and dangerous. Others see the proviso as a 'missing link' that, having been found, necessitates a treaty, or a new constitutional preamble or specific clauses in a bill of rights. At the very least, as Lee Godden concludes:

if the humanitarian impulse that prompted the inclusion of the Proviso to the Letters Patent is to have any meaning today, it needs to be reconfigured as an important gesture of reconciliation and respect for indigenous peoples' rights to occupy land and waters and for a more inclusive voice in the Australian nation that acknowledges indigenous sovereignty as a regenerative force. Australian governments might do well to consider the Proviso to the Letters Patent a little more carefully.

Restorative justice requires some atonement to indigenous Australians. Director of the Indigenous Law Centre Megan Davis suggests that an indigenous bill of rights, modelled on the UN declaration of the rights of indigenous peoples, should be adopted. This would be one means of addressing what indigenous leader Mick Dodson describes as the 'fundamental disrespect' for Aborigines in the constitution and in subsequent legal and political development. But there is a fundamental disrespect among politicians, newspaper editors and conventional thinkers towards any form of protection of legal rights, and it may be better to join the demand for a statutory charter – in the state as well as in the nation – that would show appropriate respect for Aboriginal claims and aspirations. There are many suitable models: my own draft *Statute of Liberty* proposes a preamble by which the Australian people declare that they are:

> **Humble** in acknowledging the first owners and occupiers of this unique continent whose ancestors have walked about on its earth for many thousands of years before British settlement;
>
> **sorrowful** for the dispossession, discrimination and degradation they have endured and
>
> **resolved** hereafter to respect their relationship with the land and to atone for past wrongs by future equity.

A special right for indigenous people might read as follows:

> Indigenous people have distinct cultural rights and must not be denied the right, with other members of their community:
>
> i) to enjoy their identity and culture;
> ii) to maintain and use their language;
> iii) to maintain their kinship ties;
> iv) to maintain spiritual and material relationships with the land and waters according to their customs of old.

In 1901 the founding fathers of the Commonwealth excluded Aborigines from counting in their own country. They were left to the mercy of the states. In 1967 the Australian people voted overwhelmingly to make them part of their own nation, but all that was legally achieved by this referendum was that they were counted in the census and the federal government was given the power to make special laws for them, which would not necessarily be for their benefit. Indigenous rights serve as the basis for a treaty, but my own view is that dignity will only be vouchsafed to our half a million Aborigines if they are given the right to vote for their own parliamentary representatives – two extra senators, perhaps, who might even come to hold the balance of power. It would be infinitely preferable to have that balance held by men and women of the character and integrity of Noel Pearson, Larissa Behrendt, Marcia Langton or Mick Dodson, rather than by the unimpressive senators who have ended up holding it in recent Australian history – the likes of Brian Harradine or Steve Fielding or the Australian Democrats. The advanced nations that have most successfully included their indigenous people – New Zealand and Mauritius, for example – allow them to vote their own representatives into the parliament. It works, but sadly such constitutional change is outside the imagination of most Australian politicians.

Putting these promises in a contemporary statute that has legal force, to the extent of requiring all other laws to be interpreted consistently with it, would be a belated beginning in delivering on the promise of the proviso. Law is not (as the aphorism goes) the prisoner of history, other than in the sense that history can liberate law from the chains of statutory jargon and misapplied precedent, and infuse it with a meaning that permits justice to be done, according to hard-won values that are imputed or implied.

The proviso reflects a 'Grotian moment' in which Australians should take pride: a determination by the political founders of the free state of South Australia that settlement should from the outset provide fair and equal treatment to all indigenous peoples and to their descendants. Governments and courts should make this promise meaningful today.

WAR STORIES

Chapter 12

FOR A TUMUT SCHOOLTEACHER, BLOWN UP AT BAPAUME

We have lost direct contact with World War I: all its survivors are now dead, long after their comrades who fell at Gallipoli or the Somme. 'Fell' is a weasel way of putting it – they usually died doubled-up in their blood and their excrement, screaming with pain or twitching in death agonies. On British ceremonial occasions, summoned by an embossed card that says 'Dress: medals', I wear the small golden wings bequeathed by my grandfather, a member of the Australian Flying Corps. In March 1917, he was stationed near Bapaume, in France, where his brother Bob was blown up along with eighteen other Australian soldiers, victims of a double-cross. The Germans evacuated the town, but left tunnels under the town hall packed with dynamite, which they exploded when it was full of civilians and Australian soldiers. Grand-Uncle Bob was a schoolteacher from a small country town in New South Wales called Tumut. What he thought he was doing fighting for France is one question, and another is whether his sacrifice receives today more than a Gallic shoulder-shrug.

The latter question was answered in March 2011, when the town of Bapaume showed its gratitude by tracking down relatives of the nineteen Australian soldiers who died in the town hall bombing and inviting us to the unveiling of a memorial.

I took the Eurostar to Lille and taxied down the lanes along which these men had marched in 1917 as they sang 'Tipperary' and 'Mademoiselle from Armentières' while trying to divert their eyes from the open mass graves on either side.

At Bapaume, our wreath-laying ceremony was dignified by a slow and mournful rain; the town band played Australia's national dirge and then uplifted us with 'La Marseillaise'. Afterwards, on behalf of the Australian families, I offered these thoughts.

My great-uncle Bob and his mates – nineteen young Australians – died here in Bapaume ninety-four years ago, blown to smithereens by the explosives packed in a tunnel underneath the town hall. Private Albert Edward 'Bob' Beattie had an office in the basement, so I assume he died instantly, unlike so many other poor wretches from both sides in this dreadful conflict. His body was not recovered until 1931, fourteen years later, when excavations located his bones and identified him by the name inscribed on his watch. Back in Australia he had been a country schoolteacher, and the watch had been presented to him by his admiring schoolchildren, before he went off to the war. It was sent to his still-grieving family, who loaned it for display at the local RSL, where it was stolen.

There was no conscription in Australia in 1917. Bob volunteered because he thought it the right thing to do. He had no connection with France and no particular love for this country. There was no threat to Australia that made this war of any security importance. Yet they volunteered, and Bob, the teacher in Tumut, helped recruit his former pupils. He had bad eyesight and was himself turned down several times, until the vast graveyard of the Somme demanded more occupants. So they took him on a troop ship to France, arriving in December 1916.

For three months he fought in the trenches, with Bapaume just over the next ridge. His medical records show the minor diseases from which they all suffered – scabies and diarrhoea

– although he did not contract anything from the Mademoiselles from Armentières. But he saw a few weeks of France in springtime. And he served in a division that won high praise in an official French communiqué that congratulated the Australians for their courage and skill in 'daily extensive assaults, faultlessly carried out and successful in securing numerous prisoners'. Historians note that French officials are always sparing in their praise, particularly for other nationals, and the Australian 'peaceful penetration' operations around Bapaume were masterful. They ensured the German retreat.

The German retreat from Bapaume was codenamed 'Operation Alberich'. It involved a scorched earth policy, poisoning the wells, cutting down the fruit trees and, in particular, constructing these fatal tunnels underneath the town hall, packed with explosives. British Intelligence intercepted the cables and discovered the operation was named 'Alberich' – but British Intelligence was not intelligent enough to connect it with the malevolent dwarf of German legend who features in Wagner's *Ring Cycle*, spending much time constructing underground tunnels.

I suppose we can take some satisfaction from the fact that almost a century later, this kind of treachery is now a war crime. Setting time bombs to go off at a time when civilians as well as soldiers will be killed was a tactic deployed by armies that all believed they had God on their side, yet played devilish tricks on each other that are now contrary to international humanitarian law.

The plaque I have unveiled today commemorates the sacrifice of men who came from Australia to die – like five million from other countries – in the great and futile war. The English war poets, in their anthems for doomed youth, envisaged their bodies lying 'in some foreign field which is forever England'. This is a ridiculously English conceit that Australians do not share. Our relatives lie in a field that is forever France, a country that they came to liberate from an invader, a country that has itself done much for the cause of liberty (as the playing of 'La Marseillaise' today so vividly reminds us). It had been unlawfully occupied by a country that had done very little, and had committed two monstrous war crimes – the unprovoked aggression against Belgium (an invasion conducted with unrestrained savagery towards civilians) and the decision to unleash U-boats in unrestricted submarine warfare against ships packed with civilians. The German leaders who made these decisions should have been prosecuted after Versailles, and would have been, had the British, French and Australian demand for justice not been overruled by that intellectually superior fool Woodrow Wilson.

My grand-uncle's death, and the death of his comrades, and those on both sides of this vast and pointless Armageddon in the fields of Western France and of Belgium, have never been requited: there was no responsibility for mass murder levelled at the end of the First World War as a means of deterring a second. These men have had no justice, and no justification. These men, in the words of Leon Gellert, an Australian poet there at the time, were:

> Men moving in a trench, in the clear noon,
> Whetting their steel within the crumbling earth;
> Men, moving in a trench 'neath a new moon
> That smiles with a slit mouth and has no mirth;
> Men moving in a trench in the grey morn,
> Lifting bodies on their clotted frames;
> Men with narrow mouths thin-carved in scorn
> That twist and fumble strangely at dead names.

> These men know life – know death a little more,
> These men see paths and ends, and see
> Beyond some swinging open door
> Into eternity

They thought it was the right thing to do at the time, although by late 1916 Bob must have known the odds against ever returning to teach in Tumut. He went to war because he wanted his life to mean something, to stake it for those who were under attack.

His sacrifice, and that of his eighteen mates, gives meaning to their photographs in our dusty family albums. On behalf of the relatives of the victims of the Bapaume town hall atrocity, I thank you for looking after the bodies of our young men and for remembering the lives they gave up to free your own relatives from the invader.

Chapter 13

YOU'VE GOT TO BE CAREFULLY TAUGHT: OUR SOUTH PACIFIC

The Australian Opera staged South Pacific *in 2012, directed by Bartlett Sher, and I provided this note for its program. Opera programs, unlike newspapers, are large and expensive and sometimes become collectors' items – they are usually read afterwards by audience members who want to relive, or possibly understand, their enjoyment of the show. It was an opportunity to talk about 'our' South Pacific – tales from my father's logbook – and about Hammerstein, whose seemingly homely but subtly humane lyrics had made it just possible to conceive of a black president of the US – someday. It was a pleasure to reread James Michener's* Tales of the South Pacific, *with its laconic conversations between marines and nurses and natives, set against a brilliant backdrop of jungles, oceans and heavens.*

The show was a palpable hit, not least because of the chemistry between its leads, Lisa McCune and Teddy Tahu Rhodes, which continued offstage and into the gossip columns. The opera company had been a bit coy about staging a Broadway musical (and even more coy, subsequently, about admitting that the show had been its best money-spinner ever). They were pleased to have it pointed out that South Pacific *certainly possesses the fundamental quality of opera, namely that the music knows more about its characters than its characters know about themselves.*

South Pacific has a special resonance for Australians. This struck me when I first saw American director Bartlett Sher's 2008 production at the Lincoln Centre. On stage is a Curtis P40 – the Kittyhawk that Australian fighter pilots, my father included, flew in the air war against the Japanese. The map on the scrim, radiating north-east from Townsville, identifies in precise callig- raphy the Pacific islands over which their battles were fought. I had seen this map before, among my father's memorabilia: it had been printed on a silk scarf issued as a navigational aid – when low on fuel, it would help him avoid crash-landing on islands occupied by an army infamous for its Samurai sword execu- tions of Australian airmen. This chart, with Moresby and Milne Bay and Morotai, right across to Guadalcanal and the Treasury Islands, is the setting for James Michener's *Tales of the South Pacific*, the book from which Oscar Hammerstein drew his plot.

It could have come from my father's log-book. Like Joe Cable, he was a young 'Lieutenant' (the Yanks pronounce it differently) who was barely twenty-one when commissioned to fly for the legendary 75 squadron, which had kept the Japanese at bay in New Guinea in the period from the fall of Singapore to the battle of the Coral Sea – that terrifying forty-four days when Australia had to fend for itself. Afterwards, our forces were effectively under US command, playing a crucial part in revers- ing Japanese gains in New Guinea, Borneo and the Solomons.

Australian forces in the islands had exactly the preoccu- pations depicted in the musical: grass skirts, nurses and the occasional concert parties. Grass skirts were universally sought after: native women would arrive wearing dozens at a time, and sell them for prices that increased as they peeled them off. In these all-male combat-zones in the tropics, hospital nurses provided the only female company – the young flyer's logbook notes their arrivals and departures and excitedly reports the task assigned to him on one occasion, namely to organise their toilet facilities when they arrived for a mess dance.

'The loneliness! and the longing,' sighs Michener's aviator, 'throwing words into the night on a far off Pacific Island as stars blaze over the silent sea'. This particular sadness could only be relieved by alcohol – 'grog runs' were essential to the well-being of all allied units, as some of their commanders recognised (in the musical, Captain Brackett has his secret stash). Some fine Australian pilots (including our top gun, Clive 'Killer' Caldwell) were unjustly court-martialled after the war for providing this service.

Then there was the horror and the terror of the combat when it came. My father, seventy years on, cannot forget the stench of Japanese corpses in the trenches on some recaptured islands – when not flying the men would dash to the nearest beach to escape it, laying up, in that pre-sunscreen era, the melanomas of their future. Malaria (which Joe Cable contracts on Bali Hai) was endemic, as was dengue fever and gastroenteritis: pilots flew with an empty gumboot in the cockpit to serve as a toilet. There were bullets to contend with, in the air from 'Zeke' – the nippy Japanese zeros, although it was worse to be caught on the ground in a surprise attack. My father's log laconically notes 'One of our P-38's holed in tail plane by what appeared to be a New South Wales government railway bolt – our scrap metal returns.' As indeed it did, thanks to 'Pig-Iron Bob' – pre-war prime minister Robert Menzies, who had insisted on pre-war scrap-metal sales to aggressively militarist Japan.

Australians who fought with the American forces in the Pacific did find their discipline difficult to accept – especially their obsession with rank, which features in the musical's plot. Australians fought as equals, especially in the RAAF, where distinctions between officers and others had no meaning when they were flying dangerous missions. My father was appalled when he brought his flight into land at a US base after a hair-raising sortie, to find that those of his pilots who were non-commissioned were refused access to the Officers' Mess. MacArthur criticised Anzacs for indiscipline, until his own troops performed so badly at Buna that the AIF had to save his campaign – at the cost of two thousand Australian lives.

South Pacific captures some of the comedy and a little of the cruelty of my parents' war (my mother was a WAAAF in

Townsville). But by the time I saw it at the Lincoln Centre, in the run-up to the 2008 presidential election, it had acquired a new fame – it had become the Obama musical. It was the hottest ticket in town (twice the price of a top seat at the Met) as audiences flocked to celebrate the seed of anti-racism that Rodgers & Hammerstein had planted in American popular culture in 1949, a time when the very idea of a black president was inconceivable. Americans had been carefully taught, by Jim Crow laws and segregation, to hate and fear 'people whose skin is a different shade'. But Hammerstein recognised that they could be carefully untaught. The story of Nellie, the little nurse from Little Rock (the Arkansas town that was a Broadway byword for backwardness) who confronts and overcomes her learnt bigotry against 'coloured' people, was a daring parable for a time when the poison of McCarthyism was starting its spread. Especially when supplemented by the sub-plot of a Princeton war hero torn by his love (consummated behind the theatre curtains) for a Eurasian.

This was challenging for a middle-brow Broadway audience, and Rodgers & Hammerstein came under mounting pressure, during the show's try-outs, to cut the song 'You've Got to be Carefully Taught'. They refused because, as James Michener recalled, 'the authors replied stubbornly that this number represented why they had wanted to do this play, and that even if it meant failure of the production, it was going to stay in.'

For all the tunefulness of 'Bali Hai' and 'Some Enchanted Evening', the short song 'You've Got to be Carefully Taught' is the moral climax of the show. It lasts just over a minute and is sung by Joe Cable in a sarcastic attack on the roots of the racism that will blight his and so many other lives. The lyrics might have been written by Woody Guthrie or the young Bob Dylan but would have had little impact as a 'protest song' – lodged in the nation's most acceptable middle-class entertainment, this plea for tolerance was itself made to appear acceptable and morally right.

In the McCarthy period it was held against Hammerstein (the lyric was condemned as subversive by right-wing politicians and his passport was temporarily withheld) but he got away with it. He did make a few concessions to his audiences' comfort zone and was persuaded to remove in rehearsals some lines that drew attention to Nellie's racist upbringing in the South. Bartlett Sher has restored them, much to the benefit of the drama. For example, Nellie's accusation that Emile's first wife was 'coloured', a line dropped in 1949, now serves to electrify the closing scene of the first act, and alerts the audience to the depth of the prejudice she must overcome by the end of the show.

Although Oscar Hammerstein was an active member of civil rights groups, he was too astute an artist to preach: his anti-racist message succeeds because of its understatement. The other didactic musical of 1949, *Lost in the Stars*, has been rarely performed despite Kurt Weill's exquisite music: the book is unremittingly serious. This is musical comedy, after all, which allows for only a grain or two of truth among the chaff. Not that there can be any objection to its performance by an opera company: as Clive James remarks, these musicals 'are essentially operas but with easier arias and plots that add up'. *South Pacific* certainly possesses the fundamental quality of opera, namely that the music knows more about its characters than its characters know about themselves.

Of course, some of the sentiments are dated. 'There is Nothing Like a Dame' sounds sexist, although if you look at the pictures of the dames on the fuselages of allied war planes in any Second World War combat zone, you realise its authenticity. I don't much like the romantic ending, where the French planter gets the girl and colonialism seems to continue happily ever after. The French planter is a particularly unattractive figure in the Pacific and other oceans, exploiting the indigenous people (Bloody Mary is right to call them 'stingy bastards') using native women as sex slaves (the real Emile de Becque had eight children from several concubines) and denying them democracy (France, in respect of New Caledonia and other possessions, still refuses to acknowledge their right to self-determination).

My other regret about Hammerstein's love story is that his script does not include the words with which Michener's de Becque clinches his proposal that the nurse should share his plantation: "'Nellie,' he said quietly, scarcely audible above the lorikeets, "in the hottest months you could always go to Australia.'"

For all my association of this musical with my father's war and my own youthful recognition of the roots of racism, I can play Trivial Pursuit. Did you know that the very first Broadway production booked Hayes Gordon to sing in the chorus, the actor who later played such an important part in Australian theatre as director at the Ensemble Theatre? Or that Sean Connery was one of the Seabees in the original London show – the future James Bond, bellowing out his need for a 'girly, womanly, female feminine dame'? Or that the original tune for the song after Cable's lovemaking with Liat was 'Getting to Know You' – thankfully postponed until *The King and I* and replaced by 'Younger than Springtime'? Clive James still enthuses about seeing the first Australian production when he was in short pants ('I had already memorised some of the lyrics before I left the theatre'), while lucky visitors to the inner sanctum of Barry Humphries' home in London will be played the last remaining acetate of George Sanders singing – heart-rendingly – 'This Nearly Was Mine'.

Bartlett Sher has come up with a great production of a great show by stripping away some of the sentimentality (and the hallucinogenic colours) of the film version, and restoring some lines that were just too uncomfortable for audiences in 1949. He puts the war centre-stage because, as Hammerstein said, 'racial prejudice fades away in the face of something that's really important'. But for my generation – the children, many of us born of wartime romances – it's a reminder of something else, as our own children enter their twenties in a world free from great wars. At their age, my father was nursing planes running out of petrol past storm clouds through which they could not fly, over islands occupied by vengeful Japanese soldiers. Perhaps Nellie's optimism about the future was not so cock-eyed after all.

Chapter 14

44 DAYS

Australia played a comparatively minor role in the First World War. Gallipoli was a disaster – lions led by British donkeys. There was valour, too, in those young Australians who refused to fight, resisting the nasty 'white feather' campaign that named them and sought to shame them. That is not to say that the war had no purpose. I am broadly with Clemenceau, the French prime minister, who when asked by a German diplomat at the signing of the Armistice, 'Who knows what history will make of all this?' replied, 'History will not say that Belgium invaded Germany.'

I was always chosen to make the Anzac Day speeches at school, trying to find some comfort and meaning in the corpses piled up in Sniper's Alley (including those of several great-uncles). I wished we had better war stories to tell.

I knew of one, and as the fiftieth anniversary of the battle of the Coral Sea approached in 1992, I thought it would be a good idea to document it before its heroes died of old age. So I took to the ABC the story of Australia's 'few' – the fighter pilots who won the air war against Japan over forty-four days in Moresby in 1942 between the fall of Singapore (15 February) and the Coral Sea engagement. Unfortunately, the ABC's documentary department was too busy with its own commemorative feature – a program about how difficult life was for communists in

Australia in 1942. So I went straight to its CEO, David Hill, who greeted my idea with enthusiasm: 'What a wonderful story. We'll put it out at prime time. All you have to do is find the money and make it, and the ABC will show it.'

The cost would be $100,000 (a lot in 1992). So I went cap in hand to the Coral Sea Committee, which stumped up $50,000, on the condition that I made no criticism of General MacArthur. As he had spent much of the war defaming the fighting qualities of Australian soldiers this was a bit rich. I still needed another $50,000, so I next pitched the idea to Peter Abeles, who had taken over Ansett Airlines and hence owned Hayman Island, its luxury resort, which was in need of tourists. I offered to put it on the world map – in return for $50,000, I would arrange for my client Salman Rushdie – lying low after the fatwa – to hide at Hayman and promote it once he had left. Abeles thought for a minute, and replied, 'I'll give you $50,000. But on one condition, that you promise me that Mr Rushdie will never go near Hayman Island.'

We made our documentary, 44 Days, *travelling to Jackson Field at Moresby and to a 75 Squadron reunion at RAAF Williamstown in the Hunter Valley, New South Wales, where the veterans recalled the aerial combat in their Kittyhawks. Their story is now better known, but there are many others (the Battle of Milne Bay in New Guinea, for example, which was the first Japanese land defeat) that deserve telling by 2017, which will be seventy-five years on from those fear-filled days in 1942 when Australia had to defend itself, because no one else would.*

The forty-four days between the fall of Singapore and the battle of the Coral Sea was the period John Curtin described as 'Australia's darkest hour', when the nation had to fend for itself after the British collapse and before the US army forces could mobilise in its defence. It was a time of panic – Darwin was heavily bombed and as the Japanese forces swept through

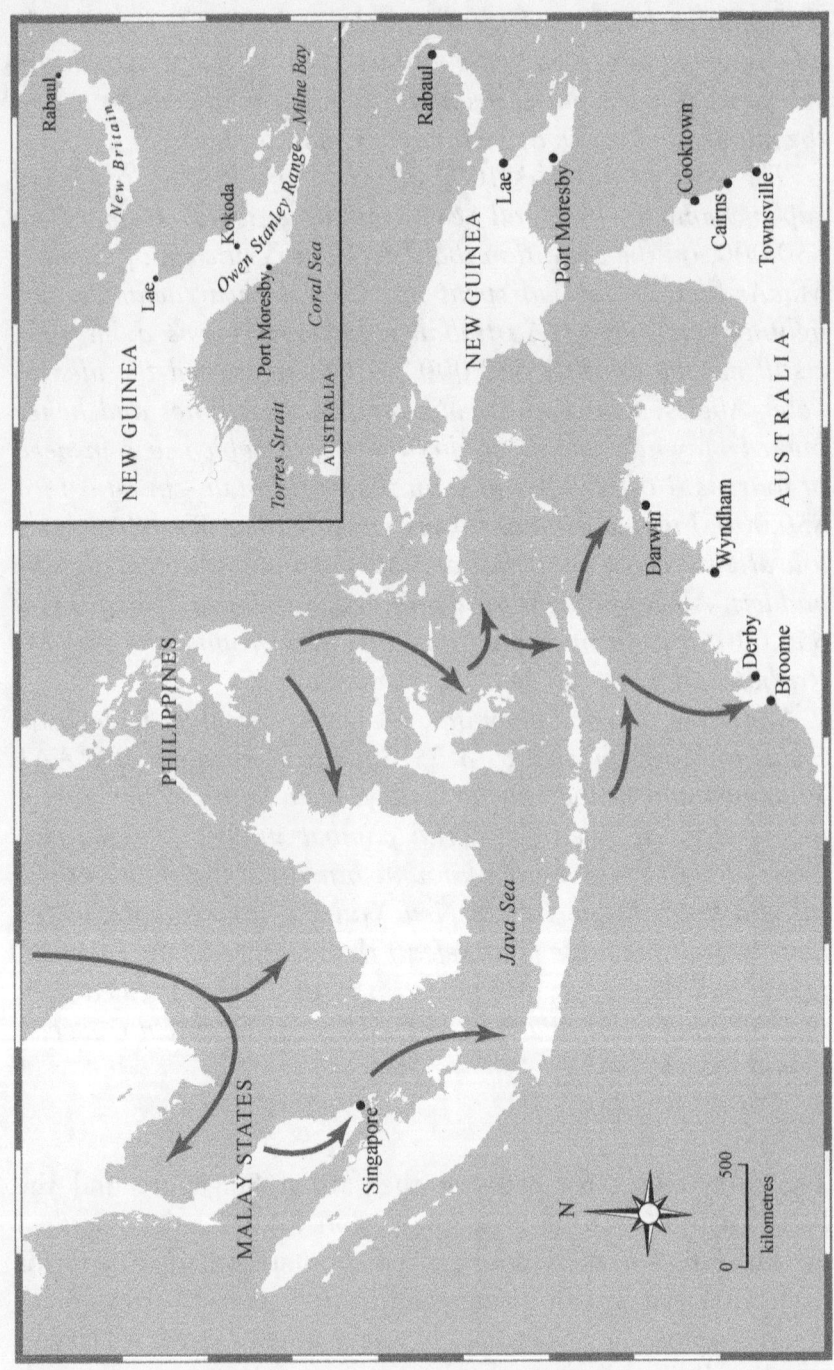

Southeast Asia to reach New Guinea, there came the sickening realisation that North Queensland could not be held. The beaches of Townsville were covered in barbed wire, but strategic thinking identified 'the Brisbane line' as the only line that could realistically be drawn against an invasion until American forces, fighting a losing battle in the Philippines, retreated to shield the eastern coast of Australia. Until then, its defence depended on Port Moresby, gateway to the Coral Sea, connected by the Kokoda Trail across the Owen Stanley Ranges to the northern towns beginning to fall to the Japanese.

Nippon's yomp through South East Asia had been made possible by its air power – the heavy-duty 'Betty' bomber and the ultra-manoeuvrable 'zero' fighter, and once Japan captured Rabaul, they began to bomb and strafe Moresby. Only Australian air power could save the port city, but Australia had no air power – not a single fighter, let alone a fighter squadron.

The background to that scandal was the incompetence of successive Australian governments, which between the wars allocated only ten per cent of the defence budget to the air force (sixty per cent to the navy). To this strategic blindness Robert Menzies, Liberal Party prime minister between 1938 and 1941, brought a manic anglophilia: in 1940 he seriously damaged the RAAF by appointing a blimpish Briton (Sir Charles Burnett) as its commander, who refused to believe that Orientals could fly proficiently. These two proceeded enthusiastically and systematically to remove almost every experienced pilot in Australia, and sent them as our contribution to the Empire Air Training Scheme. Australians flew, navigated, gunned and died for Britain in Europe, Burma and the Western Desert, but they were not permitted to return to any form of active service in Australia.

Menzies and his Melbourne Club colleagues, for whom the cathedrals of Europe were more important than northern Queensland, stuck to the 'Save Europe First' strategy, even though it risked losing Australia. As war clouds gathered at home in 1941, Menzies strutted and fretted for the first five months in London, hoping that his genius would be sufficiently obvious to others beside himself and earn him a place in Churchill's war cabinet. He even agreed to send Australian troops to an entirely predictable disaster in Crete – predictable because they had no air cover. On his return, his cabinet decided to leave Australia's air defence in the hands of the British Air Ministry, which had vaguely promised to send some planes if Australia came under threat. It was a promise it never intended to keep, as cabinet should have realised. So it came to pass that Australia, by the time of the attack on Pearl Harbor in December 1941, had no fighter aircraft – merely some home-made 'Wirraway' trainers, quickly and easily destroyed whenever they were forced into combat.

Fortunately the Liberal government collapsed and in October 1941, John Curtin became prime minister. It took this old conscientious objector – he had been jailed back in 1916 for opposing conscription – to recognise the peril and to reverse Labor policy by directing that conscripts should be sent to fight, if necessary, in New Guinea.

The chain of events in early 1942 had made this fight inevitable: the Japanese forces swept down the Malaysian peninsula and overran the Philippines. Then they aimed a series of psychologically devastating hammer blows at Australia:

- 15 February – the fall of Singapore: 15,000 of our troops taken prisoner;
- 19 February – the bombing of Darwin: 250 dead, and ships and aircraft destroyed;
- 1 March – loss of the battle of the Java Sea: 1500 Australians drowned when HMAS *Perth* sunk;
- 3 March – the bombing of Broome, Wyndham and Derby: 24 aircraft destroyed;
- 8 March – successful Japanese invasion of New Guinea, fortifying their bases at Rabaul and at Lae, only 200 miles from Moresby.

On 15 March the Imperial War Cabinet met in Tokyo, to discuss whether Australia should be invaded. The navy was in favour, the army against (their supply lines were stretched) and no final decision was taken. In the immediate future, the plan was to attack and capture Moresby (and then Fiji and Samoa), bomb Cooktown and Townsville, and blockade the communication lines between the Australian mainland and the American Pacific bases.

Meanwhile, Australia was vulnerable: the Americans had not arrived and Churchill had refused Curtin's pleas to allow the AIF to return. So, in January, an ill-trained and unprepared militia force of conscripts was rushed to garrison Moresby, the potential stepping stone to Queensland. New Guinea was Australia's largest colonial possession, inherited in trust from the League of Nations, but Moresby, the capital, had been left to become a stagnant colonial backwater, ruled by lazy linen-suited administrators who had made little effort to educate the natives, other than as their servants. The two thousand young conscripts turned to jelly once the bombings began in February: Osmar White, war correspondent for the Queensland *Courier-Mail*, compared the 'rats of Tobruk' with 'the mice of Moresby', who were 'confused, unequipped, inadequately rationed. As the bombings continued, they started to ask, "Where the hell are *our* planes?"'

The story of how Curtin defied Churchill and Roosevelt to bring the 7th Division home is well known. Less dramatic, but just as important, is how he bombarded both leaders with cables demanding fighter aircraft. Australian lives had been lost in Crete through lack of air cover, he argued. Singapore, Ambon and Rabaul had been lost for the same reason. 'Give us Spitfires and Hurricanes,' he begged at first, and then suddenly a new word, Kittyhawk, enters the top-secret cablegram vocabulary. He repeats it relentlessly: 'Give us Kittyhawks.' Washington objects – 'Does Australia have the pilots to fly them?'

'Australia has the pilots to fly any number of Kittyhawks that are likely to be available,' Curtin replied.

Providentially, a US cargo ship bound for the falling Philippines was diverted to Sydney, and seventy USAF crates were
landed at Darling Harbour. Inside them, the new Kittyhawk
fighters, never before flown by Australians. Twenty-four of the
planes were quickly constructed, and a motley collection of air
and ground crew hastily summoned from around Australia.
A fighter squadron was formed – on 4 March. It was called
75 Squadron, perhaps in an attempt to fool both the Japanese
invaders and the Australian people into thinking that there were
at least seventy-four more where it came from.

By sheer good fortune, several of Australia's best airmen
were at home on leave from their squadrons on the Western
Desert. One was John F. Jackson. At thirty-four, the oldest
fighter pilot in the RAAF, 'Old John' had learnt to fly
crop-dusters at his family property in southern Queensland.
He was a prosperous grazier and had heavy family responsibilities, but joined up at the outbreak of war and had already
won a medal for singlehandedly shooting down three German
bombers in one engagement. To him would fall the task of
leading the Kittyhawk squadron, piloted by youngsters culled
from weekend fliers, crop-dusters and raw recruits with good
eyesight, against the air aces of Japan, veterans who had
already won the air war over Manchuria: they refused to wear
parachutes and flew the nippiest and nastiest fighter of the
time, the Mitsubishi Zero.

75 Squadron's first problem was to get its planes from Sydney,
where they were being assembled, to Townsville. These kids had
not flown in a Kittyhawk before; they had no radios, let alone
any radar. Recklessly, they were ordered to ferry their planes
north – and as luck would have it, they struck a severe storm
over Newcastle. Three planes crashed and two pilots were killed,
as the new squadron just made it to Evans Head. If 75 Squadron
could not even reach Queensland, how could they hope to fight
the Japanese who now controlled the skies over Moresby?

The survivors reached Townsville, and there was no time
to mourn the tragic loss of two airmen. In North Queensland,

the schools had closed and the beaches were covered in barbed wire, as civilians streamed south to escape the predicted invasion. 75 Squadron was given one week to get its act together – one week for the pilots to learn how to fly their Kittyhawks properly, to fire its guns, to master the deadly craft of aerial warfare, before flying off to save Moresby, Australia's front line.

By March 1942 the Japanese advance had reached Lae, a township only 190 miles to the north, across the high jungle-thick mountains of the Owen Stanley Ranges. When the Japanese bombs began to fall, it became obvious that Moresby could not survive without air defence. Osmar White reported that:

> If the Japs come, organised defence will not last more than 48 hours. Early in March there was a rumour that Australian fighter squadrons with P40 Kittyhawks were due to arrive anytime, and morale rose sharply. But as the weeks passed, and the Kittyhawks did not come, it began to lag again. Then for days there were rumours that the Kittyhawks would arrive tomorrow, so they became known as 'Tomorrowhawks' and eventually as 'Neverhawks'.

The day the 'Neverhawks' finally came was 21 March. The Moresby airstrip was guarded by frightened Australian machine-gunners – conscripts whose own nerves had been shot to pieces after weeks of being bombed and strafed by enemy planes with a monopoly on the sky. So when the first four Kittyhawks lowered their flaps to land, the troops immediately assumed that these new aircraft were Japanese. They opened fire, severely damaging two planes and almost killing one pilot. It was *not* an auspicious beginning.

But barely one hour later, 75 Squadron's luck kicked in at last. A Japanese 'Betty' bomber approached, stooging complacently over the town. Two pilots – Wilbur Wackett, a Melbourne University student, and Barry Cox, a Sydney stockbrokers' clerk, raced for the two serviceable Kittyhawks and took off to

intercept – while all of Moresby watched, including war correspondent George Johnston:

> An hour after the first Kittyhawks landed a Jap heavy
> bomber came over on reconnaissance. Two Kittys took
> off, intercepted her over the mountains, drove her back
> and after a brilliant attack, shot her down in flames into
> the harbour. First real evidence of aggression in this war.
> Whacko!

Osmar White described the scene:

> the bomber faltered, and streamed straight down in the
> sky with a ribbon of white smoke behind it. It crashed
> with a mighty explosion. We onlookers fell on one
> another's necks, howling hysterically with joy. From miles
> around, men came roaring up to the airfield in lorries,
> cheering and laughing. They stared with a mixture of
> awe and disbelief at this first fighter squadron. Its arrival
> was really an event of immense importance. Now there
> would be some sort of fight, instead of a hopeless bloody
> walkover.

That night in his tent, John Jackson devised a daring plan
for the squadron's first combat mission. He was pretty sure the
Japanese bomber had been destroyed before it could radio back
to its base the news that the fighters had arrived. So the next
morning the enemy planes would be lined up on the airfield
at Lae, ready for their usual unopposed bombing attack on
Moresby. That was where 75 Squadron would seek them and
strike.

In the darkness before the dawn, ground crew prepared nine
Kittyhawks. At first light, John Jackson led his men to their
machines. They flew high over the mountains, out to the sea
on the other side, then dived through the low cloud to within
a few feet of the airstrip, to take the enemy by surprise. It was
a brilliant strategy, and inflicted the worst loss on Japan of any
single engagement in the conflict thus far. Twelve warplanes

were destroyed on the ground, and two Zeros shot down in the air. One Australian pilot was killed and Wilbur Wackett, who had shot down the bomber the day before, was forced to ditch in the sea, ten miles off the coast from Lae. He swam ashore – through a school of sharks – and despite contracting malaria, walked back to base through the jungle.

The next day, and in the following weeks, the Japanese responded in kind, invariably with more aircraft than the outnumbered Australians who rarely had more than five serviceable Kittyhawks able to go aloft at any one time. The days settled into a pattern. Johnson would wake before dawn, take off and fly a dangerous reconnaissance mission over the Japanese positions on the other side of the mountains. On his return, and usually about midday, the call would come from 'golden voice' – a coast-watcher perched in a tree overlooking Lae – reporting the take-off of a Japanese attack mission. That would give the pilots twenty minutes to scramble their craft and reach sufficient altitude – at least 20,000 feet – from which their Kittyhawks could dive on the attackers. This, together with its firepower, was the plane's great strength – good pilots could hold it in a dive, fire at the target and then cut the motor and twist away from any Zero on their tail. The Mitsubishi-built Zero was the best single-seat fighter of its time, only half the weight of the Kittyhawk and hence much more manoeuvrable. It climbed faster, turned more sharply and could fly much higher; as Jackson always said, 'Never get into a dogfight with a Zero.'

Jackson's leadership of his men, including the hundred or so ground crew vital to keeping the Kittyhawks in the air, gave the first spring of hope that the RAAF could fight this war; to its shame, several hundred men had deserted, in fear, after the bombing of Darwin, and the RAAF had originally been included in MacArthur's cruel assessment: 'Australians will not fight.' In Moresby, flying conditions were appalling, with low cloud and heavy rain on most days, swarms of malarial mosquitoes and disgusting rations (tinned bully-beef, mainly) that triggered spasms of gastroenteritis. At twenty thousand feet, pilots in the grip of malaria made use of their flying boots as a toilet for diarrhoea and vomit and spent much of the time fighting physical pain as well as watching for Zeros coming out of the sun. But for all this, not a man quailed: Johnson's calmness, dedication and conviction saw them through. Then, out of the blue, Johnson himself was shot down.

On 17 April he took off at dawn for his regular reconnaissance over enemy territory – a dangerous mission he always insisted on performing alone. He was jumped from behind, out of the rising sun, by three Zeros, which shot up his engine and forced him to ditch in the sea. His adventures for the next two-and-a-half weeks he recounted in a letter he wrote to his wife and children when he returned to base:

> My aircraft sank in a few seconds. I was out in a flash but the oxygen tube held me for a while. I started off for land with the three Japanese flying around and around me and I had a few anxious moments waiting for them to strafe me. After what seemed an eternity, they went away. As I was swimming in, a croc poked his snout at me but didn't approve and turned away. The natives ashore seemed frightened, but two good lads, mission-taught, offered to guide me. I knew the Japanese would send a search party straight after me so the lads packed their belongings and we hurried away. Hadn't gone far before we sighted Japanese boats so we went into the jungle, swimming creeks in my clothes and struggling through swamp, down to my waist in slime and mud. I decided to push on though nearly done in.
>
> I had shed my shoes and socks swimming in from the aircraft and my feet were pretty bad. When we came to a stony river crossing my feet wouldn't work at all and they had to carry me across. It rained most of the night and I was drenched, although they made an umbrella for me out of big wide banana leaves.
>
> Just after we left I heard a shot and knew the Japanese were on our trail and I limped on. Providence alone has

saved me. My aircraft was shot to ribbons. The croc turned away and I have two wonderful helpers.

Next day we got away early – travelled through a lot of villages and saw one very good singsing. The male dancers with not much on, wearing fearsome looking head-dresses, mostly with birds of paradise feathers, dance around in a circle beating their hollowed drums with lizard or snake skin stretched across one end.

23/4/42 – later a plane just arrived to pick me up. Then yesterday I was flown back to Moresby. Had a hot reception. Was about to land when three Japanese made a surprise attack. Aircraft I was in got full of holes. Had tip of my finger grazed. Just a mere scratch. Providence surely guided and protected me all through.

Jackson's return filled the squadron with joy. He appeared in the mess with his bandaged finger (the tip shot off rather than merely 'grazed'), apologising for turning up two weeks late for the dinner to celebrate the Distinguished Flying Cross just awarded for his efforts against Rommel. Osmar White attended, and saw what Jackson's devoted men could not:

His big body was sick but his complexion was still ruddy. His hands and eyes were still rock steady. Yet whoever looked at the man with friendly eyes that night saw one weary in soul. Too long in the shadows had etiolated the strong stem of his resolution to live. I have never seen a man who needed more desperately some gentleness to make him feel again, as living men should, that the face of death is terrible, and to be feared. He had done more than conquer fear – he had killed it.

On any view, Jackson should have been sent home for rest and recreation – no man could make death-defying decisions at twenty thousand feet after a twenty-day hike through the New Guinea jungle. But the two moronic officials who occupied non-combatant positions above the Squadron Leader – they are called 'Wing Commanders' although they had no command in the air – had other plans, now he was no longer invincible.

They called him in for an angry confrontation over operational tactics. These 'commanders' had not ventured a word of thanks or support to the pilots and ground crew who had achieved so much after just six weeks. Instead, and incredibly, they told Jackson that his 'hit and dive' tactics, which had protected the Kittyhawk from the more manoeuvrable Zeros, were mistaken. They accused him of cowardice for refusing to dogfight.

There is no first-hand account of that meeting, but his pilots remember – it astonished them, because he had instilled in them never to shoot it out with a Zero – how he came back to the mess and announced that they were now going to dogfight, and he would show them how. They recall no trace of anger or bitterness in his voice, and I suspect that the decision reflected the one tragic flaw of this otherwise all-Australian hero, namely that he was at heart a conservative who would always obey orders. He lacked the larrikin streak, or the distrust of authority, or perhaps the confidence in his own opinion that would have helped him to rebel to save his life.

The next morning, 'golden voice', the coast-watcher, reported that eight bombers and fourteen Zeros were on their way over. The squadron by now was down to only five Kittyhawks, and Jackson should not have been flying at all, but unhesitatingly he scrambled his men: odds of 4:1 against were not infrequent. This time, unusually, the other pilots heard him turn the air blue over the radio as they intercepted the enemy, his tracer blazing on the Zero in his gun sights as he felt the bullets from the Zeros on his tail.

Two of the five Kittyhawks failed to return that terrible day. Barry Cox and John Jackson were missing, and one wrecked Kittyhawk has been sighted on a hillside. John's brother, Les Jackson, and the squadron doctor Bill Deane-Butcher, headed for that hill. As the doctor laconically recalled,

[W]e set off for the crash site. On the way we met an
army vehicle coming towards us. They said they had
located it and the remains had been recovered but there
was little to recover. We didn't know which pilot it was.
Barry Cox was a very small man and John was a big
man. They said they'd found a foot with a boot on it.
Les asked the question: 'What size was the boot?' They
replied it was a very large boot.

Les Jackson took his brother's place, but he was not of the same
calibre – although he fought on throughout the war, he had
alcohol problems and a maniacal wish to avenge his brother,
which sometimes caused him to put other pilots in danger.
Besides, the forty-four days were almost up, and American
squadrons were now arriving in Moresby and American aircraft
carriers were confronting the Japanese fleet in the Coral Sea.
After forty-four days the squadron was down to only three
serviceable planes. For their last mission, Les Jackson asked
for two volunteers to fly with him, and every pilot stepped
forward. Fortunately for the two who drew the short straws,
their Kittyhawks were destroyed that night in a surprise raid. So
Les Jackson took off alone, but failed to find the Japanese fleet
below the cloud over the Coral Sea, where they were battling
the Americans. He flew to Cairns and made for the nearest pub.

At the end of its epic defence of Moresby, 75 Squadron had
lost half its pilots and was down to its last plane. But it had
destroyed four times as many enemy aircraft, put heart into the
ground troops (a heart they were soon to show at Kokoda) and
delayed the invasion for just long enough for the American fleet
to turn the tide in the battles of the Coral Sea and Midway.
What is more, they had created what should have become a
legend, had their achievement not been ignored for fifty years.

There is nothing in Australian war history that is quite
like the story of John Jackson and his young pilots – ordinary
Australians from all walks of life, who joined that tumult in the
clouds over Port Moresby in March and April of 1942. They

were fighting for their families and their friends and their lost brothers, and for the first time – and it was the most crucial time – they more or less won.

They had no national anthem to sing, no war machine to support them, no padre to convince them that God was on their side. There was, however, a poem they used to recite – the first my father ever taught me – written by a nineteen-year-old Canadian airman just before he was lost in action. It gave some comfort to these young airmen as they revved their machines for what they knew could be their last flight.

> Oh I have slipped the surly bonds to Earth,
> And danced the skies on laughter-silvered wings;
> Sunward I've climbed and joined the tumbling mirth
> Of sun spit clouds – and done a hundred things
> *You* have not dreamed of – wheeled and soared and swung
> High in the sunlit silence. Hov'ring there,
> I've chased the shouting wind along, and flung
> My eager craft through footless halls of air . . .
> Up, up the long, delirious burning blue
> I've topped the windswept heights with easy grace.
> Where never lark, or even eagle flew –
> And, while with silent lifted mind I've trod
> The high untrespassed sanctity of space,
> Put out my hand and touched the face of God.

I was to encounter this poem again in an English honours exam paper at Sydney University. It was alongside 'An Irish Airman foresees his death' – much the better poem (by W. B. Yeats), but one I would not imagine fighter boys ever reciting. We were meant by our ivory-towered examiners to compare the two, and explain how superior the Yeats was in every way – except (as I pointed out, at the risk of failure) to those for whose actual experience of war in the air it offers some meaning and some hope.

It did that for John Jackson, truly a great Australian in the tradition of Arthur Phillip – a man who was authoritative and wise and tender and loving at the same time (I have read his letters to his wife and children), a born leader who took the greatest risks himself and inspired his men with both courage and devotion. Had he lived he would have led the squadron he formed later in the year in the battle of Milne Bay (the first victory by combined Australian land and sea forces over the Japanese) and probably ended up after the war as a Country Party MP. But his memorial is of some significance: it is Jackson Field, now Moresby International Airport, named in his honour at the insistence of General MacArthur – the highest praise that man could ever bring himself to give to an Australian.

Chapter 15

HICKS IN GUANTANAMO

My friend Dick Smith, a true patriot, is radical only in his devotion to his country: his political allegiances sat quite happily with John Howard's style of conservatism. But he could not understand why, for five years, the Howard government utterly abandoned an Australian to indefinite detention at Guantanamo Bay. Tony Blair kicked up such a fuss about this 'legal black hole' that all British prisoners were repatriated. Dick asked me to help David Hicks but I soon concluded that the law was irrelevant to his plight. He was in Guantanamo not because he was guilty, but because he was the only white man left, and it suited the US to keep him there for as long as his supine government did not object.

The Liberal party, I am reliably informed, has a weathervane that warns when its policies need to change, namely when they begin to alienate the wives of doctors. By 2007, this key suburban focus group began telling its pollsters that Hicks had been in prison without trial for too long. So for electoral reasons it became expedient for Hicks to be offered release if, to save everyone else's face, he agreed to plead guilty to a charge ('providing material support for terrorism') of which he (and most legal experts) believed he was innocent. The cynicism of this deal between the US and its most fawning ally would have had 'Doc' Evatt spinning in his grave: when will our country ever have the confidence to do the right thing on those occasions when the US is in the wrong?

Before his release came about, in the 2006 Kenneth Myer lecture at the National Library, I had vented some spleen at the bush lawyers who conceived this unlawful prison and at our political leaders, who appeared at that point to be unperturbed if an Australian were held there indefinitely. As the case of Julian Assange reminds us (see chapters 35 and 36), it is the government's duty to assist Australians in peril to obtain a fair trial in foreign courts. That is the promise it makes on our passports and must honour, however inconvenient it may be to allies, who might thereby learn not to take Australia for granted.

The term 'bush lawyer' is Australian slang for a hick counsellor, ignorant of the law. Thanks to recent decisions of the US Supreme Court and inquiries into torture at Abu Ghraib, it has been given a wider meaning, to denote the lawyers in US government service who have misunderstood or misrepresented the fundamental rules of human rights in their advice to President Bush. Their mistakes have been so damaging that the British attorney-general has taken to tendering his own advice to the White House about Guantanamo Bay – namely to close it. The case of David Hicks should provide his Australian counterpart with an opportunity to do likewise.

It is, let us remember, a war crime to commit a 'grave breach' of the Geneva Conventions. Article 8(2)(a)(vi) of the Rome Statute of the International Criminal Court, to which Australia (but not the US) is a party, defines such breaches to include 'wilfully depriving a prisoner of war or other protected person of the right of fair and regular trial'. The US Supreme Court has now declared Hicks to be a person protected by the Geneva Conventions, and there must come a point at which Australian law officers who wilfully authorise or approve or acquiesce in an unfair and irregular trial of an Australian citizen, or no trial at all, become complicit in a grave breach of international law.

No doubt Australia's attorney-general, Philip Ruddock, like the US president, merely accepted the advice of the US government lawyers that Guantanamo detention was lawful. Now that excuse is unavailing. At first, all the president's lawmen advised that Guantanamo was not on American soil, so due process did not apply. That argument was rejected by the Supreme Court in the *Hamdi* case in 2004, ruling that habeas corpus, the great writ that has run for five hundred years to require the state to justify imprisonment, could be brought by detainees held on offshore islands.

Next, the Bush lawyers advised that the Geneva Conventions did not protect the detainees because Afghanistan was a failed state, or because they were not wearing military uniforms when captured, or because the Geneva Conventions were 'quaint' and 'obsolete', or because the president as commander-in-chief could override them. Last month [June 2006], the Supreme Court in the *Hamdan* case shredded these arguments as well, when it decided that the Conventions were part of US military law. Were the Bush lawyers abashed? Not at all. One of them, Professor John Yoo, complained: 'The court is attempting to 'suppress creative thinking.'

He was one of the 'creative thinkers' who approved interrogation techniques such as 'waterboarding' (the process that mimics drowning) and 'using detainees' individual phobias', such as fear of dogs. Other Bush lawyers approved techniques ranging from prolonged subjection to cacophonous noise to sexual humiliation and 'other scenarios designed to convince the detainee that death is imminent for him and/or for members of his family'. This was not 'torture', they advised, because torture required pain comparable 'to physical injury such as organ failure, impairment of bodily functions or even death'.

These 'creative' techniques were used at Guantanamo when the base was assumed to be a Geneva-free environment, but the inquiry set up under former secretary of state James Schlesinger after the Abu Ghraib torture photograph scandal found that, once taught to military interrogators, torture techniques 'migrated' with them to Abu Ghraib and other prisons in Iraq, where they were adapted by 'sadists on the night shift'. This kind of 'creativity' produced an inhumane environment to which no one should be subjected, certainly not for years on end.

Ruddock at least believes that Hicks should some day be tried – but for what, exactly? The US would, in theory, be entitled to try him for a war crime, but so far he has faced only a generalised charge of a conspiracy based on his presence in the ranks of those who fought for the Taliban, which was the de facto government of Afghanistan. It is not a crime to enlist in the army of a government – even a government as unpleasant as the Taliban – otherwise all soldiers on a losing side would be guilty and peace agreements would never be negotiated.

Since the *Hamdan* decision, Bush lawyers have been back at work drafting legislation for a new tribunal to replace the 'special military commissions' – the sad little Star Chambers that were struck down by the Supreme Court. Their early drafts provide no reassurance that these replacement tribunals will secure 'the rights of fair and regular trial'. A trial cannot be regular if judges and jurors owe obedience to the detaining authority, and the draft legislation provides for trial by US army officers, not by judges or jurors. They cannot be fair with procedures that still prevent the defence from challenging prosecution evidence and that admit evidence obtained by torture. At common law, based on the *Magna Carta*, a criminal process cannot be fair if it is delayed through no fault of the defendant for more than five years (the point at which, the Privy Council has held, any death sentence must be commuted). Inevitably, the new tribunal will be subject to Supreme Court challenge, which will take several years to resolve. Hicks and other detainees cannot be faulted for challenging the fairness of the process.

The advent of new forms of terror and new forces to inflict it on the innocent challenges democratic societies to respond with legal processes that do not abandon our cherished values.

In some respects, the American record is impressive: internal documents show how strenuously the attempts to evade Geneva Convention protections were opposed internally by US military lawyers. They were denounced by bar associations and defeated – eventually – in the courts and (in the case of torture) by John McCain's work in Congress. But the process is lengthy and unpredictable.

The White House, on present indications, cannot bring itself to grant foreign detainees the 'fair and regular trial' by juries in state courts, as afforded to US citizens, nor the court martials afforded to its own soldiers. Nor will it choose an acceptable alternative, such as trial by independent and/or international judges.

Given Australia's obligations under the Geneva Conventions and the Rome Statute, and the history of demonstrably erroneous advice that the White House has received on interrogation, due process and treatment of foreign prisoners in Guantanamo, it may be time for the Australian attorney-general to stand up to the Bush lawyers. He could echo the advice of his British counterpart: not only is closure of Guantanamo right in principle, it is right because 'the historic tradition of the US as a beacon of freedom, liberty and of justice deserves the removal of what has become a symbol of injustice'.

Chapter 16

SEND IN THE DRONES

The abiding American fear of the sight of black body bags returning from some foreign field – Vietnam, and later Iraq and Afghanistan – has led to the anxious development of methods of waging war without human casualties. Bombing from fifteen thousand feet over Kosovo caused no loss of US military life, although on the ground eight hundred Kosovars died as a result of imprecise targeting. The drone, originally a reconnaissance craft, is now armed with hellfire missiles and laser-guided bombs and is 'flown' – in fact, controlled – by a large team of operators twelve thousand miles away. There are more man hours 'flown' by CIA-controlled drones than by the US Air Force, and more 'pilots' are being trained for unmanned aircraft than for conventional war-planes. They have become the state assassin's weapon of choice, and the states that have chosen thus far to use them are America, Russia and Israel, although others will follow.

Australia is only tangentially involved in 'targeted killings' – when, for example, the stolen passports of its nationals are used by Mossad hit squads. But the new US bases on Christmas Island and at Darwin may provide a useful HQ for drone controllers: would their presidential 'licence to kill' be valid in this country? The White House claims that drone executions

have weakened Al-Qaeda, but it has forgotten the parable of
the dragon's teeth – the furious anti-Americanism these killings
arouse. The White House does not get this: at its 2011 Corres-
pondents' Ball, Obama joked about his advice to boys keen on
his daughters: 'I have two words for you . . . Predator drones.'
The laughter, from American journalists who have never
bothered to disturb their readers with the dangers of drone
warfare, was not shared in Palestine or Pakistan.

President Obama, on receiving the Nobel Peace Prize,
boasted that 'even as we confront a vicious adversary that
abides by no rules . . . the United States of America must
remain a standard-bearer in the conduct of war'.

Just what standard is being raised by executing suspects
without trial, together with anyone else in their immediate
vicinity, is the subject of this article, written for the New Statesman *in June 2012. Obama did not directly address the problem*
until a speech in mid-2013, promising to remove drones from
secret CIA control and to impose stricter limits on 'collateral
damage' (i.e. killing civilians). But the drone deaths continue,
often with civilians and children as the victims.

In war, it has for centuries been lawful to kill enemy commanders. As Alberico Gentili, Regius Professor of Civil Law at
Oxford during the reign of James I, explained, 'A man who is
dead renews no war' – a thought that comforted Cromwell as he
viewed the body of Charles I.

More recent allied commanders have been reluctant to
target their opposite numbers, for fear that this would unite
the enemy's people and provoke reprisal assassinations. In the
1970s, US Congressional Committees exposed comical CIA
plots to murder Fidel Castro – sending him exploding cigars
and poison pens — and the outcry led both Presidents Ford
and Reagan to ban political assassinations under Executive
Order 12333: 'no person employed by or acting on behalf of the
United States Government shall engage in, or conspire to engage

in, assassination.' This comports with the Fifth Amendment to the US constitution, which protects 'any persons' (not just US citizens) from being 'deprived of life . . . without due process of law'.

Until 9/11, the legal position was clear: in war, active combatants could kill and be killed, subject to rules about surrender and prohibitions on taking life by treachery, poison and so on. This 'war law' – ironically called International Humanitarian Law (IHL) – applied only to conflicts between opposing armies simultaneously and legitimately invoking the right of self-defence. Otherwise, confrontations with insurgents, rioters and terrorists were not matters for IHL at all: they were to be governed by human rights law, which generally allows police to use reasonable force (and if necessary, lethal force) to apprehend armed criminals.

Human rights law is much less permissive than IHL. When three IRA members were shot dead on Gibraltar by British security forces, the European Court held that the UK had denied them the right to life because its intelligence services had jumped to the overhasty and mistaken conclusion that they were armed. In the case of known members of terrorist organisations, the 'reasonable force' requirement exercises a necessary and humane restraint over the trigger-happiness of security services. This is exactly why it has suited the US, Russia and Israel to pretend that their rhetoric about the 'war on terror' is taken literally enough to engage the law of war, which (unlike the rule of reasonable force) allows terrorists to be killed without much compunction.

'Targeted killings', then, are lawful if the target is an enemy combatant at the time of armed conflict between states. In times or places of peace they will be unlawful unless the force used is reasonable to prevent crime or apprehend criminals. Otherwise, they amount to extra-judicial killings in breach of human rights law.

The states that deploy targeted killing methods argue that they are at war. As Harold Koh, US Solicitor-General, puts it:

> As a matter of international law, the US is in armed conflict
> with Al-Qaeda, as well as the Taliban ... in response
> to the horrific 9/11 attacks and may use force consist-
> ent with its inherent right to self-defence ... including
> by targeting persons such as high level Al-Qaeda leaders
> who are planning to attack us.

This bold and bald statement begs many questions. How can
you have an 'armed conflict' ten years after a terrorist atrocity
unless there is some organised enemy, rather than a random
collection of terrorist groups? What actual criteria are used for
putting names on the secret assassination list: is it enough to
be sympathetic to terrorism, or married to a terrorist, or to be
anti-American? To provide shelter or funds to terrorist groups?
What is the required degree of proof (is it enough that guilt is
likely, or on the balance of probabilities, or beyond reasonable
doubt?)? There are no accountability mechanisms – no inquests,
sometimes not even a casualty list, although the US usually
announces, and celebrates, when it hits a 'high-value target'.

There is, of course, no fairness or due process to enable the
potential victim or his relatives or any outside body to challenge the accuracy of the information on which the targeting
decision has been made, or the decision – by shadowy intelligence operatives – to place him on the target list. The Senate
Foreign Relations Committee reported in 2009 that the Pentagon's approved list of 'prioritised targets' contained 367 names
and had been expanded to include fifty Afghan drug lords
suspected of donating money to the Taliban. Suppose the suspicion was unreasonable, or the donation had been at gunpoint,
or had been of a negligible amount? What the Pentagon is doing
is secretly sentencing people to death, for an unproven crime.

The Israeli Supreme Court is the only tribunal to have
confronted the legality of targeted killing, at a time (2006) when
234 Mossad targets had been members of Hamas and the other
153 were civilians who got in the way. The court contented itself
with general comments about limiting the targets to dangerous

and dedicated terrorists, and gave out some obvious precautionary precepts: 'well-based information is needed'; 'innocent civilians are not to be harmed'; 'in case of doubt, careful verification is needed before an attack is made'.

The reality is that innocent civilians very often are killed, and that 'verification' always seems careful to the minds of the targeters. The Israeli judges and officials seem morally content to risk civilian lives: after a one-ton bomb was dropped on a building in Gaza City that killed many civilians (a result that was obviously foreseeable) in order to assassinate Salah Shehadeh, a Hamas military leader, the inquiry into the incident merely noted 'shortcomings' in evaluation of information. This was plainly a case of manslaughter by gross negligence. The Israeli defence force said that lessons had been learnt, but not about civilian casualties – later when it executed by missile Sheikh Yassin, the wheelchair-bound Hamas spiritual leader, it killed eight others outside his mosque.

In similar vein, the CIA's anxiety to kill Al-Qaeda leader Al-Zawahiri led to a drone attack on a village in Pakistan where he was mistakenly thought to be hiding, and eighteen civilians were killed. There was no explanation, no accountability and no compensation for what the CIA calls a 'decapitation strike'. The more valuable the target, the less care that it takes about decapitating civilians. The US Government admits to killing about 550 unarmed civilians in strikes over the past ten years – other estimates put the figure as high as four thousand. An internal study for the government of Pakistan of drone killings in tribal areas between 2006 and 2009 confirmed at least 147 victims, ninety-four of them children.

All this is justified – by the Obama administration as fervently as by its predecessors – as an exercise in self-defence under Article 51 of the UN Charter. But this article grants the right only against armed attacks (or, more controversially, imminent attacks) by other states, and not by terrorist groups. If the fight against terrorism is squeezed into this war-law paradigm, an irony results. The Geneva Conventions and customary rights and protections must apply to terrorist and to law enforcer alike. If it is lawful to kill bin Laden, Al-Zawahiri, and Hamas commanders, then it must equally be lawful for them to kill their opposite numbers – the US commander-in-chief, his generals, his secretaries of state and his allies (even the queen of England, as head of state of a US ally, may qualify as a legitimate target). The president would certainly be classed as a 'combatant' under the very law that his solicitor-general applies to leaders of the Taliban and Al-Qaeda, thereby dignifying them to a degree that is both unreal and unacceptable. Gangsters who deliberately take the lives of innocent civilians in order to spread terror deserve to be treated like dangerous criminals and shot down whenever necessity requires, and not treated in law as if they were warriors matched in combat with great states.

What is the position under human rights law? It would obviously be a breach of the right to life if terrorist sympathisers were targeted to deter others, or if anyone was killed in circumstances where it was reasonably possible to arrest them. It would be reasonable to kill terrorists hell-bent on missions to blow up civilians, or engaged in conspiracies to kill them. But the record of drone attacks demonstrates that frequently individuals are targeted when they present no clear or imminent danger, and strikes are often launched that foreseeably cause the deaths of civilians.

Drone killings in the tribal areas of Pakistan and in Yemen have taken the lives of targets who are armed and involved in conspiratorial meetings and councils of war, and others who have merely been attending weddings and funerals or emerging from hospitals or mosques, and the lethal missile has taken its toll of family members, mourners and bystanders. In Pakistan there have been cases where pro-government leaders, their families and children and even army soldiers, have been killed by mistake in drone attacks that have seriously damaged US relations with a politically tense, nuclear-armed nation that is not at war with America.

There was a lack of protest in the US until a drone strike in Yemen targeted an American citizen, Anwar Al-Awlaki, rumoured to be Al-Qaeda's operational leader in the area. The rockets were fired at his pick-up truck, in which he might have been picked up rather than bombed to pieces, along with several others who may or may not have been terrorists. Obama's lawyers concluded that Executive Order 12333 did not prevent the killing of a suspect in an armed conflict between the US and Al-Qaeda, and that notwithstanding the Fifth Amendment's prohibition on the arbitrary deprivation of life this constitutional right could not avail a US citizen who joined an enemy force.

This last point is correct as far as it goes, but the Fifth Amendment must entitle a citizen or his family to know whether he is on a death list and to apply to have himself taken off it. Yet when Al-Awlaki's father sought judicial review of the secret policy that had authorised the killing of his son, the judge told him he did not have standing. If a father does not have standing to challenge a targeted killing, who does? In the UK he would have been entitled to an inquest, as would the family of the website editor killed with him, and international courts have repeatedly held that the 'right to life' implies a right to an inquiry whenever a life is violently taken by a government agency.

In this respect the Obama administration seems to have given the CIA carte blanche to choose targets for execution and to carry out these executions without answering for civilian casualties. It would appear that the CIA does not bother with combatant/civilian categories: Yemen, for example, is not a war zone; many suspects fall into the civilian class, being preachers and sympathisers and friends; those who press the hellfire buttons in Nevada do not pause to consider whether their targets are engaged in combatant missions or not. However, there is no point speculating about the criteria for listing or executing: these are secret CIA prerogatives, beyond the jurisdiction of the courts or the disclosure provisions of the *Freedom of Information Act*.

The battlefield utility of drone technology means that it will be widely used in future conflicts, and by states less scrupulous than the US and Israel. Drones will become more compact, and more difficult to detect or shoot down – already there are plans for bird and even insect-size drones, capable of crawling inside homes or squatting on window ledges to listen and send 'kill' messages to their bigger brethren hovering in the sky above without the need for any 'pilot' in Nevada to press a button. There is an urgent need for the US to make its drone operations more principled and transparent in the following ways:

1) By moving responsibility from the CIA to the Department of Defence, which is more accountable and bound by the Geneva Conventions and amenable to the *Freedom of Information Act*;

2) There must be transparency both in respect of the target list and the criteria for listing, and an opportunity for those listed to surrender or to seek (through friend or father) a judicial review of whether the evidence against them proves that they are the sort of active terrorist or combatant who belongs on the list;

3) Rules of engagement must exclude any killing if civilians are likely to be present;

4) Rules must prevent killing of a target who can be neutralised in other ways, (e.g. if there is a reasonable prospect of capture or arrest).

There is a sense here in which international law has failed: neither the UN Charter nor the Conventions nor the customary norms of the courts have provided intelligible and satisfactory guidance for waging asymmetric warfare. Hence the silence of states on the subject, and even an earnest request, by the UN's Human Rights Committee, that Pakistan should take legal action against the US to clarify the law.

The way forward may in fact be to find a way back – to the principles of reasonable force and proportionality that govern most domestic laws dealing with treatment of violent criminals, and could be applied to terrorist groups, even if armed political forces like the Taliban continue to be dealt with under the law of war.

At present many of these killings can only be described as summary executions, the capital punishment of the Red Queen ('sentence first, trial later'), which deny the right to life, the presumption of innocence and the right to a fair trial. No one can question the right of law enforcement officers to kill cornered terrorists or those who are caught in the act of taking or preparing to take innocent lives, but not when there is an alternative non-lethal solution – when capture is possible or surrender is on the cards. Targeted assassination amounts to the premeditated murder of suspected criminals, and the more imprecise the target – in the sights of a drone rather than a soldier's rifle – the more likely that it will amount to the manslaughter of unsuspected civilians.

FREE SPEECH

Chapter 17

THE RIGHT TO KNOW

Tom Stoppard's aphorism 'I'm with you on the free press, it's the newspapers I can't stand' is heard a lot these days, at least in Britain, where the criminal behaviour of the tabloids has done great damage to press freedom. There are some legitimate restraints on that freedom, in the interests of accuracy and of fairness to people whose privacy should not be invaded unless there is a genuine public interest in exposing their behaviour. But in Australia, editors and journalists face legal restraints that other leading democracies (including the UK) find unnecessary. It was against these restraints that I aimed a lecture in Sydney in 2007 that opened the 'Right to Know' campaign against media secrecy laws, although I reminded its sponsors (the main newspaper and broadcasting groups) that taking investigative journalism off the legal leash should be balanced by some protection for individual privacy.

The years roll by, and privacy is still not legally protected and the free speech infringements by gag orders, over-broad defamation claims and attempts to identify sources continue. The debate seems to have degenerated: in March 2013 the then Minister for Communications brought down some weak and ill-conceived laws to regulate not the press but the Press Council, and all the Murdoch papers went into hysterical overreaction, likening them to the tyranny of Stalin and Hitler and Ivan the Terrible (whose pictures featured on the front page of the tabloids, as if they were alive and well and members of the Gillard government). No space was allowed for anyone who might argue that readers have a right to know whether a news story has another side. Which it often does, when editors take upon themselves the political and social beliefs of the proprietors, who pay them for piping and call their tune. That is, of course, the right of those who own newspapers. But when they vilify individuals, the victims should be entitled to a right of reply (at the very least, to have a 'letter to the editor' published). And a media ombudsperson, preferably, rather than a cumbersome self-regulating body like the Press Council, should be empowered to hear complaints that newspapers have published serious factual inaccuracies and to order publication of corrections if they have. This form of regulation cures abuses of free speech by the simple expedient of ordering more speech.

It may, however, be some time before I am invited to launch a 'fair speech' campaign.

It is a privilege to be invited to offer some home thoughts from abroad about law and journalism, about finding a *media via* between two professions that are in danger of colliding. That seems to be happening a lot in Australia lately: courts have imposed over a thousand gag orders on the press; journalists are punished for refusing to betray their sources of news, no matter how important that news may be to the public; a claim for freedom of information can be trumped by a conclusive ministerial certificate; freedom of speech is not a right but no more than a fragile 'implication' from the constitution – an 'implication' meaning something we are afraid to express or to say loudly and clearly, in the way the United States does in its First Amendment.

When claims to censor and suppress are made for reasons of convenience or expediency, free speech usually gives way – there is no principle, no presumption, made in its favour. And before you know where you are, you are – well, thirty-ninth in the world in the press freedom ratings and slipping – below all the countries of Europe, below Bolivia and Estonia, South Korea, Latvia and Costa Rica. And, I am rather ashamed to say, even below Britain.

It is ironic to think back twenty years, when I persuaded the publishers William Heinemann that the place to publish *Spycatcher* was Australia, because I had more confidence that the courts there would allow it – which they did. But today the freedom to publish is roundly and regularly upheld by the highest court in the UK, in language that is never heard from our High Court – other than vaguely and from the usual dissenting judge. It is, as I shall explain, the language of human rights, fashioned from the struggles of courageous journalists and publishers in centuries past.

So how is it that Australia, a nation that prides itself on its outspokenness and frankness and on telling it like it is, has a less free press than Malta and San Marino? At a time when the dark tailors of public relations spin the most fabulous fancy dress for our political leaders, we must rely more than ever on journalists to play the part of the small boy in the fable, pointing out that the Emperor has no clothes. Here are a few thoughts as to how law and lawyers might better connect with journalists and editors in providing to the Australian people the facts they need to make democratic decisions.

I offer them with some diffidence: I am not a journalist, although there was a time when I worked for the *New Statesman* and was tempted to become one. My eventual career choice was a form of life insurance: I noticed that, in the law, the older you get the more distinguished you are assumed to have become. With journalists, it's the other way round. And you need some skill to be a good journalist – to be a lawyer, as John Mortimer explains, all you need is common sense and relatively clean fingernails. To be a good journalist, Nick Tomalin famously said, you need common sense, a little literary ability and rat-like cunning.

I grew up in Sydney's Eastwood – long before Maxine McKew descended on it to campaign against John Howard (she is still doing her normal job, I suppose, although she gets out more often). In those days it was a suburb of lower-middle-class respectability. We took the Fairfax *Sydney Morning Herald*, which proved we were more respectable than other families who took the Packer *Telegraph* and infinitely more respectable than those who read Mr Murdoch's *Daily Mirror*, which my mother refused to have in the house. It was read, she noted, by those men in our street who beat their wives.

Many years later, one of my early cases at the Old Bailey was to plead for a madam – Cynthia Payne, Madam 'Cyn' – who ran a brothel in leafy Wimbledon. I pointed out to the judge that when the police raided, they had found a peer of the realm, MPs and company directors, barristers and solicitors and several vicars. Despite (or because of) my efforts, she was jailed for two years, and the story of British hypocrisy went round the world and was later made into a film (*Personal Services*). I was telephoned by my mother, tipped off by a wife-beating neighbour, and she said, 'You've finally made the front page, darling. It was in the *Daily Mirror*. Thank goodness they spelt your name wrongly.' When my client was released from prison she was whisked to a BBC News studio and asked why she had not revealed the names of her famous clients. She thought for a moment and said, 'Well, me morality's low but me ethics is high.' A distinction that has eluded philosophers, but may not be a bad credo for a journalist.

Growing up in Eastwood, in that severely moralistic Menzies era, I think I owe my lifelong aversion to censorship, my abiding sense that it is always counter-productive, to the New South Wales education department. It issued all state schools with an edition of *The Tempest* – the text that was set for our Leaving Certificate. When I read the state school edition, it seemed a very flawed, strangely inhumane and racist play – Prospero's unmotivated cruelty to poor Caliban made a mockery of the brave new world he was trying to create. On the train to school,

I noticed that GPS schoolkids had a different edition – a larger edition with more pages, which I promptly went out and bought, and found in it a very different and wonderful play. Because the wowsers in the New South Wales education department had decreed that we state school kids would have the *bowdlerised* edition, where all reference to Caliban's attempted rape of Prospero's daughter, a fulcrum of the plot, had been surgically removed. Indeed all references to sex – all implied references to sex – had been taken out. Even, would you believe, Prospero's great speech in favour of chastity before marriage had been *entirely* cut:

> If thou dost break her virgin knot before
> All sanctimonious ceremonies may
> With full and holy rite be ministered,
> No sweet aspersion shall the heavens let fall
> To make this contract grow; but barren hate,
> Sour-eyed disdain and discord shall bestrew
> The union of your bed with weeds so loathly
> That you shall hate it both. Therefore take heed
> As Hymen's lamps shall light you.

If only my wife and her school friends in Cronulla had been allowed to read that, *Puberty Blues* would have been a different book.

It was a strange experience, growing up in Sydney in the sixties, reading the newspapers in the morning then going to university or work to hear what was really happening. The Askin government was irredeemably corrupt and so was the New South Wales police force. But these were subjects that could never be mentioned in newspapers because of the defamation laws.

I spent my early days as an articled clerk at a prestigious law firm, running briefs to QCs to defend Packer papers against the cunning of Clive Evatt (brother of the 'Doc'), usually unsuccessfully because defamation law then required the media to prove

not only the truth of its statements but also that they were for
the public benefit. I remember one case in which we proved that
the Labor party had rigged a local election, but Clive convinced
the jury that this revelation was not for the public benefit
because it was only a small electorate.

The defamation laws threw a blanket of censorship over
the political and social practices of the time and the result,
interestingly enough, when so much was suppressed, was that
Sydney became a hotbed of rumours – unpublished, so uncon-
fronted and undemolished. Occasionally, one of them proved
true, but often the press proprietors and their editors actually
colluded with public figures to keep unsettling facts from the
public.

I had first-hand experience of this at Eastwood Anglican
Church where I was confirmed by Sydney's archbishop, an
Englishman named Gough. He preached a sermon that also
made the front page of the *Daily Mirror*, about how 'the
younger generation was wallowing in a mire of immorality'.
There wasn't much wallowing in Eastwood, I'm afraid, but
what all the newspapers suppressed was that this archbishop
had been doing so much wallowing himself that he was being
cited in divorce petitions all over the eastern suburbs. Not a
word was said by the *Sydney Morning Herald* as the church
shifted its promiscuous primate back to England, but in
Catholic churches throughout the state the scandal was avidly
whispered in the confessionals. A city where the media was
prevented from publishing news became a rumour mill where
reputations were blasted in conversations but were safe in
print, where allegations could not be published and hence false
allegations could not be refuted.

The suppression of news that was the feature of Sydney in
the sixties came about as a result of our inheritance and faithful
replication and application of the common law of England, and
it is right to say that the London I encountered in the seventies
was much the same, as a result of judge-made laws of defamation and contempt, obscenity and blasphemy and official secrecy.

And there is a mystery here that we need to solve, because it was in Britain, long before Australia was settled, that the principles of free speech were established. Established in history, in the chant of the mob outside the Old Bailey as publishers were acquitted of seditious attacks on George III, established in rhetoric and in literature but never in law.

Freedom of the press was in fact first achieved with the abolition of licensing in 1640, as the Stuart monarchy tottered and England descended into a civil war that helped to produce the early fundamentals of democracy – parliamentary sovereignty, judicial independence and some religious toleration. When the Presbyterians, who were never very tolerant, tried to reimpose licensing on the press, John Milton pointed out that the attempt to keep out inconvenient truths and evil doctrine by licensing is 'like the exploit of that gallant man who thought to keep out the crows by shutting his park gate'.

In his great *cri de coeur*, the *Areopagitica*, 'give me the liberty to know, to utter and to argue freely according to conscience, above all liberties', Milton first fashioned a rationale for media freedom that was taken up centuries later by John Stuart Mill and then by judges of the US Supreme Court and finally last year by judges of the highest court in England. It is the concept of a 'free marketplace of ideas' where falsehood and evil doctrine, however initially seductive and dangerous, would eventually be driven out by truth. Freedom to publish rumours can actually serve the public good by provoking correction: 'and though all the winds of doctrine were let loose to play upon the earth, so truth be in the field, we do injuriously, by licensing and prohibiting, misdoubt her strength. Let her and falsehood grapple: whoever knew truth put to the worse in a free and open encounter?'

So back in 1643, we had the immortal vision of the blind poet: the cure for abuse of free speech is more speech so the truth eventually emerges. That became the catchcry of the Levellers, polemical investigative journalists who risked their lives to expose abuses of power in Cromwell's republic, and whose leaders were acquitted of treason and sedition by sympathetic juries. The eighteenth century brought other courageous journalists and publishers. There was John Wilkes, the MP and printer, who exposed the corrupt government of George III: they jailed him for obscenity after his enemies read his 'Essay on Women', a parody of Alexander Pope, to the House of Lords:

> Life can little more supply
> Than just a few good fucks, and then we die.

For the first time, a four-letter word was uttered in parliament, in the 1750s, and the peers shouted 'go on, go on'. They jailed Wilkes for sedition but he lived to be a popular Lord Mayor of London.

Then, of course, there were the courageous printers who dared to publish Tom Paine's *Rights of Man*, the first human rights textbook. The mob carried his barrister, Lord Erskine, in triumph from the Old Bailey, chanting, 'Freedom of the press.'

But why has this rich history, in which press freedom is associated with liberty and democracy and progressive reform, never come to be reflected in English law? It was never entrenched because judges were members of a reactionary upper class who had no stomach for criticism, and in the Victorian era they fashioned the laws of libel and contempt to provide this class with exorbitant protection – especially from popular newspapers that had started up to cater for the mass readership produced by the educational reforms of the 1850s.

There was also a complacency induced by the right to trial by jury – juries had, after all, acquitted the Levellers and some of the publishers of Tom Paine. The most influential constitutional theorist of the twentieth century was A. V. Dicey, Oxford Professor of English law, who said that freedom of speech in England was no more than what twelve shopkeepers on a jury would allow – but this ensured that anything worth publishing would be acquitted. It didn't, of course, but Dicey's mistaken assumption deterred all reform of libel and blasphemy laws.

So, wrapped in this cocoon of complacency, free speech turned into expensive speech, with a libel law fashioned by judges who lived their lives in gentlemen's clubs in Pall Mall, in an age when escutcheons could be blotted and society scandals resolved by writs for slander. When I started doing libel cases in Britain, the leading cases were still about allegations of cheating at cards or shooting foxes – terrible libel to say of a chap that he *shot* a fox, because a gentleman only hunts a fox down with dogs.

The lack of any public interest defence caused real problems in distributing American papers, which had been freed in the US by the great case of *New York Times v Sullivan* to publish important statements about public figures so long as they were not reckless towards the truth. You could not publish the same book on both sides of the Atlantic. I worked with William Shawcross on his book *Sideshow* and we had to make twenty-two cuts of criticisms of US officials before it could be published in the UK. There was the famous occasion when *Time* magazine censored from its British edition Daniel Moynihan's aphorism about Henry Kissinger, 'Henry doesn't lie because it's in his interests, he lies because it's in his nature.' American public figures flocked to forum-shop, to sue in the plaintiff-friendly British courts. US courts then refused to enforce British judgments on the grounds that English libel law was antipathetic to the First Amendment.

Something had to be done – English defamation law caused problems throughout the world, because it was part of the English 'common law' that was imposed on the fifty-four countries that had been colonised by Britain. Its rigour was exploited by the powerful, especially in Singapore where Lee Kuan Yew enriched himself by suing any political opponent who ventured the mildest criticism. He always won, of course, because he had appointed judges who genuinely believed him above criticism. Eventually the only newspaper that refused to grovel was the *Wall Street Journal*.

In one case in 1988, on that paper's behalf, I cross-examined Lee for three days and the judge said he was increasing the damages because of the hurt I had caused to his feelings. The Malaysian Bar Association put out a press release saying that this was the first evidence that Lee Kuan Yew had any feelings. The CEO of Dow Jones, the owner of the *Journal*, said that the company disagreed with the verdict, so Barry Wain, the Australian editor of the *Journal*, was immediately prosecuted for contempt of court by the Singapore government.

At least Australia is still ahead of Singapore in the press freedom index, although the Singapore courts justified Barry's conviction by inference to a decision by our High Court, on one of its off days, to jail union leader Norm Gallagher for 'scandalising' its judges by overreacting to an anti-union decision. The Gallagher decision, incidentally, remains a disgrace to the Australian judiciary. Britain has now abolished the crime of 'scandalising the judiciary', and Scotland has done away with its law against 'murmuring judges' – why are Australian judges so insecure that they keep a law that threatens their critics with jail?

In other Commonwealth countries, the lack of any public interest defence in the law of defamation became recognised as a problem. The High Court in Australia – the Mason court – suddenly discovered a free speech implication in the constitution. The constitution doesn't mention freedom of expression but it establishes democracy, for which free speech is obviously necessary. *Ergo* there was an implication that the media could have reasonable freedom to discuss political and governmental matters, without attracting defamation writs.

Well, that was progress. There were only three problems. First, it was completely unhistorical – our founding fathers, at Federation, deliberately decided against adopting any of the civil rights clauses of the US constitution because they wanted no rights in the Australian constitution that could ever be used by Chinese labourers or by Aborigines or by any people of colour. It's all there in the federation debates – Higgins and Isaacs, later

High Court judges, warning the delegates that civil rights were dangerous because they might assist coloured workers to come to Australia or to insist, if they got there, that they should be treated fairly. These views make uncomfortable reading now but they deprived us of any express rights in our constitution for due process or humane treatment or free speech.

That problem the Mason court overcame, in a libel case brought against the ABC by David Lange over a program that he thought indicated he was unfit to be prime minister of New Zealand. Its judgment rejected any First Amendment-style 'implications', but struck down laws that did not permit the media to make reasonable statements about politicians and about 'governmental matters', an ill-defined and limited category. The implication did not extend very far – it did not cover areas outside politics, namely reporting business or religion or on any other institutions. One of the early cases decided that the implied freedom of political speech did not cover speech about the NRMA – and you can't get much more political than that. It did not cover media moguls, a class that included such highly litigious criminals as Robert Maxwell, Conrad Black and Alan Bond, who constantly issued libel writs against their detractors. Say what you like about Rupert Murdoch, you can always say what you like: the great thing about him is that he never sues.

I only hope his conquest of Dow Jones will be received more politely than his takeover of the *New York Post*. A few months after he had turned it into an American version of the *Daily Mirror*, he was surprised to find that while his readership went up, his advertising fell. Bloomingdale's had pulled its ads so he asked its CEO why it wasn't still advertising in the *Post*. 'Because, Mr Murdoch, your readers are our shoplifters.'

But I digress. *Lange* was a recognition by the High Court of the inadequacy of British defamation law. What achieved a reform of that law in Britain was the adoption of the European Convention of Human Rights by the Blair government in 1998. It contained a clause – Article 10 – that guaranteed freedom of expression, the right to receive both information and opinion, subject to exceptions that were 'necessary in democratic society' to protect other rights. Not 'convenient', not 'expedient' but *necessary* to answer a pressing social need. What this did was to create a presumption in favour of free speech, which could only be overridden if this was essential to protect other rights. All previous legislation and all common law had to be interpreted, if at all possible, consistently with this right.

Now the common law of defamation – and defamation means any criticism that lowers you in the estimation of others, under a law that requires the media defendant to prove truth and that allows no public interest defence – obviously could not stand. The judges in England looked at *Lange* and said it did not go far enough because it only protected speech about politicians. There had to be a broader defence so they created one out of the old defence of qualified privilege: the media still had the burden of proving truth, but if it was a matter of real public interest that they couldn't prove because, for example, their sources would not come forward, then they had a defence if they could show that they acted responsibly. This concept of 'responsible journalism' was to be judged by ten tests: the extent of the public interest in the story, the reliability of the source, the urgency of publication, whether there had been the opportunity for a response, and so on.

This appeared to be progress and in Australia in 2005 the test of responsible journalism was enshrined in Section 30 of the *Uniform Defamation Act*. Tragically, what was seen as a great advance in 1998 turned out to be a snare and an illusion. It sounded great but the ten tests became ten tripwires and if you fell at one, you lost the defence. It just didn't work. So last year the British judges swept away the antiquated notion of journalists having a privilege and re-stated it as a full-blooded public interest defence, available to the media if the story was important and had been published responsibly, without sensation or exaggeration; corrected immediately if it proved incorrect; and so on.

The test case involved a story from the *Wall Street Journal* not long after 9/11 about how Saudi Arabia was cooperating with US requests to monitor banks and businesses suspected of being used to get funds to terrorists. Many influential Americans thought the Saudis were not helping at all but the *Journal* had an outstanding Arab-speaking journalist in Jeddah who had cultivated enough business and political sources in that highly secretive society to discover the prominent names who were being monitored and he named them, which was essential to give credibility to his story. One of them sued and the trial judge said that he lost the defence because it wasn't necessary to name the names. They could simply have been referred to as 'prominent business identities' – that old device the Sydney media uses when it means someone like the late Abe Saffron. I took the case to the highest court, the House of Lords, which applied the presumption in favour of free speech and accepted that in important stories like this, the names *were* the news. No longer did libel law require the subterfuges and cover-up devices when matters of real importance were being reported.

That case – *Jameel v Wall Street Journal Europe* – brings British libel law into line with the First Amendment. It's an example of how a freedom of expression guarantee, entrenched in the law, can in the hands of good judges provide greater latitude for responsible investigative journalism on issues of public importance while withdrawing that special protection from slipshod or incompetent journalism and from trivialisation and sensationalism.

That is one example of how Britain is still ahead of Australia despite our recent reform. Another example – and perhaps the main reason why we are so low in the ratings – is the protection of journalist sources. Here in Australia, ruled by old British common law, there is no protection. Whenever I return, there seems to be a journalist being threatened with prison or punishment for refusing to dob in a source – in the recent case of two *Herald Sun* journalists, a source for an important story of how John Howard's cabinet reneged on a promise to pensioners.

Here, too, British law changed in Britain, indeed through-out Europe, because of the free speech guarantee in the European Convention on Human Rights. A young journalist was slipped a document – I suspect by an old girlfriend – about a company restructure. He telephoned to ask the company for its comment and the next thing he knew he was hauled into court and ordered to name the source of this breach of confid-ence. We appealed and the appeal judges smiled benignly and ordered him to put the name of his source in a brown paper envelope to be opened only if he lost his appeal in the House of Lords, the final English court. We resisted that temptation and lost unanimously in the House of Lords, but then took the case to the European Court of Human Rights. There, at last, we succeeded and now the ruling protects journalists in every country in Europe from identifying the source of their news stories. The court said:

> Protection of journalistic sources is one of the basic conditions for press freedom ... without such protec-tion, sources may be deterred from assisting the press in informing the public on matters of public interest. As a result the vital public watchdog role of the press may be undermined and the ability of the press to provide accurate and reliable information may be adversely affected ... Such a measure cannot be compatible with Article 10 of the Convention unless it is justified by an overwhelming requirement in the public interest.

You don't get that sort of language in Australian courts, simply because it is alien to the common law, a law made by English judges who now *do* use that language because of the *Human Rights Act*. There are certain exceptions – if the journalist has been made a conduit for a criminal offence, or if necessary to establish innocence at a criminal trial, but by and large the value placed on news-gathering by the free speech guarantee would protect journalists in England in cases where they have no protection in Australia.

The Australian government, apparently conscious of how we are lagging in this respect, has produced a draft shield law, but it is unlikely to be effective. It does not protect whistleblowers and actually makes them more vulnerable because it only operates where the journalist can prove (i) that the source would suffer harm, and (ii) that the nature and extent of the harm outweighs the desirability of the evidence being given. Well, pardon me, but how on earth is the journalist to prove that the source would suffer harm, in particular the nature or extent of that harm, unless he gives details of the source – and details sufficient to show that the source would be harmed would usually be sufficient to allow the source's identification. A golden rule in all these cases is: give no information at all otherwise you will find your source identified and prosecuted, or sacked, or concreted under a motorway. This draft bill is no way forward: it's a trap.

Then there is the problem of the *Freedom of Information Act*. Here we had a genuine Australian first – we were the first Commonwealth country to adopt the US–Scandinavian method of open government, promised by Whitlam and implemented under Fraser. In this respect, the UK has followed our lead. But now this groundbreaking Australian effort has been left behind and our *FOI Act* looks overcautious and outdated. It has worked quite well for individuals, giving them access to personal data, but it bars access to cabinet documents and even to documents merely submitted to cabinet. Worse still, any government minister can issue what is termed an exemption certificate, blocking access.

That's what Mr Costello did when the *Canberra Times* sought to obtain documents about the First Home Owners Scheme and the extent to which it had been rorted by wealthy home owners. Costello's reason? 'Because the release of the documents . . . will confuse or mislead the public and encourage ill-informed speculation and debate.' Ill-informed speculation and debate meaning, I suppose, that it will encourage criticism of Mr Costello. Well, the High Court – narrowly, by three votes to two – decided that the exemption certificate was conclusive.

As long as one ground was advanced to support the claim for secrecy, that was enough. The minority – Justices Gleeson and Kirby – pointed out that the government could always come up with one ground for suppression that seems reasonable despite the fact that there are many more, and more reasonable, grounds for transparency. If reasons on both sides could not be balanced, then media applicants could never succeed. This is obviously correct and the majority decision really does allow a government to neuter FOI by shrouding embarrassing documents in ministerial exemption certificates. It is not a decision that would have been reached if the court had been required under a bill of rights to make a presumption in favour of free speech, which would require all judges to interpret legislation so far as possible to effectuate freedom of access to information.

One development in censoring the news media that seems indigenous to Australia is the extraordinary increase in suppression orders issued by courts, stopping the reporting of evidence. Ten years ago there were less than a hundred, and today, so I am told, over a thousand. This is disturbing because of the fundamental principle of open justice – that justice must be seen to be done. That has been the rule of the common law even before *Magna Carta*. Publicity is, as Jeremy Bentham put it, 'the very soul of justice . . . it keeps the judge himself, while trying, under trial.'

John Henry Wigmore, the great exponent of the law of evidence, saw the open justice principle as the most basic guarantee that trials would get at the truth: witnesses are more reluctant to lie when they know their evidence will be reported and that others will come forward to confound them. The highest courts of Canada, America and Britain have added further reasons: the education of the public in the way courts work, for example. Publicity is often embarrassing and inconvenient, of course, and a case can often be made to a soft-hearted judge to keep particular people or evidence out of the newspapers, but open justice is a principle, not just a sentiment, and these claims must be resisted. The very number of suppression orders made in

Australian courts suggests that they are not being resisted – the media have had to battle to obtain the release of newsworthy information, at one extreme the identity of convicted murderers and paedophiles to, at the lower extreme, the affidavit revealing that Eddie McGuire wished to 'bone' Jessica Rowe.

There does seem to be a growing antagonism between judges and the media in Australia, and the media may be partly to blame. That is the view of two judges who cannot be accused of lacking sympathy for free speech – Michael Kirby and Geoff Eames – who have spoken out to deplore ignorance of and distortion by media commentators. Well, many media commentators are ignorant and distorting, and paid to provoke, and it may be a mistake for judges to take them too seriously – nobody else does – but to the extent that there is a genuine lack of comprehension and distortion in coverage of the courts, that has to be addressed by both sides.

There is something missing here. The sedition law has been revived, with its archaic definition that incriminates writing that 'brings the government into hatred and contempt' or 'stirs up class hatred'. Mark Latham seems to get away with it, but would an outspoken Muslim preacher? It does exercise a chilling effect by making artists and theatres subject to police powers. And licensing of the press is back, the bane that John Milton killed off forever in England in the seventeenth century. Mr Ruddock plans to extend censorship to a new category: 'books that glorify terrorist acts'. So don't write a sympathetic biography of Robespierre, or of Nelson Mandela.

Of course terrorism has brought emergency laws, which provide a vast increase in police powers including powers to detain and investigate journalists. They have not been used against the press in Britain because they are subject to the safety net of the *Human Rights Act*. Here, there is no safety net.

Something's missing, something is out of whack. Sure, journalists aren't being killed, editors aren't being horsewhipped, newspapers aren't being closed down. But there is a disturbing pattern of a slowly eroding right to procure newsworthy information – an example of the systemic defect in the common law. We are the only liberal democracy left that does not have a guarantee for freedom of expression. Why not? Partly because the media itself has not been supportive. It's a great irony that a measure that enhances all fundamental rights, not only of the people to receive information through the media but of people when they are unfairly treated by the state, should be viewed with a suspicion verging on paranoia by some Murdoch editors.

'It undermines parliamentary democracy,' chorus ill-informed commentators – well, not in any other parliamentary democracies it hasn't. 'Our rights can be protected by parliament, not judges.' Do you really believe that? Parliament might rectify the odd abuse spotlighted by the media, but the true beneficiaries in the UK have been ordinary people – thousands of them – whose rights have been trampled on by bloody-minded or incompetent officials.

A bill of rights on the UK model does not allow courts to override parliament or to strike down legislation, as in the US. It merely requires judges to interpret legislation and develop the common law, if they can, according to fundamental principles of individual liberty. If they can't, then they issue a declaration of incompatibility – a signal to parliament that here is a wrong they cannot rectify. And it is an interesting fact that all those columnists who witter on about a 'bill of wrongs' never notice that the Conservative party in Britain, while critical of the European Convention, is not opposed to a bill of rights. On the contrary, it wants a British bill of rights with more protection for free speech, open justice and trial by jury.

At the end of the day, under any legal regime, there will always be exceptions to the free speech principle, when the presumption will be overridden. There is no right to shout 'fire' in a crowded theatre, and those who use speech to urge violence or persuade suicide bombers should be prosecuted and punished for incitement to murder.

As for privacy protection, we are all entitled to live some part of our life – the part that concerns home and family – behind a door marked 'do not disturb'. And that applies to public figures as well. Protection is needed against publication of intimate personal facts, medical records and the like, against bugging and secret surveillance, always subject to a strong public interest defence. This balance between privacy and press freedom should be satisfactory although there are inevitable grey areas. In one case, in Britain, a disturbed man walked into a town centre and slashed his wrists, an act captured on CCTV that led to his rescue. The police wanted to show the video of his suicide attempt on television to promote their case that there should be cameras in all public places. The man, now fully recovered, argued that his moment of mental anguish should not be put on show for entertainment or for police advertisement. What do you think? The final court, reversing the penultimate appeal judgment decided that his moment of madness must remain private. These are difficult questions and courts will not always reach right, or consistent, answers but I think it's a mark of a civilised society if they are permitted to try.

One journalist did go to prison this year in the UK. He was the *News of the World*'s 'royal' correspondent, a task he accomplished by tapping into the telephone lines at Buckingham Palace and gathering electrifying news about Prince William's dental appointments and his father's conversations with the Soil Society about self-fertilising the garden at Highgrove. The reporter pleaded guilty – there is no free speech defence for hacking telephones to obtain tittle-tattle – and he was jailed for three months and no one protested, not even the reporter. His editor fell on his pen and resigned, out of shame, you might say, if it hadn't been the *News of the World*.

The point is that a media that wants and needs the freedom to publish newsworthy facts must accept some limit on its right to rifle the intimacies of citizens' lives. So long as the exclusion zone is limited to the bedroom and the bathroom and the changing room, the school, the hospital and the grave.

I have been trying to explain why Australia's media freedom ratings have slipped and will continue to slip because of this

systemic defect caused by our failure to make legal provision for
a right that is fundamental to democracy, but that same failure
has, I think, been responsible for another decline in Australia's
significance: in the international power and persuasiveness of the
jurisprudence emerging from our courts. It's not perhaps often
recognised that there have been times when Australian court
judgments carried enormous weight in the world – certainly
throughout the Commonwealth: the Owen Dixon court in the
fifties and the Mason court in the eighties and early nineties. If
there were an Olympic medal for teams of judges – and why not,
since there are Olympic medals for taekwondo and beach volley-
ball – the Mason court would have won gold year after year.
The quality of its jurisprudence was the best in the world at the
time – it was often quoted; it had persuasive force throughout the
common law world.

But times move on and the courts of other major countries
now base their decisions on human rights principles, and our
courts cannot contribute because we have no human rights
principles enshrined in our law. So I have noticed this decline
in their relevance – when the liberty of the subject is at stake
in courts around the world, Australian decisions are quoted
less often or not quoted at all (except the pathetic decision in
Gallagher's case, which is quoted because it favours repression
of speech critical of judges). The calibre of Australian judges
and lawyers remains as high or higher than anywhere else, but
parliament has failed to provide them with the modern machinery for the job of safeguarding the liberty of the subject. That is
why the judgments of Australian courts are now of little consequence in the world.

George Orwell, in the introduction to *Animal Farm*, defined
freedom of speech as the right to tell people what they do not
want to know. Then his left-wing publishers refused to print
the book because they feared it would upset Stalin. Freedom
of expression can be upsetting, can be uncomfortable and
shocking, but at a time when not only governments but most
other powerful institutions in society are setting up defensive

barriers to frank communication, and paying propagandists to 'manage media risk', we need some legal encouragement to transparency.

Chapter 18

RUPERT THE BARE

The Murdoch tabloids in Britain operate as the equivalent of Saudi Arabia's morality police, watching and besetting celebrities (as well as the nonentities who happen to be related to or having relations with them) in order to sniff out and condemn extra-marital activities. The now defunct 'Screws of the World' bribed the police to tell seedy celebrity secrets, hired thuggish private eyes to 'surveil' (James Murdoch's euphemism for sex snooping) targets ranging from Prince Harry to Harry Potter (actor Daniel Radcliffe and his parents) and illegally hacked the phones of thousands of agents and lawyers (including lawyers acting against News of the World*) and parents stricken with grief over the murder of their children. The conduct was so outrageous that Rupert, together with his son James and tabloid editor Rebekah Brooks, was summoned in July 2011 to testify before a Parliamentary Select Committee, on what he was famously to describe as 'the humblest day of my life'.*

The scandal exposed 'self-regulation' of the press as a confidence trick that could no longer inspire confidence: it had totally failed to instil any sense of ethical conduct in editors in the business of tabloid infotainment.

Yet sexual sensationalism is what the public wants in Britain – it is an excessively prurient society, its members addicted to

Sunday morning schadenfreude *as they read of other people's grief and emotional or sexual entanglements. But it has only been able to do so because, with the harlot's prerogative throughout the ages of power without responsibility, the British press cowed the British institutions that should have stood up for the rule of law. It bribed policemen and prison officers and intimidated MPs, who kept saying that it was 'drinking in the last-chance saloon' – which was allowed to become the longest swill in history.*

I've acted both for and against the Murdoch press. Murdoch's biographers have described him as a man avid for both scandal and profit, who would usually call his editors from New York to find out what stories they were about to publish and how much they had paid for them. So in those hacking years, many in Britain wanted to know, did he ever inquire about the six-figure sum that his editors and executives were paying to their industrial-scale hacker, Glen Mulcaire? Did Murdoch never wonder about how his tabloid sleuths could uncover such intimate personal details?

The parliamentary hearing lasted over three hours. It was diverted when a protester threw a shaving-cream pie, and Wendi Deng sprang (crouching tiger, hidden dragon-lady) to her husband's defence. It was a memorable event in British parliamentary history, and might have been more memorable had the committee's lacklustre MPs taken some advice on how to cross-examine a media mogul. My advice to them was published on the day before the hearing, on Tina Brown's news website the Daily Beast.

Rupert Murdoch's appearance tomorrow before a Parliamentary Select Committee is drawing the kind of international attention usually reserved for royal marriages. The committee, appropriately enough, is for 'culture, media and sport', and the Elizabethan sport that public anticipation calls to mind is that of bear baiting: a powerful, blinded beast maddened by small dogs. That would be to underestimate Rupert, who has been rehearsing for days, and certainly to overestimate the forensic ability of members of the select committee's MPs, who are selected only by virtue of their inability to obtain any promotion in their parties.

The main constraint will be the British sense of fair play: Ms Brooks is charged with conspiracy to hack unlawfully and to corrupt police and the Murdochs themselves may follow her into the finger-printing room. So 'the Wapping Three' have a right not to incriminate themselves. They will be tempted to attend with a row of QCs – a purse of silks, so to speak – but this would be a public relations error. If Rupert ever says 'I will not answer that question on the grounds it could incriminate me' News International shares would go into freefall.

The committee hearing may well disappoint, because its procedures as well as its members are not cut out for cross-examination. US Senate committees have counsel and investigators, and their questioning can last hours and be very searching. UK Select Committees have few staff and limited time: just ten minutes for a few questions from each committee member. There can be no effective cross-examination, which usually requires sustained questioning over several hours before it can be effective. 'Laying the ground' is the most important part of the art. In court, it might go like this:

> Mr Murdoch, would you agree that it is important for a proprietor, or at least his senior executives, to ensure that when payments are made for stories, you get value for money? Is it not the case that you frequently telephoned the *News of the World* editor – usually on a Thursday – to check what payments had been made for particular stories? Did you ever stop this practice or delegate it to another executive? Did that executive report to you? So the buck stopped with you, and the knowledge of where the bucks went came to you. We are told that £130,000 was paid in one year to Mr Mulcaire – which

of you [the Wapping Three] asked about this payment? You must have been anxious to know what benefit the company was getting from such a large expenditure?

This is the line of questioning that 'Operation Weeting' – the curiously named Scotland Yard inquiry – should be following and the committee may think that such questions on its part would sail too close to the legal wind. It could, however, reasonably ask who is taking care of Mr Mulcaire:

Did News International pay Mr Mulcaire's legal expenses when he appeared at the Old Bailey? Is it still paying his legal bills? Is it making any other payment to him or offering him any advantage? Has it advised him about remaining silent? Will News International renounce all dealings with Mr Mulcaire and any other private eye or policeman with whom it has contracted? And will it urge them to stand up and publicly tell the whole truth about their dealings with News International?

Although the witnesses are not on oath, and so cannot be prosecuted for perjury, Select Committee appearances can be a useful way of putting the powerful on the spot. One line of questioning to which the Murdochs cannot take exception could be about their sincerity:

Last Thursday, Mr Murdoch, you gave an interview to the *Wall Street Journal* in which you said, in effect, 'I regret nothing.' A few hours later your strategy changed and you regretted everything. You parted with Les Hinton and with Rebekah Brooks, took out full-page 'sorry' ads and humbly apologised to the Dowler family, whose dead daughter's phone had been hacked. How can your sudden apologies possibly be sincere, when they are so blatantly part of the new damage limitation strategy?

There can be no legal objection to questions from this culture committee about the culture in the *News of the World* newsroom:

Were you shocked, Mr Murdoch, that your editors and journalists did not apparently know that it was a serious crime to pay a policeman for information? Just two weeks ago News International made a public statement that it had made 'inappropriate' payments to police. Why could you not bring yourself to admit that those payments were criminal? There are no payments to serving policemen for information that are not criminal, are there? Back in 2003, Ms Brooks, you admitted to this Parliamentary Committee that *News of the World* made payments to police, but dunderheads that we are, we failed to follow this up. Let us do so now. Who made these payments, when and to whom? And by the way, how did you come to know that they had been made? Did you approve them?

It would be legitimate to move to the question of whether the secrets for which they were paid were in the public interest:

Mr Murdoch, your journalists broke the law by bribing police and hacking phones. It has been suggested that the public interest may justify such breaches of the criminal law. Can you give us one – just one – example of a story of such great public interest that has come from a bribed policeman and could not have come any other way? Any story of genuine public interest that came from an illegally hacked phone and could not have been obtained from another source? If you cannot answer, Mr Murdoch, I suggest that the stories obtained by these illegal methods were all trivial tittle-tattle, invasions of personal privacy without any public interest justification. These crimes were committed for circulation-seeking sensationalism.

The committee would have no problem quizzing the Wapping Three over their attitude to self-regulation:

You paid a million pounds or so each year to the Press Complaints Commission – was that viewed as insurance against proper regulation? Did you ever reprimand an editor found guilty of breaching the PCC code of conduct? Did News International ever arrange for training in ethics for its journalists and editors? Did it ever give instructions to editors to publish PCC adjudications prominently and not in small print towards the back of the paper? Les Hinton drafted the PCC code of conduct but did News International ever bring it to the attention of its journalists?

The committee chairman may eventually have to stop this line of inquiry in the interests not of fairness but of not labouring the obvious: everyone knows that the PCC has been a confidence trick. All this may well be undramatic – the public expect the committee to go for the jugular. Like this:

> Do you remember Digby Bamford, Mr Murdoch? Let me remind you – Digby was the thirteen-year-old schoolboy who committed suicide after you published his thirteen-year-old girlfriend's diary in the Sydney *Daily Mirror*. It was back in 1964, just after you had taken over your first big city paper and you published a thirteen-year-old's diary 'in the public interest', so you said, of revealing teenage promiscuity in state schools. Except the girl turned out to be a virgin and the boy killed himself from the shame that followed your invasion of her privacy. Let's face it, Mr Murdoch, your career took off by publishing a thirteen-year-old schoolgirl's diary. Should it not end with the hacking of a thirteen-year-old murder victim's mobile phone? Isn't it time for *you* to go?

If the committee has a Clarence Darrow among its members he might go on:

> There were more Digby Bamfords in your life, were there not? Do you ever lose sleep over those who killed themselves because you had invaded their privacy, or that of their loved ones? Remember Samantha McAlpine, age

fifteen, who danced with *Top of the Pops* and whose 'leatherette-bound diary' was said by *News of the World*, just after you took it over, to prove promiscuity among young dancers at the BBC? She committed suicide the next day and later the coroner declared her to be a virgin and her diary 'fantasy'. Then at much the same time there was the dedicated Welsh schoolteacher who committed suicide after the paper named him as a participant in a 'caravan sex party'. More recently, of course, there was Max Mosley's son. Have you ever counted the number of people your privacy-invading journalism has killed? Or is that an unfair way of putting it? I would not like to be unfair to you, Mr Murdoch. How would you put it? Collateral damage from breaches of privacy committed in the interests of profit?

This line of questioning might rattle the Wapping Three: Rupert will need to convince the public that he actually has a conscience and is sincere in his apologies. He might be well advised to burst into tears and say, 'We all make mistakes.'

The committee should avoid foreign ownership questions, which will make them sound parochial or xenophobic or both. They could, however, usefully ask why his Australian papers are so much more ethical (in the past, he has said that he would not like his mother, the late Dame Elisabeth, to read his English tabloids). It would only be fair to give Rupert the opportunity to remind the committee – and the world – that he is simply catering for the peculiarly prurient English desire for a Sunday-morning snigger at the sex lives of others. This is true, up to a point, and Rupert should seize every opportunity to exculpate News International by pointing out that his Australian and American papers do not need to cater to the English addiction to celebrity sex secrets. Rupert, notwithstanding his US tax domicile, remains Australian in voice and mind and if the committee is to play a race card, it should be done lightly:

You are, Mr Murdoch, a great Australian – in the sense, perhaps, that Attila was a great Hun. Tell us – in fifty years' time, whom do you think your countrymen will honour more for his contribution to media freedom – you, or Mr Julian Assange?

Chapter 19

LADY CHATTERLEY AT FIFTY

I received my first cabinet 'leak' when I was a pimply school-boy. It came from a neighbour, the dapper Fred Osborne, who was Minister for Air (and for much hot air) in the Menzies government. He spilled a secret, as my father was giving him a lift home, about why the Australian government decided to ban Lady Chatterley's Lover: *'Because it had been cleared in Britain we all assumed it would be unbanned – we pretty much followed Britain in everything. But then Bob Menzies stormed into the cabinet room. He said, "Gentlemen, I am not going to let my wife read this book. Nor should you." We were so in awe of him that we all immediately voted to ban it.'*

In an excess of solicitude for Dame Patty, the government even banned the transcript of The Trial of Lady Chatterley, *a Penguin book containing a transcript of the trial. A copy fell into my hands after an enterprising Sydney bookseller arranged for his friends back in Britain to write it out by longhand on aerogrammes, and dispatch it to Australia as personal mail so it would elude our smut-sniffing customs censors. The book was then reconstituted and printed in a samizdat edition. Although endowed with all the thrill of forbidden fruit, the only desire it aroused in me was to study law and one day practise it at the Old Bailey.*

In November 2010, I contributed this essay to Penguin's fiftieth anniversary edition of Lady Chatterley's Lover.

The most impactful verdict in the history of jury trials was delivered at the Old Bailey half a century ago. It was the acquittal, in November 1960, of Penguin Books for publishing *Lady Chatterley's Lover*. This was the gateway through which the sixties swung; as Philip Larkin memorably observed in his much-quoted lines in 'Annus Mirabilis':

> Sexual intercourse began
> In nineteen sixty-three
> (Which was rather late for me)
> Between the end of the *Chatterley* ban
> And the Beatle's first L.P.

It certainly marked the beginning of the end for censorship of the written word. It was a victory for liberal humanitarianism over the dead hand of those described by George Orwell as 'the striped-trousered ones who rule'. The fiftieth anniversary of the verdict provides an occasion for remembering the forensic tactics that achieved it.

Under English common law (followed in Australia), the publisher of any book that contained any 'purple passage' that might have a 'tendency to deprave and corrupt those whose minds are open to such immoral influences' was liable to imprisonment. Literary standards were set at what was deemed acceptable reading for fourteen-year-old schoolgirls – whether or not they could, or would want to, read the novel in question.

Merit was no defence: in 1928 *The Well of Loneliness* by Radclyffe Hall was destroyed by a magistrate who realised to his horror that one line in the novel ('and that night they were not divided') meant that two female characters had been to bed together; he said this would 'induce thoughts of a most impure character and would glorify the horrible tendency of lesbianism'. The prosecution had Rudyard Kipling attend the court, in case the magistrate needed a literary expert to persuade him to 'keep the Empire pure'.

Censorship of sexual references in literature was pervasive in England. In the 1950s four major publishers were prosecuted for works of modern fiction – three were convicted. In this period, books by Henry Miller, Lawrence Durrell, Cyril Connolly and others were available only to those English (and Australian) readers who could afford to travel to Paris to purchase them.

In 1959, the Society of Authors finally persuaded parliament to pass a new *Obscene Publications Act* with a preamble that promised 'to provide for the protection of literature and to strengthen the law concerning pornography'. The distinction was to prove elusive, certainly to the attorney-general, Reginald Manningham-Buller. In August 1960 he read the first four chapters of *Lady Chatterley's Lover* on the boat train to Southampton and wrote to the DPP approving the prosecution of Penguin Books ('I hope you get a conviction'). The key factor in the decision to prosecute was that Penguin proposed to sell the book for three shillings and sixpence: in other words, to put it within easy reach of women and the working classes. This, the DPP's files reveal, was what the 'striped trousered ones' refused to tolerate.

The choice of *Lady Chatterley* as a test case was inept, but it suited the anti-intellectual temper of the legal establishment, and for conservative politicians, conviction of the publisher would mean the defeat of an impeccably liberal cause.

The prosecutors were complacent: they would have the judge on their side, and a jury comprised of people of property, predominantly male, middle aged, middle minded and middle class. And they had four-letter words galore: the prosecuting counsel's first request was that a clerk in the DPPs office should count them carefully. In his opening speech to the jury, he played them as if they were trump cards: 'The word "fuck" or "fucking" appears no fewer than thirty times; "cunt" fourteen times; "balls" thirteen times; "shit" and "arse" six times apiece; "cock" four times; "piss" three times.'

But what the prosecution failed to comprehend was that the 1959 Act had wrought some important changes in the law. Although it retained a 'tendency to deprave and corrupt' as the test of obscenity, books had now to be 'taken as a whole' – i.e. not judged on their purple passages, and only in respect of persons *likely* to read them, i.e. not fourteen-year-old school-girls. Most importantly, the Act provided that even if the jury found that the book tended to deprave and corrupt it could nonetheless acquit if persuaded by literary experts that its merits outweighed its obscenity.

So Penguin's solicitor threw himself into the task of recruiting expert witnesses for the defence – rounding up thirty-six who testified and another thirty-six 'waiting in the wings'. He did not have total support from the literary community: amongst the rejection slips sent to the solicitor came a curmudgeonly note from Evelyn Waugh:

> I have not read *Lady Chatterley's Lover* since it first came out. My memory of it is that it was dull, absurd in places and pretentious. I am sure that most of its readers would be attracted by its eroticism. Whether it can 'corrupt' them, I can't tell, but I am quite certain that no private or public 'good' would be served by its publication.

Enid Blyton would have made a sensational witness for the defence, but she declined – saying that she did not dare disobey her husband:

> I'd love to help Penguin Ltd – they are doing a fine job with their publications – but I don't see how I can. For one thing I haven't read the book – and for another thing my husband said NO, at once. The thought of me standing up in Court, solemnly advocating a book 'like that' (his words not mine – I feel he must have read the book!) made his hair stand on end. I'm awfully sorry – but I don't see that I can go against him . . . while I am against too much censorship of books, I really cannot go

against my husband's most definite wishes in this ('To think of <u>my</u> wife standing up and advocating the reading of pornographic books – a well-loved author for <u>children</u> – you'd be condemned by every parent!').

Later, after the case had been lost, the attorney-general pretended that the Crown had disdained to match the defence 'bishop for bishop and don for don', but this was a lie. In fact, the prosecutors made desperate attempts to find anyone of distinction who might support a ban on Lawrence's novel. Their first choice, once again, was Rudyard Kipling – until a DPP's clerk discovered that he had died many years before. T. S. Eliot turned them down, and so did F. R. Leavis (although he also refused to testify for the defence). Helen Gardner, reader in English Literature at Oxford, told the DPP that the book 'is the work of a writer of genius and complete integrity' and offered her testimony to Penguin.

It is a measure of the narrowness of legal education in England in those days that the possibility that Lawrence was a writer of genius had simply not occurred to the lawyers in the DPP's office or to the team of Treasury Counsel, a pampered old Etonian set of barristers who conduct major prosecutions at the Old Bailey before their inevitable elevation to its judicial benches. Its leader, Mervyn Griffith-Jones, had no interest in literature: he was the incarnation of upper-middle-class morality, obsessed with the book's danger to social order. His famously asinine question 'Would you allow your wife or even your servants to read this book?' was asked rhetorically and with utter sincerity by a representative of the ruling class that really did expect their wives to lie back and think of England and its servants to stay obsequious and entertain no ideas above their station (especially not the idea of possessing their master's property, i.e. his wife).

Griffith-Jones's assumptions about society reflected his station in it and as the trial developed he seemed more scandalised by adultery – and with a servant – than by the four-letter words that had preoccupied him at the start. Ignorant of the facts as well as the facts of life, Griffith-Jones failed even to recognise Lawrence's paean to anal sex ('not very easy, sometimes, you know members of the jury, to know what in fact he is driving at in that passage'). After the trial the Warden of All Souls' College, Oxford, John Sparrow, wrote an article in *Encounter* claiming that the jury would have convicted had the prosecutor been able to identify which passage was being driven at, but he too did not understand the new law. Under the 1959 Act, 'purple passages', even on the subject of anal sex, no longer necessarily meant a guilty verdict. Jurors had to ask themselves the common-sense question of whether the publication as a whole would do any harm, and if so, whether its literary merit might redeem it.

The tactical superiority of the defence team was evident from the outset. Gerald Gardiner QC was the cause célèbre advocate of the time, and in a daring move on the first day he declined the judge's invitation to invoke the sexist law that allowed an all-male jury to be empanelled in all cases involving sex. He actually used his right of challenge to ensure that three women sat on the jury. He realised the danger that an all-male jury might be over-solicitous towards women in their absence and he calculated that the prosecutor's paternalism would alienate female jurors.

Gardiners' forensic performance was a master class in modern barristering. He eschewed the histrionics of Old Bailey hacks like Edward Marshall Hall ('Look at her, gentleman of the jury. God never gave her a chance – won't you?'). Instead, he addressed the jury in powerful but straightforward language, respecting them but never condescending or playing obviously to their sympathy. He firmly indicated that they, not the judge, were responsible for the verdict. This was crucial, because the judge's prejudices were apparent from his language and his body language.

Had there been no jury, Mr Justice Byrne would certainly have convicted. He identified 'the tendency to deprave and corrupt' in Lawrence's approval of adultery. To describe, in

1960, how characters could enjoy adultery without suffering for it, would 'tend to corrupt that fundamental sense of morality which is essential to the well-being of a nation'. So the judge directed the jury to consider whether the book 'portrays the life of an immoral woman'; to remember the meaning of 'lawful marriage' in a Christian country, and to reflect that 'The game-keeper, incidentally, had a wife also. Thus what the ultimate result there would be is a matter for you to consider.'

Lawrence's characters had come to life as if they were standing before the divorce court in the days (and the trial was held in the days) when divorce was only granted on proof of a 'matrimonial crime'. This confusion was evident in Lord Hailsham's speech in the parliamentary debate that followed the verdict:

> Before I accepted as valid or valuable or even excusable the relationship between Lady Chatterley and Mellors, I should have liked to know what sort of parents they became to the child . . . I should have liked to see the kind of house they proposed to set up together; I should have liked to know how Mellors would have survived living on Connie's rentier income of £600 . . . and I should have liked to know whether they acquired a circle of friends, or, if not, how their relationship survived social isolation.

So far as Byrne and Hailsham and Griffith-Jones were concerned, the function of the modern novel was that laid down by Oscar Wilde's Miss Prism: 'The good end happily, the bad end unhappily – that is what "fiction" means.' The acquittal was a victory for moral relativism and sexual tolerance, as well as for literary freedom.

~

No other jury verdict in British history has had such a deep social impact. Its publication was attended by what many years later was described as 'the *Spycatcher* effect', namely that the attempt to suppress a book through unsuccessful litigation serves only to promote massive sales. *Lady Chatterley* sold three million copies. A jury – that iconic representative of democratic society – had at last given its imprimatur to ending the taboo on sexual discussion in art and entertainment, and its verdict was the gate through which the sixties swung.

Within a few years the stifling censorship of the theatre by Lord Chamberlain had been abolished, and a gritty realism emerged in British cinema and drama. Homosexuality was decriminalised, abortions were available on reasonable demand, and in order to obtain a divorce it was unnecessary to prove that a spouse had committed the 'matrimonial crime' of adultery. Judges no longer put on black caps to sentence prisoners to hang by the neck until dead.

There were more anti-censorship battles to be fought, however, because the equipoise of the establishment in time absorbed the shock of the verdict and interpreted it as relating only to literature that was both great and English.

In 1970 the 'striped-trousered ones' determined to punish the ideas of the 1960s by jailing the long-haired editors of *Oz* magazine, charged not only with obscenity but with 'conspiracy to corrupt public morals'. *Oz* was neither literature nor pornography, although its multi-coloured pages contained elements of both to attack hypocrisy and, in the words of the prosecutor, 'to promote dope, rock and roll, and fucking in the streets'. A six-week Old Bailey trial in the summer of 1971 built on *Chatterley* precedents and the defence called witnesses who were 'expert' in matters never before subject to forensic analysis: George Melly was an expert on 'revolutionary chic', Edward de Bono on lateral thinking, Richard Wollheim on philosophy and Marty Feldman on humour.

The defendants beat the conspiracy rap but the jurors (average age sixty, and the last who had to own property to be on a jury) convicted them of obscenity after the judge told them that it meant no more than 'indecency' – a misdirection that ensured the editors were free after a successful appeal. But in the meantime the judge imprisoned them, so their heads could be shaved and then examined by psychiatrists. There was an almighty cultural collision – *The Times* received more letters about the *Oz* trial than about the Suez Crisis. An obscenity law that could be used to punish anti-establishment ideas lost all respect in the eyes of a younger generation that would soon take its seats in jury boxes. In 1972 the property qualification was abolished, and the age for jury service was lowered to eighteen.

In 1977, the final curtain fell at the Old Bailey on the battle to liberate the written word. A shabby little paperback, *Inside Linda Lovelace*, was defended by experts (including the Oxford professor of jurisprudence) attesting to the sociological merit of studying the trajectory of the star of the 1972 porn film *Deep Throat*. The judge (who had led a sheltered life) instructed the jury that 'if this book is not obscene within the meaning of the Act, it might well be difficult to imagine anything else that would fall within that category'. The jury (average age twenty-five) quickly decided that the book was not obscene, and their verdict ended the prosecution of the written word for obscenity. The Home Office endorsed the view of its Departmental Committee in 1979 that the *Inside Linda Lovelace* decision demonstrated the fool-ishness of using the criminal law to prohibit the distribution of books, and of the counter-productiveness of making the attempt. *Inside Linda Lovelace* had sold only six hundred copies before the trial, but, thanks to the *Spycatcher* effect, eight hundred thousand sold like hot cakes within a fortnight of the verdict.

It was ironic that, in the meantime, Penguin Books was to become the first victim of a new force for suppression of liter-ature, far more terrifying than the sarcasm of an Old Bailey prosecutor or the sentencing power of an Old Bailey judge. On St Valentine's Day 1989, the Supreme Leader of Iran pronounced a lethal *fatwa* on Penguin Books and Salman Rushdie and all others involved in publishing *The Satanic Verses*. This act of terrorism required courage of a much greater order, but Penguin again stood firm, keeping the book in circulation despite the murder of one of its translators and the wounding of another. Fear of reprisals by religious fanatics is now the 'elephant in the room', which produces much self-censorship of creative writing.

Fifty years ago, Penguin CEO Allen Lane suffered a lot of personal abuse and put his company in peril for a principle: 'My idea was to produce a book that would sell at the price of ten cigarettes.' Books have increased in price even more than cigarettes over the past fifty years and caused a lot less harm. Indeed, the message of *Lady Chatterley's Lover*, half a century on, is that literature of itself does no harm at all. The damage that gets attributed to books – and to plays and movies and cartoons – is caused by the actions of people who try to suppress them.

Chapter 20

WE NAME THE GUILTY MEN

This Hypothetical *about media ethics was conducted for Channel 9's* Sunday *program in 1984, a time when relations between press and politicians were particularly heated. There were then three media empires – Murdoch, Packer and Fairfax – so my imaginary mogul was called Kerry Murfax. This may have been a mistake – certainly the proprietor of Channel 9 and his lawyer (one Malcolm Turnbull) took exception, although had they watched until the end they would have seen Kerry coming up roses.*

The program's non-appearance became a cause célèbre (for several years the Channel 9 press office claimed it was 'still being edited') but it had the result that ABC chairman Ken Myer asked me to do Hypotheticals, without censorship, on the national broadcaster.

This program was recorded in Sydney early in 1984. Like all my Hypotheticals, it was unscripted and unrehearsed: I think up a few storylines, walk in and direct the conversational traffic between panellists who cannot predict the questions, just as I cannot guess their answers. This proved a prophetical Hypothetical. Shortly after it was recorded came the Costigan Report, the murder of a judge's wife, the exposure of a bribe-taking by the New South Wales Minister for Prisons, the campaign against Mr Justice Murphy and the prosecution of the National Times *for publishing a secret government report. The program was never put to air.*

GEOFFREY ROBERTSON (Moderator)
Welcome, ladies and gentlemen, to a land where press is free, trial is fair and news is plentiful. Much of that news is provided by you, the employees of the Murfax organisation – a media octopus whose newspapers, radio and television stations are all dedicated, at the insistence of your proprietor, Kerry Murfax, to the proposition that the public have a right to know.

One thing that the public doesn't know at the moment is a little something about a judge of the High Court – a little something that he likes late at night in the privacy of his own home. It's called cocaine and it's illegal. Gerald Stone, is this a story that you want to publish?

GERALD STONE (Producer, *60 Minutes*)
On *60 Minutes* we don't do a story unless we can think of a title for it.

MODERATOR
Think of a title.

STONE
'How High the Judge.' (Laughter)

MODERATOR
And having thought of that title, you want to go with that story?

STONE
Oh yes, I'd call my people in and I would say, 'Look, we've got a potentially great story.'

MODERATOR
Let me tell you a little more about this judge. He's Mr Justice Benchmark. He's a man of unblemished rectitude – he's never been involved in politics. He's lived a shy and retiring life and

his judgments are renowned throughout the common-law world. He's a great Australian. Are you going to really destroy this man?

STONE
Well I don't know whether what we'd do would destroy him, but I think it might put him in balance.

MODERATOR
Trevor Kennedy, would you want to publish that story?

TREVOR KENNEDY (Editor, *Bulletin*)
I think it's a very important story. Cocaine is a drug that supports a rather unpleasant infrastructure of organised crime and all other sorts of things. By using cocaine the judge supports that.

MODERATOR
You're part of the law-enforcement network? You're going to enforce the law of cocaine against this judge?

KENNEDY
We're part of the information network, which simply exposes the truth about as many things as we're able to.

MODERATOR
But what's the public interest in this particular truth?

KENNEDY
Well, the public interest is simply in knowing what big and important people do.

MODERATOR
But cocaine isn't having any influence on his judgments. They seem to have improved recently. Maybe judges go better with coke? (Laughter)

KENNEDY
We are obliged to bring to account, surely, those people who occupy those positions – in a much more strenuous way than if you are some typist in the High Court typing pool.

MODERATOR
Is this the view you take, Creighton Burns?

CREIGHTON BURNS (Editor, *Age*)
Yes. I'd also be concerned because a judge in a High Court might find himself, from time to time, judging a case that involves people associated with organised crime and also other cases that involve drugs.

MODERATOR
What about the great Australian cricketer, the fast bowler Geoff Hamstring, who, you also understand, likes a little sniff before he goes out and knocks down wickets?

BURNS
He's a pretty marginal case. It depends how close he is to the end of his career, I would have thought. (Laughter)

MODERATOR
We're in the middle of a finely balanced Test series against England. Are you going to publish?

BURNS
If we look like winning, I think probably not. (Laughter)

MODERATOR
Gerald Stone, would you go with the story on the cricketer as well as the judge, or would you make a distinction?

STONE
I don't want to make a value judgment. I don't even know whether it's wrong to take cocaine but I think that if it's illegal then it's a story.

MODERATOR
If it's illegal, it's a story. You're not worried about the prospect of ending both their careers?

STONE
No, because I settled that long ago. I know that journalism can

create a lot of harm, but I also think that in the long run it does more good by publishing the truth.

MODERATOR
The information that you have is from a dealer called 'The Snowman', who has taped his telephone deals with various celebrities. There's the judge, there's the cricketer . . . you will name them. There's another person on this tape that the dealer has supplied to you. You listen to the tape, you recognise the voice. 'I want fourteen ounces and I want it quickly.' Trevor Kennedy, it's your proprietor, Kerry Murfax. Is he a public figure?

KENNEDY
Yes.

MODERATOR
You're going to expose him?

KENNEDY
Well, we've certainly got a problem. (Laughter) That's obviously a decision that in the final analysis is going to probably be made by the proprietor.

MODERATOR
So you're going to ask the proprietor – 'Do I expose you, sir?'

KENNEDY
Well, it begs the question, certainly.

MODERATOR
And, Mr Jones, might there be a problem with the Australian Broadcasting Tribunal rule that a proprietor convicted of a criminal offence can't hold a TV licence?

PADDY JONES (media solicitor)
That certainly could be a major problem, yes.

MODERATOR
Senator Button, from your knowledge of the media, wouldn't you find it surprising if our enterprising editors and journalists were prepared to expose their own proprietor?

JOHN BUTTON (cabinet minister)
I would find it highly surprising.

MODERATOR
Trevor Kennedy, I'm sure you would give the man a chance to answer?

KENNEDY
Certainly.

MODERATOR
Your proprietor is overseas at the moment, so you'll have to wait a few weeks. In the meantime, let's take a closer look at the problems caused by cocaine. No longer is it an expensive sophisticate's drug: they've started to cultivate coca fields in South Java, and cheap cocaine from secret factories in Indonesia has found its way south. It's in Sydney in a big way – in the schools, in the streets. It spawns crime and corruption, drug dependency and despair. There's call for the government to act – and the government acts in time-honoured fashion: it appoints a Royal Commission, chaired by Judge Julian Knott. Now Jana Wendt, you get a story from a totally reliable source that there is an international hitman in town after the judge. He and his family are at risk.

JANA WENDT (Reporter, *60 Minutes*)
I would certainly want to investigate that story, depending on how high my source was.

MODERATOR
He's very high and very confidential. Judge Knott lives at Bluegum Avenue, Killara, five minutes away from your tele-vision studio, Gerald Stone; and as it happens, a camera crew are passing Bluegum Avenue, Killara, on their way back to the studio and they see something happening. What they see, and what they film, is difficult to describe in words – it is the body of Judge Knott's wife, Annabelle, being lifted into an ambulance. Part of her head is shot away, blood dripping; the twelve-year-old daughter, Melissa, screeching with grief, is being pulled away by a neighbour. Do you want to use that picture?

STONE

I wouldn't even ask the question. I mean, it's there: a judge's wife in New South Wales killed like that in front of her family. I mean, it would be astounding if we tried to suppress that type of –

MODERATOR

Of course. Creighton Burns, on the front page of the *Antipodean*, there'd be a picture of the twelve-year-old girl clutching at the body?

BURNS

Yes, probably because it's well known now that the extent of organised crime is such in the state of New South Wales that judges get bumped off by hitmen employed by organised crime. This is pretty dramatic stuff.

MODERATOR

Trevor Kennedy, would you agree with that decision?

KENNEDY

I think so, definitely. The Vietnam War was stopped by television bringing home to people the drama of that event. We've heard a lot about the good and bad of television – and the simple fact that you actually demonstrate the reality of these things to the audience is, by and large, counterbalanced by any arguments that might be advanced in the sort of esoteric interests of taste and all these other sort of –

MODERATOR

Esoteric interest of taste. Is there another interest at stake here, Robert Hayes?

ROBERT HAYES (law reform commissioner)

Well, I think the children and the family have to live with that footage and the way it is presented. They're at their most extreme moment. What they say and how they react is recorded forever. That's a terribly legacy for them to have to live with and carry around, particularly as you really don't have to portray it photographically to bring home to people the enormity of the problem. Indeed it becomes almost like a further episode of M*A*S*H or something, just another part of the endless run of television series. So in a sense it trivialises it; it makes it even more meaningless.

MODERATOR
Creighton Burns, what's your answer to that?

BURNS
A judge's wife is gunned down by a paid thug. I tell you, it's got to the point where unless we take dramatic measures nobody is going to do anything about organised crime. That's our justification, isn't it?

HAYES
Yes, well there's nothing to stop you printing the story. But I think the graphic portrayal on television of the children is another matter.

MODERATOR
There's a lot of news tonight. There's the story of the judge's wife killed in Killara. There's been an earthquake in Chile: a few dozen people dead; the state government has just announced an election in six weeks' time. And then there's some good news. Dr Peter Jekyll and his Australian team have produced the world's first test-tube triplets. Princess Di is pregnant again and George Negus has announced his engagement. (Laughter) Discuss how you are going to run those stories.

BURNS
Well, Dick, I don't care about Negus's engagement – that's his fifth engagement in two years isn't it? (Laughter) I mean, I don't think we can keep on running with that. The election and the judge's wife are the problem. My feeling is that we lead the paper with the murder of the judge's wife and we run the election announcement as the lead-out.

RICHARD HALL (journalist and author)
No choice about the shortlist. We've got the election and the

judge's wife. I think I'd put the judge's wife along over the top and the election down the left.

I think Princess Di goes back a bit too.

PETER BOWERS (political editor, *Sydney Morning Herald*)
Come on, there's only one story, there's only one picture. You put the picture of the judge's wife all over page one, at least over the top half; then see how much is left for newsprint. We all know that.

MODERATOR
Over at the ABC, Richard Carleton, I guess Princess Di is the lead? (Laughter)

RICHARD CARLETON (journalist, ABC)
We'll run with the judge tonight too.

BOWERS
'Judge's wife gunned down'. It's the only story. Come on.

MODERATOR
It's the only story and it creates a great deal of political concern and embarrassment. Three weeks before the election, Trevor Kennedy, you get a copy of the Cocaine Commission's draft report. And there's a paragraph in it, an interesting paragraph, which says, 'We heard a number of allegations in secret session to the effect that money from the cocaine trade had gone to government ministers. We were in no position to investigate this because it was outside our terms of reference but we would recommend that policy Inquiries into this matter continue.'

KENNEDY
Something as insubstantial as that in the course of an election campaign ... I think that something as insubstantial, in the terms that you have put it, would be fairly doubtful.

BOWERS
We have a draft report from the Royal Commission. Okay. You publish ...

MODERATOR
Richard Carleton, is the ABC going to publish?

RICHARD CARLETON
No. For the very same reasons that Trevor put forward – too insubstantial.

BOWERS
But where's the risk? You've got a document; and if you're satisfied beyond a reasonable doubt that it is a legitimate document, one that's about to be published, then you're bound to publish it. Come on.

MODERATOR
Three weeks before the election, Paul Landa, Judge Knott comes to you. He says, 'Look I'm terribly worried. There's a leak from my Commission. We're dealing with some very, very sensitive matters. We've got a mole somewhere in the Commission who sent to the *Sydney Morning Bugle* our draft report. Can we get the document back? Our forensic boys think that if we can, we can trace the source.'

PAUL LANDA (Attorney-General, New South Wales)
Well, if the document was stolen then certainly they could set in train procedures with the police – to have the theft investigated, track it down if they find who stole it, arrest them and seize the document.

MODERATOR
Mr Littlemore, you are the Solicitor-General. Would you advise Mr Landa that there is a way they can get this report? They want to get the draft back so they can submit it for forensic tests to decide where it came from, because the copies were numbered. This will help them trace the disloyal employee in the Commission.

STUART LITTLEMORE (barrister)
Well, my advice to you, Mr Attorney, is that there is no problem about that. The police are always entitled to seize stolen goods in the course of an investigation of a crime.

LANDA
But they have to satisfy a court that they are investigating an
allegation that it was stolen.

LITTLEMORE
You should be able to organise that.

LANDA
Well, it's not a question of organising it. I mean, I would launch
an immediate inquiry . . .

MODERATOR
You'd send Superintendent Doberman into the offices of the
Sydney Morning Bugle?

LANDA
My word.

BOWERS
And we'd get a splendid picture of you doing it. (Laughter)
Three weeks before an election and he's going to put on a political kerfuffle? What's in the document? What have they got to
hide? Why are they getting so worried? Three weeks before an
election!

MODERATOR
Does Superintendent Doberman get that document? Or do you
destroy it?

BOWERS
You can't destroy a document, but I wouldn't hand it over to
police. If there's a court order saying, 'hand it over', then of
course you'd be bound to hand it over. But make them go the
full hog in the court case and fight it in open court.

MODERATOR
The court has just ordered you to hand it over.

BOWERS
Well, you hand it over.

MODERATOR
You hand it over. You know that it's numbered, that your source will be exposed by handing it over?

BOWERS
What do you want us to do – operate outside the law?

MODERATOR
I don't know: you're the journalist, you've got your ethics. Would you hand it over, Richard Hall?

HALL
No.

MODERATOR
Why not?

HALL
I think the source – the person who risked their job, their future and their career has entered into a kind of contract of confidentiality with you when they handed it over, and that it is your obligation to live up to that confidentiality. If that puts you on the spot, too bad.

MODERATOR
He's the editor, you're the news editor. Tell him.

HALL
I think the gung-ho approach is all very well, but you've got to put something back in terms of ethics. If you enter into that relationship with your source and they have trusted you, then it's for you to protect them. I would have burned the document.

BOWERS
We didn't burn it, we've got it. The person who gave it to us isn't naïve; they knew what they were letting themselves in for in trusting you.

HALL
You should stand by your source.

BOWERS
But the paper's reputation is at risk. We have published, we should have destroyed the document. We didn't; we've got to hand it over.

HALL
In this sense, morally the paper is an extension of the reporter, and it's bound by the reporter's contract with the source. I don't see how you can wriggle out of it.

MODERATOR
Geraldine Paton, as publisher you hold the purse strings. If you don't hand over this document the court will fine you – how much, Mr Jones?

PADDY JONES (solicitor, Channel 9)
Sufficient to get the document eventually, I would have thought.

GERALDINE PATON (publisher, the *Australian*)
Can we have a retrospective burning, perhaps? (Laughter)

JONES
I wouldn't advise that. I don't think you've got any choice but to obey the order. Geraldine, I think it is an impossibly difficult position for the reporter concerned – but I think at the end of the day you can't just flout a court order.

MODERATOR
You hand the document over, and Superintendent Doberman traces it to Miss Sarah Mole, a twenty-three-year-old typist on the Commission. She photocopied the secret document and she is charged with sending it to the *Bugle*. Richard Hall, do you resign?

HALL
Oh yes, no choice.

MODERATOR
Creighton Burns, the *Antipodean* writes an editorial about these events. What does it say?

BURNS
We're talking about the *Bugle*, so we get very pompous. (Laughter) We say that if it had been us we would have checked our sources more carefully and that we wouldn't have published without being absolutely certain that it was somebody more reliable than a mere typist . . .

BOWERS
Come on. We had the document. We don't talk about reliability. We're talking about official documents. You've published tapes that you've got no way of proving . . .

BURNS
Not true, not true, not true.

BOWERS
Don't adopt this 'holier than thou' attitude.

MODERATOR
Senator Button, you're the Minister for the Media. Do you make any statement about these events at any stage?

BUTTON
No, certainly not. I would . . . I would prefer these people be left with their moral dilemmas.

MODERATOR
You are very concerned about this leak because you are in charge of the Australian government's negotiations with Indonesia, negotiations that are detailed in Part Two of this document. Part Two gives details of the Australian undercover agents in South Java who have found the cocaine fields; it deals with Judge Knott's suggestion to pay money to the military rulers of South Java to get the cocaine fields destroyed and to relocate the people who are working there, just as the Americans did with the heroin corps in Turkey. Gerry Stone, here is a story that has got panoramic, visual appeal, hasn't it?

MIKE CARLTON
And overseas travel. (Laughter)

STONE
We've got this document, Jana. I don't know how good it is, but I do think it's worth taking a punt. I've got the names and locations of people who are alleged to be Australian agents dealing in the cocaine business. I think we should go to Indonesia under maybe some pretext of doing a fluff story about the tourist trade in Bali or something like that. Go there, and see if you can make contact with these fellows, see what they're doing, see if we can get anything for the record because I think we're sitting on a very good story.

JANA WENDT (reporter, *60 Minutes*)
Do we go with the story?

STONE
Well, let's see what you bring back.

MIKE CARLTON
Why are you sending Jana and not George Negus?

STONE
George just got engaged, remember. (Laughter)

MODERATOR
General Buldoza, the military governor of South Java, is the man to whom the Australian government is thinking of giving a great deal of money in an effort to eradicate the problem, but in the knowledge that much of it undoubtedly will end up in his pocket.

WENDT
I would be very interested to speak to General Buldoza.

MODERATOR
Senator Button, ASIO gets wind of Jana Wendt's foreign trip.

MODERATOR
She has a copy, it would seem, of this secret document. What action do you take?

BUTTON
I would send somebody from ASIO with her.

MODERATOR
So you put an ASIO man on Jana's tail. She talks to General Buldoza, she gets lots of colour film of the South Java cocaine fields and the temples. *60 Minutes* is going to do this story based on Part Two of the secret document.

BUTTON
Well, if one couldn't abort the television story in Java, then I would seek to take similar action against *60 Minutes* as was taken against the *Bugle* earlier on.

MODERATOR
Have a word with Mr Littlemore. Is there any way you can stop this film?

LITTLEMORE
What about a D-notice? Why can't you issue a D-notice?

BUTTON
Well, in those circumstances, given the contents of the document, yes I can.

MODERATOR
There's a D-notice on your film, Gerry Stone.

BOWERS
Don't take any notice of that. It's voluntary.

MODERATOR
(to Stone) It's your decision.

STONE
Yes, I would be torn by that. I might, under those circumstances, observe a D-notice.

MODERATOR
You would observe a D-notice. Richard Carleton, at *Four Corners* you've made this film, you're in the same position as

Gerry Stone. What do you do about the D-notice that has just been slapped on you?

RICHARD CARLETON
Well you either observe it at *Four Corners* or you go. It's as simple as that.

STONE
I must say that if the government has got to a state in which it is asking me to basically put in abeyance every rule I know is holy in journalism, and says 'Trust me', then I am willing to do it once. But I don't know whether I would be willing to do it twice. It's different from the question of the judge's wife who got slain in a Sydney street. That's such a clear-cut case of public interest that I would publish. But if you come to me as a government and say 'Look, trust me, it really is a matter or security', then I have to say, 'OK, I won't broadcast. But next time I don't know.'

MODERATOR
Creighton Burns, you published the story about the judge who indulged in cocaine. Why are you not publishing this story about another judge's attempt to stop the cocaine trade by bribing an Indonesian general?

BURNS
Because the Royal Commissioner has invented a master plan that will stop a considerable social evil in society. And when you expose the judge for smoking cocaine, you'd do so because you want to expose a social evil.

MODERATOR
Respect the integrity of officials, Gerald Stone?

STONE
No. The greatest blot of my career as a journalist was being in a situation where we went along with the Bay of Pigs invasion with Jack Kennedy – because we thought that we were going to be on a good story by following the invasion, you see. So instead

of publishing the plans of the invasion, what we said was, 'Hold on, if we don't say anything about it, we can be there and film the troops as they come into Cuba.' So I don't trust governments that much.

MODERATOR
Well, nonetheless, although you don't trust governments, you at Channel 9 obey the D-notice and Richard Carleton at the ABC obeys the D-notice. So are our television people craven? Peter Bowers? You're a man who believes in 'publish and be damned'.

BOWERS
Well, just a minute. Talk about double standards! A few minutes ago Gerald Stone and just about every other journalist around this table were condemning me for not disobeying the Supreme Court order to hand over a document and, God help us, in the next breath now they're ready to obey a D-notice – which is purely voluntary and which everybody knows is phoney and just there to protect the government.

MODERATOR
So you wouldn't obey a D-notice?

BOWERS
Of course I wouldn't. But by the same token I would make a value judgment. Of course there's a national interest; of course we can't put ourselves outside a national interest. We're all Australians, and we're not going to put the national interest at risk unnecessarily; we're not going to put Australians at risk because even people who work for ASIO and ASIS are still Australian.

MODERATOR
Let's move on to something that the papers are interested in and that the public is interested in. Judge Knott is running his Cocaine Commission, but how is he coping after the murder of his wife? Mark Day, I can tell you exactly how he is coping. I am Ken Paparazzi, freelance photographer. I have got some

photographs here of Judge Knott coping, with the help of that famous actress Katie Bombshell. They are at a private pool in Palm Beach; she's topless and he's breathless. (Laughter) Interested?

MARK DAY (editor, *Strewth*)
My word I am. I'm delighted that the subject has got off all this pompous esoteric nonsense and that we have got back into real journalism – which is about people and their human failings. And I am delighted to see that the judge has some human failings as well.

MODERATOR
And are your readers going to be delighted to see them as well?

DAY
All the time you have been going on about D-notices I have been out interviewing George Negus and his fiancée, and praying that it is Jana Wendt. (Laughter) You know *they're* important things that people want to know about. Now these pictures, are they in focus?

MODERATOR
Yes, they are.

DAY
Good. Where were they taken?

MODERATOR
They were taken by telephoto lens from another house overlooking the private pool.

DAY
How old are the girls?

MODERATOR
Katie is a mature woman. Her new film, *Picnic at Snowy River*, is opening next week. Are you going to publish the pictures in *Strewth*?

DAY
Yes.

MODERATOR
Jana Wendt, you are interviewing Katie Bombshell for *60 Minutes*. Do you ask her about her relationship with the judge after *Strewth* publishes these pictures?

WENDT
I think that under those circumstances there would be no way that I would avoid asking Katie Bombshell a question about the judge.

MODERATOR
If those topless pictures were not of Katie Bombshell but of Jana Wendt, how would you feel?

WENDT
All I could say to *Strewth* is that it would not be worth their while. (Laughter)

MODERATOR
But would you be angry, upset?

WENDT
I think any individual would be perturbed by the fact that they were published topless, yes.

STONE
What worries me is the acceptance that a nude photo of Jana published by somebody who happens to see her in a backyard swimming pool can be published by *Strewth*. I don't believe that's the case; and so I'd go to Paddy. I would have thought that Jana has a case. I mean here she was, just lounging by a swimming pool, and somebody takes a picture of her and publishes it in *Strewth*. Don't we have a case about that?

JONES
No, not on that basis alone. She has got no cause of action.

STONE
To publish a photograph of a woman bare-breasted who is only in the privacy of her home – whether she is Jana or somebody else – and to splash that on a newspaper ... you tell me that woman has no recourse under law?

JONES
That's the position.

STONE
Can't she say that it has subjected her to ridicule by her friends?

JONES
I can't see how you could make that meaningful.

STONE
Oh well, we'll get another lawyer. (Laughter)

MODERATOR
You've got Mr Littlemore. Try counsel's opinion.

LITTLEMORE
I would give you the same advice. I think you have a very good solicitor.

MODERATOR
Robert Hayes, would the Law Commission have something to say about an incident like this?

HAYES
Yes, it would. I think that photographing people from a private place in their private activities ought to be unlawful. It isn't presently, but it ought to be.

MODERATOR
Mark Day, you are doing some research into Judge Knott's old cases and as you go through the back issues of *Strewth* you discover that there was a case way back in 1954 where he defended a young doctor, Dr Peter Hyde, who was acquitted on an abortion charge. There is a photograph, and the doctor looks

remarkably like Dr Peter Jekyll, the man who has just produced the world's first test-tube triplets. It would appear that when he was a very young man he was perhaps mixed up in an abortion racket, or at least that was what he was charged with. Is this an interesting story?

DAY

Yes, it is. I would get one of our best reporters to go down that burrow and see what he can find.

MODERATOR

Well Richard Hall has resigned from the *Sydney Morning Bugle* and is now the chief investigative reporter for *Strewth* – give him his orders.

DAY

OK, Dick, get out there and see what you can find, because if we have a former abortionist now leading the world in test-tube baby programs, that's a damned good story.

HALL

Oddly enough, I find myself on Mark Day's side. Jekyll's a public figure, he is a member of the medical profession, we can establish he's changed his name by deed poll. I don't happen to believe that to have been involved in abortion cases is morally bad. In fact, I think if you wrote about a doctor now involved in some form of medical breakthrough, and you were able to say that at one stage he was charged with what a significant proportion of people accept now, that's part of the process of changing public opinion.

MODERATOR

Creighton Burns – would you publish?

BURNS

Not if he was acquitted. No, I wouldn't.

MODERATOR

Why not?

BURNS
If he was convicted I figure that there would be a stronger case for at least investigating the story. I am not sure that I am very moved by the name change; that seems to me something that people are entitled to do for all sorts of reasons.

MODERATOR
The difficulty is that at the moment there is a ferocious campaign against legalising abortion. The Right to Exist campaign, chaired by Mrs Lily White, is fomenting a massive opposition. She's known in the media as 'The White Nile'. (Laughter) She's charismatic and formidable. Richard Carleton, you're about to interview her and you discover that when she was twenty-five, some twenty years ago, she herself went to this abortion clinic. Is that the sort of matter that you would raise with her?

RICHARD CARLETON
Life is getting difficult as the night goes on, isn't it? (Laughter)

Ah . . . yes.

MODERATOR
You think it right to raise that?

RICHARD CARLETON
By way of a question, yes. I think it is a very interesting question, and you would have the audience on the edge of their seats.

MODERATOR
You're not 'live' as it happens – you're doing the interview the day before transmission. You ask the question and to your surprise she says, 'Yes, I did have an abortion when I was twenty-five. I was raped, you see.' Are you going to comply with her request to edit that out?

RICHARD CARLETON
I'd have to go to my boss.

MIKE CARLTON
You go in hard . . .

MODERATOR
You'd go in hard, Mike Carlton, if she was on your radio program?

MIKE CARLTON
You build every possible charge of hypocrisy out of it. 'Why is it right for you to have an abortion twenty years ago, when today you are saying no to abortions?'

MODERATOR
You are prerecording this interview with Mrs White and she answers you: 'It's true. Twenty years ago, I went to an abortion clinic, because I had been raped. I stayed one night in that dreadful place that Dr Jekyll used to run, and I realised I couldn't face it. I left, without having the abortion. I had the child; my boyfriend, Peter White, stood by me and married me. My daughter is now twenty and at Melbourne University. She doesn't know Peter isn't her father. She doesn't know her real father is a rapist. Please don't transmit this interview.'

MIKE CARLTON
You've got a problem. I would keep tape rolling and I would say: 'OK, different ground rules. Let's take it again, but we are going to get you into that abortion clinic.' Now we can get around it . . .

MODERATOR
How can you get her into an abortion clinic without the fact that she is pregnant?

MIKE CARLTON
No, we have taken her in there, we are going to agree that she has been in there and, ah –

MODERATOR
What, just to look at it?

MIKE CARLTON
You have got to twist her arm a little because this woman has had no hesitation whatsoever in twisting the arms of other

women who have sought abortions. She has been brutal, she has been vicious in her campaign and I would put that question to her: 'Is it not understandable why other women are tempted?' I would say, 'Why are you so perfect and angelic?'

MODERATOR
She was tempted and she resisted it – she had the child. But the child doesn't know that its real father was a rapist and it's impossible for you to put that to her without revealing it. We weren't worried about the sensibilities of twelve-year-old Melissa and her right to privacy as she was screaming with grief; why are we worried about Mrs White's daughter?

MIKE CARLTON
You've got me. I would probably have to stop and go back to a fellow journalist and discuss it.

MODERATOR
Go back to Gerry Stone and Creighton Burns.

MIKE CARLTON
All right. Gerry, listen. I have just been in the studio, I have interviewed this woman, she has admitted that yes, she went to an abortion clinic, that she has a twenty-year-old daughter whose father was a rapist. What the hell do I do with it?

STONE
I know how you feel and, yes, we are going to hurt the daughter, we're going to hurt the mother, but I mean don't you have a duty – having got that story – to let it out for all the other hundreds of thousands of people that are involved in the abortion debate?

MIKE CARLTON
That's what I wanted you to say. We'll go and finish the interview.

BURNS
Wait a minute. I'm really concerned about the future of that twenty-year-old girl. I think it's pretty rough to publish that.

I think what we say to Mrs White is: 'Right, we will kill this story but you will never appear on radio again on this station.'

MIKE CARLTON
Oh, go away.

BURNS
And we'd start a campaign –

MODERATOR
Blackmail?

BURNS
That's not blackmail . . .

MIKE CARLTON
Yes, it is. I mean I would resign rather than say that.

MODERATOR
Peter Bowers, you will publish anything. Will you publish that?

BOWERS
No, I wouldn't.

MODERATOR
Why not?

BOWERS
Well, I have to live with my conscience.

MODERATOR
That's the first time we have heard the word 'conscience' used all evening.

BOWERS
I would be worried. I mean, the woman was raped after all. So I am worried. We all make dreadful, appalling mistakes; and we all make messes of our lives. We live it down, and twenty years later someone wants to put us on trial again. Not only that, but innocent twenty-year-old girls who don't know that their fathers are rapists get ruined for the sake of a story. Well, I just think that you have got to draw the line somewhere.

STONE

This is the most amazing thing to me. I mean here we are sitting around having a drink, and we're all talking about Mike's problem and what to do with this story . . . I mean, where do you stop? Somebody says, 'Yes I did in fact kill somebody and steal their wife, but I never let her know about it, so therefore I don't want her to know about it.' I mean, you can't allow yourself to be tangled up –

BOWERS

I am not telling Mike Carlton what to do, I am not telling Gerald Stone what to do. I am just saying what I would do.

MIKE CARLTON

Maybe we just say to the woman, 'We'll give you two days to tell your daughter and then we run the interview.'

MODERATOR

I am afraid, Mike, now you've told so many journalists that the story's got out and it's in *Strewth* this week and they've scooped you all. (Laughter)

DAY

Unless either party confessed, we wouldn't have published.

MODERATOR

You would have told the daughter yourself? (Laughter)

DAY

No, no, no. Not at all. We would have sought the confession from the mother after she had told the daughter; we would hope that she would have done that. We would have also searched for the father. Maybe he was still around. We would have spoken to the husband, we may –

MODERATOR

You would have got everyone in that story. (Laughter) Let's move on, because at last we have a suspect for the murder of the judge's wife. John Smith his name is – and boy, does he have a chequered past. He has got a record as long as your arm: rape, assault, armed robbery. He was a member of the Nazi Party in the sixties, he was last sentenced for armed robbery in 1970 and turned in the dock and screamed at the prosecutor, 'I'll get back at you, you bastard.' The prosecutor was Julian Knott QC. Smith came out of prison a few years ago on the early-release scheme, and he's been dealing in cocaine. He's mentioned in the Knott report as one of the big dealers. He's got every reason to kill the judge's wife. You know all this, Peter Bowers. Do you publish it while the man is on the run? He is just a suspect but you've got his photograph and all the information.

BOWERS
The police of course have requested our cooperation and that we publish a great many of these details, because this fellow isn't just somebody on the run – he's a dangerous public menace. And in the public interest we are bound to publish as much information about him as we can to protect the public, and we will do so.

MODERATOR
Stuart Littlemore, you're going to get the defence brief. Are you concerned about all this publicity?

LITTLEMORE
Oh yes. It's already almost impossible for him to get a fair trial.

MODERATOR
Peter Bowers gets a telephone call. 'Mr Bowers, this picture of John Smith that you just published looks like my neighbour. Do you think I should go to the police?'

BOWERS
Of course.

MODERATOR
'He's gone on holiday, but he left me the key to his house so I could water his plants.'

BOWERS
Get thee behind me, Satan! (Laughter)

MODERATOR
'Do you think I should go to the police and give them the key?'

BOWERS
I'd like to say, go to the police. But I'm very fearful I'd say, 'Give us a look inside the house first.'

MODERATOR
Richard Carleton, the call has come to you at the ABC.

RICHARD CARLETON
I've got problems.

MODERATOR
What are you going to say to him?

RICHARD CARLETON
Go to the police.

MIKE CARLTON
I'll come with you! (Laughter)

MODERATOR
'You want to come with me to water the plants?'

MIKE CARLTON
Sure. Let me come with you.

MODERATOR
'You're from 2GB, so it must be all right.' (Laughter)

MIKE CARLTON
Yeah, of course.

MODERATOR
All right, we'll go in. 'Gee, interesting books on the shelves'. Do you open the closet, have a –

MIKE CARLTON
No, I touch nothing. Not a thing do I touch. I just look and stick it all in my head.

MODERATOR
You've got a lot of information that the other ace reporters haven't. They are still waiting for the police to arrive.

MIKE CARLTON
Silly.

MODERATOR
Is there anything illegal in what our investigative reporter has done here?

LANDA
The possession of the key implies permission to enter so I doubt whether there is a trespass. Mike is wandering around freely – I think he has a scoop.

MODERATOR
He gets the scoop, he puts out on his radio program and in his columns the story of what he saw in the murderer's house. Which rather upsets Mr Peter Jones, who owns that house. Mr Jones is a travelling salesman who has been away on holiday. He bears quite a resemblance to John Smith, but he certainly isn't John Smith. He goes to you, Mr Littlemore. 'I'm very unhappy to have my home portrayed as that of a murderer. My little habits hanging in the closet being described in lurid detail by Mr Carlton.'

LITTLEMORE
Well, Mr Carlton has got very large problems, hasn't he?

MODERATOR
Tell us about them.

LITTLEMORE
Well, the trouble with defamation is that unintentional defamation is just as bad as intended defamation. It doesn't matter where you aim, it's where you hit. Now they've hit my client and really depicted him as a murderer.

MODERATOR
Paddy Jones, you're defending Mike Carlton.

JONES
Well, that's a difficult brief. I'd have to pay Stuart a lot of money.
I mean, obviously you're in a difficult situation, aren't you?

MODERATOR
Well, Mike is.

JONES
I'm being paid, so *I'm* all right. Stuart, we'd like to resolve the
matter involving Mr Jones as quickly and as amicably as we can.
We'd obviously be prepared to apologise in the most fulsome
terms and we would also like to make a payment without any
admission of liability in order to get rid of the claim. I am
instructed to put $70,000 to you.

LITTLEMORE
Well, this is a case where my client is not interested in money.
He says it's his reputation he wants back and there isn't any
money that can buy that for him and he wants to know what
you will do for him.

MIKE CARLTON
Paddy, I'll do this terrific apology. (Laughter)

MODERATOR
How do you do the apology?

MIKE CARLTON
With every evidence of sincerity. I go on at some length about
Mr Jones being an upright citizen and though we grievously
admit our error, we believe we were acting in the finest public
interest and that we deeply regret any hurt, bother, interference,
stress et cetera, caused to Mr Jones, who we believe to be a
blameless and upright citizen.

MODERATOR
Satisfied, Mr Littlemore?

LITTLEMORE

My client says that people who heard the first report didn't necessarily all hear that. Not only that: a lot of the people who have heard the defamation about my client have heard it from other people, and it's been discussed for forty-eight hours before the station comes up with this insincere apology with a laugh in the middle of it.

MIKE CARLTON

And a commercial. (Laughter) I could impersonate the Prime Minister and get Bob Hawke to apologise. We could pay Bob Hawke to apologise for us. (Laughter)

MODERATOR

The answer is: he can't get his reputation back, can he?

LITTLEMORE

Well, that's what troubles him.

MIKE CARLTON

What does he want, a musical? (Laughter) The terrible thing about this is that this is the way lawyers really talk.

LITTLEMORE

That's how lawyers talk because that's the sort of talk that publishers understand. It always gets back to money.

MODERATOR

While the lawyers are talking, the real John Smith is convicted of murder, and is sent to jail for life. Judge Knott marries Katie Bombshell and gets appointed to the High Court after the vacancy left by the premature retirement of Mr Justice Benchmark. *60 Minutes* continues to top the ratings and Jana Wendt, like the good reporter she is, never reveals her source. Although you did have some anxieties, Jana, about that telephone call you got way back from the high official concerned about the judge's security. This person you remember, who was very high up, very confidential, very reliable . . .

WENDT
I certainly would love to know.

MODERATOR
It was Judge Knott himself, setting up a media cover story to divert suspicion from himself that day he murdered his wife. (Laughter) But what of our proprietor, Kerry Murfax? He's just back from overseas, and Trevor Kennedy is at this very moment waiting outside his office to confront him with the evidence that he ordered cocaine from The Snowman. 'G'day, Trevor. Come to see me about the falling circulation of the newspaper?'

KENNEDY
Hi, Mr Murfax. We've got a matter here that I think you will be deeply interested in.

MODERATOR
'About time. What is it?'

KENNEDY
It concerns yourself and it raises allegations that you have been involved in the cocaine trade.

MODERATOR
'In the cocaine trade!'

KENNEDY
Yes. It suggests . . .

MODERATOR
'I'm not involved in the cocaine trade. I've never been involved in the cocaine trade.'

KENNEDY
Now look, I believe you. (Laughter) This other fellow says that you have been, and he has produced a significant amount of evidence to substantiate the point.

MODERATOR
'That telephone call with The Snowman. Okay, I did order that cocaine. What are you going to do about it?'

KENNEDY
Well, in that case, how do you think we ought to handle this story? (Laughter)

MODERATOR
Your proprietor gives a long laugh – a sort of *proprietorial* laugh. 'I did order cocaine on that telephone call. But it wasn't the first call I had from The Snowman. He rang me asking me if I wanted to buy cocaine. I immediately went to the police. They said, "String him along, act as a decoy, *pretend* to buy it." So of course when he called back I ordered it, and the police were listening on the extension. I wouldn't break the law, because I would lose my television licence and you'd all be out of work.' (Laughter)

Where there's smoke, ladies and gentlemen, there's usually fire. But sometimes, there's only a smoke machine.

HUMAN RIGHTS

Chapter 21

TEACH THE CHILDREN WELL

I attended a primary school in Eastwood, a respectable lower-middle-class suburb of Sydney, and found myself selected at age eleven for what was called an 'opportunity class'. I was never quite sure what it was an opportunity for, but it did have a remarkable teacher, Lionel Phelps (later to become Chancellor of the University of Southern Cross), who made us read the Sydney Morning Herald *every day and criticise the doings of grand men with middle names, like John Foster Dulles and Robert Gordon Menzies.*

Mr Phelps's political provocations might not pass muster today, when teachers are meant to have no views about anything, but he taught us to think. His example often comes to mind when I talk to teachers, which is always a pleasure because I come from a long line of headmasters – of Fort Street and Sydney Grammar; and my grandfather, Harry Beattie, was head of a one-teacher school at Marshall Mount, just outside Dapto.

This speech was to a conference of state schoolteachers in 2009, at which the new Minister for Education, Julia Gillard, set out her pitch. I offered some thoughts about state schooling, and how it should incorporate an education in human rights.

The state education that shaped my life and the lives of many others deserves not only to be supported but celebrated, at a time when upon it depends the future of seventy per cent of our young Australians, including most young Australians who, through learning difficulties and cultural differences, are particularly vulnerable to exploitation and abuse.

It is an exciting time to have a government committed to creating an educational revolution, a government that recognises 'the central role that education plays in the economic and social strength of our nation'. I joined in the applause for education minister Julia Gillard as she promised that her government would not quail at the economic malaise, and would deliver funding increases for primary and secondary schools at least, if not for universities. She spoke with alluring alliteration of 'equity and excellence', although she did not ponder the problems of achieving excellence in schools that still teach creationism and intelligent design, or inculcate sharia attitudes to the detriment of women.

As for equity, this current political buzzword, let me tell you – as a long time equity practitioner – it means basic fairness, and in that sense our funding arrangements are certainly not fair to the state sector. What the minister did not say – and perhaps it is still too difficult in Australian politics to say it, is: PUT STATE SCHOOLS FIRST. First among equals, it may be, but FIRST. Let others catch up, let others get ahead – competition in education, as in other professional services, is fine. But a real revolution in education will only come when a government ensures that its state schools set the standard for excellence. Then, and only then, will you have equity.

State education, after all, is one of Australia's greatest achievements. We were among the first of nations to establish a free, compulsory and secular educational system, right back in the 1870s, when state governments were imbued with the ideals of the Gladstonian era of improvement. State education was one of our most important borrowings from Britain, championed here by a visionary autodidact, Sir Henry Parkes. But back in the 1870s, secular education provoked religious reactions. Protestant churches set up their own schools to inculcate the fear of God, at least in the sons and later the daughters of the rich. Catholics were predominantly Irish, in those days, and were genuinely concerned that secular state schools might imperil the hold over the souls they wished to save and more importantly, according to Manning Clark, they wanted to promote their own version of Irish history. So they insisted on setting up their alternative system. These were exceptions – acceptable exceptions, given freedom of parental choice – to the great and enduring principle of free secular education. As proponents of that principle, we have had debates – we still have them – about achieving excellence through various forms of selective schooling. The debate has ebbed and flowed and it flowed quite aggressively during my own schooldays.

As a pupil in an opportunity class, my card was marked to go to a selective school, Fort Street, where a distant relative – John Dettman – had been a famous headmaster. But suddenly the New South Wales Education Department changed its policy, and we were streamed off to a new non-selective school that had just opened at Epping. My parents were inconsolable and offered to pay for me to go to Sydney Grammar. I refused. I would like to think of myself at age eleven as a precocious progressive, firm in my support for state education, but I have to admit that principle nothing to do with it. I simply worked out that I could spend an hour longer in bed if I went to Epping, so there I demanded to go.

We had some great teachers, including a mischievous history master who had read his A. S. Neill and suggested that I should wag school and spend my days instead in the Mitchell Library. I took his advice, and came second in the state – to a boy whose father set the exam paper. (Some things you never forget.) Fifteen years later, would you believe, my rival and I had our first books published by the same British publisher, at the same time. Mine was about rigged trials of IRA suspects, his was a defence of General Pinochet's torture policy. Mine did not

sell, except in Ireland, while his sold voluminously because the
Chilean Embassy bought fifty thousand copies. Once again, I
had come second.

So that was the danger of state education in my day, and
today as well. Whether it was state censorship on grounds of
morality or grounds of cost (the bowdlerised edition of Shakespeare was cheaper), it is the kind of behaviour to which states
and their officials are always prone. So it is right to have an
alternative to state education, if only to keep it up to the mark.

We were not really disadvantaged by attending state schools
– we weren't bullied, we weren't buggered, we weren't indoctrinated into religion or forced to join the cadets. But we were not
led to believe that we were any good, and certainly were made
to feel inferior to the confident GPS kids we met on the train.
Until the leaving results came out and we read our names in the
Sydney Morning Herald ahead of theirs in the honours lists.
What we were lacking, I think, was confidence. It came out at
university tutorials as well. The old school tie, for no rational
reason, had induced a degree of self-confidence and a degree of
self-assertiveness in our private-school rivals.

That shouldn't have been the case then, nor should it be now.
Public education should compete effectively in the parental
marketplace. Not only is it free, it has the great advantage of
secularity. In a world where dogma is becoming the greatest
threat to rationality, surely secular learning should be regarded
as a plus. Not to mention diversity – the value of children and
teenagers mixing with a wider variety of fellow human beings
from different social classes, different ethnic groups and levels
of advantage and performance. And the virtue of locality. The
virtue that I intuited at age eleven – the saving of so much time
on trains and buses. That doesn't seem to count with too many
of today's parents.

I should make clear that I believe in a mixed educational
system, and in the right of parents to choose the kind of education that shall be given to their children, subject to the right
of the state to set curricula and to intervene if schools are

performing inadequately or teaching intolerance. Indeed, I defended Summerhill, A. S. Neill's remarkable little school in Essex when OFSTED, the government inspectorate, tried to close it down. One of Neill's basic beliefs was that children come to embrace education and really learn – but only when they want to, so they must not be forced to attend class. OFSTED decided to close the school down – because pupils were not being forced to attend class! It was quite a joy to cross-examine these ignorant inspectors, and to call evidence from the astrophysicists and philosophers and Hollywood actresses who had graduated from Summerhill. Not a school for everyone's children, but one that has led to important insights into how children learn.

And I've never been impressed by the current veneration of the state system in Finland by Australian educationalists. Having attended an education conference there, I was deeply unimpressed not by the schools so much as by the streets of the capital, Helsinki, where you can walk up and down for days without seeing a non-white face. This is a country that alone in Europe refuses to take refugees – a monocultural society with the worst cuisine, the worst weather and the highest suicide rate in the world. After the recent school shootings, the Finns are questioning their own system, and should begin by questioning their social values.

I have been talking about education in the sixties when state education was reasonably well funded and respected, and I have watched from a distance with some horror at the way in which successive federal governments have pump-primed the private schools at the expense of the state sector and how state schoolteachers have become whipping boys and whipping girls for all sorts of ideological grievances. It was famously said, by the public servant in charge of the great 1944 Education Reforms in Britain, that his job was, as he put it, 'To die in the last ditch to prevent politicians getting their hands on education.' Well, today their hands lie so heavy on education we must crawl out of that ditch and point them in the right direction.

There has been a massive political interest in education, in Australia and elsewhere, since 9/11. The idea seems to be that public education can be used to erect some talismanic barricade against attacks on Western civilisation. There was already a perfectly sensible interest in the teachings of civics or citizenship and a perfectly reasonable debate about 'values education', which suddenly metamorphosed into a demand to teach 'Australian values'. Then of course there was the demand from the History Summit to teach Australian history. No bad thing in itself, but it emerged from that summit in triumphalist tones, as if accepting the Panglossian notion that Australians live in the best of all possible worlds and demanding that history serve as the narrative of how we got there.

I don't entirely discount these initiatives. They represent deeply felt community aspirations and it's important not to be too cynical about them. Teaching civic values has been advocated by great educationalists since Aristotle. But you should ask: whose values? The word came down from the previous education minister, Dr Brendan Nelson, to teach 'Australian values', and he even prepared a list of Australian values – care and compassion; doing your best; fair go; freedom; honesty; trustworthiness; integrity; respect; responsibility; understanding and tolerance.

These are not Australian values, they are universal values. Values that are enshrined in the *Universal Declaration of Human Rights* and in its progeny, the Conventions against torture, against apartheid, against racism, against discrimination. It certainly is time they were taught, but in terms of the philosophy behind them; why they were necessary; how they were fought for; how they were enforced; how they are spoken about and debated. Here I think we do have the makings of a discipline, a body of rights language that students can absorb as part of the progress of humanity and can use to give them confidence at their present stage of teenage uncertainty and in their future life.

But with the demand for Australian values, there is also the demand to have Australian heroes. The first role model suggested by Dr Nelson, Simpson and his donkey, rather proves my point.

The minister was apparently ignorant of the fact that Simpson was not Australian but was in fact a Yorkshire trade unionist, an illegal immigrant and a republican. He loathed Australia; he only volunteered in order to get a free passage back to England where he planned to desert. Frankly I don't think that makes him any less of a hero; it just proves the point that the values of humanity are universal. They have been ever since the Good Samaritan left Samaria.

By all means hero-worship Simpson, although that is not, in fact, his real name (it was John Kirkpatrick). Dr Nelson's mistake emphasises one objection to the teaching of values – that they are subjective. There are other arguments against them – from Karl Marx (who thought that human rights were bourgeois rights) and from Nietzsche, who denied that objective truth was capable of being known to any individual human mind.

To that cynicism, there are two answers. The answer of Immanuel Kant, who identified those principles of morality that are sufficiently or categorically imperative so as to be universally binding, and the answer given by modern liberal philosophers like John Rawls and Ronald Dworkin who argue that there are certain moral values such as justice and equality about which a democratic society can never be neutral. Moral education should be based on initiation into a rational morality constructed on these fundamental values. Bernard Crick, the architect of citizenship courses in British schools, pointed out that there are key concepts – political literacy, freedom, rights, justice – without which students are unable to comprehend the modern political context in which they live. They must be initiated into a 'rational morality' constructed on these fundamental values.

There may be little controversy now about the importance of preparing children for the world. The common and agreed National Goals for Schooling in Australia has as Goal 6, 'the development in students of the capacity for judgment in matters of morality, ethics and social justice'. Goal 7 requires dissemination of knowledge that will enable students to participate as active and informed citizens in our democratic society within the international context. That means teaching democracy, teaching the rule of law and the rights of citizenship. The first three focus issues identified by Tony Vinson (in his recent report on disadvantage in education) were: how should Australian society develop participatory, critically minded and just citizens? How do we guarantee that children have an equal opportunity to learn and fully develop their capacities? How do we ensure that the principles of social justice are guaranteed and that public education strengthens the influence of these principles across society? I would answer Tony's questions by saying we should do this by enacting a charter – a Statute of Liberty – and by teaching its provisions in a compulsory citizenship course.

There is a particular course that state education could and should teach, a course that will not only empower its students but give them the confidence that we lacked, back in Epping – the confidence that comes from learning and maintaining the rights and responsibilities of citizenship, of Australia and of the world. In the UK, it is called human rights education, but of course, the idea of teaching civic virtues can be traced back to Aristotle. Remember his great argument for public education in Book VIII of his *Politics*:

> Supervision of education must be public and not private: public training is wanted in all things that are of public interest. Besides, it is wrong for any citizen to think that he belongs to himself. All must be considered as belonging to the *polis* for each man is a part of the *polis,* and the treatment of the part is necessarily determined by the treatment of the whole.

How should public education today teach Aristotle's civic virtues? According to Article 26(2) of the *Universal Declaration of Human Rights*:

> Education shall be directed to the full development of the human personality and to the strengthening of respect for human rights and fundamental freedoms. It shall

promote understanding, tolerance and friendship among all nations, racial or religious groups, and shall further the activities of the UN for the maintenance of peace.

It is important to study educational discoveries and developments in other countries over recent years. Groundbreaking research in Canada – the Cape Breton Project in 2002 – was replicated in Hampshire schools between 2005–2007 and has now been approved for introduction to all British schools. 'Teaching citizenship through human rights' is the name of the course, which will be delivered by citizenship teachers, many of them signed up to a separate initiative by UNICEF UK entitled 'Rights Respecting Schools'.

The 'Teaching citizenship' course aims to link the concept of universal human rights with everyday experience, focusing on what rights mean to young people. Teachers are being trained to bring human rights to life, exploring concrete issues such as poverty and discrimination and facilitating challenging debates about identities, diversities and rights and responsibilities.

It is a carefully thought-out course of twelve one-hour lectures for twelve- to fourteen-year-old kids. It begins very simply by inviting them to consider a new set of school rules: are they fair or not? Then they have to explain why not and draft alternative rules. The new rules are predictable: teachers may hit students at any time; students must convert to the head teacher's religion; teachers can go through students' bags at any time and examine their property; anyone who criticises the new rules will be punished; students cannot talk to each other or stand in groups of more than two during school hours; students can be expelled at any time without reason. They will not be entitled to argue or appeal the decision; teachers can take any trainers or mobiles from students and keep them for their own use; students whose names start with the letter 'R' cannot come to school ever again and will instead clean public toilets eight hours a day. The reasons for unfairness are set out and it is explained to students how they contravene rules in the UN Declaration of Human Rights.

The second lecture period discusses the human rights story with a special reference to the Holocaust and slavery and some of the horrors of recent times. The third focuses on classroom games, play and hypotheticals to understand how human rights might help produce a more peaceful world. The fourth lecture zeros in on the *Human Rights Act* passed in the UK in 1998: students are shown how it applies to public bodies including their own state school, hospitals and old people's homes and to the police. The example that they discuss is an actual one of a couple who had been married for sixty years and then were put in separate care homes. They were reunited thanks to the *Human Rights Act*. Further lectures explain the UN Convention of the Rights of the Child, which has particular relevance to schooling, and indeed to children's rights to be respected and not molested. They look at balancing rights (free speech against religion, etc.).

Another lesson, also of particular relevance, concerns identity profile and privacy, what is termed 'the right to forget' and have old and embarrassing Facebook facts deleted. A further session comes back to an important issue in classrooms, namely homo-phobic bullying. This is a particular problem where so many teachers and parents simply do not face up to the fact that young people at age fifteen or sixteen may have developed a homosex-ual identity and the terrible misery that is inflicted upon them by their peers as a result.

The final session encourages students to take action on a particular matter by writing letters to the editor, phoning radio call-back programs, fundraising, filmmaking, lobbying the local council, organising a peaceful protest, lobbying their MP or organising some information event on some issue that affects them or moves them. This has a potential for blow-back, but so far so good. Throughout the course students are shown how it all ties in with the *Human Rights Act*. Kids here could have a great time bothering Alan Jones.

The really interesting thing about this course is how pilot projects have been so successful. Assessments highlight benefits that include:

- Behaviour improvement;
- Increase in attendance;
- Decrease in exclusions;
- Classroom and school atmosphere is healthier;
- The school environment is respected to a greater degree;
- Students demonstrate a heightened awareness of the broader community and social issues;
- Teachers feel empowered and many are reminded about why they came to the job.

That summary is produced in the UK by the Ministry of Education (the Department for Children, Schools and Families) and the Ministry of Justice – two departments not normally given to great enthusiasm about anything.

Of course it is not uncommon for young people to say 'that's not fair', but they may begin to say that on behalf of other young people in Australia and the wider world, for example those suffering physical or mental abuse or discrimination who cannot access education, healthcare or adequate food. Then the universal nature of human rights and our mutual responsibilities begin to be understood. Human rights education is not all 'doom and gloom' – there are many positive stories, particularly in local newspapers, of people in the community standing up for the rights of others on the issues of homelessness, discrimination against minorities or protecting the environment.

UNICEF UK's 'Rights Respecting Schools' program starts at primary level. Schools win awards by showing that they are teaching civics and human rights in ways that permeate the school ethos. Kids learn their rights, feel included, increase in self-esteem – by aged ten they are learning to negotiate their language and their thinking skills are being extended and they are learning that responsibility means not to bully or harm their peers. They can realise the consequences of their actions, use human rights as a framework for moral judgments and begin to criticise the wielders of power. The ethos is taken from the UN Children's Rights Conventions.

The assessments by school supervisors and OFSTED suggests that a 'Rights Respecting Schools' program improves relationships between young people: there is much less falling out, greater readiness to take responsibility – kids look out for one another more. The atmosphere in the classroom encourages adventurous teachers and has helped language development. Young people grow to expect to have a say in their own learning – they like the fact that it derives from a 'higher authority' that is not school-based. The values at this very basic point are acceptable to all faiths and to most parents and adults working with children and it gives coherence to school policies that enhance school leadership.

So there is growing evidence that such work:

- Improves pupils' self-esteem;
- Enhances pupils' moral development;
- Improves behaviour and relationships;
- Produces more positive attitudes towards diversity in society and reduction of prejudice;
- Helps pupils develop as global citizens;
- Increases the job satisfaction of teachers.

In these ways, universal values can, I think, be taught as part of the Australian story. My concern about the somewhat parochial insistence upon Australian values and Australian history is not so much the underlying political agenda as its triumphalist flavour. We need to understand where these values come from and the capacity for their use in everyday discourse and everyday life. Disciplines of maths, science and geography may themselves be value-free, but education itself is not.

In his 1984 book *Personal and Social Education in the Curriculum*, Richard Pring reminds us about the story of the head teacher who would send her new teachers this letter:

Dear Teacher,

I'm a survivor of a concentration camp. My eyes saw what no man should witness: gas chambers built by learned engineers, children poisoned by educated physicians and infants killed by trained nurses. Women and babies shot and burnt by high school and college graduates. So I'm suspicious of education.

My request is: help your students become human. Your efforts must never produce learned monsters, skilled psychopaths, educated Eichmanns. Reading, writing, arithmetic are important, but only if they serve to make our children more human.

It's surely time to put that insight back into and onto the public school curriculum. Human rights is not history because it isn't past; it's not law because it's still in flux; it's not philosophy, although it does provide some ethics for our time. Nor is it religion because it pays no heed to the supernatural and it's not politics because it's not populist. It is, however, drawn from all these disciplines, and more, in its efforts to define and enforce human values. Values about which a democratic society can't be neutral. It also has the capacity to induce the self-confidence that comes from a sense of dignity because these rights sustain and reflect the dignity of the human person. For students in our state schools, and teachers as well, they serve to show that privilege is an anachronism, dogma destruction, freedom is a birthright and discrimination a wrong that should never be suffered. To the advantages of state education with its secularity, diversity, locality, let us now add humanity.

Chapter 22

TOSCA AND THE TICKING TIME BOMB

'Torture,' said Fortescue, a sixteenth-century English jurist, 'is something that is done by the French.' And it was, for centuries after 1641, the year parliament abolished the king's 'Star Chamber', with its brandings and pilloryings and ear-splittings. A proud tradition in England, but too good for the colonies, where the British army tortured relentlessly in Oman and Malaysia and Kenya, and later in Basra.

The US was worse after 9/11 with its secret rendition program, which ferried terrorist suspects to secret cells in client countries – Egypt, Morocco, Poland and Romania – where they were viciously beaten and mutilated. George W. Bush could dissemble – 'We don't do torture' – while CIA officials supervised torture outside the jurisdiction. (This equivocation was more deplorable than the one for which his predecessor is remembered, namely 'I did not have sexual relations with that woman.')

Wherever armies fight, and whenever 'terrorists' are suspected, the temptation to torture has proven irresistible. Pinochet was a prime example of a ruler who used the foulest tortures – not to discover information that might save lives, but to terrify his opponents. I acted for Human Rights Watch in the case that brought him to some kind of justice, and it taught *me that torture can work – but at a price that only a scoundrel could ever believe to be worth paying. My arguments were set out in the introduction to a book titled* Torture, *published in 2005 by Human Rights Watch.*

Before I became a human rights lawyer, my only encounter with torture came from attending performances of *Tosca*. In Act II, the judge gives a nod (it's a non-singing role) and the politically suspect painter is escorted to an off-stage torture chamber: his pain-wracked notes traumatise his girlfriend during her interrogation by Scarpia, chief of the secret police. To end the torture, Tosca reveals the hiding place of Andreotti, a republican, who is promptly located and killed by Scarpia's death squad. Meanwhile the tortured tenor, who has hobbled back to centre stage, overhears the news of Napoleon's victory over the royalists and lets out of his lungs that great operatic paean to liberty: 'Vittoria!' Its incandescent high C seemed a pretty convincing refutation of the case for state-approved torture, showing that it serves only to inspire defiance and martyrdom.

But not so fast. Let's update Puccini. Suppose Scarpia is 'one of us' (dress him as Donald Rumsfeld) while Andreotti is an 'enemy combatant' recently escaped from Guantanamo, and last seen being equipped in some way by a sacristan – sorry, mullah – in Act I, which is set in the local mosque. Are our sympathies now, ever so slightly, with the judge who – in a legal process advocated by Alan Dershowitz – nods for the torture to start and picks up his pen to record the expected confession? Put Tosca in a burqa, give Cavaradossi a few flying lessons in Florida, and the audience may wish, ever so faintly, to bring back Lynndie England and the alsatians fresh from Abu Ghraib.

In real life, terrorists don't have girlfriends (more's the pity) and the female of the species (e.g. the 'black widow' suicide bombers from Chechnya) can be not only deadlier than the male but hold out longer under interrogation. Tosca, the tender-hearted but air-headed diva (today, she'd be a UN 'goodwill ambassador'), informed on Andreotti because she wanted to stop the suffering of the man she loved. In such cases, torture works.

English common law always refused to adopt the infliction of pain as a device for inducing admissions or proving guilt. There had been exceptions, of course, notably for treason: in the National Archives today you can see how the handwriting on Guy Fawkes's confession trails away after stretching on the rack leaves him too weak to hold the pen. But in the seventeenth century, the Star Chamber (the king's torture chamber) was abolished (1641); 'cruel and unusual punishments' were outlawed in the *Bill of Rights* (1689) and habeas corpus, the fundamental right to challenge state detention, was in 1679 given such statutory force that three centuries later it could still be applied by the US Supreme Court, when pointing out to the Bush administration that due process extended to offshore islands. These safeguards against torture, achieved at a time when it was an established and routine part of criminal justice throughout the continent of Europe, were a form of humanitarian constitutional progress in which we should take Anglo-American-Australian pride.

Just because we have laws against inhumane treatment does not mean they are always obeyed. Suspects are often beaten up in the cells, but at least the common law rules permit cross-examination of police at trial and a rejection of any confession that cannot be proved voluntary. Those suspected of ordinary crime are now protected in Australia and the UK, by rules requiring tape recording (and even video recording) of police interviews.

Special regimes that have been enacted for detention of terrorist suspects, however, often do not afford these protections, and it is in this context, when 'the gloves must come off', that infliction of pain is most tempting for interrogators. In Birmingham in 1974, a few hours after IRA bombs in crowded pubs had killed thirty young people, a number of Irishmen had confessions extracted through force, by police who believed them guilty and were thus consumed with righteous fury. After 'the Birmingham Six' had served almost two decades in prison, the wrongful convictions were finally overturned – but the damage that the case did to the reputation of British justice was incalculable.

Many governments approve the inhumane treatment of detainees 'in the interests of national security'. That was the case in Singapore's 'Marxist conspiracy' detentions in 1988, when the ISD (its secret police) rounded up a group of young lawyers, Catholic aid workers and women playwrights, detaining them for years without trial and subjecting them to what Home Affairs Minister (now Prime Minister) B. G. Lee admitted was 'psychological pressure to get to the truth of the matter . . . the truth would not be known unless psychological pressure was used during interrogation'.

This 'psychological pressure' was described by the detainees who became my clients: it amounted to sleep deprivation (for up to twenty hours), standing for interrogation in cotton pyjamas under sub-zero blasts from an air conditioner; being doused with cold water and enduring threats to have their loved ones arrested for similar treatment.

These 'psychological pressures' were cunningly chosen so that they would leave marks on the mind but not on the body. But what 'truth' did they elicit? My clients said what their paranoid interrogators told them to say: 'I am Marxist-inclined . . . my ideal society is a classless society . . . I was made use of by . . . [insert name of suspect that the ISD wanted an excuse to interrogate].' These 'confessions', made by frightened middle-class idealists to win respite from the deep freeze, were anything but the truth, because the truth in their case was of no interest to conspiracy-fixated interrogators.

We should not underestimate the effect of torture on the weak, the innocent or the mere sympathiser. It can produce amazing results – false admissions to crimes carrying life imprisonment or even death. In the 1930s, Stalin's show trials fooled the world because every defendant's confession was word-perfect. In *Darkness at Noon*, written in 1940, Arthur

Koestler imaginatively attributed to these old Bolsheviks an urge to sacrifice themselves for communism, but the truth we now know to have been more mundane. Before the trial opened, they spent months on 'the conveyor', a disorientation technique in which denial of food and sleep produced suggestibility and acquiescence in the fantastical script written by the prosecutor. They were told at rehearsal that if they changed their lines in the public court room, their wives and children would be killed – and they knew that Stalin's willing executioners were not bluffing.

'The conveyor' has been followed, in the grim argot of state sadism, by 'the parrot's perch', 'the telephone', 'the airplane', 'waterboarding', 'the Liverpool', not to mention old standards like the cattle prod, the cigarette burn and the electrode attached to the genitals. Some years ago I had the privilege of representing Human Rights Watch in proceedings against General Pinochet, and I have kept a copy of his indictment. It contained thirty charges, of which the following are typical:

> That you on or about 29th October 1976 being a public official, namely Commander-in-Chief of the Chilean Army, jointly with others intentionally inflicted severe pain or suffering on José Marcelino Gonzalez Malpu, by applying electric current to his genital organs, shoulders and ankles and pretending to shoot his captive naked mother in front of him, in purported performance of official duties.
>
> That you jointly with others intentionally inflicted severe pain or suffering on Irma del Carmen Parada Gonzalez by:
>
> (a) stripping her of her clothes;
> (b) applying electric current to her mouth, vagina and breasts;
> (c) subjecting her to rape by two men;
> (d) putting her hands into chemicals and introducing them into a machine causing her to lose consciousness;

(e) forcing her to eat putrid food and the human remains of her dead fellow captives; in purported performance of official duties.

That you in 1974 being a public official, namely Commander-in-Chief of the Chilean Army, jointly with others intentionally inflicted severe pain or suffering on others by the employment of 'Papi', a man who had visible open syphilitic sores on his body, to rape female captives and to use on them a dog trained in sexual practices with human beings, in purported performance of official duties.

Given these charges, it is interesting to recall the distinguished people who demanded that Pinochet should never face them. His freedom to live happily ever after was championed by Mrs Thatcher and Dr Kissinger (of course), by Jesse Helms and George Bush Snr (as you would expect) and regrettably by the pope and the pope-in-waiting (Cardinal Ratzinger). Even, and incredibly, by Pinochet's mortal enemy, Fidel Castro, who declared the arrest 'an affront to national sensibilities'. In Australia, John Howard was bewildered at how Pinochet could be prosecuted: he evinced surprise that the law had changed so much since he had studied it.

The law – international human rights law – *has* changed, to the extent that states now owe a duty to the international community to investigate and punish any breach of the absolute prohibition in Article 5 of the *Universal Declaration of Human Rights*: 'No one shall be subjected to torture or to cruel, inhuman or degrading treatment or punishment.'

The 1984 Convention against Torture and Other Cruel, Inhuman or Degrading Treatment or Punishment has now (by the year 2013) been ratified by 153 states. It requires torture suspects to be put on trial or else extradited to a country that *will* put them on trial. Torture is defined by the Convention as the intentional infliction of severe pain or suffering, whether physical or mental, by or with the consent of a public official (excluding the imposition of lawful punishments). The Convention prohibits 'degrading treatment', and there have been several unsatisfactory attempts to draw a distinction with torture. The case most commonly quoted was brought in the European Court of Human Rights by the Republic of Ireland against the UK over 'in-depth interrogation' to which internees in Belfast in 1970 were subjected by the British army. They were hooded and forced to stand for several hours spread-eagled against a wall, while questioning was interspersed with discombobulation from sleep-deprivation and high-pitched noises. The Court held that this treatment was degrading although it did not amount to torture, which was defined as 'deliberate inhumane treatment causing very severe suffering'.

In cases brought against the fascist military junta in Greece, the court had no hesitation in finding that electric shocks, *bastinado* (beating of feet so as to produce pain and swelling), genital assault, burning with cigarettes and sticking pins under nails would all cause pain of sufficient cruelty and intensity to satisfy this definition. In 1999 it emphasised, in a case brought against France, that repeated beatings during police interrogation, causing severe pain over a period of time, amount to 'torture' rather than to 'inhuman treatment'.

For the purposes of the European Convention, the distinction between 'torture' and 'inhuman treatment' does not matter other than for calculation of damages. Both techniques are prohibited. But post-9/11 pronouncements from US officials seize upon the distinction, and declare that the war on terror justifies 'inhuman or degrading treatment' which does not amount to 'torture'. They claim that certain intentional forms of suffering, euphemistically called 'augmented techniques of coercive interrogation', may be inflicted upon terrorist suspects. But the Geneva Conventions, which protect prisoners of war, specifically prohibit 'outrages upon personal dignity', and the Convention prohibits 'cruel, inhuman and degrading treatment'.

The US hides its outrages in military euphemisms: *forced standing* for hours on end; taking advantage of *individual phobias*; *environmental manipulation* (this may involve *adjusting temperature* – presumably as they do in Singapore); *dietary manipulation* (i.e. temporary starvation); *deprivation of light* and *deprivation of auditory stimuli* (blindfolding, or solitary confinement in a darkened cell); *stress positions* (painful shackling and contortions), *forced nudity* (especially in the presence of Alsatians); *isolation* (solitary confinement for thirty days); *working dogs* (one way of taking advantage of *individual phobias*, i.e. the Arab fear of dogs).

The period of US occupation of Iraq will be worst remembered for the obscene pictures of American soldiers enjoying themselves by subjecting detainees at Abu Ghraib to violence and degradation. An army investigation found numerous instances of 'sadistic, blatant and wanton criminal abuses' and the 'sadists on the night shift' received prison sentences ranging from three years (Lynndie England) to ten (Charles Graner). Their behaviour mimicked the more juvenile obsessions of American pornography: victims were forced to masturbate and have sex with each other while leering GIs taunted and humiliated them. Even more serious were the torture pictures – of hooded men hanging from hooks and naked Arabs screaming as Alsatians growled at their genitals. More serious still were pictures of two corpses wrapped in cellophane and packed in ice, in cells plastered with blood.

These torture pictures proved a disastrous own goal for the war on terror, because they became recruiting posters for Al-Qaeda throughout the Middle East. The pretence that they merely depicted the doings of a few rotten apples in an otherwise wholesome US military barrel was soon belied – not only by the official 2004 Schlesinger Report into Defense Department operations, but by a paper trail that showed first how Bush administration lawyers had wilfully misinterpreted the law to approve the use of inhumane interrogation techniques for Guantanamo detainees, and secondly how these techniques had 'migrated' to Iraq, borne by military intelligence officers who naturally assumed that they could get away in Abu Ghraib with what had been approved in Guantanamo. Although the inhumane techniques they had been taught did not extend to forcible sex or harsh beatings, the lessons had left an expectation that the Geneva Conventions were irrelevant and that prisoners could be cruelly treated so long as they were not caused permanent physical injury.

Bush lawyers have in this respect proved bush lawyers. Jay Bybee (now a federal judge) assisted by John Yoo (a Berkeley law professor) defined torture so tightly ('extreme acts of an intensity akin to that which accompanies serious physical injury such as death or organ failure') that pulling fingernails would not qualify. Alberto Gonzales (the US attorney-general in 2005) thought that Islamist jihad 'renders obsolete Geneva's strict limitations on questioning of enemy prisoners and renders quaint some of its provisions', and advised that Guantanamo was beyond the reach of habeas corpus. They turned a blind eye to international law, and believed the US government was entitled to withhold due process from men who are not American citizens and are not imprisoned in the US, and to subject these non-Americans, once located in an offshore limbo-land, to treatment that could qualify as inhuman or degrading.

This approach is not merely provincial, it is counter-productive because, as Senator John McCain points out, it sets an unhappy precedent for captured US servicemen in future wars whose lives may depend upon strict compliance by their captors with the Geneva Conventions.

It puts British and Australian soldiers in peril, too. Those of our fathers and grandfathers held prisoner in Nazi Germany were treated with some dignity, thanks to the Geneva rules relating to POWs. Many were maltreated by the Japanese (who, contrary to myth, were well aware of the rules) but at least some of their captors were punished after the war. Later, in Korea and Vietnam, patchy compliance with the Conventions saved at least some Australian – and many US – lives. That is why we dishonour and diminish the Geneva Conventions at our peril. 'Obsolete' they may be in part (the right of prisoners to smoke cigarettes is certainly outdated and the privileges for officers reflects an antiquated British class system). 'Quaint' they may seem, but only to those ignorant of how they were influenced by the Holocaust. 'The American people are never going to pay for Taliban prisoners to have a musical instrument!' fumed a White House spokesman, failing to appreciate that this rule a) came about because of the importance of orchestras in Jewish ghettoes like Terezin and b) that the Taliban hate music.

The rationale for the rule against torture is not only that it dishonours the state and the legal system that permits it, but that it is counter-productive: much of the evidence elicited will be unreliable, and public sympathy will swing behind victims and their cause. Why then was the Bush administration so keen to permit it and so insouciant about criticism – which Donald Rumsfeld dismissed as 'isolated pockets of international hyper-ventilation'? There was certainly a post-9/11 feeling that the Geneva Conventions were obsolete in this 'new' war on terror, during which information might have to be obtained quickly from captured suspects in order to foil bombings and other atrocities. The 'ticking time bomb' scenario was always quoted, involving a suspect who knows where the bomb is hidden and is not prepared to give the vital information voluntarily. Is it justifiable to torture it out of him in order to save lives – a moral end that would justify unlawful means?

The problem with the hypothesis, of course, is its unreality: fanatics privy to such knowledge either stay silent because they welcome torture and death as martyrdom, or are sufficiently hardened or pain-wracked to supply false information, which distracts police while the time ticks away. The official who orders the torture may think his judgment is moral when in reality it is perverse. James Schlesinger posited a 'minimum harm rule' for the interrogator: do not inflict more pressure than is necessary to get the desired information, but never cause permanent damage and always be prepared to take the consequences. The danger of a minimum harm rule, however, is that interrogators will always ratchet up the pain if they do not get

the desired answers. Schlesinger recommended a professional
ethics program to equip military leaders with a 'sharper moral
compass for guidance in situations often riven with conflicting
moral obligations'. While ethics education is always welcome,
an education in legal obligations, explaining why the law
prohibits torture and cruel and inhuman treatment, would be
more appropriate.

Certain forms of torture often work, especially the kind practised by Pinochet and Hussein where spouses, parents and even
children were maimed and violated within the sight and hearing
of suspects with information their interrogators wanted to
extract. But torture of this kind is so bestial that a Western state
could never sanction it: the only torture that US officials could
authorise – 'stress positions', exploitation of dog phobias, and
Category III techniques (to use the US government's terminology) – will not terrify the real terrorist, and top commanders in
Iraq have admitted that they learned little about the insurgency
by using these techniques.

The Red Cross estimated that seventy-five to ninety per cent
of the detainees had no connection with the insurgency and
no useful information to offer in any event. Yet every Iraqi
subjected to ill-treatment had a dozen or so relatives – sisters,
brothers, parents, wives and children – who became in consequence committed to a blood feud against 'the invaders'.

Multiply this number by the number of prisoners ill-treated
and the number of Iraqi civilians shot accidentally or through
'pre-emptive' action in Fallujah and other flashpoints, and the
reason why so many Iraqis who were well disposed to the overthrow of Saddam came to oppose the US military can readily
be appreciated. The most significant intelligence tip-off – the
whereabouts of Saddam Hussein – came from treating an
internee kindly.

Abu Ghraib may have been characterised by James
Schlesinger as '*Animal House* on the night shift', but on the
day shift, in interrogation rooms, it was institutionalised ill-
treatment, approved at the very top by the US Secretary of State

for Defense. The Americans may have learned little about the insurgency, but would-be insurgents certainly learned something about Americans. As one popular (and initially pro-US) Shia preacher put it in mid-2004, at Friday prayers:

> It was discovered that freedom in this land is not ours. It is the freedom of the occupying soldiers in doing what they like ... abusing women, children, men and the old men and women who they arrested randomly and without any guilt. They express the freedom of rape, the freedom of nudity and the freedom of humiliation.

The rhetoric was provocative, but it drew corroboration from the torture pictures from Abu Ghraib, ironically supporting the message that Iraqis had to fight for their own freedom, against their own liberators. President Bush rightly said that the Abu Ghraib photographs 'do not represent America', but they caused America a massive loss of respect and moral authority. (In Iraq, they fuelled a bloodbath that continues today, almost every day.)

The Schlesinger Report explained how the ill-treatment permitted for Afghan detainees in Guantanamo Bay where the Geneva Conventions were claimed not to apply had 'migrated' to Iraq, where the Geneva Conventions applied with full force. The 'message in the field' was that no distinction should be drawn on grounds of geography: intelligence personnel trained to terrify Arabs in Guantanamo used the same techniques to terrify Arabs in Iraq.

But the Schlesinger Report never grappled with the real problem, which was why it had been necessary to depart from the Geneva Conventions at Guantanamo in the first place. It must have been obvious to those Bush lawyers who recommended this course to the president (mis-stating legal doctrine in the process) that military intelligence officers trained to use inhumane techniques in one war would use them in the next. The Schlesinger Report frankly admitted that the 'brutality and purposeless sadism' extended beyond ordinary soldiers to military intelligence personnel and occurred during interrogation sessions and not only at Abu Ghraib. There was 'both institutional and personal responsibility at higher levels', although the person most responsible – Donald Rumsfeld – had his resignation offer refused by President Bush.

Soldiers and their commanders, under pressure and under deadly threats, will always be tempted to break rules to get results. This 'stuff' always happens in wars and in countries where the occupiers are resented. The only satisfactory deterrent is to prosecute those with 'command responsibility', or at minimum to require their resignation, although the only senior officer prosecuted over Abu Ghraib was Janis Karpinski, who was in charge of the prison. Charges against interrogators should have followed, but they did not. Charges against the 'Bush lawyers' – for permitting or at least bending the law – should have been levelled, as they were at Nuremberg against the Nazi judges, but they were not. International human rights law can lay down rules but it cannot at this juncture require their enforcement against an occupying power.

~

Torture is not confined to the application of pain to induce a suspect to confess. I first encountered it in real life in the atmosphere of death row in Trinidad, when visiting black power radical Michael X after he had been sentenced to hang. There were about thirty men in monkey cages, sweating in the heat, fingers scratching through the wire, screeching and shouting at each other and at the warders. They were allowed neither education nor exercise as they waited in torment for their death warrant to be read. The victim would then be weighed and measured for the drop; the sound of his family wailing and screaming would be interspersed with the sound of the hangman loudly testing 'the trap'.

After spending a few hours on death row, it struck me that men stuck here for years were effectively being tortured, and were certainly subjected to 'cruel and inhuman treatment or punishment', contrary to the 1689 *Bill of Rights* and to the

Trinidadian constitution. Most condemned men in the Carib-
bean – as well as in the US – stay on death row for many years
before their eventual execution, and this prolonged emotional
and psychological suffering is of a different – a more extreme –
dimension of inhumanity than the actual hanging. Although the
death penalty itself is carefully protected from constitutional
challenge, the Privy Council in the case of my clients *Earl Pratt
and Ivan Morgan v Jamaica* held in due course that a prolonged
stay on death row amounted to inhuman or degrading treatment and prevented the state of Jamaica from executing them.
As a consequence, hundreds of death sentences have had to be
commuted.

I believe it is necessary to improve the existing Geneva provisions for monitoring the treatment of persons detained in the
wake of war, whether as POWs, 'enemy combatants', or as
suspected spies or terrorists. Most are at risk of torture, and
the only safeguard is the International Committee of the Red
Cross. Article 3 gives Red Cross representatives a legal right to
enter the prisons and police cells of all belligerents, to monitor
conditions and compliance. This is a task that the Red Cross
has courageously and punctiliously performed, but under a
procedure that has one fatal flaw. It is utterly confidential: Red
Cross reports are secretly sent to a country's high commanders
and are never made available to the public. The mistreatment at
Abu Ghraib was first detected early on by the Red Cross, but its
report to the US Department of Defense was completely ignored
– until it was leaked by some 'deep throat' in the department to
the *Wall Street Journal*. In how many other prisons has the Red
Cross found evidence of torture, yet cannot disclose it or speak
out when the torturers are permitted to continue?

This confidentiality seems unconscionable. If torture is a
crime against humanity (and it is), then covering it up must
always be ethically questionable. The Red Cross justifies secrecy
on the basis that if its reports were published, many governments would not allow it access to their prisons. The argument
is overstated: the Geneva Conventions give it access by right

and countries that refuse would suffer aid and trade sanctions and turn the human rights spotlight on themselves, since the refusal would signify that they had something – namely torture – to hide. But the Red Cross is adamant, with the result that its monitoring can never be a satisfactory safeguard. There are, no doubt, a few governments that would deny it access if its reports were to be made public, but surely it is time for countries like Australia, which both condemn torture and maintain that they have nothing to hide, to take the lead by *waiving* their right to confidentiality in Red Cross reports. Australia should have nothing to hide, although I suspect that we do – in Woomera, Christmas and Manus Islands and Nauru.

The paradox of torture is that all states pay lip-service to its illegality yet many – seventy-three at Amnesty International's last count – still secretly permit the practice. It will never end for terrorist suspects and prisoners of war, unless states are prepared not only to allow independent observers into their prisons, but to suffer publication of their findings. That time may be far off, but the work of organisations like Human Rights Watch brings it closer.

Chapter 23

DR HANEEF

Dr Haneef's case shows how easily panic can prejudice the press and the politicians, how officials may lie, even to a court, if they think the end justifies the means, and how even today the fate of an innocent can depend on the courage of his lawyer. These were a few of the lessons I drew in this preface to Jacqui Ewart's book, Haneef: A Question of Character.

In the great scheme of human rights atrocities, Dr Haneef's sufferings were comparatively minor: a few weeks of wrongful imprisonment and public vilification that frightened his family and has probably left psychological scars. The extent to which the Australian media followed the assumptions of police and politicians that there is no smoke without fire emphasises the point I was trying to make in the banned media hypothetical (see Chapter 20): sometimes the smoke comes from a smoke machine.

Dr Haneef was an innocent man, presumed guilty by overzealous police and prosecutors, and over-excited politicians and pressmen. That his ordeal lasted only twenty-five days was due to the courage and dedication of his lawyers and the independence of the magistrate who gave him bail and the judge who condemned the immigration minister for cancelling his visa. But the extent of government misconduct and prosecutorial incompetence gives his case a special significance for the civil liberties of all Australian citizens. At a time when the case for a charter of rights is challenged by the arguments that only elected politicians can be trusted to protect liberty, the case of Dr Haneef provides a powerful refutation.

Shockwaves were felt throughout the world when in June 2007 two young hospital doctors tried to bomb a packed London disco and later made a terrorist attack on Glasgow airport. That men professionally dedicated to the saving of life should fall prey to a barbaric creed that impelled them to attempt the mass murder of innocent civilians was both astonishing and frightening. When an Indian doctor employed by a Gold Coast hospital was briefly identified by Scotland Yard as a person possibly connected to these terrorists through a SIM card he had lent to one of their friends several years before, the reaction in Australia was panicky, dishonest and over the top. The media invented a 'sleeper cell' of medical terrorists; politicians gave self-promoting press conferences that prejudiced the defendant and hampered the investigation; senior policemen closed minds that should have stayed open and decided that because there were reasons to suspect Dr Haneef, he must be guilty.

It should in fairness be pointed out that initial suspicions of Dr Haneef were not unreasonable. It looked as though he was fleeing the country immediately after the attempted atrocity in Glasgow: only then did he book his ticket to India to see his six-day-old baby, and it was a one-way ticket; the haste of his departure was apparently evidenced by the fact that he left washing on the line and dishes in the sink. Police were right to intercept him at the airport and to subject him to a lengthy interrogation (they asked 1116 questions over a twelve-hour period) to clear up all their reasonable doubts. When his answers provided convincing explanations, as they did, he should have been released on bail, and completely discharged a few days later when it became clear that he was not implicated by Scotland Yard's inquiries in the UK, or by any evidence in Australia.

Instead, he suffered three weeks of wrongful imprisonment. He was wrongly charged, without evidence, by the Australian Federal Police and when he applied for bail false statements were made on behalf of the Director of Public Prosecutions to prevent him from obtaining release. This alone was outrageous. Then John Howard, the prime minister, doubtless sensing an early election advantage, criticised the Queensland Labor government for failing to vet Dr Haneef for terrorist connections before allowing him to work in its hospitals, while Philip Ruddock, attorney-general at the time, stirred up as much prejudice as possible by press statements. It took a courageous magistrate at a second hearing to grant Dr Haneef bail after he had been in detention for ten days.

It was at this point that the Minister of Immigration, Kevin Andrews, disgracefully contrived to keep him in detention by cancelling his immigration visa on 'character' grounds that he should have known to be bogus. (A former Supreme Court judge, John Clark, later described his action as 'astounding'.) Meanwhile no less than six hundred federal and state police were deployed in an effort to turn over Dr Haneef's life and contacts in a hunt for 'negative' information about him and to give politicians further opportunities for publicising themselves and prejudicing his case by referring to his 'terrorist associations'. And all this time, in secret and in vain, ASIO was reporting to the government that Dr Haneef had no terrorist connections at all.

One merit of Jacqui Ewart's book is that it brings home just how much power of the state was brought to bear against Dr Haneef – and how this Goliath was toppled by brave lawyering. Through smears and leaks, police and politicians had sent the media into a feeding frenzy of hostility towards the defendant. This finally abated and even turned in his favour when his counsel, Stephen Keim SC, released his 142-page police interview, in which the doctor had explained away all their suspicions. For this action Keim was vilified, especially by Ruddock, by John Howard, by Police Commissioner Mick Keelty and even by an editor from the *Australian*, Paul Kelly.

What they all seemed incapable of comprehending was that transcripts of police interviews are not confidential – on the contrary, the right of a suspect and his lawyers to publish them is a vital safeguard against abusive secret policing. Such transcripts are not usually released to the press by the defence, for the simple reason that they usually show defendants in a poor light, struggling to answer difficult questions. However, since Haneef answered every question satisfactorily, and the transcript refuted the smears and falsehoods put about by police and press, it was plainly his lawyer's duty to put the interview in the public domain. By so doing Mr Keim performed his duty to his client, and to the public and to the court, and his action lifted the miasma of guilt that the irresponsible media and the self-serving politicians had dumped upon his client. Those who complained about Keim's 'unprofessional' conduct revealed their own ignorance of what the adversary system requires of counsel in these fraught circumstances. For all the obloquy that lawyers attract (sometimes justifiably) the work of Keim and his team serves as a reminder that dedicated lawyering may be the citizen's only protection against the abuse of state power.

The case demonstrates beyond any doubt just how preposterous is the claim that liberty will be safe in the hands of politicians – the refrain from those who oppose a charter of human rights. The official report into the Haneef affair, by former judge John Clarke, was an indictment of government ministers for making 'astonishing' and 'troubling' decisions to deny liberty to an innocent person. On its publication, the *Australian* newspaper argued editorially that a charter of rights was not necessary because overzealous politicians and public servants could be exposed by the media – especially by 'the *Australian*'. 'The truth' it pompously proclaimed 'was revealed by this newspaper doing its job . . . by journalists acting on the public's right to know.' Readers of Ms Ewart's book will learn just how absurd this statement is: the truth was revealed by Stephen Keim QC through his action in releasing Dr Haneef's interview to the *Australian* journalist Hedley Thomas, who only then was able to realise how uncritical he and his fellow journalists had been of the police line that Haneef was a terrorist. Had a federal charter of rights been in place, Dr Haneef would not have been charged without any evidence in the first place, and the minister would have been advised of the illegality of cancelling his visa – and that alone would have saved the doctor at least fourteen days of wrongful detention.

But some people never learn – John Howard, for example. In August 2009, in a Menzies lecture in Perth, he condemned a charter for 'handing powers to unelected judges'. 'Trust the politicians' is his message ('I always thought a member of parliament was a decision maker and not a buck passer'). Jacqui Ewart's book enables readers to test his argument by asking themselves, after reading it, whether in the event of their unjustified arrest or some other incursion on their liberty, they would rather have their dispute with the authorities decided by the likes of Kevin Andrews and Philip Ruddock, bending the truth for political advantage, or by independent and impartial judicial decision makers like magistrate Jacqui Payne (who gave Haneef bail), or Justice Jeffrey Spender (who quashed Andrews' decision to cancel the visa). Judges are unelected precisely so they may decide without fear or favour disputes between the citizen and the state. Any charter that promotes trial by judges as against trial by politicians or trial by media should be welcomed by all thinking Australians.

Chapter 24

UNDER A BORROWED MORTAR BOARD

Barristers realise they are growing old when their judges look younger. For academics, I guess it's when they start being awarded honorary degrees. This event is a carefully choreographed ego trip: your assumed achievements are sonorously orated (if dubious, this can be in Latin) and one's failures are never mentioned. Sometimes you are even allowed to keep the gown.

But offers of honorary degrees come with a pro bono quid pro quo, *namely a duty to say something inspiring to the graduates – and, more importantly, to their mums and dads – gathered in serried ranks in front of you. Modern universities turn out hundreds of degree recipients at these ceremonies – a rite of passage in which the orator must play a part by offering a quotient of Polonius-like precepts that convey the message that education endows wisdom, and (these days) that it is worth all the expense.*

At Sydney University in 2006, these were the thoughts offered to those whose vocations as teachers and social workers were about to begin.

Mr Chancellor,

I am humbled by this honour you have seen fit to bestow on me – indeed, I wish the citation were still spoken in Latin, to spare my blushes. Perhaps it should have been spoken in Scottish – in Glasgow recently, the chairman of a meeting who spoke in a broad Scots accent introduced me as what sounded like 'a distinguished liar'.

In spite of all temptations to belong to other nations, I remain Australian. Any purpose my life has served was shaped and guided at this campus of Sydney University. It was an oasis of inspiration and disputation when I dived into it, from the springboard of Epping Boys High School, in 1964 until 1970, working for degrees in Arts and Law.

It is said that if you can remember the sixties, you can't have lived through them. In Australia the sixties didn't begin until the election of the Whitlam government in 1972, so my time here I remember all too vividly. I pay tribute to my teachers, especially to philosophers Alan Stout and Julius Stone and Tony Blackshield, and criminologists and constitutionalists like Gordon Hawkins, Duncan Chappell and Garth Nettheim. I learnt even more from three older students who had already commenced provocative public careers – Michael Kirby, Richard Walsh and the late Charlie Perkins. And of course from my own contemporaries on the SRC, friends then and friends now, like Jim Spigelman and Joe Skrzynski, Nick Greiner and Alan Cameron, Clare Petrie and Meredith Burgmann. We amalgamated the men's and women's union, we actually sued the university to establish the rights of students not to be expelled without due process; we insisted the SRC should participate in all decision-making processes that affected students. And looking out from this intellectual shelter, financially secure in our Commonwealth scholarships and funded by mandatory student union fees, we tried to challenge with law suits and protests and freedom rides some of the dead verities of the Menzies era: the White Australia policy, censorship of literature, contempt for the poor – and indifference towards Aborigines, who then were not even counted in the census.

In that distant era, learning at this university meant learning how and why to reject ideas that were cruel or obsolete or discriminatory. We left here with the notion that there was no such thing as 'pure' scholarship: that scholarship could never be pure unless it pointed a way to benefit society. That is probably why I feel so honoured to have been awarded this degree in the company of future teachers and social workers rather than of lawyers – a class whose benefit to society is more open to question.

This is your day, not mine. You have, after all, had to work for your degree. So let me first congratulate you on your success and congratulate your families for helping you achieve it, especially those parents who have not themselves had a university background. I know from sacrifices made by my own mother and father what you have had to go through and how crucial your support has been to the success of your sons and daughters, as one day they will come fully to understand – probably when they have adolescent students of their own. So don't stint on family pride: the degree your children hold in their hands is proof positive of their capacity to do good in the world.

That is the second reason for congratulations: the choice you have made at this stage to commit your talents to education or social work. You live in a country of considerable, if not yet common, wealth. Once we rode to prosperity on the sheep's back and for the future we shall apparently prosper by selling uranium to everyone, except of course to Iran. Our land abounds in nature's gifts, many still safe from developers, and the physicality of our culture is represented by our Midas touch for gold medals at games. But these are fairly easy virtues: the true test of a nation is how it treats its most vulnerable, its unformed or uninformed, even its most unprepossessing.

On that score we don't rate so highly, certainly when it comes to allotting resources to public schooling and to health and social services. So you will need your own resourcefulness to make a difference: but what a difference you *can* make. Nothing is more important, especially in the underrated sector of primary education, than teaching a child to think, unless it is identifying and rectifying the reason why the child is not thinking. There are few more valuable tasks than those that social work require, whether in helping refugees adjust or saving children from abuse or assisting disadvantaged clients to cut through the red tape of welfare entitlements.

Politicians think your virtue should be its own reward. You will be badly paid, probably, and receive inadequate practical training. You will be traduced by ignorant newspaper columnists and radio shock jocks, who will never themselves have done a real day's work in their lives but who will stigmatise you as 'do-gooders'. As distinct, I suppose, from the 'do-badders' they prefer to celebrate.

Let me offer just one word of advice: don't give them a free kick. Temper your idealism with street wisdom, never let your capacity for kindness override your judgment. It is true that poverty, social exclusion, discrimination and sheer bad luck causally contribute to the human hardships you will encounter – but some unfortunates *are* the authors of their own misfortune. I have no doubt that there is the same percentage of bad people in refugee camps and ethnic communities and welfare centres as there is in Vaucluse or Mosman. Don't think that *society* is always responsible for crime, or that underprivilege can excuse a callous lack of consideration for fellow human beings. There *are* bludgers and dole cheats, greedy shonks on welfare as well as on high salaries in AWB*; there are tribal customs that deserve to be called torture and there is misogyny in most religions, not just in Islam. Doing good is *always* the best thing to do but it does no good to permit people to avoid the consequences of reckless or selfish actions. I hope you will retain your idealism but at the same time I hope it will be tempered by a preparedness to judge and, if necessary, to condemn.

I am talking of morality, not law. It was my generation who explained that moral rules are relative, if they follow merely from tradition or religion or political affiliation. But it has been

---

* Australian Wheat Board, implicated in ripping off the UN's Oil for Food program in Iraq

an achievement of civil society in recent years to agree on a set of *universal* values, which brook no exception based on custom or geography. These universal values are based not on human *dogma* but on human *dignity*: they are universal because their denial in one country, or even in one town, affects and shames us all.

They were first listed in the *Universal Declaration of Human Rights*, that great charter by which the world said 'Never again' after the Holocaust. It was prepared by Eleanor Roosevelt, who on 10 December 1948 handed it to the Chairman of the General Assembly of the United Nations – as it happened, a famous graduate of Sydney University, Dr H. V. Evatt. He had been a crucial supporter of the Genocide Convention, which had been introduced the previous day, and a few months later came the Geneva Conventions for protecting prisoners of war: they formed that great post-war human rights triptych, setting out the basic principles by which state action should be judged. We have been slow to enforce them on an international level: only since the Pinochet case in 1999 did we work out ways to put tyrants on trial for mass murdering their own people. Those of us who work in Africa know the truth that eludes lachrymose Irish pop singers: unless we first eradicate civil war and corruption, we will not make poverty history, we will make poverty inevitable. But we are making a start, as last week's surrender of Charles Taylor to my court in Sierra Leone shows.

Back in Australia we are often apt to forget the wise words of Eleanor Roosevelt, as she handed the *Universal Declaration of Human Rights* to Dr Evatt:

> Where, after all, do universal rights begin? In small places, close to home – so close and so small that they cannot be seen on any maps of the world ... Unless these rights have meaning there, they have little meaning anywhere. Without concerned citizen action to uphold them close to home, we shall look in vain for progress in the larger world.

Unfortunately, in Australia there has been unthinking resistance to adopting the device that in other countries now serves to make human rights a reality, which enables them to be taught proudly to children in schools and used by social workers to ensure their clients have access to health, education and housing. It is called a bill of rights and it provides a way of taking court action to force governments to deliver on them. Its first five years in the UK have seen disadvantaged groups benefit – mental patients, the disabled, school children, prisoners and so on, but the greatest beneficiaries have simply been citizens tangled up in red tape, unable to obtain their entitlements because of bureaucratic incompetence or bloody-mindedness.

Since a bill of rights has proved so important as a measure of fair governance and for educators and social services in the UK and Canada, in New Zealand and throughout Europe, why is it resisted here?

Politicians fear it would restrict their power to govern as they like, while senior public servants fear it will put pressure on them to treat members of the public fairly. These are bad arguments, although they tend to prevail among a people who have been made scared of constitutional change. They are told to be happy with things the way they are: 'If it ain't broke, don't fix it.' This is an idiotic argument against improvement, which would have us still flying around in DC3s, driving golden Holdens and playing LPs. The case for standing still, for avoiding change even when it is going on all around us, plays on our own insecurity, so we allow ourselves to be comforted by the notion that in Australia we live in the best of all possible worlds, and those who want to improve it are 'do-gooders' – or worse, 'intellectuals'. We pay lip-service to the notions of liberty and fair play, but refuse to entrench them in our constitution. So first, perhaps, we should entrench them in our culture, in the way we teach our own history.

This is a subject about which neo-conservatives have become very concerned. They think it is being taught too provocatively in schools, in ways that give the impression we have not yet arrived in the best of all possible worlds. But I want to suggest that you teach Australian history and citizenship more provocatively, and perhaps more truthfully.

For example, teach that Ned Kelly was a multiple murderer, that Gallipoli was a military and moral disaster, attributable to knee-jerk obeisance to stupid British generals. Teach that John Howard's own heroes – Menzies and Fadden – were imperialists whose incompetent leadership imperilled Australia in its darkest hour. And don't over-venerate the Whitlam years: remember the financial disasters and how dishonest ministers placed the economy in the hands of a shady black marketeer.

Ask cultural questions – is our fabled 'mateship', for example, any more than a protective sexist ritual for emotionally inarticulate males? As for our constitution, explain that it was drafted by men who thought like Pauline Hanson, obsessed with racial purity: they spoke of Aborigines in the Convention debates as if they were native animals and they argued 'Australia' into existence for the purpose of stopping Chinese immigration and to prevent Queensland planters from importing 'Kanakas' from the Pacific Islands.

But remember, there are inspiring and amazing people and achievements in Australian history, although teachers rarely mention them. As well as disasters like Gallipoli, we should remember triumphs like Milne Bay, when Australia's fledgling fighter pilots and outnumbered AIF turned the tide of battle against the hitherto invincible and barbaric Japanese forces. We should celebrate apolitically John Curtin's steadfastness in that 'darkest hour'; our children should be taught the vital contribution 'Doc' Evatt and his team made to the post-war world order, and yes, even to applaud John Howard's finest hour, his commitment of troops to East Timor – an exercise so potentially dangerous that the US funked it.

Teach our children proudly, from whatever countries they come, about how Australia pioneered universal suffrage and votes for women and maternity allowances, and invented the secret ballot and the basic wage, and how miners at Broken Hill achieved the thirty-five-hour week for workers in dangerous jobs fifty years before that idea caught on overseas. Ours was the first Commonwealth parliament to introduce a *Freedom of Information Act* and comprehensive court oversight of public service decisions.

These achievements might proudly reflect a society that determined to give its people an entrenched legal right to a 'fair go'. That means the law must come into it: if we are to preserve our right to a 'fair go' in a way that citizens understand and public servants and politicians respect, then this entitlement must be written into law. If 'rights' are not capable of enforcement then they are not 'rights' at all, but empty promises. Although we talk with some pride of our freedoms, we have never taken the opportunity to set them down in writing in any covenant, by which those in power promise the people they will not restrict them. Australia is the only advanced democracy in the world that offers no constitutional protection for the rights of its citizens. There is nothing about human liberty in our constitution that we can point to with pride, or happily invite our children to recite in school. We will not, I fear, have an interesting future until we tell of a more inspiring past, a past where we participated in, and sometimes led, human progress.

'Teach the children well' sang Crosby, Stills, Nash & Young in the sixties. It became one of my generation's anthems, a kind of promise that our children would embrace different values, would be inspired by the real truths of our history to press for legal rights to liberty and fair treatment, so that we could move forward as a society: if we could not do good, we could at least do better. But we have failed to make rights meaningful and enforceable at that domestic level where Eleanor Roosevelt and 'Doc' Evatt knew they would be most needed. The challenge to teach our grandchildren well now falls to you; you are too young to be Generation X or Y, perhaps you are Generation Z – alphabetically, our last chance. I wish you every success.

Chapter 25

THE GREAT CHARTER DEBATE: FATHER FRANK'S CARAVANSERAI, WITH A STATUTE OF LIBERTY

The first Rudd government, in a flush of idealism, appointed a commission under Father Frank Brennan to consider whether Australia should have a charter – a bill of rights. It reported in due course that this would, on balance, be a good idea, especially to provide some degree of justice and fairness to those who would otherwise 'fall through the cracks' – the poor, the sick and the disadvantaged. But by this time, the enemies of the poor, sick and disadvantaged – the Liberal Party, the Catholic Church, the Murdoch press and Bob Carr – had effectively killed it by alarmist and spurious arguments.

I refuted them in a book entitled The Statute of Liberty: How Australians Can Take Back Their Rights. *It still surprises me that lesser academics and self-styled constitutional 'experts' can describe a charter as 'a danger to democracy', overlooking the fact that other advanced democracies – Canada, the UK, the US, all countries in Europe and even New Zealand – have bills of rights that have not endangered their record for representative government.*

In the event that the debate returns, which it most probably will after a few years of Prime Minister Abbott, here is an article I wrote in 2009 about the Brennan Commission's Report followed by my draft of an Australian 'Statute of Liberty'.

Father Frank's Caravanserai

The most remarkable feature of Frank Brennan's *National Human Rights Consultation Report* is its projection of the voices of 'ordinary people' (a somewhat condescending phrase, used by lawyers to describe people who are not lawyers). These voices are alternatively laconic, passionate, revelatory and querulous, all dialogue guaranteed verbatim, as heard by Father Frank's caravan on its travels from Paraburdoo to Mindarie and thence to Yarrabah. They speak of hospitals that turn away patients, police stations that ignore reports of crime, and even a public toilet in Alice Springs that charges an entrance fee high enough to deter you-know-who.

The consultation committee's brief, according to the attorney-general's office, was to 'conduct a nationwide consultation to examine the protection and promotion of human rights and responsibilities in Australia'. The report's simple finding is that our wealthy and allegedly egalitarian society disrespects many classes of its citizens. Most serious is the plight of those who 'fall between the cracks' – the homeless, the aged, the mentally impaired and physically disabled, children in care and indigenous Australians living in conditions of 'third world disadvantage'. The committee also found that the Great Dividing Range is more than a geographical barrier: there is a massive difference in basic health, education and welfare-service provision between those who live in cities and those who live in rural or remote areas. These indignities and iniquities would be ameliorated, the report's authors reason convincingly, by the adoption of a federal bill of rights.

In other words, those who oppose a charter – including, most stridently, the editors of and many of the commentators in the *Australian* – are hostile to a measure that, on all the evidence, offers some chance of betterment for the poor and oppressed. The onus now falls on those commentators to demonstrate that their objections – political, for the most part, or lawyer-phobic – are sufficiently weighty to outbalance the evident public good of improving the lot of our downunderdogs.

Brennan finds little substance in their objections. A 'lawyer's banquet' a charter most certainly is not: most of the human-rights work would be done by community legal centre lawyers, who are paid less than cadet journalists. The argument that judges will be empowered to override parliament is convincingly refuted: the charter model endorsed by Brennan would merely enable judges, if the language of a statute is ambiguous, to assume that parliament intended the meaning most consonant with human rights. In dealing with controversial issues such as euthanasia, abortion, gay marriage and so on, parliament would remain supreme.

Reactions to the Brennan recommendations so far have been knee-jerk political. Many of its antagonists condemn the idea of a charter because they believe it is some kind of left-wing plot. For Liberals, this delusion may be an ideological hangover from John Howard's day, but it is philosophically mistaken. A bill of rights is an impeccably conservative idea. The great right-wing thinkers – going back to Edmund Burke, William Blackstone and Albert Dicey – all cherished rights that limited the power of government and were entrenched in the common law (that is, the law that is made by judges). Winston Churchill, in his impassioned speech to the Hague Conference in 1948, urged the adoption of a bill of rights for every country in Europe in order to protect democracies 'guarded by freedom and sustained by law' where 'the people own the government, not the government the people'. It was Churchill who insisted on establishing the European Court of Human Rights, building upon a proposal first made at the 1946 Paris Peace Conference by Dr H. V. Evatt. Two top advisers to Britain's conservative prime minister, David Cameron, recently published a pamphlet in praise of bills of rights under the title 'Churchill's Legacy'. Someone should send a copy to the Queensland Liberal senator and shadow attorney-general George Brandis, who keeps warning that a charter would be 'inimical to democratic values'.

Senator Brandis has come some distance in the course of the Brennan consultation: the Liberals are still opposed to

Churchill's legacy, but Brandis is all for human rights education (which should be the government's highest priority, in Brennan's view) and now wants 'a comprehensive audit of existing legislation, to identify and repair gaps in human rights protection under existing law'. What he does not appreciate is that existing legislation is a morass of technical and pettifogging verbiage; simply 'auditing' (that is, reading) it will not reveal the human rights problems it can cause in practice. Only a charter can do that; if a charter were in place, the courts would operate as true auditors, either by interpreting ambiguous legislation in conformity with human rights, or by declaring it incompatible with the rights guaranteed by the charter and referring the matter back to parliament. That is a real audit. How many more years in opposition will it take for the Liberals to realise that it is a very good thing to have a check on government power?

Many years, if the New South Wales government is anything to go by. In a state where government incompetence is exceeded only by government corruption, the penny still has not dropped. The New South Wales Labor Party's ferocious opposition to a *Human Rights Act* is not unconnected to its fear of being called to account for the indignities in its hospitals, care homes and other public services, not to mention the corruption that leaches from one of its right-wing factions. As for the National Party, it might have been expected to welcome the Brennan Report's exposure of the discrepancies between city and country, and to do voters in remote areas a favour by declaring its support for a charter. Instead, its members shout 'left-wing plot', failing to recognise that a charter would serve the interests of their constituents.

The truth, of course, is that human rights are apolitical. A charter will disfavour whichever party is in government because it will be used to expose maladministration and to offer some protection to minorities from unfair or oppressive treatment. Ideally it would be introduced with cross-party support, although that seems many years away. The education Brennan advocates may in time produce greater awareness of a charter's benefits, and will in any event help to produce more engaged citizens. (Human rights courses in Canadian and British schools have been credited with doing exactly that, while reducing bullying and encouraging better behaviour and greater respect for students from ethnic minorities and even for teachers.)

One deficiency of the report is its failure to concentrate on rights that have emerged through the Australian experience, rather than those handed down by international treaties. The problem is that the easiest way to introduce a federal charter is as an exercise of the federal parliament's external affairs power – that is, as legislation implementing international treaties that Australia has already ratified. Such treaties tend to be of the 'lowest common denominator' variety, and would give the charter a foreign rather than Australian flavour. For this reason, many human rights experts in England now want to replace the European Convention on Human Rights with a *British* bill of rights.

In the history of the struggle for human rights, Australia has some great stories to tell, beginning in 1787 when Captain Arthur Phillip devised the 'First Law' that asserted 'there will be no slavery in a free land and hence no slaves' many years before William Wilberforce achieved the abolition of slavery in Britain. The subsequent emancipist battles for the right to vote and for trial by jury, and Chief Justice Forbes's declarations striking down Governor Darling's censorship of the press, are worth celebrating, as are the egalitarian passions of the Eureka Stockade and the Great Shearers' Strike of 1891, and Henry Parkes's commitment to secular state schooling. Eleanor Roosevelt recognised that Australia contributed more than any other nation to the definition and development of the principles enshrined by the *Universal Declaration of Human Rights*.

We were the first to guarantee the minimum wage, the forty-hour week, paid holidays, long-service leave and even the fabled 'smoko', harbinger of the right to 'down time' at work. Doc Evatt and his delegates ensured that rights to health, education and welfare – the very rights most needed, according to Brennan, by those on the margins of our modern society – were included in the *Universal Declaration of Human Rights*, which calls upon all nations to protect human rights through domestic legislation. Tailoring such a domestic law to our own experiences, rather than anchoring it in the simplistic miasma of UN conventions, is the best way forward.

Brennan's most notable failure, at the end of a very long day (five hundred pages and many thousands of kilometres: this was a journey to rival that of Priscilla, Queen of the Desert) is the absence of any draft of his proposed bill of rights. Exhaustion, perhaps, accounts for this – his committee achieved a great deal in just nine months. But since the proof of the pudding is in the eating, we should at least see the dish before deciding whether to partake.

~

Here, then, is my recipe for the pudding – a fully fledged and up-to-date charter, an Australian Statute of Liberty – although it begins with Arthur Phillip's first law for the Great South Land. It comes with a preamble, which might alternatively serve as a template for a new preamble to the Australian constitution, of the kind currently sought by Aboriginal groups who want to be mentioned in it, with the approval of Prime Minister Abbott.

Of course, drafting preambles can be difficult, as John Howard discovered. Notwithstanding help from poet Les Murray, his stumblebum effort put to a referendum in 1999 ('We value excellence as well as fairness, independence as dearly as mateship') was roundly rejected.

The greatest of all preambles began, in Thomas Jefferson's first draft of the Declaration of Independence, 'We hold these truths to be sacred and undeniable'. When he read it to Benjamin Franklin, the latter shook his head – 'smacks of the pulpit, Mr Jefferson, smacks of the pulpit. They are . . . *self evident* are they not?' Jefferson agreed, and the rest is history – US history, at any event, recited now by every child of school age.

Here, our horse-and-buggy constitution offers no such inspiration: my wet-Sunday-afternoon effort is an attempt to illustrate how it might.

Statute of Australian Liberty

Preamble

Whereas the people of Australia, united in one indissoluble Commonwealth, declare it the democratic duty of their parliaments and elected bodies and government officials to uphold, protect and advance their hard-won liberties, and being:

> ***Humble** in acknowledging the first owners and occupiers of this unique continent, whose ancestors have walked about on its earth for many thousands of years before British settlement;*

> ***Sorrowful** for the dispossession, discrimination and degradation they have endured and **resolved** hereafter to respect their relationship with the land and to atone for past wrongs by future equity;*

> ***Proud** nonetheless of our progress from penal colony to a free nation of boundless opportunity, unrestricted by divisions of class or caste or private wealth, and an example to the world of the ever-present possibility of reformation of the human spirit;*

> ***Dedicated** to democracy as defined in the federal constitution, under which all who have a stake in the nation shall have a say in its governance;*

> ***Grateful** for the British legacy of liberty first planted in this country by Governor Arthur Phillip, for Magna Carta's great promise that to no one will justice be denied or delayed, for jury trial and the importance of free speech, for a common law that presumes innocence and abominates torture and for the way these fundamental*

*freedoms have been nurtured and embellished by gener-
ations of Australians;*

Cognisant *of the achievements of our country in providing better ways of working through labour rights and
collective bargaining and the basic wage;*

Invigorated *by a creative culture that encourages innovation and the development of new ways of working and
enjoying life;*

Mindful *that rights entail responsibilities, and that
Australia expects its citizens to show tolerance, respect
and mutual consideration for their fellows, to abjure
violence and embrace peaceful change, and willingly to
share community burdens for the common good of the
Commonwealth;*

Determined *that all shall have a stake in the prosperity
of this nation and those most in need shall have a moral
and legal claim on our compassion;*

Inspired *by the Anzac tradition of preparedness to fight
for freedom, internationally and in our region, against
any movement that threatens to extinguish the rights of
humankind;*

Respectful *of the* Universal Declaration of Human
Rights, *in the drafting of which Australia had the privilege to participate, and of all the treaties we have ratified
to uphold the dignity of individuals in this nation and
throughout the world*

*hereby resolve that the liberties our forebears struggled and
sacrificed to achieve and which are set out in the following
29 paragraphs shall hereafter inure for the benefit of all who
live in this land.*

CHARTER OF AUSTRALIAN LIBERTY

1. FREEDOM FROM SLAVERY

That there can be no slavery in a free land and hence no slaves.

2. PROHIBITION ON TORTURE

No one shall be subjected to a) torture or b) to cruel or inhumane or degrading treatment or punishment.

3. RIGHT TO LIFE

Every person has, after he or she is born, the right not to be arbitrarily deprived of life. Any loss of life attributable to agencies of the state must be carefully and independently investigated. No death penalty shall be exacted in Australia.

4. FREEDOM FROM COMPULSION

No one shall be compelled to work except by order of a court. There shall be no conscription for military service other than in a national emergency and in that event with provision for conscientious objection. No one should be subjected to medical or scientific experimentation unless they give free and informed consent.

5. RIGHT TO BE SET AT LIBERTY

No one shall be detained or imprisoned other than in compliance with the law and every detained person shall have the right to bring an action for habeas corpus, namely to be produced speedily before a court and to be set free unless the detaining authority can prove its actions are lawful.

6. RIGHTS ON ARREST

No one shall be arrested or imprisoned for debt or for inability to perform a contractual obligation. Persons arrested or detained on a criminal charge:

i)   *shall be informed promptly, and if practicable in a language they understand, of the reason for their arrest and the details of any charge;*

ii) *must be brought before a court as soon as practicable and in any event within forty-eight hours of arrest. In terrorist*

*cases, parliament may provide for up to seven days'
detention, renewable by judicial order for a further seven
days.*

iii) *shall be entitled to legal advice while in custody prior to
their first court appearance;*

iv) *shall be entitled to have any interviews with police or
persons in authority recorded by electronic means or by an
independent third party;*

v) *shall be entitled to apply to the court for bail, which
if granted on security or by surety shall not be for an
exorbitant amount.*

7. THE OPEN JUSTICE PRINCIPLE

*Every court in the land shall be open to the media and the
public, unless it be established beyond reasonable doubt that
justice cannot be done other than by their exclusion for part
of the proceedings. In any such case, the judgment of the court
shall be made public.*

8. RIGHT TO TRIAL BY JURY

*Every person charged with an offence carrying a maximum
sentence of more than two years' imprisonment has a right
(which may be waived) to be tried by a jury.*

9. THE RIGHT TO FAIR TRIAL

i) *In the determination of civil rights and obligations or of
any criminal charge every litigant or defendant is entitled
to a fair and public hearing within a reasonable time by an
independent and impartial tribunal established by law.*

ii) *All persons charged with criminal offences shall be
presumed innocent until proved guilty according to law.*

iii) *Every person charged with a criminal offence has the
following minimum rights:*

    a) *to be informed promptly, in a language that they
understand and in reasonable detail of the nature and
cause of the accusation;*

b) *to have adequate time and facilities for the preparation of their defence and to have the opportunity to communicate with legal representatives;*

c) *to attend their own trial and defend themself in person or through legal assistance of their own choosing or, if they have not sufficient means to pay for legal assistance, to be given it free when the interests of justice so require;*

d) *to examine or have examined witnesses against them and to obtain the attendance and examination of witnesses on their behalf under the same conditions as adverse witnesses;*

e) *to have assistance from an interpreter, free of charge, if they cannot understand or speak the language used in court;*

f) *to put the prosecution to proof of guilt;*

g) *if convicted, to have the right to ask a higher court for leave to appeal on reasonably arguable grounds against conviction and/or sentence.*

10. NO PUNISHMENT WITHOUT LAW

i) *No one shall be found guilty of any crime on account of any act or omission that did not constitute a criminal offence under Australian or international law at the time it was committed. Nor shall a heavier penalty be imposed than the one that was applicable at the time the offence was committed.*

ii) *No person may be punished more than once for the same offence.*

11. FREEDOM OF MOVEMENT

i) *Every person lawfully present in Australia has freedom to move across state borders and to choose where in the country to live. Every citizen of Australia shall be entitled to an Australian passport and, subject to any court order, may leave the country with a guaranteed right to return.*

Every holder of an Australian passport shall be entitled to consular assistance if detained or arrested in a foreign country and to such efforts and representations by the Australian government as may ensue that his or her rights under this charter are respected. Every person accepted for residence in Australia shall be afforded the opportunity to become an Australian citizen.

ii) *Australia will entertain asylum claims from any persons who come to or within its jurisdiction and allege they are refugees under the Refugee Convention 1951 and can establish they are fleeing from a country where they have a well-founded fear of being persecuted in a way that will endanger their life or that of family members for exercising human rights of the kind protected by this charter. A precondition of such claim must be a proven willingness to accept the rights and the responsibilities set forth in this charter.*

iii) *No person shall be accepted for naturalisation or citizenship unless he or she can demonstrate an understanding of this charter and can swear or affirm that they accept its responsibilities and its rights.*

12. FREEDOM OF EXPRESSION AND THE RIGHT TO KNOW

(i) *Everyone has the right to freedom of expression, which includes the right to hold and express opinions and to receive and impart information and ideas without interference by government.*

(ii) *Practitioners of journalism shall have a right to protect their sources, subject only to overriding considerations of public interest.*

(iii) *The above rights shall be accorded especial importance in any civil court proceedings in which it is properly invoked.*

(iv) *This right shall create a presumption in favour of publication, rebuttable only if the restriction sought to be placed upon it is necessary in the interests of a democratic society to guard against incitement to crime or disorder, or to safeguard national security, or to enable other citizens to stop lies being told about them or falsehoods being published which relate to them, or to preserve confidential information, or to protect privacy as defined in Article 13.*

(v) *Citizens have a right to know about the workings of their government. In addition to their rights under* the Freedom of Information Act, *and subject to (iv) above, all cabinet papers and other government documents shall be made available for public inspection within ten years from their creation.*

vi) *This right may be invoked by media corporations on behalf of their journalists and editors, and/or on behalf of their readers, viewers or listeners.*

13. RIGHT TO PRIVACY

Everyone has the right to have his or her home and law-abiding family life respected and to prevent the passing on, or publication of, intimate personal details, or the disclosure of personal matters concerning children in their care. Public authorities shall not interfere with the exercise of this right unless such interference serves the public interest and is in accordance with legally prescribed data protection principles or ethics codes promulgated by statutory or professional bodies.

14. FREEDOM OF THOUGHT, CONSCIENCE AND RELIGION

Everyone has the right to freedom of thought, conscience and religion; this right includes freedom to change religion or belief and freedom, either alone or in community with others, to manifest religion or belief in worship or other forms of observance and to expound the tenets of that religion to others. This freedom shall not extend to religions or other movements that preach hatred or incite violence and shall not protect religions from criticism made by persons exercising their free speech rights under Article 12.

15. RIGHT TO OWN PROPERTY

i) *Everyone has the right to own property alone as well as in association with others.*

ii) *Nobody shall be deprived of his or her property arbitrarily.*

iii) *There shall be no confiscation of private property by the state other than when it is in satisfaction of a judgment debt or if it is reasonably suspected to be the proceeds of crime.*

iv) *The state may acquire private property but only upon just terms.*

16. RIGHT TO WORK

i) *Everyone has the right to work, to free choice of employment and to safe and healthy conditions of work and to protection against unfair dismissal.*

ii) *Everyone, without any discrimination, has the right to equal pay for equal work.*

iii) *Everyone who works has the right to fair remuneration, ensuring for their family an existence worthy of human dignity, and supplemented, if necessary, by other means of social protection.*

iv) *Everyone has the right to form and join trade unions for the protection of their interests and in the course of that protection to have trade unions represent them in collective bargaining.*

v) *Everyone has the right to rest and leisure, including reasonable limitation of working hours and periodic holidays with pay.*

17. RIGHT TO WELLBEING

i) *Everyone has the right to a standard of living adequate for their health and wellbeing, including food, clothing, housing and medical care, and necessary social services and the right to security in the event of unemployment, sickness, disability, old age or other lack of livelihood in circumstances beyond their control.*

ii) *The government is required to take reasonable legislative and other measures, within its available resources, to achieve the progressive realisation of the rights in (i) above.*

iii) *Everyone has the right to due respect when treated in any hospital or nursing home or care centre or medical surgery, and where practicable to give informed consent before undergoing any invasive surgical procedure.*

18. RIGHT TO EDUCATION

i) *Everyone has the right to education. Education shall be free and compulsory at primary level and until an intermediate secondary level. Technical and professional education shall be open to all, and higher education shall be equally accessible on the basis of merit.*

ii) *The government is required to take reasonable measures, within its available resources, to make technical and professional education and higher education progressively available and affordable.*

iii) *Education shall be directed to the full development of the human personality and to the strengthening of respect for human rights and fundamental freedoms. It shall promote understanding, tolerance and the values that are set out in this charter, and shall include teaching about the history of these rights. Such teaching shall include objective accounts of the history of Australian Aborigines and Torres Strait Islanders, of their dispersion and degradation during the colonial period, and about the Stolen Generation.*

iv) *Parents have a right to choose the kind of education that shall be given to their children, subject to the right of the government to set curricula and to refuse approval to schools where teaching is or is likely to breach (iii) above.*

v) *Government may, but has no duty to, subsidise private schooling: it has a primary duty to ensure educational excellence in schools provided by the state.*

19. THE RIGHT TO DEMOCRACY

Every citizen, and every resident and/or taxpayer, over the age of eighteen has the right and must have the opportunity, without discrimination:

i)   *to take part in the government in Australia, directly by standing for parliament or by voting, freely and secretly, for chosen representatives;*

ii) *to have access, on terms of equality and merit, to the public service and to all public offices, including the office of Head of State in any Australian republic.*

20. RIGHTS OF PARLIAMENTARY REPRESENTATIVES

(i)   Speech in parliament shall be free and may be reported by the media with absolute freedom.

(ii) MPs shall be entitled freely to communicate with their constituents, and vice versa. An MP's parliamentary office shall not be subject to search or interference, save with the permission of the Speaker of the relevant House, who shall, if practicable, seek the assurance of the Attorney-General that the search is necessary to the investigation of a serious crime.

(iii) Parliament shall not be disturbed, and MPs shall not be subject to arrest or other forcible process in parliament or its precincts, except by the permission of the Speaker, once the Attorney-General has confirmed that such action is necessary for the investigation of serious crime.

(iv) In all other respects, MPs shall not be above the law.

21. RIGHT TO EFFECTIVE JUSTICE

Everyone whose rights and freedoms are violated shall have an effective remedy by way of access to a court or a tribunal empowered to apply the provisions of this charter. The aforesaid court or tribunal shall give a reasoned decision, in language comprehensible to lay persons.

22. PROHIBITION OF DISCRIMINATION

i) *Everyone is equal before the law. In all laws made or to be made, every person may be bound alike; and no tenure, estate, charter, degree, birth or place shall confer any exemption from the ordinary course of legal proceedings whereunto others are subjected.*

ii) *The enjoyment of the rights and freedoms set forth in this charter shall be secured without discrimination on grounds of age, disability, sex, sexual orientation or gender identity, race, colour, language, religion, political or other opinion, national or social origin, association with a minority, property, birth or other status.*

iii) *In the implementation of government policy, public servants shall in all decisions that involve the rights stated in sections 16 to 18 above, bear in mind their duty to narrow the gap between rich and poor, and to narrow the gap between indigenous people and the rest of the community.*

23. RIGHTS OF CHILDREN

i) *Every child has the right:*

    (a) to a name and a nationality from birth;

    (b) to family care, parental care, or adequate and appropriate alternative care if removed in accordance with law from a dangerous family environment;

    (c) to be protected from maltreatment, neglect, abuse or degradation;

    (d) to be protected from exploitative labour practices;

    (e) not to be detained except as a matter of last resort and then only for the shortest time necessary, for that detention.

(ii) *A child's best interests are of special and particular importance in every matter concerning the child.*

(iii) *Every person under eighteen who is detained pending or during trial or after conviction must be segregated from detained adults.*

24. RIGHTS OF DISABLED PEOPLE

The government shall ensure, within its available resources, that all persons who are disabled shall be vouchsafed full enjoyment of the rights set out in this charter without discrimination or diminution on the grounds of their disablement. They shall have the right to live in their community, with choices equal to others, and to participate in their community, and shall in particular have:

(i) the opportunity to choose their place of residence and where and with whom they live to the same extent as others;

(ii) access to a range of in-house, residential and other community support services, including personal assistance necessary to prevent isolation from the community;

(iii) access, on an equal basis and in a way that is responsive to their needs, to community services and facilities that are made available to the general population.

25. RIGHT TO A PRISTINE AND HEALTHY ENVIRONMENT

Everyone has the right:

(i) to an environment that is not harmful to their health or wellbeing;

(ii) to have the environment protected, for the benefit of present and future generations, through reasonable legislative and other measures that:

  (a) prevent pollution and ecological degradation;

  (b) promote conservation; and protect native flora and fauna, and areas necessary to maintain biological diversity and ecosystems;

  (c) secure ecologically sustainable development and use of natural resources while promoting justifiable economic and social development;

  (d) preserve properties and places of historic or cultural significance;

*(e) establish a planning system that ensures that encroach-
ments upon areas of natural beauty or heritage value are
not approved unless by fair, transparent and non-corrupt
process, which takes that value into account;*

*(iii) to timely and adequate assistance if threatened by fire,
flood, cyclone or other natural catastrophe.*

26. DEROGATION IN TIME OF EMERGENCY

*In time of war or other public emergency threatening the life of
the nation the government may take measures derogating from
its obligations under this charter to the extent strictly required
by the exigencies of the situation. However, there shall be no
derogation from Articles 1, 2(a) and 3.*

27. SPECIAL RIGHTS OF INDIGENOUS PEOPLE

*Indigenous people have distinct cultural rights and must not be
denied the right, with other members of their community:*

i)   to enjoy their identity and culture;

ii) to maintain and use their languages;

iii) to maintain their kinship ties;

*iv) to maintain spiritual and material relationships with the
land and waters according to their customs of old.*

28. DUTIES OF AUSTRALIANS

*i)   Everyone has duties to the community in which alone the
full and free development of their personality is possible.*

*ii) In the exercise of these rights and freedoms, everyone
shall be subject to such limitations as are determined by
law for the purpose of securing the recognition and respect
for the rights and freedoms of others and for meeting the
just requirements of public order and general welfare in a
democratic society.*

*iii) Nothing in this declaration may be interpreted as implying
for any group or person any right to engage in any activity
or to perform any act aimed at the destruction of any of the
rights or freedoms set forth in this charter.*

iv) *All persons present in Australia, (however briefly) have a duty (unless relieved of it by diplomatic or other immunity, in which case they have a moral obligation) to obey the law.*

FREE THINKING

Chapter 26

CREATIVITY: THE TONIC FOR A NATION

Jesus Christ insisted that it was harder for the rich to get to heaven than for a camel to go through the eye of a needle. Salutary though it may be to imagine Clive Palmer, Rupert Murdoch, Gina Rinehart and others pitch-forked into hell, this is not a message that Australian churches dare utter. They never suggest that any who wish for eternal life and earn more than a few million dollars per annum might give this money to the poor or even to less traditional charitable objects like the creative arts. That may be part of the reason (the other part may simply be acquisitive greed) why very wealthy Australians for the most part acknowledge no obligation to be philanthropic, other than in Kerry Packer's sense of funding every hospital, ambulance and kidney donor that might someday come to the aid of their own carcass.

American billionaires in this respect are different, although it may just be that there are more of them. Should we call on corporate Medicis to fund a new generation of renaissance men (and women) or ask the government to sell Blue Poles (the only sound investment Whitlam ever made) at a massive profit to subsidise struggling Australian artists? Was John Howard right to object to a jazzed-up version of our 'sacred' national anthem? Questions about philanthropy as a spur to creativity,

*raised at a forum in 2008 convened by the Australia Council
and UBS bank, opened with these remarks.*

Should successful businesses contribute to the arts? Americans
think so, but were shaken by the experience of an art exhibition hosted by a profitable New York supermarket. It closed
the show in panic when a nice portrait of the president turned
out, on closer inspection, to be made up of chimpanzees. The
problem, apparently, was the artist's insinuation that George
W. Bush may not have been created by God, but might have
evolved from an ape. It was Kafka who said that the duty of an
artist was 'to wield his pen like an icepick, to smash the frozen
sea inside us'. So corporations that support artists may get back
more than they bargained for.

I'm sure that Australian businesspeople understand the
provocative purpose of art in a more sophisticated way than the
prime minister, who claims that Sydney Mayor Clover Moore's
proposed disco version of the Australian national anthem will
lower the tone of the city's New Year's Eve celebrations. I had
always thought the phrase 'girt by sea' was appropriate only to
the name of a ladies' retirement home – what joy to hear it is
to be the chant of a conga line around Circular Quay.

Australia has advanced fairly well, from Sir Les Patterson
to Arts Minister Helen Coonan in just two decades. The Arts
is now an $8 billion industry, an asset to tourism, a source of
national pride (four Oscar nominations this year) and an intellectual export. Most of London's great museums, ballet companies
and arts centres are run by Australians. So you would think
that culture, so vital to our sense of identity and community, so
crucial to our fun and our mischief, would be nurtured financially by government and by business.

If you think that, you would be wrong. Government in
Australia devotes less than one per cent of its spending to the
arts – less than 0.5 per cent if you subtract the ABC and SBS.
Business donates $1.5 billion annually to charity, but of that a

mere $70 million goes to the arts and $40 million of that is for sponsored events. Asked about benefit their companies obtained from arts donation, forty per cent of executives said 'We get signage' and thirty-five per cent said 'It's the free tickets.'

But let's not be censorious. All company directors – Ray Williams excepted – know of the strict legal duty to use share-holders' money only for the benefit of the company. So it's important to explore new ideas about how businesses and the wider community can benefit from their involvement in the arts. In 2002, Richard Florida, a US professor of economic develop-ment, published a seminal book, *The Rise of the Creative Class*, in which he argued that creativity was not confined to artists; it was shared by scientists and professionals who recognised how innovation and adaptability were the keys to economic advancement.

The function of the creative class in every society is to develop new ideas, technology and methods of problem-solving – its members include those top professionals in business, finance, law and public administration who bring an independ-ent, educated but individual judgment to bear on finding ways through intellectual or administrative mazes. Florida's thesis, in short, is that technological, cultural and economic creativity is interlinked and inseparable, providing a rationale for corporate involvement in the arts and indeed for government encourage-ment of that involvement.

There is another emerging rationale, which might be crudely called 'the payback principle'. Those who have taken large profits from society have a moral duty to plough some of them back – into community education, welfare and culture. In the US, Bill Gates and Ted Turner are examples of a trend that draws on Puritan fundamentals: good works are a precondition for salvation, not as a means of buying your way into heaven but as demonstrating, in life, that you are the sort of person who deserves election to that great boardroom in the sky.

For this reason, philanthropy is suddenly coming out of the closet. Once, donors insisted on anonymity, afraid of attracting begging letters and burglars. Now, if you have a heart you must wear it on your sleeve. 'The latest fashion accessory,' cynics may sneer, but the moral responsibility of the rich to demonstrate that they have given some of their wealth for the public good is increasingly accepted – certainly by Australian employees, who say they do not wish to work for 'heartless' companies, and increasingly by consumers and shareholders. It may soon be recognised by accountants as essential to a corporation's goodwill. In that event, of course, it will be necessary for the arts to argue the case for its own share in corporate payback. This can be hard: employees, offered a corporate 'match' for money they raise for their favourite charities, invariably nominate sick children, followed by cancer research.

What must be explained is how support for the arts, as part of charitable giving, contributes not only to a happier community but a healthier one as well. We are still at an early stage in understanding the impact of different forms of human expression. Classical music is recognised as having a therapeutic effect on mental conditions and even delaying the onset of Alzheimer's disease. Only last week the National Health Service in Britain announced that doctors would be permitted to prescribe books in place of anti-depressants – prose instead of Prozac. Will visits to the GP be quite the same again? 'I'm not sending you back to the sanatorium – here's a ticket to the *Ring Cycle*.' Or perhaps, 'Erectile dysfunction? I'll write you a prescription for the latest Kathy Lette novel – it's cheaper than Viagra.'

Company directors should be aware they have greater freedom to donate to the arts than previous interpretations of the law suggested – so long as the donations objectively furbish the company's reputation and goodwill and are not designed as a trough in which they can wallow. Arts institutions, too, must curb greed and discriminate: sometimes there is reason to beware geeks bearing gifts. The Guggenheim is a laughing stock after allowing motorbike manufacturers to sponsor an exhibition called 'The Art of the Motorcycle', and for allowing Armani to pay for an exhibition of its designs and pretend it was high art. Above all, any increase in corporate giving must not be used as an excuse for the federal government to withdraw its funding even further.

What would life be like without art? Like sex without foreplay, or cappuccinos without froth? No metaphor works because life without art is simply unimaginable, and movements that seek to suppress culture invariably fail. It seems safe to say that the more collective or individual expression there is in a country, the more confident, happy – even healthy – is the common weal. So here's hoping that government and business leaders join the conga line swaying to the disco version of the national anthem: it would provide some assurance that Australia has really advanced.

Chapter 27

ALL THE GLOBAL ATHEISTS

It is rare, except in the last act of the Ring Cycle, *to celebrate a world without gods, but in April 2012 a long weekend in Melbourne's massive Convention Centre drew four thousand unbelievers to sit at the feet of Richard Dawkins and others of the secular priesthood. Christopher Hitchens had promised to attend if he was still alive: he had died, alas, in December 2011. A lecture I gave in his memory provided an opportunity to salute an old friend and to reprise arguments in a book he had encouraged me to write –* The Case of the Pope *– about how the Vatican state's condoning of sex abuse by priests amounted to a crime against humanity.*

The scene was set for this lecture by Cardinal Pell, who had reassured Dawkins a few days before that atheists could indeed be admitted to heaven. At the time, Mitt Romney was looking good for the US presidency, Bob Brown had announced his belief in extraterrestrial communication, Craig Thomson's brothel-creeping had been exposed by the media and you could filch a joke from The Book of Mormon *(the newly opened Broadway musical) without getting rumbled. It was also an opportunity to bang the drum for a Royal Commission into the sexual abuse of children, which was set up shortly afterwards.*

It's wonderful to join this celebration of reason and humanity, this Global Convention of Atheists. I'm not really an atheist – I'm a lawyer, so I can argue both sides of the question. But it's a great time to be an atheist in Australia, now that Cardinal Pell has declared, on *Q&A* this week, that atheists can go to heaven. So what's the point of being, for example, a Catholic, when you can get to paradise without attending midnight masses or Sunday sermons, without choking on stale communion bread or running the risk of your kids being molested by the local priest?

After death you have to go through what George vaguely describes as 'some sort of purging process', after which St Peter hands you your keys to that vast transcendental hotel where hip replacements come free on the after-life disability scheme and you can recover from the endless repeats of parliamentary question time you were forced to watch during your time in purgatory. So atheists can get to heaven, but I'm not sure about lawyers. God has to draw the line somewhere.

It's an honour to offer some remarks in memory of Christopher Hitchens, over whom death shall have no dominion. If we were to adopt Alain de Botton's curious idea that atheists should have their own cathedrals, he'd be up there in the stained glass, along with Voltaire, Schopenhauer, Mary Wollstonecraft, Charles Bradlaugh and George Bernard Shaw. But secular sainthood is the last thing he would have wanted: he was a humble man who saw himself merely as a jobbing journalist, positioning himself as the small boy who pointed out that the Emperor had no clothes – whether the Emperor happened to be the queen or Mother Teresa, Dr Kissinger or Bill Clinton, the pope or God himself. Or herself. He disdained money, of which he never made much, and he cared nothing for literary prizes or awards – he just kept trucking and writing. In fact, he said that the accolade that most delighted him had been bestowed by Kathy Lette. He was staying with us one Christmas at Palm Beach, and since *Puberty Blues* was one of the few books he hadn't read, he made the mistake of challenging her to a race in the surf, from which he emerged dumped, dishevelled and defeated.

'Don't worry, Hitch,' she said. 'You still look like a spunkrat.'

For those curious about the title of his autobiography – *Hitch 22* – Salman Rushdie has reminded us that it picks up the pieces of one of the word games we played at the first coming of Monty Python – thinking of book titles that never quite made the final edits such as: *The Catcher in the Wheat;* or *For Whom the Bell Rings;* or *To Kill a Hummingbird;* or *Mr Zhivago. Hitch 22* might have been the first draft title for *Catch-22,* so he appropriated it for his unassuming and honest account of a life enjoyably spent puncturing the hypocrisy of others.

Hitch had a passion for fairness, and for righting, by writing, historical wrongs. One of his first and best books is *Imperial Spoils: The Curious Case of the Elgin Marbles.* It's sadly out of print, though it would have a big market here in Melbourne, the Athens of the south. Well, at least in the sense that there are more Greeks in Melbourne than there are now in Athens. I was recently hired by the Greek government to lead a team of international lawyers to launch an action against museums in Britain, Germany and France to recover the looted Parthenon friezes and I found that Hitch's book is still the most compelling factual and historical statement of the case for their return. Unfortunately the retainer was cancelled when Greece collapsed into Euro debt: its government did not think it was a good time to be suing the very countries it was depending on for its bailout.

There is, throughout Hitch's journalism, a consistent passion for justice, for the post-Nuremburg idea that political and military leaders who mass-murder their own people should face retribution on earth rather than in hell or in history. Hell (if it did exist) would constitute a serious breach of the Convention against Torture, and history, as Richard Nixon pointed out, depends on who writes it. So the idea of putting on trial those responsible for crimes against humanity appealed to Hitch.

We had become friendly at the *New Statesman* in the seventies and our daughters had been flower girls at Salman's wedding – I can't remember which one – and he heard that I'd been arguing the case for putting General Pinochet and Idi Amin on trial.

'Take it a step further,' he challenged me. 'Why not the trial of Henry Kissinger?'

Well, he went on to make a pretty good case for that – in his book *The Trial of Henry Kissinger*, and then a documentary film. Some years later I suggested he might have more luck with a charismatic evangelical that hardly anyone knew about, who was killing and enslaving children in Northern Uganda. This was in 2005 when Joseph Kony was actually in Uganda. Hitch caught the next plane, and then went bravely into the jungle to meet Kony's victims and some of the killers, producing his most blazing and brilliant piece of investigative journalism, 'Childhood's End: An African Nightmare'. This is how he described the running children:

> They are running for their lives from the Lord's Resistance Army. This grotesque zombie-like militia, which has abducted, enslaved, and brainwashed more than 20,000 children is a kind of Christian Khmer Rouge and has for the past 19 years set a standard of cruelty and ruthlessness that even in a region with a living memory of Idi Amin, has the power to strike the most vivid terror right into the heart and other viscera. Here's what happens to the children who can't run fast enough . . .

Read this, if you read nothing else, because it is a model of passionate and factual journalism getting at a truth that, six years later, the video about Kony that has just gone viral never admits – namely the perverted biblical basis for his atrocities and the support he has had from crazed evangelicals in the US.

The brainwashing and brutalising of children was one of Hitch's abiding concerns. That was why he called me eighteen months ago with a question about the news reports on child sex abuse in the Catholic Church. 'Could this amount to a crime against humanity? Might the pope – arguably – be accountable, under international law?'

It was at his prompting that I wrote the book, *The Case of the Pope: Vatican Accountability for Human Rights Abuse,* which

sought to answer these questions. They are timely ones here in
Melbourne where Justice Cummins has urged a Royal Commission into paedophile priests. According to Victorian Police, at
least forty of their victims have committed suicide in the last
ten years. In that period sixty-five priests have been convicted
and a further fifty-three have been the subject of compensation
payments – that's 118 molesters, most with multiple victims,
and they are only the ones who have been outed so far. That
means thousands of victims, just in the state of Victoria. The
case for a Royal Commission is compelling.

Church Sex Abuse

The appalling facts of child sex abuse within the worldwide
Catholic Church are now well established – by judicial inquiries
in Ireland, which have described it as 'endemic' within boys'
schools; by studies in America, which implicate up to ten per
cent of the Catholic priesthood; by revelations in England about
misbehaving monks; and by scandals in Europe, which have
exposed the guilt of bishops and even cardinals. The practice of
moving molesters to different parishes – greener pastures with
unsuspecting flocks – is legendary, and it's clear that the Vatican
has routinely and knowingly approved the transfer of paedophile priests to third world countries, especially to Africa where
the moderator of the African churches recently said, 'They sent
us wolves in sheep's clothing.'

In the last thirty years, well over 100,000 children have been
bewitched, buggered and bewildered by priests. When parents
or victims complain, those wrongdoers are protected by canon
law – the law of the church, which requires the case to progress
in utter secrecy without reporting it to any outsider, least of all
to the police. And when a priest is found guilty under canon
law, even of hundreds of offences, he receives no punishment –
only something called 'penance', which involves an order to sing
Hail Marys or to say prayers for the victim.

But victims don't want prayers, they want justice. And they
certainly do not get justice from the church, which hides their

offences to protect its reputation, and especially to protect its finances. That is why the Vatican refuses even now to impose mandatory reporting to police or law enforcement agencies. In some places – including Victoria – the church says it will report voluntarily, but only if victims consent. There's the catch-22, because it's very easy to discourage victims by bullying them, or by telling their parents it would be an ordeal and they should let it be dealt with 'within the family', leaving the guilty priest still in holy orders and liable to offend again. This is what Justice Cummins condemned in his recent report, pointing out that 'Crime is a public, not a private, matter.'

I am glad to say that as a result of human rights demands, the law is changing. In Britain a few months ago a Court of Appeal rejected the church's argument – one that has succeeded in Australia – that priests are not employed by bishops. It ruled that bishops are vicariously liable for the sexual misbehaviour of their priests and are legally bound to compensate for the pain and suffering they cause. The judgment was based on the 'immense power and trust' with which priests are endowed in respect to children. Even more significant is the conviction in Philadelphia of a church official, Monsignor Lynn, for the crime of aiding and abetting three of his priests to rape boys that he placed under their care knowing these priests had paedophile propensities. This is the first case where criminal law has been deployed against those who are most to blame – those in the church hierarchy who keep silent to protect the church's reputation and its money. Highest of all of those figures, of course, is Pope Benedict.

Justice Cummins urges that a law be passed imposing a mandatory reporting duty on bishops, priests and church workers, except for information divulged in the confessional. I don't agree with an exemption for the confessional: why should the law endow this religious ritual with the cloak of confidentiality? There can be no confidence in iniquity. There can be no justification for any exemption from the law for a private ritual whereby priests confess their guilt and receive absolution from one of their mates – 'Brother, can you spare a crime?' I suppose the answer often is 'Sure, brother. Just pray that the kid doesn't commit suicide and his parents don't go to the *Age*.'

Forgiveness, we must insist, is the prerogative of victims, not of prelates.

I don't want to sound like Derryn Hinch. I have defended paedophiles and had excrement put through my letterbox for doing so, and I know these men can do good as well as ill. But there is a deeper question, and it concerns the legitimacy of allowing any religion to indoctrinate children at a very early age by priests whom they are encouraged to believe have supernatural powers. The Catholic Church has this problem in particular because it takes children at the age of seven to communion, an awesome experience in which the priest as God's agent performs the miracle of changing bread and wine into the body and blood of Christ. Then at the same age, the impressionable and anxious child is forced to confess to sin, under fear of hellfire. He receives salvation from the God-priest. The victim's reverence for the priest is why he unflinchingly obeys his confessor's sexual requests. Children have such emotional and psychological respect for the molester – they obey him because they are conditioned to obey.

For weak-willed, sexually confused or infantile priests, the temptation to abuse this power over unformed minds is difficult to resist. That is the real reason why child abuse happens so often in the Catholic Church, much more than in other religions that do not confirm children until they reach teenage-hood. Of course, the power of priesthood can lead to abuse in all faiths – there is currently a rabbinical scandal in New York and there have been serious failings in the Anglican Church. But if the Vatican wants to minimise child abuse, it must raise the age at which it commences formal indoctrination. This is the real challenge to the Vatican – take your hands off children until they are old enough to think for themselves, and old enough to resist.

In my view this is actually a requirement of international law. Article 14 of the Convention of the Rights of the Child insists that children have a right to freedom of thought, conscience and religion, which should mean freedom from religious indoctrination until they are old enough for critical understanding, and big enough to give molesting priests a swift kick in the cassock. Of course young children can be exposed to religion and told about it from an early age. But the law should ban any formal induction into the supernatural, by confession, confirmation or communion, until the age of at least thirteen.

The Vatican accepts no responsibility for abuse by its priests. Its top officials blame the scandal on 'aggressive secularism', on 'homosexual infiltration', on the permissive culture of the sixties, on Jewish journalists at the *New York Times*, on journalists in general, on 'modernity' and, of course, on the devil. The Vatican is a power in the world because it is, or claims to be, a state and its bogus statehood is accepted without demur by otherwise sensible countries like Australia and by the UN, where it opposes all measures designed to improve the status of women or to encourage family planning or to deal with the scourge of HIV by the supply of condoms.

In unholy alliance with Muslim states, especially Iran, it condemns homosexuality as evil and opposes abortion under any circumstances, even to save a mother's life, and of course it tried to stop UN agencies from supplying morning-after pills to women raped by Serb soldiers. A few years ago Joseph Ratzinger orchestrated a program to threaten Catholic politicians with excommunication if they failed to oppose abortion or IVF or embryo experimentation, particularly if they supported gay marriage because, he said, homosexual acts are a 'serious depravity'. These threats have already been made to Nancy Pelosi and Joe Biden, so if Tony Abbott becomes prime minister it's the kind of spiritual blackmail he may have to resist.

This is doubly outrageous, because the Vatican is a Santa Claus state – no matter how many believe in its statehood, it simply does not exist as a matter of law. It claims its statehood was created by the Lateran Treaty between Mussolini and Pope Pius XI in 1929, but that was a squalid deal between the dictator and a pro-fascist pope in order to secure fascism in Italy. In law, a state must have territory: the Vatican has none – it is merely a palace with a museum and gardens. A state in international law must have a permanent population, but the only residents of the Vatican are celibate clergy and nuns. No one gets born there, except by accident. There are no Vaticanians, no 'people' to form a team to enter the Olympics or play in the World Cup. Even the papal guards are Swiss. It would be comic were it not for the damage the Vatican does to human rights and to the progress of women in the world. It is no more a state than Disneyland, which is larger and has even more outlandish costumes.

But of course the Vatican is a political convenience. Here in Australia, the ambassadorship to the Vatican has long served as the dumping ground for inconvenient Catholic politicians – Vince Gair and Brian Burke, for example, and, later, ex-Howard deputy prime minister Tim Fischer. For the last three years we've paid millions of dollars to provide round-the-clock security for Tim Fischer. The idea that anyone would notice Tim, let alone want to bump him off, is pretty odd. But he's just retired from this position, so there's an opportunity for the government to get rid of Craig Thomson – simply appoint him as Vatican ambassador.

We have a new, incredibly expensive embassy in Rome for the ambassador to the Holy See, which Australian tourists are not allowed to enter. I'm one of the few who have actually been inside it. It's at the top of a lovely old building just below the Castel St Angelo – you look up through its glass ceiling and see the ramparts and expect Floria Tosca to come crashing down at any moment. But it's no use at all to Australians who have their passports pickpocketed when they are looking up at the Sistine Chapel – an increasingly common occurrence. They have to walk a few hundred yards down the road to the Australian Embassy to Italy, where until recently Amanda Vanstone was ensconced. That proverbial mug, the Australian taxpayer, pays for two embassies within two hundred yards of each other. What makes this even more ridiculous is that Ireland, that most

Catholic of countries, is now closing its embassy to the Vatican to save money – because it's useless, the prime minister says, and because of the way the Vatican's papal nuncio deceitfully tried to cover up the church's child abuse in Ireland. The Irish were so furious about his behaviour that the Vatican had to withdraw him. They sent him as nuncio to Australia where he is now safely hidden in the bosom of Cardinal Pell.

Human Rights and Atheists

Well, let me move on, at this Global Convention of Atheists, to bring you some good news about the developing human rights jurisprudence that is insisting that atheists be accorded the same rights and privileges as the religious: there must be no discrimination between believers in God and believers that there is no God. This is an interpretation that flows from the wording of Article 18 of the *Universal Declaration of Human Rights*: 'Everyone has the right to freedom of thought, conscience and religion.' And from Article 18 of the International Covenant on Civil and Political Rights, which guarantees 'the right to religion or belief'. *'Or belief'* I emphasise – atheism is a positive belief. Hence the ruling by the Human Rights Committee that 'Article 18 protects theistic, non-theistic and atheistic beliefs, as well as the right not to profess any religion or belief'.

So, as a matter of international law, which upholds the rule that states must not discriminate between holders of different religions or beliefs, atheists and agnostics can claim the same privileges and protections as believers, and laws must not specially privilege religions.

Now this is important to understand, in order to refute the increasingly shrill claim by the churches that they are being subjected to 'aggressive secularism' or 'militant atheism' by court rulings that there cannot be prayers before council meetings, or that Christians cannot wear their crucifixes at work, or that homosexual couples may not be denied the right to adopt.

There is nothing 'aggressive' or 'militant' about these rulings at all – they are simply cases brought by atheists who claim the same equality rights as Christians, or are concerned to ensure that Christians are not privileged by reason of their religion. This was the basis of the great secularist decision by the European Court in the case of *Şahin v Turkey,* upholding a government ban on the wearing of headscarves at universities. 'Freedom of conscience and religion is a precious asset for atheists, agnostics, sceptics and the unconcerned' as well as for believers, but it did not protect every religiously motivated action. Wearing a head-scarf at an educational institution, the court said, 'might have some proselytising effect, seeing that it was imposed on women by a religious precept that was hard to reconcile with a prin-ciple of gender equality' and could not be reconciled with 'the message of tolerance, respect for others and above all, equality and non-discrimination that all teachers in a democratic society should convey to their pupils'.

This decision is criticised by churchmen who regarded it as the high-water mark of 'militant secularism' but it simply makes the point that in a democratic society, any sexist or superstitious practice can be denied privileged protection, whether it arises from religion or politics, or from trade unions or freemasonry, if it infringes the rights and freedoms of others, especially the right to equal treatment.

The complaint about 'militant atheism' is not only used by Christians – we heard it recently and very loudly from the Hindus living in Wales. They were upset when the Welsh Assembly (the provincial government) ordered the slaughter of Shambo the sacred bull, who belonged to a Hindu temple. Poor Shambo had bovine TB, posing a threat to all Welsh meat. I made the sugges-tion that Shambo the sacred bull might be put on a sacred barge and sailed into the Irish Sea, beyond the jurisdiction of the Welsh assembly, as well as any proximity to Welsh cows. Meanwhile, to the chagrin of their fellow Christians, Mr and Mrs Bull – an evangelical couple who ran a guesthouse – were ordered to compensate two gays in a stable civil partnership whom they had turned away from their stable door late at night. I have always acknowledged the parable of the Good Samaritan as one of the inspirations for human rights, but I just wish that more Christians would take it seriously.

There are many examples in many countries of special privileges for the religious and it's time they came under attack from human rights lawyers – the angels' advocates. Here in Australia they range from Anglican prayers in parliament to the closure of bottle shops on Good Friday. But the law of most consequence is that relating to tax, which exempts any organisation if it is a religious institution.

The High Court has ruled that to be a tax-exempt religion requires only a belief in 'a supernatural being, thing or principle'. So it ruled that Scientologists are tax exempt, as of course are Jehovah's Witnesses, Hillsong and the Free Deist Community of Australia and, for that matter, the Lord's Resistance Army were Joseph Kony to set up with other Christian cults in Toowoomba.

This is plainly unfair – Human Rights Watch has been trying for years to get government approval for tax-exempt status but that is incredibly difficult if you are a secular do-gooder. It is automatic if you are a religion, however crazy. If we had a federal *Human Rights Act* with anti-discrimination protection this state of affairs could be challenged – which is doubtless why George Pell and others campaigned so ferociously against a bill of rights. If you can't lick 'em join 'em, I say: atheists foundations should qualify for tax exemption by declaring their belief in Christopher Hitchens. They could turn him into an L. Ron Hubbard figure, worshipped through his sacred books – although this might be taking Alain de Botton's idea too far.

A better answer would be for governments to pass laws requiring the major tax-break religions, with their churches partly built on public money, to offer some public service in return. I have often thought, when driving through the countryside, that it would be really useful to require churches to offer public toilet facilities to passing motorists – when caught short you would always know where to go by looking for the nearest steeple.

But the proper answer to this egregious discrimination is to abolish tax breaks for all religions – they are businesses after all, and should pay the going rate in corporation tax. No government need go as far as Henry VIII and seize the wealth of the monasteries. Although come to think of it, instead of a carbon tax we could have a steeple tax, refundable in heaven. But I can't envisage an Australian parliament taxing the churches anytime soon, since our parliamentary day begins with not one but with two prayers: the Lord's Prayer and a special prayer wherein Almighty God is humbly beseeched to vouchsafe his blessing, so that its deliberations will lead 'to the advancement of Thy glory'.

But here's an interesting thing: section 116 of the Australian constitution actually says, 'The Commonwealth shall not make any law for establishing any religion or for imposing any religious observance.'

So how on earth – or in heaven – does the parliament get away with imposing Anglican prayers at the start of every day? It can't do so by law, because that law would be unconstitutional, so very sneakily, and in my view unlawfully, they have provided for Christian prayers by way of internal parliamentary standing orders. Can they subvert our constitution like that? Someone should bring a case. Where are our devil's advocates?

Section 116 goes on to provide 'No religious test shall be required for any office or public trust under the Commonwealth'. This is terrific but, er, what about the office of our head of state? This is occupied by the British monarch, a personage defined by the 1701 *Act of Settlement* as a member of the family carrying the genes of the seventeenth-century German protestant princess Sophia of Hanover. The *Act of Settlement* requires that the monarch – this is the head of state of Australia, remember – should be a communicant member of the Church of England and indeed the head of that church.

Supporters of William as the next king hope that his father, rather than becoming Charles III, will declare himself an atheist or some form of vegetable worshipper, which would rule him out. But quite clearly the monarchy itself is a breach of Section 116 because the queen, as our head of state, occupies an office or public trust under the Commonwealth. That's the interpretation you might get if laws had to be interpreted, so far as their language allowed, compatibly with human rights standards. As they do not, our judges would probably rule that the queen occupies an office *over* the Commonwealth, requiring Ms Gillard, our atheist but elected prime minister, to be reigned over by the unelected head of the Anglican Church.

Mullahs without Mercy

These absurdities would appeal to Hitch – one of his early works was *The Monarchy: A Critique of Britain's Favourite Fetish*. But they are merely comic relief when compared to the terrible cruelty that faces atheists in many parts of the world where atheophobia (that's a real word – I've checked with Stephen Fry) is rampant.

Atheists in some Islamic countries are persecuted as apostates, under the most despicable provision of Sharia law that carries the death penalty for male apostates and life imprisonment for female apostates. In Saudi Arabia atheists are locked up and given three days to repent, and if they don't they are executed. Understandably, all of them repent. Egypt's persecution of atheists is unlikely to end under the Muslim Brotherhood.

In 1997, Alaa Hamed served a year in prison there for writing a novel (*The Bed*) deemed to contain atheistic ideas. In 2006, the Algerian parliament passed a new law, imposing a sentence of between two and five years in prison for any atheist who criticises Islam. In Jordan atheists must associate themselves with a recognised religion to obtain ID papers; in Indonesia they have difficulty registering births and marriages; and in Pakistan Christians as well as atheists are threatened with prison – even death – for blasphemy.

These laws are in blatant contravention of the *Universal Declaration of Human Rights*, which expressly guarantees the right to change one's religion. Let us, at this Global Convention of Atheists, pause a moment to salute all those who today, throughout the world, are risking imprisonment and death because they share our non-belief.

There is no country in the world that has killed more atheists in recent years than Iran, run by mullahs without mercy who will soon be capable of acquiring a nuclear weapon. This is a subject upon which Hitch, had he lived, would have undoubtedly waxed, because it may be the gravest problem the world faces over the next few years: the bomb in the hands of people whose religious beliefs may incite them to use it.

Let me explain. In August 1988 the Ayatollah Khomeini was forced, so he told his people, to drink the bitter cup of poison – a truce in the seven-year war with Iraq. In secret, he issued a *fatwa* requiring all political prisoners who were *Moharab* – enemies of God – to be killed. There were many thousands – atheists, Marxists, mujahideen – in Iranian prisons. For them the death committees, headed by a religious judge, came to the prisons under supervision by the army commander, Rafsanjani and the then president, Ali Khamenei, who is today Iran's supreme leader. They sentenced to death all men and many women whom they deemed after a two-minute hearing to have no belief in Allah. These prisoners were blindfolded and ordered to join a conga line that was led straight to the gallows. They were hanged from cranes four at a time or in groups of six from ropes hanging in front of the stage in the prison assembly hall. Some were taken to army barracks at night, directed to make their wills and then shot by firing squad. Their bodies were doused with disinfectant, packed in refrigerated trucks, and buried by night in mass graves. Months later their families were given plastic bags with their few possessions, and ordered never to look for their graves or mourn for them in public.

In this period at least seven thousand non-believers were massacred. This was the worst single crime in recent history involving the mass murder of political prisoners – worse than the Japanese death marches, worse even than the killing of Muslim men and boys at Srebrenica. These were long-term political prisoners, whose only crime was not to believe in the God imposed upon them by the theocratic government of Iran. That government lied to the UN about the massacre and still tries to cover it up by preventing the victims' families from mourning at the sites of the mass graves.

The perpetrators of this atrocity are mostly still alive and in high office in Iran's theocracy and judiciary. The Ayatollah Khomeini died the followed year, after his public *fatwa* on Salman Rushdie, but the other perpetrators of this crime against humanity have been promoted and rewarded – most blatantly Ali Khamenei, president in 1988 and now the Supreme Leader, a man accurately described by Hitch as 'a semi-literate megalomaniac'. They are the men that in 2009 broke the Green Revolution, killing many and torturing protestors at Evin Prison in Tehran. These were the men who, it is undisputed, sought nuclear weapon technology from the AQ Khan network and elsewhere. These are the men who are now progressing towards a full nuclear fuel cycle, a position from which their scientists can readily switch to produce nuclear weapons. Ali Khamenei denies that intention, but he is a mass murderer who lies when his lips move.

The WikiLeaks cables show how Saudi Arabia and Jordan have been pleading with the US to strike Iran, and Israel may do so unilaterally or with US support within the next few years. Of course Israel has the bomb – about 120 nuclear bombs it is said. Why shouldn't Iran build some too?

Iran is a theocratic state that not only kills atheists but is constituted under a particular Islamic belief that has no counterpart elsewhere. It is the Shia belief – shared by the Supreme Leader and most of the other mullahs, and by the revolutionary guards and the *Basij* militias (the thugs who killed Nedā Āghā-Soltān and so many others in 2009). It is a belief which turns upon the re-emergence of the Twelfth Imam, currently said to be in 'occultation' (some form of hidden existence) – who will destroy all the *Moharabs*, the atheists and members of other faiths – and will establish the Islamic millennium. Peace and justice for all except atheists and members of other religions, including Sunni Muslims. What Iran's religious texts say is that this second coming will be triggered by chaos and their description of the chaos that will trigger it (after a 'scream from the sky') sounds suspiciously like a nuclear war.

So the fear is not that with a nuclear weapon Iran will try to wipe out Israel, but that some fanatical 'Supreme Leader' will one day relish the opportunity to create the kind of chaos that will trigger the second coming of the Twelfth Imam. This is a fear that has led Jordan and Saudi Arabia to urge a US attack on Iran, although I would rather see the UN set up a court to prepare an indictment for all those who perpetrated the mass murder of the atheists in 1988. After all, if this regime is allowed impunity for mass-murdering unbelievers, it may one day decide to mass murder them again.

~

So Hitch, where are you now to make sense of all this? Looking down, perhaps, from Cardinal Pell's heaven to see Iran, the nation that wants the Twelfth Imam to return in nuclear chaos, opposed by an America with nine thousand nuclear weapons soon in the keeping, perhaps, of President Romney. He's a Mormon who believes that when he dies he will go to his own planet, from where, I suppose, he will be able to communicate with Bob Brown. He believes that Jesus visited upstate New York in 1823 with golden plates inscribed with the Book of Mormon. It's a book that was very rude about black people when God wrote it in 1823, but in 1978, so Mitt Romney believes, God contacted the head of the Mormon Church in Salt Lake City and said he had changed his mind about Afro-Americans. Well, it's a crazy world, ladies and gentlemen, and it could get a lot crazier, which makes it a special joy to celebrate the memory of a man who tried so hard to make it a saner place.

Chapter 28

THE QUEEN AND I

One of the more arcane duties of a Queen's Counsel is to advise the monarch, when called upon, free of charge. I have for that reason taken the liberty of regaling her from time to time in public print, although whenever we accept her invitations to Buckingham Palace, my wife and I are berated by Australia's more common commentators (Gerard Henderson and Andrew Bolt) for somehow betraying our republican principles. They do not seem to understand either the virtue of politeness or my wife's point about the Royals: 'Of course they are dinosaurs, but who wouldn't want to see dinosaurs in their natural habitat?'

But the queen, like Rupert Murdoch, seems disinclined to follow the sensible steps of Pope Benedict into a comfortable retirement, and we must await her passing before republicanism lives again in Australia. Let us only hope that it returns with a less parochial argument than last time, i.e. that we need an Australian as head of state. What we need is a head of state elected by Australians, who might sensibly choose Richard Branson or Angelina Jolie – but might well choose Wills and Kate.

Here are some republican thoughts offered in the UK press on the occasion of their nuptials in 2011.

The Royal wedding highlights the absurdity of the constitutional arrangements which require Australia – and Britain, for that matter – to be reigned over by a family of white Anglo-German Protestants. The real reason why religious, racial and sex discrimination inherent in the monarchy remains untouched is through fear that the royalist tapestry would unravel if a single thread were pulled. But if this were ever the case, what could republican ideology – which has scarcely advanced in Britain since the 1650s and seems 'on hold' in Australia – offer in replacement?

The bedrock of both nations' constitution is the *Act of Settlement* of 1701, a blood-curdling anti-Catholic rant which enshrines the genes and protestant religious beliefs of Princess Sophia of Hanover in the line of succession to the throne. This means that any monarch who holds communion with the Church of Rome or who marries a Papist – heaven forbid a Muslim or a Methodist or a Scientologist – is immediately dethroned. The Act imposes anti-meritocratic race discrimination: no one unrelated to this German family (the Windsors changed their name from Saxe-Coburg Gotha during the First World War to disguise their familial relationship with the Kaiser) can aspire to the crown.

In further breach of the UK's *Human Rights Act*, this primitive 1701 law adopts the feudal principle of primogeniture (inheritance down the male line), so that if Prince William and Kate produce a daughter, she will be relegated to the bottom of the stately pile, below any subsequent male heirs.* If Charles III were to convert to Catholicism (or have a sex-change operation) the crown would go first to his male children then to his male brothers and their family, ahead of their older female sisters.

Why should the office of head of Australia go to any members of this Anglo-German dynasty, merely because Princess Sophia, three centuries ago, won 'Britain's Top Sperm' competition?

---

* David Cameron hastily changed this law in 2013, just in time for the arrival of the royal baby, who has turned out to be a boy. So barring accidents or a new referendum, the Australian head of state will, for almost a century following the departure of Queen Elizabeth, be a hereditary male.

Tom Paine pointed out the absurdity of an hereditary poet or an hereditary mathematician (today, he might have added an hereditary airline captain), although he failed to take into account the entertainment value provided by a hereditary family of royals. Speaking of which, there is still the *Treason Act* of 1361, which was the instrument for Anne Boleyn's beheading, and will constrain Kate by criminal law after Charles becomes King: it punishes (until recently, with death) any party to adultery with (and including) the wife of the heir to the throne. I once had to advise Kate's deceased mother-in-law, Diana, about this medieval nonsense, during her dalliance with James Hewitt.

These constitutional laws are obsolete and obnoxious, and in some cases very silly – for example, ownership of every wild swan in the UK is vested in the monarch, and in the case of 'the royal fish', the head of every whale, sturgeon or grampus landed in the kingdom belongs to the king, and its tail belongs to the queen. You may not find the monarch's immunity from legal action quite so amusing, however, if you are run over by a royal motorcade.

Why has reform not seriously been attempted? The Blair and Brown Labour governments claimed it would be too hard, because the Commonwealth would need to be consulted and countries like Jamaica and Australia were besotted by royal tradition. David Cameron at first repeated this nonsense about the Commonwealth wishing to block change (but when Kate's push came to shove, not even David Flynt objected). In fact, Commonwealth countries do not need to be consulted at all: if they still wish to be reigned over by the British royal family they must take it as they find it, after it has moved into the twenty-first century.

In any case, it is an open secret at the Commonwealth Secretariat that Charles will not be the next head of the Commonwealth when the queen retires – they are looking for someone more inspiring. Mandela was once the favourite candidate, but now the crown will probably go to his wife, Graca Machel, or to Aung San Suu Kyi (Burma was once part of the empire). If the queen holds on until 2016, the role of titular head of the Commonwealth could be offered to ex-president Obama, who had a Kenyan father. The refusal to invite the Obamas to the Royal Wedding was an oversight that may not have been unconnected with the possibility that Barack and Michelle would look good to the 'Black Commonwealth' as its future leaders, rather than Charles and Camilla.

In the meantime, where stands republicanism in Britain? Its A-level politics course teaches feminism, anarchism, conservatism, multi-culturalism, socialism and ecologism, but republicanism is not on the syllabus, perhaps unsurprisingly, as there has been little intellectual advance since John Cooke's *Monarchy – No Creature of God's Making* (1652) and Harrington's *The Commonwealth of Oceania* (1657).

Some years ago the *Guardian* began a legal campaign to challenge the monarchy – we had some initial success when law lords commented that the un-repealed sedition laws which sent Irish republicans to Botany Bay in 1848 could never again be enforced, thanks to the *Human Rights Act*. But the paper could not find a Catholic in line to the throne who was prepared to challenge the discrimination in the *Act of Settlement*. Although there are quite a few German Catholics in the line of succession, all those contacted declined to bring a test case, because they feared they would no longer be invited to take tea at Buckingham Palace.

As part of that campaign, there was much discussion about how to produce a republican president. The method invariably favoured by politicians, i.e. candidates chosen by MPs, would produce a contest between political has-beens. But political lobbying to put some spent party hack on the constitutional dais can very simply be avoided, if the 1701 *Act of Settlement* were replaced by a law requiring a democratic election for head of state every five or seven years, and excluding from candidature anyone who has held government office. In Britain, that would of course permit Prince Charles to stand – he would probably win the first Presidential election unless the royal vote was split by Wills or Harry (or his sister Anne) standing against him.

That might let in Richard Branson or Helen Mirren, or Boris Johnson, or lead to victory for the inevitable 'Stephen Fry for Queen' campaign – but why not?

In the Westminster system, the role of head of state, with the duty 'to advise and to warn' is an important part of the constitutional mechanism. But Elizabeth II merely follows the directions of the government of the day. However astute she may remain in her old age at picking Derby winners, Britain lacks an elected and respected figurehead, above party politics, who could provide wise counsel to the government. One result of choosing a head of state by inheritance rather than election is that in a crisis they may lack the confidence, popularity and independence to make a worthwhile contribution to govern-ance. Good luck apart, the *Act of Settlement* and the genes of Princess Sophia will not provide – by sexist, racist or religiously discriminating descent – the calibre of leadership that could be provided by elections every five or seven years for a head of state.

The challenge for republicans in Britain today is to find a way to keep the royal soap opera running, while ensuring that public power is exercised by elected representatives or officials appointed on merit. There needs to be a written constitution, in which the Windsor family has a very small part. They would still be called Kings and Queens, would remain custodians of Windsor and Balmoral and other royal palaces, and they would still hold garden parties and have whisky jam and boot polish 'by Royal appointment'. They would still have 'royal tours' of Australia, as long as sentimental Australians were prepared to pay for them. But the monarch would be replaced, for most practical purposes, by an elected President who would represent the nation abroad, advise and warn the government, inspire the people and open and if necessary, close, the parliament.

The ancient and rotting legal foundations of this kingdom can be rebuilt, by a written constitution that keeps kings and queens but allots them the minimal and secular role of keeping harmless traditions alive, in the interests of tourism, the tabloids and David Starkey.

Chapter 29

MEA MAXIMA CULPA

Individual priests and nuns of the Catholic faith have been among the bravest human rights defenders, and their church has at different times made important contributions to halting the perverse doctrine of eugenics and to denouncing death penalties. But under Joseph Ratzinger, both as cardinal and pope, the Vatican neglected the poor of Latin America and Southeast Asia and became complicit with the politicians and generals who kept them oppressed.

Through the bogus status of statehood that it occupies at the UN, the Holy See promotes a pernicious theological agenda – that homosexuality is 'evil' and so is divorce; that women have no right to choose; that condom use must never be countenanced, and so on. These cruel doctrines are ignored by most Catholics in the West, but were promulgated aggressively by Pope Benedict XVI, the fallible leader who sacked liberation theologians but protected paedophile priests.

In February 2013 it was time, in articles for newspapers in Britain and the US, to welcome his resignation (in the first of the following articles) and to suggest (in the second) how his successor should tackle the child abuse problem. It may be doubted whether Pope Francis, who has made a favourable impression by his immediate concern for the poor, will have the stomach for these reforms. However the Royal Commission established in Australia in November 2012 might recommend that they be adopted through legislation.

Joseph Ratzinger

The resignation of Joseph Ratzinger from his office as Pope Benedict XVI, the Vatican head of state, was merely expedient – he had become too old to cope. (The queen and Rupert Murdoch might usefully follow his example.) It would have been both astonishing and courageous, a few years ago, had it been offered in atonement for the atrocity to which he had for thirty years turned a blind eye – the rape, buggery and molestation of tens of thousands of small boys (and some girls) in priestly care. Instead of this measure of accountability, he has refused even to change canon law so as to force all paedophile priests to be defrocked and to require all bishops to hand over the evidence for their crimes to law enforcement authorities.

The pope's 'command responsibility' for a crime against humanity – as widespread and systematic child abuse surely is – goes back to 1981 when he was appointed Prefect (i.e. head) of the Congregation for the Doctrine of the Faith (CDF), the Vatican body that is in charge of disciplining errant priests. For the next twenty-four years, until he became pope, he presided over a system in which the CDF regularly refused to allow bishops to defrock child molesters, and knew of and approved their transfer to other parishes and often to other countries, where they usually reoffended. Although the CDF files are a closely guarded secret, letters from Cardinal Ratzinger have emerged in several US court cases, always protective of rapist priests.

The case of Father Lawrence Murphy, for example, who molested two hundred deaf boys at a Catholic school in Wisconsin (the subject of the award-winning documentary *Mea Maxima Culpa*) led to anxious communication between local church officials and Ratzinger, who emphasised 'the need for secrecy' because he was worried about 'increasing scandal'. Although he knew Murphy to be guilty, the cardinal ordered the secret proceedings to end so that the guilty priest could die a respected member of his brotherhood.

Father Stephen Kiesle, after his conviction for tying up and sexually assaulting boys, was at Ratzinger's insistence (and against the wishes of his bishop) kept in holy orders and allowed to continue working with children whom he also duly abused. Ratzinger had claimed that 'the good of the Universal Church' justified its continued cover-up of the abuse and its continued employment of the abuser.

As Father Hans Küng, the eminent theologian, put it in his open letter to Catholic bishops in 2010, 'There is no denying the fact that the worldwide system of covering up cases of sexual crimes committed by clerics was engineered by the CDF under Cardinal Ratzinger.'

Ratzinger's policy at the CDF had always been to keep child abuse secret, even though that meant forgiving the offender. The worst case was that of Father Maciel, a bigamist, pederast and drug-taker who raped his own children but had become a close friend of John Paul II and in 2004 was invited to Rome for a papal blessing. Ratzinger was in possession of all the evidence about Maciel's regular debauchery with his young novitiates, but refused to act.

Even after he became pope, Benedict refused to defrock this monster priest or provide the evidence against him to the police. Instead, he merely 'invited' Maciel to retire and lead a quiet life in the US, away from media attention. Ratzinger undoubtedly loathes such men, but he was always the ostrich pope, the academic who kept his head in the sand until the storm hit – in Boston (2002), Ireland (2009) and now all over the Catholic world.

Pope Benedict's Vatican has been an enemy of human rights. The fiction that this religious enclave is a 'state' enables it to appear at UN conferences and to veto initiatives for family planning, contraception, or any form of 'gender equality'. Benedict himself has decried homosexuality as 'evil'. He ruled that women have no right to choose, even to avoid pregnancies that result from rape or incest; IVF is wrong (because it begins with masturbation); condom use, even to avoid HIV/AIDS within marriage, must never be countenanced. Ratzinger began the Vatican's attack on the UN in 1998 because its 'new world order' envisaged population reduction and what he termed 'the sinister ideology of women's empowerment'. There is no denying that the Vatican has been a force in international affairs, rallying the Catholic countries of Latin America to make common cause on moral issues with Islamist states like Libya and Iran – for example, to veto the UN's projected 'right to sexual health'.

As for international justice, Ratzinger has been its sworn enemy. When the UK dared to detain Augusto Pinochet, he went public and passionately defended the old torturer's right to return to Chile. He refused to sign up to the International Criminal Court, and has helped Robert Mugabe and his shopaholic wife to avoid EU travel bans by inviting them to travel to the Vatican, which is not an EU member (and cannot join because it is not a democracy).

As head of a make-believe but widely recognised state, Pope Benedict has had absolute immunity from legal action. But as ex-King Farouk famously discovered (when a court ordered him to pay for apparel acquired when he was king), this immunity is not the same after you retire. There are a number of priests who were permitted to stay in holy orders by Cardinal Ratzinger after their propensity to molest was known, and their victims would like to sue him for damages for negligence. If he chooses a retirement home outside the Vatican, the local court may decide that they have a case.

How to Stop Paedophile Priests

How should the next Supreme Leader of the Catholic Church meet its most urgent challenge: stopping its priests from sexually molesting boys? These widespread and systematic sexual assaults can collectively be described as a crime against humanity.

The church cannot atone just by paying compensation. Unless the new pope installs a policy that minimises danger to children, he – like Benedict – will become complicit in ongoing but avoidable abuse.

First, and most obviously, there must be zero tolerance for paedophile priests. They should automatically be defrocked by their bishop as soon as their guilt is established. There must be no delay, and certainly no appeal to the Vatican – it was there that Ratzinger's preference for avoiding scandal permitted so many paedophiles to be forgiven, and then to reoffend. There is ample evidence now, from Ireland, America, and Europe, that the Vatican has conspired to thwart prosecutors and protect clerical criminals.

The pope is the source of canon law, which directs that allegations of child molestation be investigated in utter secrecy, by a 'trial' loaded in favour of clerics who, if found guilty, are 'punished' for the most part by orders for prayer and penitence. This must be changed, by recognition that child molestation is a serious criminal offence that cannot be dealt with in a secret ecclesiastical procedure. Allegations must be reported to the police.

The Vatican pretends that it made this change in 2011, when new guidelines were issued reminding bishops to cooperate with law enforcement authorities. But this cooperation only needs to be forthcoming when local law *requires* it (and many countries still do not have laws compelling the reporting of child abuse). These guidelines are not incorporated into canon law: bishops are not told to hand evidence over to the police and priests are not required to inform on brothers whom they know (often through confession) to be molesting children. There is no duty to suspend a suspected priest.

Even in countries where local bishops have bowed to political pressure and announced that public prosecutors will be told of sex-abuse allegations, there is always another qualification: 'only if the victim consents'. It is all too easy for young victims and trusting parents to be counselled that the victim's best interests lie in allowing the church to deal with the matter 'in its own way' without involving the police. So priests escape prosecution because officials, in order to protect the reputation of their church, pressure and persuade families to have complaints dealt with in secret under canon-law processes.

Abolishing the role of the Vatican and of canon law in covering up for paedophile priests will take some papal courage, but will be relatively easy beside the radical changes necessary to stop the abuse from happening in the first place. The reform most often suggested is to abandon celibacy. This would not be doctrinally difficult – Christ's disciples appear to have been married, and the rule was a dogma introduced in the eleventh century and almost abolished by sixteenth-century reformers. But marriage does not 'cure' paedophilia. Moreover, many abusive priests are not paedophiles: their disordered personality can often be ascribed to conditions that would prevent them from forming satisfactory heterosexual relationships. Abuse happens because they are too weak or emotionally immature to resist the temptation.

That temptation arises because the church indoctrinates children at their earliest rational age – usually at seven – that the priest is the agent of God. Communion is an awesome miracle performed by the God-priest, and then the impressionable and nervous child is made to confess his sins and seek forgiveness from God, represented again by the priest. Father Tom Doyle explains the phenomenon of children's unflinching obedience to priests' sexual requests as induced by 'reverential fear': the victims have such emotional and psychological dependence on the abuser that they unquestioningly obey – and do not tell for many years afterward.

It follows that the only reform that would tackle the evil of clerical sexual abuse at its source would be to raise the age at which children are first given communion and confession from seven to, say, thirteen. Other churches (and the Jewish faith) leave indoctrination and spiritual commitment rituals until teenage-hood; by this stage, young people are much more capable of resisting sexual advances, and have more courage to report them.

Could a pope ever contemplate this reform? The Jesuits say, 'Give me the boy at seven . . .' and now we know what that has meant. The Vatican newspaper, worried that indoctrination at seven is not producing sufficient lifetime allegiance, has been arguing that the age of first communion and confession be reduced to five. If the new pope cannot bring himself to deliver small children from the spiritual hold of the priest, then parliaments may have to step in to protect children of tender age from immersion in religious rituals.

Chapter 30

THE LAW OF THE RINGS

The dickhead tendency in Australian official decision-making has many examples. The one that infuriated me first, as a seven-year-old tennis enthusiast, was how Lew Hoad and Ken Rosewall, who won the 1953 Davis Cup, were forced to undergo conscription at Holsworthy Barracks, with the result that they lost the Davis Cup in 1954.

You can see other examples of dickheadery scaring the coastline – Blues Point Tower, the Toaster, the Ettalong Beach War Memorial Club – although in New South Wales, outrageous planning decisions might be due to corruption rather than stupidity. Another prime example, this time thanks to ABC executives and state politicians, was their decision that the Sydney Opera House should not be an opera house but a recital hall, with a modest opera theatre attached. This theatre is far too small to accommodate the orchestra, the singers and the vision of Richard Wagner's Der Ring des Nibelungen, *a sixteen-hour epic performed over four days that provides the ultimate experience in musical drama.*

A scaled-down version was managed in a quarry in South Australia, but it was not until 2013 that Opera Australia rose to the occasion, in Melbourne, with the help of a hefty donation from Maureen ('Lonely Planet') Wheeler. Here follows my program note for the production's debut.

> I meant in the presentation of the whole Nibelung myth
> to show how, from the first wrongdoing, a whole world
> of injustice arose, and subsequently fell to pieces, in order
> to teach us the lesson that we must recognise injustice
> and tear it up by the roots and raise in its stead a right-
> eous world.
>
> Wagner, letter to Röckel, 23 August 1856

John Mortimer always said that he was glad he did not discover
Wagner until he was over sixty, otherwise he would have spent
many months of his life 'Ring-cycling', (which would have
been his only exercise). Not that the epic is suitable only for
the aged: this summer's Prom, conducted by the incomparable
Barenboim with his 137-strong Staatskapelle Berlin, received
ovations from thousands of young people standing for almost
as long as it would take them to fly to Australia. And that was
merely a concert performance. This music tingles the spine and
the brain at the same time when it is dramatised. The Ring
is the ultimate in operatic experiences, drawing any audience
prepared to engage with what Wagner called 'the emotionalisa-
tion of the intellect' into a cruel, God-ridden world that is about
to end, and (possibly) to begin again with a humanitarian order
in which individuals have learnt moral responsibility.

This might seem a portentous way of describing what to
lawyers would be an all too familiar dispute over a building
contract. Wotan has lots of freeloading children and relatives, so hires the giant firm of Fasolt & Fafner Ltd to build a
skyscraper to house them. The contract, negotiated by Loge,
his cunning but sleazy lawyer, provides that if he can't pay
on completion, he forfeits his sister-in-law to provide sexual
services indefinitely to the builders. I'm not sure how common
this sort of contract is in Australia: it might, in some states, be
void for immorality, although here in Melbourne I gather that
selling sexual services is lawful. At any event, Loge is hurriedly
summoned to find a loophole in the agreement: he suggests

expropriation of gold from Alberich, leader of the Nibelungen, which might not be considered theft since Alberich has stolen the means of making it from some women who were swimming in the Rhine. In Victoria, stealing from a thief counts as theft, but old Norse law was based on tit-for-tat and we are in very early times – the earliest, in fact. The effect of that low E-flat note on the double basses, followed individually by the horns, at the opening of *Das Rheingold* announces the creation of life. Wotan, it will much later emerge, is the god whose craving for power was attained by etiolating that creative force, ring-barking the world ash tree and leaving him only with the wisdom to will his own doom.

The pulling power of the *Ring* – the chemistry that draws aficionados back time and again to find fresh enrichment in its luminous fusion of music and myth, drama and philosophy, stems from the psychological depth of its characters, revealed in a complexity beyond the capability of any other composer–poet (although, if Milton had an orchestra . . .). Primitive demigods these people may be, fighting and loving and outwitting one another at the beginning of the sentient world, but their emotions, their social rules and their moral dilemmas are those of Wagner's time, and of ours. They possess some rough magic – a golden helmet (the Tarnhelm), Donner's thunder-hammer and the lethal tip of Wotan's spear – comparable, in our age, to the power of the internet and the tip of a nuclear missile, but they make as much of a mess of their lives as we do.

Take Wotan's opening dilemma: he is ruler of human society, a noble politician who owes his status and respect to his enforcement of the laws ('runes') that he enshrines on his spear. *Pacta servanda sunt*: contracts must be obeyed and solemn promises kept. But his megalomanic insistence on constructing a heaven to which war heroes can aspire (like devoted jihadists) requires a deceitful deal with the only giants who can build it. Extricating himself from that bargain will demean and diminish him, just as Obama's failure to deliver on his promise to close Guantanamo or Gillard's failure to junk the carbon tax shows modern politicians unable to cope with a catch-22 of their own making. Gods cannot have both their heaven and their eternal youth from Freia's golden apples (an apple a day keeps the wrinkles away): the hollow triumphal march across the rainbow bridge at the end of *Das Rheingold* presages their doom.

Wotan soon learns from earth mother Erda in Act II of *Die Walküre* that the time for gods – and for human beings to have illusions about the existence of gods – is almost up. He wills his own death, but hopes that Siegmund, his once begotten son, can save humanity by recapturing the Ring and returning the gold to nature, in the form of the river nymphs. But that creates a new dilemma: Siegmund must die, for love has led him to break another of the pettifogging rules on Wotan's spear – 'Thou shalt not commit adultery' (or, in this case, the double whammy – Thou shalt not commit adultery *and* incest, even in prehistoric Tasmania). There seems no way out of this catch-44, although Brünnhilde disobediently finds one: she cannot save Siegmund, but she can save his son, conceived in that last night of consanguineous passion, an orchestral orgasm that explodes at the end of Act 1 of *Die Walküre*. Brünnhilde's punishment is to sleep surrounded by fire until a love-smitten hero awakes her with a kiss. It sounds very *Snow White*, but Wotan's farewell to his daughter builds to one of the most moving set pieces in all opera. This is not some Disney-esque fairy story about dwarves and dragons, but an exploration of the most poignant emotion we are capable of feeling, for the loss of a loved one.

The dwarves and dragons are back in *Siegfried*, of course, together with the eponymous hero – an autistic teenager who knows no fear and is lured by the sensuousness of the birdsong to win Brünnhilde at the ecstatic climax of the last Act, reprised at the opening of *Götterdämmerung*. It is then that we learn the full story – from the Norns, the spinners of fate – and like Wotan we now know that the gods have no future. What Wagner saves to the end – indeed until after the curtain falls, when you can read about his alternative endings in this program note – is whether the fire that consumes Valhalla is merely the end of the gods (goodbye to superstition, militarism and oppression) or an end to the world – i.e. to humankind as well.

We are in the hands, let us always remember, of a revolutionary creative genius, out to challenge the injustices of a mid-nineteenth-century Europe where power over people was wielded by unforgiving churches, over-powerful armies and a privileged class of plutocrats, whose inherited wealth was now multiplied by ownership of industry. Wagner revolted not only in thought but in deed, standing on the barricades of Dresden in 1849 shoulder to shoulder with the famous anarchist Mikhail Bakunin, who went to prison. Wagner, proclaimed in a 'wanted' police poster as 'a politically dangerous person' escaped to Switzerland, where over the next few years he wrote the entire libretto of the *Ring*. He wrote under the philosophical sway of Ludwig Feuerbach, who held that all religion was fantasy, albeit a necessary fantasy for a human race that had nothing to build on other than nature. God did not create man; man had created God for comfort in his life and imagined heaven to relieve his fear of death. Thus, the end of the gods would provide the opportunity for individuals to evolve as humanitarians, to respect nature and to restrain the industrialists who despoiled it in their insatiable greed. Revolutionaries could then succeed in tearing down the petty and unjust rules of the state and the church, then would learn to love one another, and then die. This was the romantic socialist thinking that infuses the libretto of the *Ring*, as George Bernard Shaw, in *The Perfect Wagnerite*, instantly recognised. He called it 'melodramatic socialism' but took to it more kindly than Karl Marx, who thought it unscientific and 'utopian'.

Wagner later became disillusioned with revolutionary politics – the god that failed – and became immersed in the gloomy thinking of Schopenhauer, a pronounced atheist, who held that life was a tragedy, politics petty and that nothing really mattered. He analysed life in much the same way as Hobbes – it was short, brutish and nasty – but instead of concluding that a state Leviathan was necessary to put it in order, he argued that state control made it even worse. Its only consolations were art and sex, and attaining the wisdom to wish for death. That, of course, is Wotan's achieved wisdom in the *Ring* and hence Wagner's dilemma in ending *Götterdämmerung*: is it to offer the hope of a better life, or the hope of no life at all?

I favour the first (the so-called 'Feuerbach ending'), which chimes with the optimistic and iconoclastic philosophy of the younger Wagner. In this, the original version, Brünnhilde, who is about to immolate herself and become the human torch that will set Valhalla alight, tells the mysterious 'watchers' that once they have observed Valhalla's end and the return of the Ring to the Rhine:

> Though the race of gods
> passed away like a breath,
> though I leave behind me
> a world without rulers,
> I now bequeath to that world
> My most sacred wisdom's hoard –
> Not wealth, not gold,
> not godly pomp;
> not troubled treaties
> treacherous bonds,
> not smooth-tongued custom's
> stern decree:
> blessed in joy and sorrow
> love alone can be.

These words, written in 1852, sum up Wagner's original conception of the *Ring* as an attack on the injustice produced by the stultification and inhumanity of the church and the courts and the political and social tyrannies of the time, which must be overcome by disbelief and replaced by love. Later, under the bleak influence of Schopenhauer, he had Brünnhilde find her redemption in the realisation ('I saw the world end') that there will be no life after death for anyone other than nature.

Eventually he decided to cut both these alternative soliloquies and leave the audience to find its own emotional meaning. We become the mysterious 'watchers' observing on stage the pyromania at the end of *Götterdämmerung*. What do we make of the return of the Ring, of the ravens that wing towards Valhalla bearing its suicide-note, of Brünnhilde's fiery self-sacrifice and the stoicism with which the gods face their immolation? Will this mean a better world without God, or the destruction of a humanity that has failed to learn a worthy way to live? I am by nature optimistic, but as the cast take their bows I cannot help noticing that the two characters unaccounted for after the fire are Loge and Alberich – the seedy lawyer and the fallen tyrant. They will return, I fear, to pervert any new world that tries to live by love alone.

The *Ring Cycle* poses a challenge for any opera company, not only in its expense (these performances are sponsored by Lonely Planet – an apt, Schopenhauerian description of Wotan's domain). The work gains dramatic force through its staging, and the vision of conductor, director and designers. My first memory is of Ralph Koltai's centre-stage setting (for the English National Opera) of a large globe of the world, a rubber balloon strong enough to take the weight of the spherical Rita Hunter in horns and armour, while Reginald Goodall's baton lingered over every quivering bar and quatrain. Then at Covent Garden came Götz Friedrich's Marxist interpretation – which made a lot of sense – followed in later productions by time tunnels and crashed aeroplanes and, at the Met, the vast Arthur Rackham-style canvas mountains of Bavaria that had originally inspired Wagner (as well as *The Sound of Music*).

But the Met's latest effort is a value-free technological triumph, despite the shivering timbres of Bryn Terfel's Wotan, while in Bayreuth this year, Frank Castorf's meretricious production is full of expensive thrills. Brünnhilde's rock is Mount Rushmore (with Stalin replacing Jefferson), Siegfried gets drunk on schnapps rather than passion, Valhalla is the New York stock exchange and the Ring itself is an advertisement for Van Cleef

& Arpels. 'Erda gives Wotan advice and a blow job,' exclaimed *The Times* reviewer – whether in awe or horror is difficult to say, but it puts in perspective anything that Neil Armfield has in store. It will not be long before someone's *Ring* substitutes uranium for gold; makes Wotan the CEO of Rio Tinto, with Alberich keeping the Nibelungen hordes in North Korean-style subjugation. Valhalla will go up in a mushroom cloud. It might work because reactions to the *Ring* are infinitely personal: the account that has moved me least at Covent Garden was by Richard Jones: Brünnhilde's rock was an enormous orange chimney on top of a factory. But my Jewish friends were enraptured. 'This is the most deracinated production ever.'

So, inevitably, on to Wagner, Hitler and the Jews. Wagner's music still goes unplayed in Israel. Should any art that succeeds in its own terms, as art, go unappreciated because the artist held despicable views? I was brought up by Leavisites at Sydney University to value literature for its own sake, never raising my eyes from the text. I read Virginia Woolf and D. H. Lawrence, and only later read their diaries, which express the wish to have the mentally ill consigned to gas chambers – they were advocates of the perverted eugenics craze that captured the imagination of the left, as well as of Hitler, between the wars. Many great artists are cruel and tyrannical in their private life and have expressed deplorable opinions fashionable in their time: the real issue is whether these traits are discernible in their work or in its message. I can detect no anti-semitism at all in the *Ring*: the character of Mime, the duplicitous dwarf, is sometimes a candidate, but he exhibits the kind of greed shown by all who sit hypocritically at the bedside of a dying relative in the hope of an inheritance. Bringing up Siegfried, a Jewish mother he is not.

Wagner overreacted to everything in his writings, which are sometimes viciously anti-Semitic (although he regretted this towards the end of his life). His musical dramas, however, were tightly controlled, with stage and character directions that said what he meant. It is inconceivable that if he wanted Mime to be thought of as a Jew, he would not have said so. As for young

Siegfried, so often identified as the epitome of Hitler's master-race, it took W. H. Auden to point out that his low IQ (a result of incest?) and erratic behaviour hardly make him the proto-type for a superman. The only character with any resemblance to Hitler himself is the megalomanic tyrant Alberich, uncon-strained by the rules and treaties that Wotan must honour, happy to renounce love and enslave his own people to satisfy his lust for total power and unnecessary wealth. Hitler would not have noticed the parallel nor acted differently (art has its limits) if he had.

I am the last person to blame a man for the excesses of his wife, but it must be conceded that Cosima after Wagner's death turned Bayreuth into a festival that would be receptive to Nazi ideology. She was only prepared to hire Jewish conductors, singers and musicians if Aryan equivalents were unavailable. Their daughter married an odious English racist, whose writings were influential and who met and blessed Hitler. Wagner's son, Siegfried (of course), turned out gay, and covered by marrying Winifred, a Welsh orphan with an anti-Semitic streak, who fell in love with Hitler and invited him 'home' to Bayreuth so often that her children knew him as 'Uncle Wolf'. Whether she also gave him golden showers (Adolf was a urolagniac) is not known, but suspected. This intimacy with Der Führer brought lots of state funding, which is still very important (I noticed Angela Merkel in the audience this summer) but for all Winifred's kowtowing there was no nazification of the operas – not even a Swastika on the banners in *Meistersingers*. It is important to recognise (and Israel should take note) that as late as 1929 Otto Klemperer was conducting Wagner at the Jewish-dominated Kroll Opera House in Berlin (I am inordinately proud of this since I am descended from Joseph Kroll) and it was only rabid nationalists who protested.

Wagner is not responsible for Hitler and although the Nazis did exploit his musical legend, there was nothing in his operas that suggested or inspired the Holocaust. It is amusing to read accounts of the senior party members dragged by the Führer to sit for six hours in the seats at Bayreuth (which are even harder than those at the Sydney Opera House). These thugs were not interested in classical music – they yawned and dozed and scratched, and dreamed only of how to slink away to the beer halls and brothels of Bayreuth. The worst of the 'cultured' Nazis, like Dr Mengele, preferred to listen to Schubert. German armies never went into battle to the strains of 'The Ride of the Valkyries', like the US helicopter attack on Vietnam depicted in *Apocalypse Now*. Their musical inspiration was 'The Horst Wessel Song'. I have sometimes wondered whether, had Hitler not driven away Germany's Jewish scientists, they might have developed a nuclear weapon by the time he was forced into the bunker: one imagines him playing *Götterdämmerung* while ordering atom bombs to be dropped on London. That image dissolves in the face of the fact that Hitler lost interest in Wagner during the war, in favour of Lehar. The opera that consoled him in the bunker was *The Merry Widow*.

Nonetheless, in Wagner's two-hundredth anniversary year of 2013, it is right to remember the victims of the Holocaust, a crime that was eventually punished by human justice at Nuremberg. At nearby Bayreuth, in the garden beside the Festspielhaus, the nettle has been grasped: an exhibition, 'Silent Voices', has pictures and biographies of the Jewish singers and musicians who performed there in the decades before they were murdered in the camps, with an eloquent apologia for those hideous heirs of Richard Wagner who used his festival to support anti-Semitic and anti-democratic organisations in Germany. The best way to guard against the return of Alberich is to remember just how close the Nibelungen came, in 1939 to 1945, to recapturing their ring, with its power to rule the world.

ROLE MODELS

Chapter 31

FAREWELL, RUMPOLE

This obituary was written for the Guardian *in love and haste on the day of John Mortimer's death; reading it four years later fills me with awe at his achievements and gratitude that he welcomed me, and later my wife, into his charmed and charming circle around the little home and big garden at Turville Heath in Oxfordshire. He was my forensic father in the law courts and my friend outside them, and there was so much more that could have been written: the* Guardian, *which had for sixty years sympathetically chronicled his campaign against censorship and the death penalty, reviewed his plays and reported his career, published this tribute over two full pages and without cuts – a subeditor's salute to a life lived to the full. As for an afterlife, John was never sure. 'Eternity,' he would sigh. 'When will it all end?'*

The barrister, playwright and author Sir John Mortimer, who has died aged eighty-five, was a man for all the seasons that touched his Chilterns garden, where he lived as profusely as he wrote, in a spirit of unjudgmental generosity. His greatest achievement was to create, in Rumpole of the Bailey, a lawyer the world could love.

Though born in Hampstead, north London, John grew up in the house at Turville, near Henley, in Oxfordshire, that he never really left. His father was an irascible, blind barrister, the Mortimer of *Mortimer on Wills, Probate and Divorce*. His mother, devoted and stoic, read aloud to his father the sad, true stories of cruelty and passion between the wars contained in his briefs for the divorce court.

John, an only child, was sent to the Dragon School at Oxford, in a class with the historian E. P. Thompson and a 'sour-faced boy who wouldn't share his tuck', who grew up to become a severe circuit judge and model for Rumpole's adversary, Judge Bullingdon. Home from Harrow, the teenager wracked his imagination to stage theatricals that his father might 'see' – his contribution to the stiff-upper-lipped family pretence that Clifford Mortimer was not blind. In Henley, he encountered with interest the bookshop-owning lesbians who had taken opium with Cocteau, and a prim, elderly lady who had, in her youth, urinated regularly upon pioneering sexologist Havelock Ellis.

He determined to be a writer, and on leaving school joined the Crown Film Unit, devising accounts of industrial and military Britain in wartime. But his father had other ideas, a clash captured in *A Voyage Round My Father*, the account by John of their relationship that first surfaced as a play on BBC radio in 1963:

> Father: . . . if you were only a writer, who would you rub shoulders with? (*With contempt*) Other writers? You'll be far better off in the law.

> Son: I don't know.

> Father: No brilliance is needed in the law. Nothing but common sense, and relatively clean fingernails. Another thing, if you were a writer, think of your poor, unfortunate wife . . .

> Son: What?

> Father: She'd have you at home every day! In carpet slippers . . . Drinking tea and stumped for words! You'd

be far better off down the tube each morning, and off to the law courts . . . the law of husband and wife may seem idiotic at first sight but when you get to know it, you'll find it can exercise a vague, medieval charm. Learn a little law, won't you? Just to please me.

Son: It was my father's way to offer the law to me – the great stone column of authority which has been dragged by an adulterous, careless, negligent and half-criminal humanity down the ages – as if it were a small mechanical toy which might occupy half an hour on a rainy afternoon.

When Britain's other 1960s playwrights examined their fathers – Peter Nichols despairingly in *Forget-Me-Not Lane*, David Mercer bitterly in *After Haggerty* – *A Voyage Round My Father* stood out, not only for its stagecraft and for Alec Guinness's central performance, but for the unquestioning love distilled in its lines for this man who had been incapable of showing any to his son. Many young people ruin what would otherwise be talented and useful lives by devoting themselves to law, and John at the time felt himself to be one of them (he was always remarking on the irony of leaving the artificial atmosphere of the court at 4.30pm for the real life of theatre rehearsals). Yet practice of law, although it sapped the early development of his writing skills, eventually gave him the experience that produced his greatest character.

After Brasenose College, Oxford, and at war's end, love and law came hand in hand. He was called to the bar in 1948 and in the following year married Penelope Fletcher, taking on her four existing children and adding two of their own. They wrote a travel book together, *With Love and Lizards* (1957), and novels separately as he struggled to develop a practice. Soon he discovered a real talent for divorcing people (in those cruel, fault-finding days before divorce reform), and for the arcane Chancery world in which time and talent is expended in deciding the validity of a will written on a duck egg, or the charitable status of a legacy to Trappist nuns.

John's first stage success, *A Dock Brief* – set in the cells, where an incompetent barrister counsels himself and his convicted client – was rooted in his own nervousness about failure and his permanent terror at having responsibility for another's fate. For this reason, he avoided the criminal law until reform dried up his contested divorce work, and he had no alternative but to go 'down the Bailey'.

By the end of the 1960s he had a considerable reputation as a novelist (his first, *Charade*, drawing on his Crown Film Unit experience, appeared in 1947) and playwright, and he had played an important role in the abolition of the death penalty and the passage of the *Theatres Act*, which saw off that bane of the British stage, the Lord Chamberlain's power of censorship – not that his own work had ever been in danger from this quarter.

An irony of his leadership of the anti-censorship movement was his profound belief that anything at all should be capable of being said about sex, coupled with his own reluctance to deal in his work with anything other than its consequence. Sex was an amusing but bemusing fact of life: in his stage father's words, 'The whole business has been overestimated by the poets.'

This was not, one feels, an attitude shared by Penelope. Theirs was, in fact, a remarkable marriage, although its final stages were somewhat bitterly reflected by Penelope in her novel *The Home* (1971). John, typically, celebrated more of the fun and laughter in his play *Collaborators* (1973), in which the couple metamorphosed into characters played by Glenda Jackson and John Wood.

By this time, John was a successful silk – he had become QC in 1966 – having reinvented himself as an advocate in murder trials. He found a macabre fascination in the pattern of bloodstains, and acquired a singular ability to charm expert prosecution witnesses out of their preconceptions. He was the greatest cross-examiner of such experts ('the art of cross-examination is not to examine crossly') and many alleged murderers owed their liberty to his ability to draw out a doubt in the apparently closed mind of a police forensic scientist.

But nothing in the training of the English bar and bench had equipped it for the underground press, and when, in 1971, a largely unreadable magazine called *Oz* published a cartoon strip featuring Rupert Bear with an erection, its editors were treated as if they had committed treason. QCs, their cab-rank principles forgotten, fled from the proffered defence brief.

A few days before the trial – for conspiracy to corrupt public morals, an offence carrying a maximum of life imprisonment – Richard Neville and I showed John the offending publication while he was lunching a young woman, also named Penelope. They giggled. We begged him to take the case. 'Goody,' was his response.

Thus began his second life, as defender of the apparently indefensible, as creator of *Rumpole* and much else besides, and, from 1972, following his divorce, as husband of Penelope Gollop (Penny the second), and father of Emily and Rosie. Two autobiographies, *Clinging to the Wreckage* (1982) and *Murderers and Other Friends* (1994), speak of a life anchored in family, yet lived in a daily dramatic jumble of court cases, plays and television series, sharply observing the vanities of the world through the blur of diminishing eyesight.

Rumpole of the Bailey had a particular impact on the reception by juries of police evidence. It came at a time – the late seventies – when the vaudeville routine of the police 'verbal' was still in vogue. Hardened villains, immediately on their arrest, would always say 'It's a fair cop, guv' or 'You've got me bang to rights this time' or make other incriminating remarks. At least, police would tell this to juries as they read from the concocted interviews, in notebooks written much later in the police canteen. Juries would believe them, having been misled by the incredibly honest coppers in television entertainment like *Dixon of Dock Green*. But *Rumpole of the Bailey* presented a different picture. It showed how bent or overzealous police could secure convictions by forensic trickery. I remember the talk in the bar robing room at the Old Bailey during the first series of *Rumpole*: we credited the show with the new willingness of juries to acquit in such cases. In due course the law was changed and all police interviews had to be tape-recorded or videotaped.

Rumpole can also be credited with helping to change the culture of the bar. John was always amused at the prejudice against criminal law amongst the English legal establishment – as one senior judge had put it, 'the Old Bailey is hardly the SW3 of the legal profession'. Lawyers who practised in crime were looked down on and students who showed any interest in human rights (then called civil liberties) were warned that they might ruin their career. Rumpole helped the public – and the bar – to understand that the need to protect the liberty of the subject is the main justification for the profession, and certainly for its independence.

John retired from the bar in 1981. Rumpole was the barrister he wanted to be, but wasn't. He was too nervous – petrified before a big case, and diffident about his own ability in legal argument. However his final jury speeches, meticulously handwritten, were minor works of literature. Almost alone at the Bar, he could laugh a case out of court (had he stayed, he would have made a fortune in libel defences). His forensic contribution to civil liberties was effectively to end censorship for the written word, first for literature, by arguing the appeal that freed *Last Exit to Brooklyn* (the 1964 novel by American author Hubert Selby Jr, which was prosecuted under obscenity laws for its treatment of sex, drugs and violence), then by persuading the jury to reject the moral corruption charge against the editors of *Oz*, and going on to demolish, at the appeal, Judge Michael Argyle's directions on obscenity.

Of course pornography corrupted – starting with the policemen charged with enforcing the laws against it, many of whom were later jailed for taking bribes. John put on his wig and took off his glasses, so he could not see some of the trash he was called upon to defend with a success that drew rage from Mary Whitehouse and an extravagant attack from *The Times*, which claimed that no jury was immune to his charm.

The Williams committee on obscenity, reporting in 1980, agreed with Kenneth Tynan in crediting John with achieving a *de facto* freedom for the written word by his victorious defence of *Inside Linda Lovelace* (1978), a shabby little book that would have gone unnoticed had the DPP's office not decided to dignify it with a prosecution, after which it sold almost a million copies.

From dawn each day John would be at work on his supreme creation, *Rumpole of the Bailey*. Horace Rumpole had, like all great fictional characters, been composed from fragments of the real people John had worked with: his father, James Burge (a mercurial Old Bailey junior who was denied silk by the establishment in reprisal for his zealous defence of Stephen Ward during the Profumo scandal in 1963) and Jeremy Hutchinson, a mighty defence QC married at the time to Peggy Ashcroft.

In the hands of Leo McKern and Thames Television from 1978 to 1992 (after an initial appearance on the BBC in 1975), and in novels that continued till 2006, Rumpole achieved international acclaim. There are Rumpole societies of lawyers basking undeservedly in his popularity from Los Angeles to Perth. Rumpole is, perhaps, the first truly Dickensian character to emerge from the medium of television. There remains one great virtue about him – his independence – along with much that has, for good reason, passed away. If Rumpole returned today, he would still not be made a silk. The new appointments board displays a marked English nervousness about appointing outspoken eccentrics to the rank of Queen's Counsel.

John worked on, long after leaving the bar, meticulous as ever. He came to the European Court of Human Rights in Strasbourg with us in 1995 to research the law and the restaurants that feature in *Rumpole and the Rights of Man*, and more recent volumes had the bewildered barrister grappling with ASBOs and terrorism control orders. Too full of ideas to sleep, he started work on a new film or novel or play – or all at the same time – at 5 am, ending in time for long gossipy lunches with friends and family, followed by theatre and parties in London.

In the capital, he has in recent years served as culture's Queen Mother, gracing the National Theatre, the Royal Opera, the Royal Ivy and the Royal Court with his comfortingly unchanging, beaming presence. It is a sorry reflection on his political friends that he was never made Lord Mortimer of Turville, although he was knighted in 1998. The older he became, the more determined he was to cudgel his mind for any idea that might amuse a reader, while continuing to champion the causes for which he cared – the Howard League for Penal Reform, the Royal Court Theatre, and a holiday home for deprived children that he and Penny helped to establish in Turville.

Politically, his faith in liberal socialism wavered at the end. He had emerged from his one-member communist cell at Harrow to a post-war Labour party he supported with increasing conviction as the Thatcher years changed Britain for the worse. Once the joker, jotting his contributions to the satirical BBC TV comedy *That Was the Week That Was* during idle afternoons in court in the early 1960s, he and Penny teamed up with Harold Pinter and Antonia Fraser to found 'the 20 June Group' in 1987 – reviled almost as viciously in the Tory press as it was by those on the left who were not invited to join. Although saddened by the 1992 election loss, he was increasingly uncertain about Tony Blair and his talent for turning the Labour party into the war party. In 2005 he broke the habit of a lifetime, and voted Liberal Democrat.

The previous year a shoddy and unauthorised biography produced one delightful result. It stirred some embers, from which emerged, fully formed, a lost son, the hidden fruit of a sixties affair with the actress Wendy Craig. It was a happy discovery for both men, and later a proper biography. *A Voyage Round John Mortimer* (2007), by Valerie Grove, did her subject justice, capturing some of the pleasures of the Mortimer caravanserai: the long Sunday lunches at Turville in winter, the bluebell picnics in Chiltern woods every spring; the summer idylls in that part of Italy he dubbed 'Chiantishire'.

In the last years, age wearied everything except his mind.

His rotund face collapsed, his limbs and bladder gave up, bedtime became a ritual of excruciating pain, yet he continued writing and performing, as if for dear life. *Mortimer's Miscellany*, performed at the Sydney Festival in 2006, ran for a month at the King's Head, Islington, in 2007. A doctor's warning that the run might kill him only excited him at the prospect of dying like Dickens. He strove to keep his jokes up to date, although (like the law) they lagged by a decade. (Judge comes into court confessing he has left in his country cottage the judgment he is meant to read. 'Fax it up, m'lord,' says counsel. 'Yes it does, rather,' laments the judge). His own cottage in Turville Heath had acquired a conservatory for Sir Laurence Olivier to pot earwigs in the television version of *Voyage*. Every weekend until his death it became a place of laughter and gossip and gumboots and children, with friends who felt privileged (although they were never made to feel privileged) to inspect the garden and walk in the wood and sip tea and champagne and talk of everything except Michelangelo, with the Renaissance man who had been saved from terminal decadence by his Reformation wife.

Much of his work in the last half of his life, and much of his continuing happiness, was inspired by Penny the second, whose enormous strengths of decency and determination creatively challenged his own vacillation and reluctance to make moral judgments. The result may be seen in his work, and in his family: Hollywood actress Emily and model Rosie (daughters with Penny II); Radio 4 producer Jeremy and social worker Sally (with Penny I) and law/IT consultant Ross Bentley, his long-lost son.

John Clifford Mortimer, barrister, playwright and author, born 21 April 1923; died 16 January 2009

Chapter 32

VÁCLAV HAVEL, AND ALL THAT JAZZ

In December 2011, after the death of Václav Havel – playwright, philosopher and former president of Czechoslovakia – American right-wingers claimed him as their own. My old friend would have turned in his grave at the accolades from George W. Bush and the Wall Street Journal *op eds that claimed him as some kind of proto-neo con who supported unrestrained capitalism and the invasion of Iraq. On the contrary, he died cheering for Bradley Manning and the 'Occupy' movement – then current examples of his belief in 'the power of the powerless'. I provided this reminiscence for the* Daily Beast *and the* Australian *to set the record straight.*

Václav Havel struck me as the most unlikely of revolutionaries when we first met in 1986 in the smoky fug of his favourite café overlooking Prague's Vltava River. His nervousness had something to do with the secret police eyeing us shiftily from their table by the window.

But he was also concerned that his demands for the truth, to lift the Stalinist miasma that had wearily settled over Czechoslovakia, might eventually require rethinking of the democratic socialism in which he believed. So at all our meetings he would chain-smoke and agonise, but not even the threat of a return to prison (he had already served four years) could weaken his resolve to fight for freedom of thought and speech.

I was in Prague to arrange support for political prisoners. Havel's own crime had been to draw up Charter 77, a demand for human rights. By 1986, the country's rigid but corrupt communism had produced an official rate of exchange so absurdly at variance with reality that US dollars were accepted at thirty times their official value everywhere in the city. But when I tendered them to pay for our meal, Havel stopped me and explained (I kicked myself for not realising) that he would immediately be rearrested by the watching police as an accomplice in black marketeering. 'This is the first rule of being a dissident,' he instructed me. 'You must scrupulously obey the law.'

It was the first of many Kafkaesque ironies to which I was introduced by this unassuming philosopher–playwright. I visited Prague regularly in 1986–88 on behalf of the Jan Hus Society, a rainbow coalition of Western writers (ranging from Tom Stoppard to Harold Pinter), which organised funding and public support for the defence of Czech dissidents. Havel was courageously prepared to be my mentor, explaining to me which cases were important, which lawyers could be trusted to handle them, and which families most needed financial support. By this time the authorities were playing a cat-and-mouse game with him. His celebrity in the West gave him a certain protection, but he was always threatened with return to prison if his activities became too embarrassing.

Gustáv Husák's Stalinist government was doing a good job of embarrassing itself. It had just passed a criminal law against possessing a copy of *The Frank Zappa Songbook*, and an eighteen-year-old youth had already been sent to prison. 'He was a dissident,' Havel told me sorrowfully, 'before he was a man.' The government's concern about Zappa dated from 1976, when members of Plastic People of the Universe – a rock band that took its name from the songbook – were jailed in the first assault on 'alternative' culture. Now it had arrested the entire executive of the Czech Jazz Society, who had published a three-volume *Encyclopedia of Rock* with a long entry on Zappa. It was to assist their defence that I had first come to Prague to meet Havel, who explained how important the case was to his strategy of 'velvet revolution', of confronting and confounding communism with its own phoney commitments to human rights.

The genius of Charter 77 had been to argue that the Czech government's ratification of the UN's covenant on civil and political rights had imported these rights into its municipal law, pursuant to promises made by the Soviets in the 1975 Helsinki agreement. This was something of a fudge (Helsinki was a rudimentary handshake on East–West cooperation, specifically made non-binding so the US could sign) but it called the Soviet bluff: human rights appeals by dissidents could gather momentum by taking these international agreements at their face value, however much the governments that signed them lacked any intention of honouring them.

So the Jazz Society was briefly permitted to flourish, attracting more than one hundred thousand young people to its *Rock on the Left Wing* concerts, its tree plantings in honour of John Lennon and its seminars with Green parties from Western Europe. Havel's involvement with the Jazz Society gave him the support base that later came out on the streets to propel him to the presidency in 1989. But in 1986 its existence, by clinging to its supposed rights under Helsinki and through its UNESCO affiliation, had infuriated the government.

Its leading members were sacked from their jobs and then, when they continued to organise concerts, arrested on charges of 'unlicensed trading'. The government pretended to the world that this was simply a fraud case ('A crime in your country too,' Czech diplomats would tell Western counterparts) but this was propaganda: the Jazz Society was a strictly non-profit enterprise.

Havel identified this case as a crucial test for socialist legality and took me along to the trial of its chairman, Karel Srp. This was the time of Soviet-style 'telephone justice' when the trial itself was a sham: the verdict (and more importantly the sentence) was delivered in a telephone call from the party boss to the judge on the night before the hearing.

There had been sufficient fuss made about the case in the West for Srp to be given a lenient sentence – two years' imprisonment – and when we emerged on the steps of the court for Havel to announce the result to several hundred waiting supporters, they struck up a ragged chorus of 'We Shall Overcome'. 'You can always tell who are the secret police on these occasions,' explained Havel with a tight grin. 'They are the ones who know all the words.'

I have never much liked jazz – you keep thinking it will turn into a tune, and it doesn't. But it had been banned by Stalin and condemned as 'decadent' by the Nazis. What, I asked Havel, is its subversive secret? He gave his trademark grin and invited me to an 'official' jazz concert organised by the government after it disbanded the Jazz Society, in order to show it was not afraid of music. We sat through hours of sclerotic Russian 'big bands' (old men in suits playing Glenn Miller) until after midnight, when thousands of young people turned up in the cavernous Lucerna Theatre to hear Herbie Hancock and Mike Westbrook, and to laugh about the stupidity of the police. 'You see now why totalitarians distrust jazz,' said Havel. 'Because it's music you can talk under.'

It was to the Lucerna – ironically once owned by Havel's wealthy family – that his supporters flocked two years later to listen to his hoarse, halting but determined speeches about the need for a 'socialist legality' that could respect human rights and allow criticism of the state. 'We must fight with our only weapons – words,' he declared, and the words of the crowd, 'Havel to the castle', carried him triumphantly to the presidency as the dishonest, geriatric regime finally faced up to the truth and withered away. One of Havel's first actions as president was to invite Zappa to make an official visit.

Back in London, we hosted Havel at the Institute of Contemporary Arts on his first presidential trip abroad in March 1990.

After his lecture, some idiot from *Marxism Today* asked him accusingly why he wasted so much presidential time with an American rock singer. Havel seemed lost for words, but then politeness got the better of him. 'Because . . . well, because he seemed a very nice man.' It would have taken too long to explain the symbolism, too many imperfect words to conjure up for some pampered English Marxist what it was like to live under the constant threat of losing one's liberty as punishment for reading another's lyric.

Havel's presidency was plagued by smoking-related illnesses and the difficulties of keeping any socialist faith at all in a free market free-for-all. I went back to Prague to lecture on free speech but discovered that what Czechs needed most was guidance in contract law and in conveyancing of private property, subjects that had not been relevant in a Stalinist state. Havel, in and out of power over the next two decades, remained an inspiration. His speech to the Canadian parliament during NATO's bombing of Kosovo, which he justified 'out of respect for a law that ranks higher than the law which protects the sovereignty of states', was an influential contribution to the evolving principle of humanitarian intervention.

Havel was the most humble man I have worked with – and probably the most influential. He stands with Soviet dissident and human rights activist Andrei Sakharov at the head of the pantheon of people prepared to sacrifice their liberty so others could enjoy liberty as a right. Politically, he achieved his aim of revising the map of middle Europe so disastrously drawn at Yalta. Philosophically, he never quite squared the circle over which he agonised in that café by the Vltava – how to reconcile his belief in both socialism and freedom.

Chapter 33

SINGAPORE'S LION

History is usually written by, or about, winners, which is one reason why I penned the Guardian's *obituary for Ben Jeyaretnam, Singapore's perpetual loser. For half a century in this small city state, he stood – and stood and stood – for true democratic values, against a government that intimidated electorates by threatening to withdraw all their public services if they dared to elect an opposition MP.*

Ben was handed on to me as a client by John Mortimer: we took it in turns to defend his honest criticisms of Lee Kuan Yew, in front of the judges Lee had appointed – who were not so much biased as brainwashed into believing that their prime minister could do no wrong. Mind you, Lee Kuan Yew deserves some credit as dictator of an ersatz democracy who eliminated his opponents by bankrupting them with libel writs rather than using other methods of liquidation.

After the Bali bombing, Australians became attracted to the Asian 'strongman' model that Lee exemplified, although Asians, including Singaporeans, came to like it less. When Ben died in September 2008, there were only two opposition MPs in parliament, but in the 2012 elections – to the People's Action Party's horror and amazement – it only just scraped home. Perhaps Ben's legacy was beginning to work.

Joshua 'Ben' Jeyaretnam, who has died aged eighty-two, was for many years Singapore's only opposition politician, standing courageously for universal values of fairness and free speech against Lee Kuan Yew's 'Asian values' of hierarchical order, public submissiveness and government by the fittest – that is himself, his son (B.G. Lee) and his People's Action Party (PAP). Jeyaretnam, as leader of the Workers' Party, was regularly persecuted, briefly imprisoned and ultimately bankrupted by Lee's use of colonial libel and contempt laws, but he continued his struggle to make Singapore a more open and fair society.

Born into an Anglican family of Christian–Tamil descent in then Ceylon (now Sri Lanka), he was educated at St Andrew's School, Singapore, during the Japanese occupation and won, via a correspondence course, a place to study law at University College London. There, a lecture by Nye Bevan inspired his early socialist beliefs. They were put on hold while he developed a successful legal practice back in Singapore, where he became increasingly angered by the Kuan Yew government's attacks on trade unions. So in 1971 he made his political move, joining the Workers' Party, which was at that time moribund through lack of effective leadership.

His first electoral attempts failed, but his mild criticisms of the PAP government, delivered in a deep and booming voice from the hustings, infuriated Lee Kuan Yew, who in 1978 attempted to crush him with a libel case. In court, with the help of his wife, dying of cancer, and of John Mortimer QC, acting *pro bono*, Ben survived, albeit much poorer from the libel damages, to fight another day. That day came in 1981, when the electors of the constituency of Anson stood up to PAP threats to cut their public utilities and elected Ben as Singapore's first opposition MP.

This victory was the trigger for a long-running campaign to diminish and then destroy him. He was forced to pay the Kuan Yews and other PAP grandees for criticisms that would scarcely raise eyebrows in real democracies, and was fined for contempt of parliament for making allegations of the kind commonly made by MPs in other countries: Ben estimated he had paid out more than S$1.6 million in damages and costs. His bankrupt-cies disqualified him for several periods from parliament and no shops would stock his books – he was forced to sell them on street corners.

Ironically, it was Lee Kuan Yew's obsession with destroy-ing – rather than merely defeating – his opponents that led the government to overplay its hand. Not content with having Ben convicted, bankrupted and expelled from parliament, its obses-sion with humiliating him led it in 1987 to take away his right to practise law, the profession that had sustained him through-out his life. But it failed to notice an obscure clause in the *Legal Practitioners Act*, which permitted an appeal by a disbarred solicitor to the Privy Council in London.

It was there that the whole trumped-up series of charges against Ben unravelled. The English law lords reviewed the case objectively and voiced a devastating condemnation of the Singa-pore judges who had handled it, expressing 'deep disquiet that by a series of misjudgments' Ben and his co-accused had suffered a 'grievous injustice'. They had been fined, imprisoned and disgraced for offences of which they were not guilty.

The Singapore government responded by abolishing all appeals to the Privy Council, and still adamantly refuses to sign any human rights treaty that would permit any more decisions of its courts to be appealed to an international tribunal. But the Privy Council judgment in Jeyaretnam's case still resounds, as a warning to other judges tempted to fail in their task of standing up for the subject against the state.

For the last forty years, Ben pointed out Singapore's demo-cratic deficit. His speeches were not properly reported in the government-owned *Straits Times*, and any foreign newspaper that interviewed him risked having its circulation cut to four hundred copies and sold only in tourist hotels. His voice was loudest in 1988 when Lee and son (the latter as Home Affairs Minister) detained for two years without trial twenty young Catholic youth workers, lawyers and playwrights accused of participation in a 'Marxist plot'. Several were women playwrights, jailed without trial on the charge of 'singing aggressive songs and performing plays which exaggerated the plight of the poor and the inadequacies of the existing system'.

They were tortured by use of what Lee junior (who became, of course and in due course, Singapore's prime minister) described as 'psychological pressure' to extract confessions – dressed in cotton pyjamas, they were blasted for hours with freezing cold from souped-up air conditioners. With organisations such as Amnesty International banned from Singapore, Ben's voice was important in exposing the cruelty of their treatment.

Ben felt that many Western criticisms of Singapore were misplaced. They focused on its laws against jaywalking, urinating in public and dropping chewing-gum wrappers. The real concern was that the PAP had turned the city state into an ersatz democracy by suppressing well-intentioned dissent, and even the reporting of such dissent, in order to maintain its monopoly of power. Ben's views were set out in a book in 2003 by Chris Lydgate that serves as his biography: *Lee's Law – How Singapore Crushes Dissent*.

Ben was never in any realistic sense Lee's rival for national leadership. With his tailored waistcoat, watch chain and mutton-chop whiskers, he looked the model of a Gladstonian Liberal, but voters who wanted their monorails to run on time preferred PAP precision to the shambolic Workers' Party. Nonetheless, the persecution he stoically suffered gave his life a significance it would not otherwise have had.

The PAP has ruled Singapore since 1965, and Ben has been their principal opponent. He lost his seat in 2001, bankrupt again because he could not pay another $367,000 libel judgment to Lee and son.

However, on emerging from bankruptcy early in 2008, he helped to form the Reform Party and announced that he would once again stand for parliament, in an attempt to give Singapore 'rights that are most essential to our well-being: the right to speak up freely, the right to tell the government that the way things are going is wrong'.

The Privy Council's recommendation that the Singapore government pardon Ben and make amends for his wrongful conviction has, of course, been ignored. A future generation, however, will understand that he deserves not only to be pardoned, but to be honoured.

Chapter 34

MICHAEL KIRBY AT SEVENTY

Michael Kirby has been a good friend, ever since he mentored me in student politics at Sydney University back in the sixties. On his seventieth birthday in 2009 he left the High Court, and I was asked to contribute the introduction to a book in which legal academics surveyed his legacy. It was never going to be a slim volume – it ran to 996 pages. Since the tome would only be bought by his friends, it seemed safe to provide some more intimate, youthful snapshots of Michael. The last paragraph was sufficiently shocking to be tut-tutted about in the Sydney Morning Herald.

Happy birthday, Michael. At three score years and ten you have reached the age that Shakespeare allots for one life – yet as the size of this book attests, you have lived so many. It celebrates most of them, as they have impacted upon every aspect of law and its reform in Australia, as they have inspired several generations of law students, academics and practitioners, as they have served the wider community by finding reasoned ways through thickets of prejudice and ignorance and outmoded beliefs. It pays tribute to your kindness to friends and strangers alike and surveys your work for humankind: all the lives you have saved through your prescience over HIV/AIDS; how you have given the Human Genome Project its charter and provided an ethical base for modern reproductive medicine; how you have contributed to the reconstruction of war-torn Cambodia and drafted at Bangalore the international code by which judges of the world conduct their business. Life is better – in Australia, and elsewhere – because you have lived.

This book is what academics call a *festschrift* – essays in honour of Your Honour. In it you will read (if you have the time) your story so far, with predictions for the fate of all those dissenting judgments with which you have doubled the size of the *Commonwealth Law Reports* over the past decade. They recount the multifarious ways in which your decisions and law reform proposals and the recommendations in your lectures and books have reshaped thinking in the legal world. They pay tribute to your phenomenal industry, to your powers of historical exposition, to your creative imagination and ability to marshal all that is to be known under the sun on any particular subject and then to distil it into readily understood principles.

My only regret – and I am sure you will share it – is that the volume lacks any contribution from your usual critics. It would have been useful to hear from a barrister who finds life too short to read your judgments, or from a judge who disagrees with your appeals to international conventions, or from one of those newspaper commentators who find it convenient and lucrative to fill their columns with bile about you. The ironic thing about their criticism, of course, is that you relish it, as proof of the fact that your ideas are having an impact – enough to unsettle those whose vested interests they disturb. A few of your judicial colleagues have had understandable anxieties that your high profile might attract unfair criticism or unwanted attention to the bench, but we live in an age that demands greater transparency and accountability and, in any event, you have done the judiciary proud: your public image has served to reassure the public that judges are indeed judicious. (I have never known you

to be anything other than judicious, except at the Old Guard
balloon game, over which I shall draw a veil.)

There is, of course, a raging debate over judicial activism. I
take a novel position, neither for nor against, because I think all
judges are activists, especially those of your High Court brethren
who so actively deploy strict construction to reach conservative
conclusions. But the issue goes back long before your time on
that court. It was best articulated in the debate between Lord
Denning – a passionate exponent of creative law-making, and
Lord Devlin, a cool advocate of judicial restraint.* Ironically,
Devlin's own judgments were rather like yours – lengthy and full
of history, policy and principles. He had a wide-ranging, enquir-
ing mind, wore his hair long and his floral shirts bright purple,
and retired early from the House of Lords because he found his
judicial colleagues boring. Denning – on whom you have partly
modelled your own style (those very short sentences) – disguised
his massive erudition in tabloid prose and re-wrote the law of
contract and tort to serve the needs of modern society. The man
himself, alas, was stuck in pre-war middle-class morality, and
his prejudices later came to disfigure judgments that discrimin-
ated against women, denied rights to prisoners, foreigners, and
trade unionists and yielded all power to the state in matters of
national security. He refused to retire ('I have every virtue except
resignation') but then repeated in one of his books some racist
scuttlebutt he had picked up at a Temple dinner, about black
jurors being untrue to their oaths. They became my clients and
I had dutifully to draft the libel pleadings that forced him from
office.

It was Denning who made the jejune distinction – which I
am afraid you have picked up – between 'bold spirits' and 'timid
souls'. Courage and cowardice are overused words and neither
is relevant to the judicial task. In a democracy, leaving aside the

---

* Alfred Denning was the populist judge whose reforms in civil law inspired
  many throughout the common law world, while Patrick Devlin was the most
  intellectual of the judges (law lords) sitting in Britain's highest court (the
  House of Lords) after the war.

common law, parliament makes rules and judges apply them. The virtue of this approach lies primarily in its predictability – no mean thing, since those of us who urge a belief in the rule of law are made to look silly when it turns out to be the length of the Chancellor's foot. After all, as Devlin points out, most judges (with your Australian Law Reform Commission background, you are a rare exception) are ill-equipped for excursions into law-making because 'like any other body of elderly men who have lived on the whole unadventurous lives, they tend to be old-fashioned in their ideas', and anyway, learning in law is no guarantee of common sense.

What the 'judicial inactivist' school overlooks, however, is the extent to which discretion and choice are involved in curial decision-making. This is obviously so at first instance, in deciding the length of sentence or finding facts on conflicting testimony or determining whether to reject evidence that has been illegally or immorally obtained. Personal outlooks and prejudices will, sometimes unconsciously, inform these decisions. So too at appellate level, where the alternative interpretations of statute or the plasticine of case law leaves a choice – often between arguments that are good and arguments that are better. In the rarefied classroom of the High Court, there is no such thing as a judicial 'error': you do not make mistakes of logic or science, but deliver an arguable opinion that is often trumped by an opinion that is better argued. Most cases at appellate level are not straightforward – that is why they have gone on appeal – and here the art of judging becomes the art of juggling, of shading and eliding, and ultimately the art of choosing. The English language is rich with ambiguity and Australian jurisprudence is teaming with precedents: whenever legislative words have more than one meaning, or where case law points in different directions or offers different solutions, there comes the necessity for choice.

The best judges are reckoned to be those whose choices pass the Benthamite calculus, producing the greatest happiness for the greatest number. I've always thought of you as a floppy

Benthamite, refined by Julius Stone's teaching of Roscoe Pounds' methodology for weighing the interests involved in a judicial decision, but more importantly by an understanding of Ronald Dworkin's 'crucial idea' that democracy is not the same thing as majority rule: the greatest number might have to suffer a slight degree of mortification when the courts uphold the fundamental right to pursue happiness of a minority they dislike.* Although minorities are unprotected in Australia by any bill of rights, since you are a member of one of them I suspect that the choices you have made, influenced also by your lengthy experience as a law reformer, are better than most on offer. When the best choice is radical, however, you do sometimes falter: law reform commissioners tend to caution, even conservatism, because they have to craft their recommendations to suit what politicians will accept.

Critics of your work fail to grasp that a judgment is not a computer printout from fed-in facts, but a decision between competing and tenable arguments. Although law is 'settled', many issues are not – which is why they come to court. They may be thrown up by the advance of technology or the sophistication of police and criminals, or the aspiration of groups and individuals who want to live better or more convenient lives. The choice you make will affect those lives, and although your judicial colleagues say they make a 'policy' decision, these are really political decisions, in the sense that the policy is influenced by subjective feelings and philosophies. Ultimately, of course, it must measure up to the standard of justice – but which standard? For Devlin (and for Michael McHugh in *Al-Kateb*),**

---

* Julius Stone was the long-serving Professor of Jurisprudence at Sydney University, of great influence on Kirby because he taught ways of escaping from predetermined decisions by introducing policy considerations into judicial choice. Dworkin, who died in 2013, has been the most influential Anglo-American legal proponent of a rights-based jurisprudence, renowned for hard-nosed liberal solutions to moral issues.

** This was the case in which the High Court notoriously upheld – by four votes to three – an interpretation of a statute that would produce indefinite detention for asylum seekers. McHugh deplored the result, but felt impelled by the language of the statute to join the majority decision.

'justice' lies in the merit of the principle upon which the choice is made, while for Denning – (and for you in *Al-Kateb*) – it lies in the merit of the result of that choice. Which raises the question whether, in hard cases, courts should opt for just means or just ends?

There is no difficulty in rejecting the austere literalists, wilfully blind to the results of their decisions. A few of your High Court colleagues still seem to live in Diceyworld, but for grown-up judges, literalism is dead. As Lord Steyn reminds us:

> the tyrant Temures promised the garrison of Lebastia that no blood would be shed if they surrendered to him. They surrendered. He shed no blood. He buried them all alive. This is literalism. If possible it should be resisted in the interpretative process.

Activists are more appealing, but not when they echo Denning's arrogant and simplistic boast that 'I must do justice, whatever the law may be', if only because justice eventually meant for Denning what fiction meant to Miss Prism – 'the good end happily, the bad unhappily.' (The 'bad' in his anachronistic moral vision including prisoners, feminists, trade unionists and gays.) The proper approach to interstitial law reform remains more or less that of Portia in *The Merchant of Venice* – implement parliament's purpose, with an interpretation of its statute that serves the values of humanity, compassion and mercy 'as far as possible' – i.e. so far as language allows this choice. Pick from the available grab-bag of precedents the one that seems most to advance the needs of modern society, or at least fashion the common law according to universally accepted (if not universally applied) principles and values of the kind that are set out in international conventions or bills of rights.

I do not get the impression that your last ten years have been entirely happy, which is not surprising given your record of dissent. At least you have been spared the fate of that great British judge Lord Atkin, whose colleagues petulantly refused to dine with him after his famous dissent in *Liversidge v Anderson*,* which everyone now accepts as courageous and correct. Have any of your brethren dined with Johan, by the way?** Of course the High Court has never been a particularly congenial place – the spats between Evatt and Dixon are legendary, and it was Starke who said to Rich, at the cemetery as they buried Isaacs, 'You look so ill – why bother to go home?'

My only appearance there was the result of the worst piece of advice I have ever given a client. Dow Jones was looking for a court to decide the question of where an internet libel was committed – in every country where it could be downloaded (that is, all 193 of them) or, preferably and rationally, only in the place it was uploaded. 'Try Australia,' I said. 'It has a progressive High Court that might protect the internet from libel gold-diggers.'

Fat chance. After a parish pump-priming judge in Victoria, who thought 'free speech' meant speech made expensive by libel damages, we came to Canberra. There you all were, trooping in suddenly like seven black cockatoos (whatever happened to the usher shouting 'oyez'?) and then taking up your pecking order. And I do mean pecking. To the Chief's right were Hayne, Gaudron and Gummow JJ. After they had asked a few questions, they chattered amongst themselves, especially when you or Ian 'the Tub' Callinan were asking questions. 'The Tub', on the Chief's far left, could not understand the difference between newspapers and the internet: I gather from his judgment that I failed to enlighten him.

You asked most of the questions and wrote a long concurrence, showing an encyclopaedic knowledge of the worldwide web but failing to find a way of freeing it from the constraints of nineteenth-century Victorian defamation theory. Murray

---

* A wartime case in which Britain's pliant judges bent statutory language to allow the Home Secretary to jail anyone. The only dissenter was Lord Atkin, who pointed out that his brethren had become 'more executive-minded than the executive'.

**Michael Kirby's long-time partner.

Gleeson, I have to say, impressed me with his chairmanship as he struggled to keep his judges in some sort of order. Your seven–nil decision against Dow Jones has, I am pleased to say, already become outdated and is increasingly disdained by courts in Canada, the United States and Britain. Nevertheless you were prepared to debate it later with Dow Jones lawyers at a good-natured session at the Commonwealth Law Conference, a form of accountability to which you are one of the few judges to submit.

I should perhaps make this point – because no one else does. Your international work has been astonishing and outstanding – your chairmanship of the International Commission of Jurists in Geneva, projects at the Organisation for Economic Co-operation and Development and the United Nations Educational Scientific and Cultural Organization, lectures in London and your United Nations positions in New York and Cambodia and Bangalore, not to mention your famous lecture in Zimbabwe on breastfeeding.

For an Australian holding down a full-time job, to make this contribution to international civil society must come at severe personal cost. Notwithstanding the internet, the tyranny of distance exacts a heavy personal toll in jetlag and sleep deprivation. Tireless in your toil to build a better world, you have taken no payment for all this work. What is more, doing it often for cash-strapped organisations, you have insisted on flying economy class. When you arrive at Heathrow, you always take trains or buses, never a more expensive taxi. This kind of integrity is rivalled by no one I know in the field. It is a rare self-sacrificing quality, and probably contributed to your recent heart problem.

~

The editors seem to think that I may have snapshots, so to speak, from the student political album at Sydney University, or from occasional encounters since. You have told others that I influenced you at various times, but when offering you advice

I always have the advocate's sense when talking to a judge that his mind is probably made up already.

You were born in 1939 – the generation ahead of me, although we were both what my wife (a denizen of Cronulla beach) derisively terms 'Westies'. We both attended 'opportunity class', a curious invention of Darwinians at the New South Wales Department of Education, who thought that precocious boys from the city's lower-middle classes could compete with the progeny of private schools by being made to feel, at the age of twelve, separate and superior. Then came a selective state school – Fort Street, in your case. Would you have been quite so pompous in your early career had you attended a non-selective school? Perhaps your sights might have been set lower – you might have followed the career in history you have always secretly craved – and you could by now have written more books (with more television tie-ins) than Simon Schama. We should not bother about the paths we did not take into the hypothetical rose garden, except for this: had you gone to Sydney Grammar, been articled at a prestigious commercial law firm like Allens or Freehills, then married and had three children and a home on Sydney's north shore, would anyone have found your judgments in the least bit controversial?

As a Cromwellian, I can only paint a picture of you 'warts and all', so allow me to recall that we both had bad acne – yours left traces – a deterrent to social life but an incentive to scholarship in formative years. We spent too much time with our books and avoided the beach (happily for our melanoma-free skins, it now transpires). You may not have missed socialising with girls, or maybe you did: the times were painful enough for heterosexuals, and I cannot imagine how hard it was to cope with your own 'spring awakenings'.

Later generations just do not realise how tormenting it was, to be hormonal in the fifties. Outside marriage, sex was illegal (remember how they prosecuted teenagers for the crime of 'carnal knowledge'?) and homosexuality was never mentioned other than in derisory terms such as 'poofter' or 'shirt-lifter'. It was something that visiting English actors and operatic tenors occasionally did in park toilets. The only sex education at state schools was provided at 'father and son' evenings once a year, when embarrassed fathers and even more embarrassed sons would sit through some lantern slides of swimming tadpoles. This was organised through the Father and Son Movement Ltd (later incorporating Mother and Daughter Inc), a well-meaning Christian group that issued pamphlets about the dangers of masturbation, with a picture of a teenager on a rocking horse beneath the slogan 'puberty means leaving childish things behind'.

Since you were a fervent Anglican, I don't know how you coped with being told you would burn in hell for an abominable crime, but cope you did. Perhaps it was by immersing yourself in work and cultivating an image of a double-breasted, hymn-singing, pillar of society with, by the time I met you, three degrees (BA, LLB, BEc), a lucrative practice in workers' comp and a distinguished career in student politics.

When I came up to Sydney University you were still around – the student solicitor, the student senator, the saviour of students in any sort of trouble. You told me you would wake at 4.30 am, do the papers in three workers' comp cases before a day in court, and spend afternoons and evenings in voluntary legal work. This was the period of growing dissent over Vietnam, street demonstrations ('Run the bastards over,' said Premier Askin to LBJ when students blocked their motorcade) and your work with the Council for Civil Liberties was invaluable.

As a solicitor who always made himself available for the underdog, you were our local Atticus Finch – a friend indeed to anti-Vietnam and anti-apartheid protestors, to Aboriginals and immigrants who came before Sydney's irascible magistrates, several of whom were corrupt and one, at least, certifiably insane. There is a marvellous Bob Ellis short story, *My Life in the Lower Courts*, in which you make an appearance defending the young author in the celebrated case in which he was caught up his girlfriend's drainpipe and was accused of burglary at the insistence of her father, the irascible David McNicoll. Ellis changed the names in the story, as he put it, 'to protect the guilty' – so he left only yours.

Your own life in the lower courts, in Sydney's bunyip society where 'the best burglars burgle naked', must have brought you close to despair. Your beloved Anglican church was knee-deep in hypocrisy: I was confirmed in it by Archbishop Gough, who shortly after laying his hands on me denounced the younger generation as 'wallowing in a mire of immorality'. He certainly was: after being caught *in flagrante* with a Sydney socialite, the poor old Primate was shipped back to occupy the smallest parish in England. Not a word in the newspapers, of course: what really went on in Sydney was well known but never made public. The city was full of corrupt police and politicians and there was a severe intolerance of dissent. Many talented people of your generation simply left the country: I'm still not sure why you stayed.

When I became Students' Representative Council (SRC) President for 1966–67, I needed your advice on a regular basis. Jim Spigelman had returned from America full of Martin Luther King and the freedom rides – with Charlie Perkins and others, they planned a bus trip to the deep north of New South Wales. Could the SRC financially support it? With the help of your opinion, we could and did.

Then there was the help you gave me over 'the Humphries affair', that fraught conflict with the university's Vice-Chancellor (Stephen Roberts) and the Professorial Board, who had expelled a student without bothering to give him a hearing. They were paranoid about 'student power', but instead of marching upon the administration we gave them a taste of real student power: we took them to court for breach of natural justice, represented by Gordon Samuels, and we won. The student was reinstated and they were forced to have student representatives on disciplinary boards in future.

In the sixties, SRCs provided teeth-cutting forums for future participants in public life. I remember my first National Union of Students Conference in 1965 with other teenage tyros – John Bannon, Robert Holmes à Court, Richard Carleton and others. We sat around a table in the upstairs room of the Old Windsor Pub in Melbourne, as two veterans from the older generation – you and Gareth Evans – vied to impress us. Gareth was heavily into pipe smoking, affecting a Ben Chifley persona, and I remember taking a bet with Richard Carleton that in twenty-five years' time he would make it to foreign minister – in your cabinet.

You had, of course, made all the right moves for a political career. You sounded like Robert Menzies, wore double-breasted suits, sang hymns (low church, of course – 'Onward Christian Soldiers') and had cultivated close Labor connections. I had no idea that you were gay, and nor did anyone else. Did you? The realisation may have altered your career plans. I did not find out until late in the seventies, when it was reported that you had borrowed a kombi van from a lawyer for a trip to Europe with a male friend and returned it in a state that permitted a deduction to be made from the sleeping arrangements. We had figured that you simply had no time in your workaholic schedule for romance.

On 6 January 1975, I dropped in to your new chambers – a room without a view in an anonymous Commonwealth building – to congratulate you on your appointment (at the age of thirty-five) to the Arbitration Commission. I was back on a Christmas visit from London, where I had commenced practice with John Mortimer, and I was frankly a bit dubious about your decision to assume the bench – it gave you a title ('Mr Justice') that perhaps your insecurity craved, but this particular bench would provide no obvious outlet for your talents.

When you told me that Lionel Murphy was thinking of appointing you to head the Australian Law Reform Commission, I was pleased for you. You appeared to be in two minds, so I waxed lyrical about Gerald Gardiner, the great reforming Labour Lord Chancellor, who had plucked Leslie Scarman from similar obscurity in the Family Division to become a household name for his efforts at reforming a common law desperately in need of updating. Australian law in 1975 was basically still English law (incredibly, it was to be another twelve years before Gareth would abolish the Privy Council's role as Australia's highest court) and the case for law reform was irrefutable, no matter which party was in power.

I suggested a 'public hearings' model being trialled by the Canadian Law Commission – you could hold seminars and public meetings, give lectures and appear on television. This I truly believed to be the best model (I had written on the subject for the *New Statesman*) but I also had in mind its value to what I assumed would be your political career (I still had to collect on that bet with Carleton). It would, I pointed out, be the best possible way to get yourself known, travelling the country promoting changes that were obviously necessary.

Suddenly your telephone rang. You took the call and put your hand over the mouthpiece: 'It's the Attorney. He wants to offer me the Law Reform Commission. Now . . . He says for you to come up as well.'

So to the attorney-general's spacious chambers at the top of this building we took the elevator, and I guess you made your decision. Lionel Murphy knew what was good for Australia (if not always for himself). He greeted us with his lopsided Cheshire-cat grin and laughed at your by now half-hearted objections (that you were only thirty-five and perhaps should be a judge for more than a month before essaying the reform of the law). He beamed when I volunteered a few reasons why you were the best possible appointment. 'Well, it's settled then,' he said, ambling over to his large fridge, from which he extracted one of many bottles of French champagne. He poured us a glass (probably the only alcohol you have ever taken at ten-thirty in the morning) and raised a toast, 'To Justice Kirby – your first step to the High Court bench!'

Legal appointments in Australia are to some extent a matter of luck – you are in the right place at the right time and have a connection with the right political party (that is, the party in power). This is not as it should be: in my view, appointments federally and in all states should be made on merit, by an expert and apolitical selection committee, preferably after a competitive examination. Still, after your admirable work for ten years on the Australian Law Reform Commission (ALRC), both Neville Wran (your sometime leader in court) and Nick Greiner (another admirer from our SRC days) would have been happy to have you as President of the New South Wales Court of Appeal. You took that office in September 1984. The New South Wales law against the abominable crime of buggery was repealed in August 1984. A coincidence? I suspect not.

Your years as president were probably your happiest on the bench. As Denning said, when he insisted on taking the unprecedented step down from the House of Lords (Britain's highest court) to the presidency of the English Court of Appeal as Master of the Rolls, 'The chances of doing justice in the Court of Appeal are only 2–1 against; in the House of Lords, the prospects are 4–1.'

You were fortunate in having such outstanding colleagues as Bill Priestley and Gordon Samuels and slowly your judicial decisions began to filter through the fax machines to be cited in Commonwealth courts around the world. It was a real, if private, pleasure for me to introduce English courts to your decision in *Osmond* about the duty to give reasons (far preferable to the High Court decision that overruled you) and in media law I was able to cite your decision in *Raybos,* which summed up the reasons for and the basis of the principle of open justice.

Your style of judgment writing is of particular assistance to overseas common law courts and to the counsel addressing them. That is because it saves a lot of expository time to have a Kirby judgment setting out the history and the principles of the question at issue, after which your application of those principles and the interpretation of local laws that affect the result can be ignored. Your decision is not binding elsewhere but your exposition is invariably helpful. However much Australian counsel may tear out their horse-hair at Kirby J's delay in coming to the crunch, the clarity and accuracy of your stage-setting soon made you internationally respected.

That mean trick you played on me over the trial of Charles I shows both how widely you are respected by the judiciary in the United Kingdom and how difficult it is to beat you in an argument. It was the 350th anniversary of the king's trial, and you asked me to comment on a paper that you had been invited to deliver at Gray's Inn about the unfairness of the trial. I soon realised that you were quite wrong about it – it was in fact a model of fairness for its time, certainly compared with the rigged trial of the regicides come the Restoration, so my republican sympathies were engaged. But I assumed that this event would be the usual Gray's Inn revel, and I would be speaking to lots of drunken law students, so I prepared a short speech larded with the kind of jokes about Australian actresses that would appeal to that sort of audience.

You can imagine my horror as I stepped on stage to find myself staring at every law lord in the land, perched in the front row, and just behind them many Lord Justices and High Court judges. Men who have never shown the slightest interest in rejecting the knighthoods and peerages showered upon them by the monarch, the beheading of whose ancestor I was not only about to defend, but to celebrate! You smiled at my predicament and launched forth at interminable length into your unoriginal and mistaken thesis condemning the regicides. Eventually it was my turn: I took off like a kamikaze pilot and struggled through my jokes, to stony faces from the front rows.

Not content with that humiliation, you then challenged me to repeat the debate at a dinner in the New South Wales parliament chaired by Jim Spigelman. I should by this stage have smelled a rat, but the prospects of equal time and an Australian audience and at least one judge with a sense of humour were too much. I agreed, without asking about the make-up of the audience that you had cunningly invited. Were they from the League of Empire Loyalists? Australians For Monarchy Forever? Perhaps they were Fred Nile's congregation – they looked and sounded like it. In revenge I took myself off for the best part of the following year to the British library to write a book, *The Tyrannicide Brief,* expanding on my views and demolishing yours. But even then you had to have the last word – by reviewing it in the *Age.*

We have had less combative encounters. Do you remember the time when, with Enoch Powell, we addressed three thousand final-year school students in that cavernous hall in Westminster? To my surprise and slight embarrassment you pulled a small camera from your pocket and started taking pictures of everyone. I thought this a bit naff and accused you of behaving like a Japanese tourist – I hadn't realised how this had become your harmless fetish. Nobody seemed to mind, and you must by now have many thousands of such mementos. Annie Leibovitz you're not, but as a judicial hobby I guess it beats stamp collecting. Incidentally, that rather intense woman who organised the event fell utterly in love with you: she kept writing you amorous letters and poems (she was, in fact, a published poet) and then sent them to me, complaining about the formality of your responses. I thought it best, in all the circumstances, not to reply.

Your dignity in response to Bill Heffernan's false allegations set a new standard for Australian public life. Politics will always attract scoundrels, but the real revelation was the mean-minded behaviour of the prime minister, John Howard. Incidentally, everyone describes Heffernan as 'abusing' parliamentary privilege, but it was Enoch Powell, that great parliamentarian, who always pointed out that a privilege cannot by definition be 'abused' – it can only be used. In the long run, it was probably better to have the allegations conclusively destroyed rather than have them still out there, whispered *sotto voce.* Like poor John Marsden, you've been a victim of vile people with vile prejudices – at least your ordeal was soon over, unlike his, and your conduct throughout it showed your true character.

Some of your friends raise metaphorical eyebrows about your beliefs in God and the monarchy, since neither institution is readily susceptible to your rigid powers of rational exposition. I have always put them down to the Ulsterman in you – you have the views of Edward Carson, circa 1922, but without the tragic consequences.* Your religion is your own business, although I wonder how you get on with it in the diocese of Sydney, which still thinks you will burn in hell. I listened to you recently giving a masterful talk in London about the abject failure of the black Commonwealth to abolish the sodomy laws that Canada, the United Kingdom, Australia and New Zealand repealed decades ago. I couldn't help wondering how much this is due to primitive Anglican bishops who threaten to secede from the church at the slightest whiff of incense from a gay ordinand.

As for the monarchy, those Ulster Protestant roots must explain your veneration for it, because nothing you have ever said on the subject stands up to rational scrutiny. I can understand if you were put off by some of the shrill, Pom-bashing voices before the 1999 referendum, and perhaps by the inability of the republican lobby to agree on a method for electing our president. Your concern for decency and decorum in public life has a surface attraction, but we must learn to supply that ourselves – thanks to the monarchy, the British really are a race of courtiers. You harp on about the insecurity of many Australians who genuinely want to keep ties with the old country: I want to keep them too, but by building museums to house them and not by keeping in perpetuity a white Anglo-German Protestant as head of state of Australia.

Other commentators in this book give the impression that you are a workaholic (they say, euphemistically, that your 'industry is phenomenal') and that your work has been self-sacrificing and obsessive and really hard. They present you, in a word, as 'duty's slave'. What they don't know – or at least don't get across – is that you have enjoyed every minute of it. Your mouth creases

---

* Carson was the Protestant QC who led the battle to keep Ulster – now Northern Ireland – part of the United Kingdom rather than Eire (the Republic of Ireland). The consequence has been a century of sectarian violence, which is still not over.

in a tight smile, your voice quavers with suppressed laughter, you are amused by the follies of your critics and the foibles of your fellows. You pull legs, you tease, and you take teasing – in short, you are a good sport. Even in those pre-dawn hours when you craft your judgments and your lectures, you must obtain satisfaction from principles precisely stated, from critics reasonably refuted and from principles neatly extrapolated from the grab-bag of precedent. Students love your self-deprecating humour. Colleagues respect you, because of your sincerity and your kindness. Unlike most men, your enjoyment of life increases with your age.

I'm writing this as you are making your farewell tour of the law schools, which I suspect will be as final as Dame Nellie Melba's endless 'positively last' appearances. I am told that your student audiences sometimes ask you to identify the most important quality in a judge, no doubt expecting you to speak of independence, or fairness or patience. Instead, you answer 'love'.

That answer is shocking, as no doubt you intend. Love is an emotion that no one else has associated with the law. Except W. H. Auden:

> Law is neither wrong nor right,
> Law is only crimes
> Punished by places and by times,
> Law is the clothes men wear
> Any time, anywhere,
> Law is Good Morning and Good Night
> . . .
> Like love we don't know where or why,
> Like love we can't compel or fly,
> Like love we often weep,
> Like love we seldom keep.

My final regret about this book is that it is not accompanied by a CD of you performing live. These are the occasions when the wisdom in your words is audible, almost tangible, in the controlled passion of your utterance, leavened with topical (but invariably polite and not very funny) jokes and snatches of poetry. The packed audience in St Martin-in-the-Fields church, London, on World AIDS Day 1995, will never forget your delivery from the pulpit, not of a sermon but of a charter for compassionate law reform. That was your Doughty Street lecture, which brought your concerns about HIV/AIDS to the attention of the world. Incidentally, the very fact that in Britain today there are no raised eyebrows about the several openly gay High Court judges – one has just been appointed a Lord Justice of Appeal – can be attributed in part to your example.

We have not heard the chimes at midnight – you are always sound asleep, in preparation for your 4 am work schedule. But now you are seventy, and unleashed from the High Court, what next? When Denning belatedly retired, Devlin said to me, 'He'll be more of a menace off the bench than on it,' and there is always the pleasing prospect that you might get up to some mischief. But seventy is the new fifty, and I'm sure that Australia and the world will benefit from your new lease of life. Not for you, I suspect, the lucrative post-retirement career of arbitration, which attracts many Australian ex-judges (and their financial dependants). Nor do we need an instant autobiography (it's hardly necessary, after publication of this book). I foresee UN judgeships – we need your talents – and the American university lecture circuit will beckon. I hope the government will make use of you. I had half-hoped that Mr Rudd would make you Governor-General, and give Australia a Queen's man who has come out of the closet, but you were passed over for a woman.

'What is to be my destiny now?' I hear you ask anxiously of a friend you have credited with advising on your career thus far. I have given this some thought, and have come up with the perfect solution for that admixture of talents that are to be described hereafter in this book at interminable length. There is a momentous job that will hopefully be on offer in a few years' time, after Her Majesty the Queen of Australia graciously dies or retires and when Australians have the confidence in themselves to vote for a republic. It is a job that must be yours, because no one else could do it so well, or serve better to heal the divisions – all that wounded *amour-propre* of mourning monarchists.

Once again, you must be Mr President – not of the New South Wales Court of Appeal but of the Australian nation, no longer in thrall to a white Anglo-German Protestant and primo-genitured family, to another self-opinionated King Charles or to the sprogs of the Goddess Diana. No, it must be President Kirby, and if homophobes snigger that you have become 'the Queen of Australia', just make the monarchists curtsey.

ASSANGE

Chapter 35

THE CASE FOR WIKILEAKS

There have been many books written and documentaries made about Julian Assange and WikiLeaks, and I have no wish to add either to their cyber-babble or to their often slanted accounts of infighting and outfighting with a man who can be his own worst enemy. He came to me in October 2011 – a fellow Australian, and up to his neck in trouble – and I rushed back from my Sydney Christmas to secure him bail under house arrest (or at least manor-house arrest) in Norfolk. His freedom from Swedish prosecutors might have been secured, too, had he not abandoned the one legal argument that could have saved him from extradition. When the crunch came, he hightailed it to the embassy of Ecuador, where he may be staying for some time yet.

I have remained generally supportive of Julian because he is one of those gifted and mischievous eccentrics, somewhere (he thinks) on the autism spectrum, whom society should treat with a degree of appreciation. At the very least he should be credited with expanding knowledge about how military and political power really works. I deprecate a few of his decisions and connections and must confess to being pro-American (given the alternatives) but he does not deserve the denigration ('megalomaniac sleazeball' and the like) that some of his critics have been well paid to hurl at him. He has invited me to tell what I know of his Swedish experience, but that is for him to tell, eventually, to a court. I can only comment on the unfairness of his treatment in the past, and the likely ordeal that he would be put through were he to be captured or surrendered.

The first chapter of this section deals with WikiLeaks and its US adversaries. The second, some reflections about his being marooned in the Ecuadorian embassy, might take the form of a cautionary tale with the title 'Look before you leap into bed'.

Australians learnt from WikiLeaks that those who plotted to roll Kevin Rudd had their priorities: they first told the US embassy before they told Mr Rudd or the Australian public. As for Kevin, we learnt from WikiLeaks that he told Hillary Clinton that if the US ever felt inclined to invade China, Australia would be right behind it. He didn't say how far behind – a long way, if our soldiers are still not properly equipped and have to buy their own boots, something we learnt from another leak.

All you need to be a political journalist in Canberra today is a supply of leaks from disaffected public servants and politicians, and access to WikiLeaks and Wikipedia. Leaks are the stuff of journalism and without them there would be much less news available to the public. The European Court of Human Rights, back in 1996, actually declared that leakers were essential to news reporting, and that their protection was necessary for democracy and freedom of expression. What, then, is the basis for the American government's hostility to WikiLeaks, and its crushing of the organisation's principal source, Bradley Manning?

Let me make clear that I have very little in common with Julian Assange, except that we were both probably conceived on Magnetic Island, off the coast from Townsville (where my parents were stationed at the end of the war). I am a Luddite, a computer-phobe who still writes with a fountain pen, while he is a cyber-geek and a former hacker. I am a lawyer, he was a law-breaker, and still is, according to the US government. But ironically, it is to the wisdom of the great Americans that he turns to justify his behaviour: to James Madison, arguing for a First Amendment to create a nation 'where knowledge will forever govern ignorance – the people must arm themselves with the power that knowledge brings'; to Theodore Roosevelt, who called on 'muck-rakers' to destroy what he described as 'the invisible government' – the corrupt links between business and politics. The US Supreme Court refused to injunct the publication of a top-secret leak, the Pentagon Papers, because it ruled that the only protection against abuse of power was an enlightened citizenry.

Julian Assange, the man from Magnetic Island, took 'sunlight is the best disinfectant' seriously. He invented what might be termed an electronic dead letterbox, where sources could send him secret documents in complete confidence and would remain anonymous because even he could not find out who they were. There would be no problem about protecting *his* sources – they could waterboard him for weeks and he could not tell because he would not know. All he could do would be to check the authenticity of the document – and WikiLeaks, so far as I know, has never published an inauthentic document.

So Assange became the latter-day Johnny Appleseed of information, scattering it far and wide, watching it inspire revolutions, expose crooked politicians and bent policemen, provoke policy debates and make us more knowledgeable about history and context. Now, hardly a day goes by without reference in some news story to a WikiLeaks revelation.

Let me remind you of a few of them. The organisation (using 'organisation' very loosely – it is basically Julian Assange, an inveterate loner) began in 2007, publishing documents about the massive corruption in Daniel arap Moi's Kenya. Then a document was leaked from the Church of Scientology, revealing malpractice, and then documents exposing tax evasion through Cayman Island banks. Then documents relating to banking fraud in Iceland; the dangers of a nuclear accident in Iran; and the greedy price-gouging of US and British contractors after the war in Iraq.

All these revelations were of obvious and immediate public interest. In the UK, WikiLeaks revealed the names of some policemen and teachers who were members of a Neo-Nazi party. But its exposés have not always benefited liberals or the left: WikiLeaks also exposed 'Climategate', the apparent rigging of data by scientists. This gave a free kick to climate-change deniers, but WikiLeaks did not hesitate to publish.

After this came the material we now know to have been provided by Bradley Manning. It is difficult to forget 'collateral murder', the tape that showed the aerial manslaughter of two Reuters reporters and several children. Then, in quick succession:

- The Afghan War Logs: revealing far higher civilian casualties from drone attacks than the US had been prepared to admit.

- Iraqgate: no fewer than 400,000 filed reports, showing many thousand more civilian casualties than the US had admitted, and providing a treasure trove for war historians by revealing how the Iraq War had been fought on the ground, and how blind eyes were turned to torture at Abu Ghraib and elsewhere, and how US forces would sometimes hand their prisoners over for torture and murder to pro-government death squads.

At this point, there had been only muted protest from the US government. But a number of other countries had become disturbed, and had taken action to block all WikiLeaks-related websites and had threatened to jail any of their citizens caught sending material to Assange. Which countries were these? Let me list them: China, Syria, North Korea, Russia, Thailand and Zimbabwe. These enemies of freedom sensed the danger: dictators cannot cope with the prospect that their secrets might be discovered.

Then, in November 2010, came 'Cablegate', and the US could not cope either with a release of a quarter of a million of its diplomatic cables, despite their publication being 'mediated' by leading newspapers – the *New York Times*, the *Guardian* and *Der Spiegel* – with all the protections of 'responsible journalism'. Some names were redacted, and the *New York Times* nervously consulted the State Department in advance. But the burst of hysteria in America that followed publication singled out Julian Assange – this alien, this peripatetic Australian, this blogosphere Machiavelli.

Vice President Biden labelled him 'a high-tech terrorist'. Mike Huckabee, on Fox News, called him a terrorist and suggested that he be assassinated. Shock jock Rush Limbaugh yearned for him 'to die of lead poisoning – from a bullet in the brain', while Sarah Palin, shooting from the lip, said 'he should be hunted down like bin Laden' (which would at least have given him nine more years of freedom).

Later, visiting him in the Norfolk countryside when he was on bail, I would keep a wary eye open for Navy Seals. I received a few death threats from Middle America for representing him, although since they came by email I did not take much notice. There were some cooler voices. Defense Secretary Robert Gates said that Assange's actions had caused embarrassment but no long-term damage, while Hillary Clinton (tipped off by the *New York Times*) warned friendly foreign governments to be prepared for some unpleasant comments. They said, so she reported, 'Don't worry. You should see what we say about you.'

And so it came to pass that the people of Egypt and Tunisia discovered facts about the endogenous corruption of their rulers that helped to fuel the Arab Spring. That phenomenon has complex causes, but in Tunisia anger erupted among protesters when they read a cable from the US Ambassador describing the Ben Ali regime, accurately, as a political kleptocracy. It was headed 'Corruption in Tunisia – what's yours is mine'.

Once he was on bail, Assange himself worked to transmit 'his' cables to ninety different countries, alerting their people to misfeasance, hitherto hidden, in their public life. At the UN, the cables reveal Hillary Clinton's plans to bug diplomats, in breach of the Vienna Convention, and how Saudi Arabia and other Gulf States had urged the US to 'cut off the head of the snake' – the Iranian nuclear program – by bombing Tehran.

As 'Cablegate' unfolded, it revealed the most surprising secret of all – that US diplomacy is reasonably principled and pragmatic, and better informed and more objective than Western or local journalists. What WikiLeaks was doing, in some respects, was promulgating a CIA-sourced view of the world, ironically made to seem all the more credible by the US threats to silence him. This is one reason why many Western diplomats have, privately, been relaxed about WikiLeaks. President Putin was one of the first to worry and actually suggested that Assange might be a CIA agent. The 'Cablegate' releases certainly showed how heavy is the burden of world leadership that falls on the United States, under constant pressure from so many 'friendly' governments to bomb and brutalise, or at least protect them against their enemies.

Nonetheless, America was upset by dissemination of its diplomatic messages and the shrill, exaggerated voices calling for the messenger to be killed continued unhappily from the land of the First Amendment. American pride had been hurt by a pesky Australian, so they targeted him in grand jury proceedings and the military took out its anger on young Bradley Manning, treating him abominably in prison until Hillary Clinton's press spokesman, P. J. Crowley, resigned in protest. The Obama regime could not very well indict the *New York Times*, a valuable supporter of the Democratic Party, but it did three unconscionable things:

- Bradley Manning was kept for eight months in solitary confinement, naked and without blanket or pillow, awoken every few minutes for a bogus 'suicide watch'. His prosecutors hoped he would confess to being 'groomed' by Assange, and at one point, according to his lawyer, threatened him with the death penalty if he did not.

- It put the frighteners on intermediaries like Amazon, which hosted the sites of WikiLeaks US domain-name owners. (Amazon cravenly gave in to the pressure and stopped hosting the site.)

- It put pressure on PayPal, Mastercard and Visa, to which they succumbed, to stop receiving donations for WikiLeaks or Assange. (You can buy Nazi uniforms and Ku Klux Klan outfits with your Visa card but you can't donate to WikiLeaks.)

On what basis was Assange demonised? His accusers claimed that release of the cables had put 'lives at risk', and that he had 'blood on his hands'. However:

1. Almost three years have passed since 'Cablegate', and a year and a half since all the cables were released. There has been no fatality, or casualty, causally related to their publication. Several US ambassadors and cable-authoring diplomats have had to be withdrawn because of their comments about their host country, but by August 2013, at the sentencing proceedings for Bradley Manning, the Pentagon could produce no evidence that release of the cables had put any life in jeopardy, and was forced to retract an earlier claim that it had.

2. The lack of fatalities is unsurprising, and indeed to be expected, because *none* of the WikiLeaks cables was classified 'top secret' – the designation that diplomats *must* use if release would put lives at risk. The Pentagon Papers were classified 'top secret' and distributed to a small circle of officials, while up to three million people, including twenty-two-year-old soldiers, had access to the cables that Bradley Manning uploaded on a Lady Gaga disc for Julian Assange. The fact that they were not classified as 'top secret' meant their authors did not expect lethal reprisals if they were published.

3. On a point of principle, it is the responsibility of a government and of its officials, if they have sought information from people who may be put at risk by

giving it, to protect those informers – by 'top secret' classification, by encrypting or redacting their names or simply by keeping them anonymous; and if they fail to do so and the information leaks, they have a duty that arises immediately to protect those sources.

4. The information was of manifest public interest, revealing many examples of human rights violations and political corruption.

It's the government's job to protect its own sources, but this does not relieve publishers from moral responsibility when the government misclassifies or, under the rubric merely of 'secret', names individuals such as local politicians or human rights activists who have supplied intelligence to US embassies and may, if revealed, suffer some local difficulties and will probably not do so again. Assange has been accused of being an 'information absolutist', wanting to publish everything, which he denies, although any informed judgment about the accuracy of leaked intelligence requires knowledge of who has supplied it. The alternative, to 'redact' (i.e. censor) the names of CIA sources is a value judgment made by journalists who are not necessarily well placed to make it. It becomes a moral judgment: does a local politician paid to inform for the CIA deserve to be outed? Should we not redact the name of a human rights researcher who tells the local CIA case officer in some benighted country about torture, in the hope that if the information gets back to Washington something might be done to end it?

There is no bright-line solution: human rights groups have generally welcomed WikiLeaks and awarded Assange prizes, but at senior levels there is a view that WikiLeaks exposure can hinder their back-channel work. The problem, as a matter of principle, is intractable: these questions can only be answered pragmatically on a country-by-country, case-by-case basis. WikiLeaks' consequences are not always good, but on balance it has done more good than harm. By all means let governments try to protect their informants, but not by throwing the publishers of their information into jail.

~

We can all envisage situations where 'leaks' are wrong and should be severely punished, because of the criminal way in which they are obtained – by bribery or duress or telephone hacking – or because they would obviously put lives at risk (the names of spies or police informers, for example). But custodians of genuine secrets have a duty to classify them as such and to protect them, and should be open to prosecution if through negligence they culpably fail. It all comes back to a proper classification policy. If a 'top secret' class of harmful information does get out, then the first duty of government is to take steps to protect as best it can any persons whom the leak might put at risk, and then to make sure that its top-secret information is better protected in future. If it considers prosecuting the publisher – whether the *New York Times* or Assange or Edward Snowden – it must only do so on evidence that they have procured the information by bribery or corruption or, at the very least, by inciting the leaker to reveal the information contrary to his duty, and always subject to a public interest defence if the information reveals serious abuse of power. There can be no criminal blame attached to journalists or publishers who receive state secrets from those who wish to divulge them. They have an ethical duty to protect their source, although if that source is caught through his own carelessness, he will have to suffer the legal consequences. (Bradley Manning, for example, confessed to Adrian Lamo, who befriended him in an online chatroom and then dobbed him in for what turned out to be a manifestly excessive thirty-five-year sentence.)

The issue of 'incitement' has been much discussed in relation to print journalism: there can be no criticism of a journalist who receives a secret document through the post from an unknown source, or meets a known source who, without encouragement other than a meal or a train fare home, hands over or reveals the secret information. Watergate's 'Deep Throat' (assistant FBI director Mark Felt) would move a pot plant on his window ledge to signal to Woodward and Bernstein that he was ready to talk. Assange's arrangement for an electronic drop-box was the equivalent. In the Bradley Manning proceedings the prosecution suggested that the man Manning described as a 'crazy white-haired Aussie' and allegedly contacted online under the code name 'pressassociation', might have helped him navigate the contents of the Lady Gaga disc into the WikiLeaks electronic letterbox, but the same principle would apply: Assange as journalist/publisher was not forcing or paying or inciting Manning to do what he very much wanted to do in any event.

There was no evidence against Assange to warrant opening the grand jury proceedings – an oppressive mechanism long abolished in England, in which prosecutors summon jurors and witnesses to a secret room where they alone hold court and there is no judge to exercise any independent or impartial control of proceedings. The jurors usually do what the prosecutor who has summoned them requests. 'A grand jury would indict a ham sandwich,' American lawyers say, and the grand jury will doubtless indict Assange under the *Espionage Act* if and when the government wants, even though he owes no allegiance to the United States, received the information abroad and shared it with the media at the *Guardian*'s offices in London.

The US ambassador to Australia has sought to play down the likelihood of a US indictment, but his reassurances are empty so long as the grand jury is sitting – and grand juries can sit for years with prosecutors playing a cat-and-mouse game with their suspect (a grand jury indictment could coincide, for example, with Assange's forced return to Sweden, if it happens). I am not without sources in the Obama White House, and they tell me, 'We don't want Assange.' There is a beat, and then they add, 'But the Pentagon does.'

The Pentagon usually gets its way. If it gets its hands on Assange, he will not be lethally injected (although some charges under the *Espionage Act* carry the death penalty), but he will grow old in a US 'supermax' prison in order to deter other would-be publishers of ring-fenced US diplomatic data and military records. But WikiLeaks was not based in America and Assange was not an American citizen. Under the vague but broad provisions of the US *Espionage Act* of 1917, passed amid hysteria about spies in wartime, can a US grand jury's writ run anywhere in the world? We shall see. For a time he was public enemy number one in Washington and he has made some over-blown condemnations of US foreign policies and policy-makers. But he is really in no different position to any journalist who receives information of public interest from a source who is willing to go to some lengths to give it, and who really wants it to be published.

It can only diminish US leadership and dim the beacon of the First Amendment to raise that old blunderbuss the *Espionage Act* and to aim it beyond the jurisdiction at a publisher who is a national of a friendly country, who disseminated information of public interest that was not 'top secret' and was in any event accessible to three million Americans. Nor could it be helpful to America's reputation for respecting due process to amend the Act retrospectively, as Senator Lieberman has suggested, so it could more effectively criminalise Assange.

What the WikiLeaks phenomenon called for, but has not received, is a cool-headed appraisal not only of US government classification policy but of developing international media law principles for dealing with worldwide publishers of national security information. A sensible rule might run like this:

1. Citizens everywhere have a presumptive right to know what a government does in their name;

2. Governments and their public servants and contractors bear sole responsibility for protecting properly classified information and the sources who have supplied it;

3. Outsiders who receive or communicate confidential government information should not be prosecuted unless they have obtained it by bribery or duress, or illegal

hacking, or have actively incited a source employed by the government to breach his or her duty; and

4. Whistleblowers who reveal human rights violations should have a public interest defence, which would protect them if the information revealed criminal (including internationally criminal) behaviour by the state. This would cover, for example, Bradley Manning's release of the 'collateral murder' tapes – the public has, at the very least, a right to know if a war fought in its name is killing innocent civilians through illegal targeting decisions.

I do not advance these principles as definitive but as a basis for a debate that the US Justice Department should be prepared to engage in with publishers. As leader of the free world, the US cannot pretend that its policies have no international public interest. The First Amendment turns on the principle that open government leads to better government. In Václav Havel's phrase, the WikiLeaks phenomenon returns some 'power to the powerless'. If leaks are 'mediated' through the mainstream press, there will be less danger and some benefit. If the data goes raw and unredacted directly onto the net, there may be more danger but also more benefit. Governments must live with the facts of modern electronic life, and their citizens should welcome it as one way in which the bastards of the world can be kept honest, and perhaps as a prelude to their overthrow.

It should not be forgotten that the most virulent attack on WikiLeaks came in the midst of 'Cablegate', on 14 January 2011. Assange was accused of leading the protesters in Tunis astray by false claims against their incorruptible president. The speech was made by Colonel Gaddafi.

Chapter 36

ASSANGE IN ECUADOR

London has a new tourist attraction. The Ecuadorian embassy is just beside Harrods, the famous Knightsbridge department store. This elevated ground floor of a Georgian mansion block is staked out round the clock by some very bored British bobbies who seem to know that they will do nothing for the next few years other than tell tourists the time. Unless, of course, Julian Assange leans so far over the balcony while addressing supporters that he topples into their outstretched arms, thereby leaving South America and landing, instantaneously, in the United Kingdom.

International law produces such miracles: embassy premises are 'inviolable' sovereign territory under the Vienna Convention, and one of Britain's best qualities is that it actually abides by international law. So across the threshold of this pied-à-terre in Ecuador neither SAS unit nor Navy Seal may enter. When Scotland Yard picked up a rumour that Assange on dark nights would ascend to the roof to smoke Cuban cigars they prepared a snatch squad, only to be told that Ecuadorian sovereignty might extend skywards. Julian Assange has this in common with Banjo Paterson's swagman in the song that should be Australia's national anthem – he will do anything to avoid being taken alive.

Inside the embassy, there are some reminders of Ecuador: a travel magazine on the front desk, a few toy llamas, a portrait of the incumbent president, a smattering of conversational Spanish from the ambassador, a strikingly attractive woman who insists on being called 'Anna' and not 'your Excellency'. The large front room from which Assange addresses the outside world is her office; there is a function room that functions as a party space. And a corridor, at the end of which is the asylum-seeker's lair, well stocked with books, computers, a sun lamp and an exercise machine. His bedroom is a converted toilet, a space that would rival in size the prison cell to which the governments of Sweden and the United States would wish him consigned. But he is free, to do portentous things that keep his name in the headlines, like channelling Edward Snowden when he was holed up in an airside hotel at Moscow Airport, and promoting, long-distance, his unsuccessful candidacy for the Australian Senate. For all his work-aholism he has time for parties – for birthdays and celebrations of Ecuadorian national days, attended by friends and journalists and beautiful young people who often turn out to be human rights lawyers; the brilliant Jen Robinson; his loyal WikiLeaks associates Joseph Farrell and Sarah Harrison; a few peers of the realm; and admirers such as Yoko Ono and Bianca Jagger.

Sarah Harrison disappeared for a while, and his detractors put about rumours that she must have defected from her 'manip-ulative' and 'megalomaniac' boss, then she broke cover at a press conference in Moscow, as Snowden's shepherd. Assange is not, as everyone says, a 'control freak' (he has no one to control) and he is certainly not in line to become 'Australia's L. Ron Hubbard', another snarky headline that makes no sense because he has no brainwashed followers and (the most obvious differ-ence) no money.

That was an attractive feature of the international man of mystery whose baby-face first glowed from the newswires in mid-2010, after he produced the 'collateral murder' tape. His was no shoulder-slumped mugshot, but the visage of a danger-ous cherub, beaming beneath a halo of blond hair, which hid a cranium that could outwit the most powerful country in the world. He had no money nor interest in acquiring any. Among the internet generation in Europe this gave him a rock-star image, as he sang his siren song of political transparency, justice and human rights. Just how mesmeric Assange had become by mid-August of that year may be measured by the front-page reporting, throughout the world, of the allegation that he had raped a woman in Stockholm. Within a few hours seven million people had clicked on the website of *Expressen*, the paper to which the story had been leaked. There was much less publicity a day or so later, when the senior prosecutor of Stockholm dropped the charge and said there was virtually nothing else to investigate.

Then, a week later, the charge was reinstated by a 'gender prosecutor' in another Swedish city, after a secret appeal by a lawyer–politician acting for the complainant. Irrespective of the merit of the complaints, this was no way to run a legal system: prosecuting authorities should not be in the business of giving 'scoops' to tabloids and should not allow secret appeals to another prosecutor, from which hearing the suspect's lawyer is excluded. I said as much, to a journalist from *Crikey*, and in October received a call from Assange, now back in London and in hiding as the threats from America and Sweden mounted. I invited him for lunch and he came with Sarah Harrison. He was charming (save for a moment of pique when he lost an argument with my wife over the merits of Jane Austen) and when it turned out he had nowhere to stay for the next few nights it seemed only compatriotic to put him up.

Offering Julian Assange a bed for the night might have been hospitable, but it soon became clear that he was not going to sleep in it, or at all. He took up residence in the kitchen, computer on lap, curled up over it like a question mark. The only way I could get him to sleep – at 5 am – was to indicate the kitchen's glass ceiling and to point out that any police helicopter could spot him a mile away. He instantly folded his computer and went off to bed. He was paranoid, of course, but he had every reason for paranoia, given the threats emanating from American politicians and now from Swedish prosecutors who vowed to issue a European Arrest Warrant (EAW) if he did not return to Stockholm for questioning.

The next day I took him for a walk in the autumnal serenity of Regents Park (its gnarled tree-trunks had been a favourite 'dead letter' drop for British spies during the Cold War). He seemed genuinely horrified by the sex allegations – it was 'excruciating' even to talk about them. His mind was on higher things, but two women who announced that they 'wanted to teach him a lesson' had enlisted for this purpose the power of the Swedish state. He had gone to bed, separately, with both of them, at their initiative, but they later found out about each other and presented him with an ultimatum to have a blood test to prove he did not have HIV/AIDS, or else they would go to the police.

He refused to be 'blackmailed' (as he put it) and the very next day they had gone to the police and immediately the prosecutor's office told a tabloid that it was issuing a warrant for his arrest for rape. The hunt was now on: he had waited in Stockholm for six weeks before returning to London in October, but now the Swedish prosecutors wanted him back and were pressing for his arrest. They would have succeeded, had they filled in the European Arrest Warrant forms correctly. While they corrected their mistake, Assange was allowed his moment of glory at the launch of 'Cablegate', exposing American diplomacy to a fascinated world.

In early December the inevitable happened: Assange presented himself for arrest to the UK police and was taken to Wandsworth Prison, the first stage in his extradition to Sweden. By this time I was in Sydney, having been invited by the federal attorney-general to conduct a *Hypothetical* at an international conference on child pornography. There had been an uncomprehending reaction to 'Cablegate' by Australian politicians: Julia Gillard had immediately declared that Assange should be prosecuted under the *Crimes Act*, despite a famous decision of the Australian High Court in 1983 that declared that obtaining diplomatic cables (by Richard Walsh and George Munster, about East Timor) could not be made subject to a prosecution under the *Crimes Act*. So I was providently placed to advise the government (and did) both on how Australia might protect children from porn and how Assange should be protected from knee-jerk defamation by his own prime minister.

Back in Britain, my client was not enjoying the petty restrictions of prison. My wife had sent him a Jane Austen novel, but he was not allowed access to the internet and *Time* magazine with his picture on the cover was banned from the prison because it had his picture on the cover. His first bail hearing had not gone well. The Crown Prosecution Service (representing the Swedish prosecutor) endowed him with Houdini-like characteristics and suggested that well-connected supporters, such as US filmmaker Michael Moore, would be capable of spiriting him out of the country. So I was prevailed upon to return from a Christmas holiday at Bondi in order to make a new bail application in London. My old friend Richard Neville called to impress upon me the importance of freeing Assange – I could scarcely believe it had been forty years since I had helped to get Neville out of the same prison after his conviction for publishing *Oz*. What did surprise and slightly humble me was the number of 'ordinary' Australians – Qantas crew, customs officials, and the like – who had heard the reason for my departure and wished me success. They seemed proud that Australia had produced this wild-spirited genius, and certainly felt it unfair that he should suffer for revealing American secrets that mattered to the world. At present, however, he was suffering for allegedly molesting two women. But he was entitled to freedom until the Swedish extradition claim could be assessed by a UK court.

The renewed bail application, just before Christmas, came before the district judge who had turned it down the previous week. To change his mind, I had not only to refute some false allegations, for example that he had refused to be interviewed in Sweden (he had voluntarily attended a police interview at which he denied the allegations). The central fact that affected the judge's mind was that the charges facing Assange were 'very serious'. 'Rape' always *sounds* very serious, and the Swedish prosecutors (in breach of their duty under European law) had refused to make available in English their dossier of evidence. WikiLeaks had been forced to spend £10,000 translating it. So I was able to put before the court some facts about the case that had gone unmentioned in the media, and still tend to be overlooked.

It turns out that Sweden has three classes of rape – extreme, serious and minor. Assange was charged with 'minor rape' – a contradiction in terms, but that is what the Swedes actually call the allegation against him. It amounted to allegations of having consensual sex without a condom, the use of which had been an implied condition of the consent. The maximum sentence for 'minor rape' is four years, and an expert in Swedish sentencing law declared that given the circumstances of the offences the likely penalty for Assange if he were convicted would be non-custodial, or no more than a few months in prison.

In the case of both complainants, the police dossier confirmed that the sexual engagements were not merely consensual, but actively desired. Assange had come to Sweden at the invitation of a fringe political party to deliver a lecture on Saturday 14 August 2010. The first complainant, a thirty-three-year-old Social Democrat politician, told the organisers that Assange could stay in her tiny one-room, one-bed flat, giving them an assurance that she would be out of Stockholm electioneering on the Friday evening – Friday the thirteenth, as it happened. She returned, however, for no apparent reason, and took him to dinner and to bed – supplying a condom that she requested him to use, and he did.

One week later she alleged to police that at some point that evening he had torn it, or had torn it off. Oddly, given that this event is the basis of the molestation charges, she made no complaint the next morning, Saturday, when a colleague called to take Assange to his lecture. By that time she was proudly describing herself as his 'personal assistant', and tweeting to the world about how 'cool' and clever he was; tweets that she later removed. She also later removed her rather puerile blog, entitled '7 steps to legal revenge', which advised women on how to avenge themselves on 'cheating' men: 'You should use a punishment with sex involved, like getting his new partner to be unfaithful or ensure he gets a madman after him – the ideal is revenge as strong as possible.' Assange, for all his technical genius, does not appear to have looked at her blog before he leapt into bed. On Saturday afternoon, she volunteered to be his hostess at a 'crayfish party' (Swedes are inordinately fond of these lobster-and-liquor indulgences) and arranged it for that evening in his honour. Witnesses confirm that she insisted he stay with her, despite others offering to put him up.

She did not complain to the police until one week later, after learning that he had spent the next Monday night in bed with the second complainant, a twenty-six-year-old self-confessed 'groupie', who told police she had attended Assange's lecture in the hope of attracting him – an objective in which she succeeded all too well.

This second complainant took him by train to her flat in the suburbs on the Monday night, and took him to bed, where he fell asleep and began to snore – to her annoyance, as she tweeted at the time to her rather voyeuristic friends. However, during the course of that night they had intercourse three or four times. On one occasion, when she was 'half asleep' as she put it, she asked whether he was wearing anything and he laconically replied, 'I'm wearing you.' She did not object at the time but later inferred that he was not wearing a condom.

Her friends had read that he had spent some time in Africa so they advised her to have him take a test for HIV/AIDS. Her only way of contact was to call his personal assistant – the aforesaid first complainant, the self-styled expert on revenge. That's when this 'personal assistant' called a journalist friend of Assange to make a menacing demand: unless he took a blood test for HIV/AIDS, both women would go to the police.

The journalist told police that he called Assange, who reacted with shock and said he was willing to take a blood test but did not want to do it as a result of blackmail. The next day (Friday 20 August) the first complainant directed the second to a police officer, who just happened to be her political colleague and 'Facebook friend'.

In the course of the interview that ensued between this policewoman and the second complainant, the policewoman informed her that Assange would be charged with rape. She reacted to this news by fainting. Nonetheless, a few minutes later, an *acting* prosecutor, without further investigation, issued the warrant, and in breach of the rules revealed the fact to *Expressen*. Its scoop the next day – 'Assange Wanted for Rape' – went live to millions throughout the world. Two days later Stockholm's senior prosecutor cancelled the arrest warrant and publicly stated that there was no basis to pursue a charge of rape.

I have given but a cursory summary of the ninety-eight-page police dossier – it can be read in full on the internet. It included some eerie photographs of what looked like a jellyfish but was in fact a condom, supplied to the police by the first complainant, who said she had found it on the floor of her flat, two weeks after Assange had stayed on Friday the thirteenth, and it might have been the one he ripped, or ripped off. There was a lab report, from a lab that reported that it had no experience of examining condoms, but it could have been torn. This hardly amounted to corroboration of the first complainant's story, but the photograph gets a surprised laugh from the audience when it appears in the *WikiLeaks: We Steal Secrets* documentary.

So, this was not 'rape' as that term is normally understood. Whether it was an offence did not matter for the purposes of EAW extradition (Sweden had ticked the 'rape' box on the warrant, which was enough) but the very use of the word 'rape' gives a false impression of malice and violence.

I should make clear that I believe that it *should* be a sexual offence for a man deliberately to deceive a partner whose consent has been conditional upon his use of a condom. That is the real allegation Julian Assange has an obligation to answer in Sweden, if (but only if) he can receive a fair trial.

~

Under Swedish law, victims are entitled from the outset to their own lawyer, paid for by the state. The two complainants chose Claes Borgström, a controversial Social Democrat politician, Sweden's former 'gender ombudsman', who had notably called for a ban on football matches with Germany because the country had legalised prostitution (a position that would prevent Melbourne teams playing against Stockholm United). This man secretly contacted a 'gender prosecutor' in another city, Gothenburg, who was well known for her publicly stated view that prosecution of men charged with sex crimes is socially worthwhile even in cases in which the defendant is acquitted.

Under a secret process, from which Assange's lawyer was entirely excluded, this 'gender prosecutor' reinstated the rape charge and then took over the case. Assange obediently remained in Sweden throughout these events, turning up voluntarily to the police station to answer questions at an interview on 30 August. He denied the allegations, and waited until the new prosecutor informed his lawyer on 17 September that he was free to leave the country.

It was not until 28 September that Assange did so – for a long-arranged event in Berlin, after which he flew back to London. There, he heard that the prosecutor wanted him to come back to Sweden to undergo a second police interview. He offered to answer police questions by telephone (the first complainant, after all, had made her complaint by telephone), by video-link from Scotland Yard's special video suite, by Skype or in person with police at the Australian or the Swedish embassies in London. The prosecutor refused, although these methods of interview are regularly used in Sweden and other countries when witnesses and suspects are abroad. She was determined to get him back to Sweden, and there was little doubt that, whatever he said in that interview, she planned to arrest him immediately afterwards.

Assange declined her invitation to return (which never came with an offer to pay his expenses) so she in turn reached for an EAW, which makes extradition between the UK and the main states of Europe almost as easy as extradition of suspects between Victoria and New South Wales.

~

The new bail hearing was jam-packed with journalists – hundreds attended from all over the world, straining and craning to see the embodiment of freedom captive in the court dock. I supported their request to allow, for the first time, tweeting from a courtroom, and it was granted: Assange's first legal precedent in favour of freedom of speech. The atmosphere was tense throughout, but the information from the police dossier put the allegations in perspective and character witnesses refuted any idea that he was some kind of sex pest: bail was granted. The hundreds of tweets announcing his imminent release, however, proved premature: the Swedish prosecutors, demonstrating their hostility, insisted on appealing to the High Court, a move that kept him in prison for a few more days. Their appeal failed and it was 6 pm on Thursday 16 December when Julian Assange was released – just in time for the evening news.

He stood on the steps beneath the gothic archway of London's High Court, his white hair dazzling in the television lights, speaking across the sheaf of microphones to a large crowd of supporters as a light snow began to fall. I can be seen in the background, spoiling the iconic picture by looking at my watch (Julian *can* go on . . .). He spoke impressively, and after a week in which 'Cablegate' revelations had wholly occupied the quality press of Western countries, this looked like his finest hour. A car to Norfolk had been laid on, and I advised him to take it and lie low and write his autobiography.

I arrived home about 11 pm, and turned on the BBC's *Newsnight* program to receive an electric shock. There he was, in a dressing gown, clutching a cup of coffee on a garden seat in the snow, answering questions from a female presenter – 'Why don't you just apologise to these women?'

A couple of days later he was on breakfast radio with the BBC's top attack dog, John Humphries. 'Humphries handed him a shovel and he dug his own grave,' said one commentator. I caught part of this interview in a Bangkok airport lounge, en route to resume my family holiday, and had to agree: by giving interviews but refusing in them to answer questions about the complaints, he looked evasive, and attempts at a humorous shrug-off – 'A gentleman never talks about sexual relations' – sounded ridiculous since he was being accused of not being a gentleman. There had to be a convincing answer to what had now become an insistent question: why didn't he simply go to Sweden and face down his accusers?

When the judge had asked me that question at the bail appeal, I had had a readily acceptable lawyer's answer: he was entitled to object to a warrant that would curtail his freedom, and he stood on that right. So can anyone, but Assange was a public man, a leader of opinion and by now, by virtue of his power at least to embarrass every government with which the US had diplomatic relations, he was a force in the world; arguably (at least his supporters would argue) a force for good – for transparency and justice. There are few countries in the world that have, at first glance, a better reputation for transparency and justice than Sweden – why didn't Assange rush back voluntarily to clear his name?

There are a number of answers to this question, the first being that this will simply not be possible in Sweden, where all rape trials (including allegations of 'minor rape') are held in secret. This, so the 'gender prosecutor' explained to the court in a written statement, is so that 'the complainants may give evidence in confidence' – i.e. confident that their testimony, and any cross-examination that may undercut or demolish it, will never be revealed to the public.

This means, to those familiar with the Anglo-American tradition of open courts, that justice will not be seen to be done, and may therefore not be done at all. It means that if lies are told, members of the public who know the truth will not come forward, because they will not know that those lies are being told. In Sweden, only the verdict is published, and sometimes the judge's reasoning, but where the evidence has not been heard or published, it will be impossible to know whether the reasoning is reasonable. 'Publicity,' in the words of Jeremy Bentham, 'is the very soul of justice: it keeps the judge, while trying, under trial.' While it is understandable that efforts should be made, especially in rape cases, to comfort alleged victims, that can best be done by limiting questions about their personal life and (in certain cases) granting them anonymity. Otherwise, open justice requires testimony in public.

From society's standpoint, the Swedish practice is wrong – the public is entitled to details of the case, and publicity serves the deterrent purpose of criminal law. To deny open justice to Assange would not only be unprincipled, but absurd: statements by his accusers concerning his sexual behaviour, made in intimate detail, had been leaked to the media from the prosecution, published in skewed and selective detail by newspapers, and placed on the internet for anyone to access. No trial could be 'fair' unless it permitted the public to observe how Assange challenged that evidence, how he gave testimony himself and how his own witnesses testified.

There is another curiosity of Swedish criminal justice that will render Assange's trial unfair. There is no jury – only a judge and three part-time 'lay judges', who participate in and vote on the verdict. Astonishingly, they are selected not at random but by the main political parties and are, for that reason, very often retired politicians. As it happens, the major opposition party – the Social Democrats – has as its active members the first complainant and her lawyer and the policewoman who decided to issue the warrant. How could a member of that party judge him fairly? As for the government, the prime minister, the chancellor and other ministers in the coalition government all launched quite outrageous public attacks on Assange for criticising Swedish legal procedure. The very notion that he will be tried by superannuated politicians is unacceptable – all the more so as they will try him in secret, so any bias they actually show will be undetectable.

Swedish legal practice presents a further problem for Assange:

he will not be allowed bail. Are Swedish prisons inhumane? Yes, says the European Committee on Torture (which should know): in 2009 it issued a report drawing the Council of Europe's attention to Sweden's ill-treatment of foreign prisoners, particularly in Gothenburg – the prison where Assange is likely to be held.

The reality of Swedish justice belies the country's squeaky-clean image, that of a nice, neutral nation that has given the world such treats as IKEA and ABBA. A closer look – for example through the eyes of the novelist Stieg Larsson – shows a different side to this small country (population nine million) or at least a hidden underbelly. It has the highest reported level of violent rape in Europe, for example (a statistic that Amnesty International has deplored), and allowing complainants to give evidence in secret has not produced more convictions.

But Sweden must be saluted in one important respect: its courts (and those of several other Scandinavian countries) hold a genuine belief in the possibility of reformation. Thus a mass-murderer such as Anders Breivik (who killed seventy teenagers in Norway) can be sentenced only to twenty years, and those guilty of rape and murder and burglary receive much lighter jail terms than anywhere else. This partly explains a certain complacency about the quality of criminal justice in Sweden – it is merciful and collaborative, with a socialised system that provides every suspect with a publicly paid defender. But Assange's assigned counsel was handling two hundred other cases. Socialism is difficult to reconcile with an independent defence bar: there is not the adversarial practice found in Australian or American courts, and no tradition of challenging the state. The failure to challenge the continued practice of secret justice in rape trials is a good example of this acquiescence: most defendants are happy to have the sordid and brutal details of their behaviour shielded from public view, and so their lawyers do not complain. Even the bad practice of political appointment of lay judges had gone unchallenged in Sweden until it was criticised at the Assange extradition hearing.

~

It is rare to overcome an EAW. The leading countries of Europe agreed, sensibly, to make extradition between them for criminal offences very easy. All that is required is for a 'judicial authority' in one country to issue an EAW and send it to police in another country, who will arrest the suspect and, subject to any flaw in the warrant, or so long as that trial will not be flagrantly unfair, dispatch him or her to stand that trial. The technical points usually run at these extradition hearings would be unlikely to avail Assange: the British prosecution authority ironed out the initial mistakes and the Swedes ticked all the right boxes. They had, for example, ticked the box on the form confirming the crime for which he was sought was 'rape'. We could not complain (although we tried) about the fact that he was only wanted at this stage for questioning, or about the fact that he had already been questioned, or about the rejection of his reasonable offer to undergo that questioning at Scotland Yard or at the Swedish or American embassies, or by Skype.

The Swedes wanted him, and he had only two realistic defences. One would have to go to the Supreme Court of Britain (which meant another year or so in the UK) but was unlikely, ultimately, to succeed. The other *could* succeed on appeal, so long as the district judge found that his trial would indeed be held in secret.

The first of these defences was simple. The warrant had not been issued, as law required, by a 'judicial authority'. It had been issued by a prosecutor. To say that a prosecutor is a 'judicial authority' is a contradiction in terms. Every first-year law student is taught that judges must be impartial figures, as distinct from prosecutors – the more partial the better – who are employed by the state with the job of getting convictions. So what was Britain, the proud upholder of the tradition of judicial independence, doing treating a prosecutor as if she were an independent judge? Parliament should never have agreed, and so far as a study of parliamentary proceedings can prove anything, it seemed that British MPs really thought, when they passed the EAW law, that the UK would only enforce warrants issued by real judges. But this argument – important enough to require the attention of the Supreme Court – overlooked the fact that many states in Europe combine judicial and prosecutorial functions in one official and allow that official to issue warrants. Therefore the entire EAW system would be undermined if the first Assange argument was ultimately upheld. From the outset I rated its prospects at no more than about twenty-five per cent (and so it proved: the Supreme Court ultimately rejected the argument, five judges against two).

The only real hope was to prove that Assange's trial in Sweden would not be fair. This depended on a finding of fact from the district judge to the effect that all the evidence would be heard in secret. We knew that this was the invariable practice at rape trials in Sweden, although there was no statute that required it. I could hardly believe that the practice had never been challenged, either at appellate level or under the European Convention of Human Rights (which guarantees an open trial by independent and impartial judges) but that indeed was the case – one explanation, as I've already suggested, is that most defendants prefer it that way.

There was the additional matter of these politically appointed lay judges, who would have to be carefully watched: publicity was required 'to keep the judge, while trying, under trial'.

At the hearing, we called a retired appeal judge from Stockholm and a senior Swedish prosecutor who testified that rape trials were indeed invariably held behind closed doors. The district judge accepted that this was the long-standing practice, 'certainly alien as far as our system is concerned'. Crucially, he concluded that:

> any trial in this case would be heard by four judges, one professional and three lay. The lay judges are chosen by political parties ... the evidence will almost certainly be heard privately. There has been considerable adverse publicity in Sweden for Mr Assange, in the popular press, on the television and in Parliament.

This factual finding was exactly what we wanted, even if the district judge failed to see that closed courts and political judges were not merely 'alien to our system' but should be alien to all systems. His reasoning was illogical, and open to appeal. He said that 'if the Swedish practice was a flagrant breach of human rights, I would expect there to be a body of cases against Sweden confirming that'.

This is a bad argument – novel cases are brought all the time to successfully challenge time-honoured practices as inconsistent with human rights rules. Although there had been no specific case brought against Sweden, the European Court has made many rulings against closed courts in other countries. Even in terrorist cases, where witnesses might be at risk, the court has said that publicity is 'indispensable' and in a recent case against Croatia, concerning a public figure whose alleged sexual affairs had been discussed in the media, the court insisted that considerations of privacy or 'dignity of witnesses' could never justify closing the court doors, because it was in the interests of the general public that justice should be seen to be done. So the prospects of appeal success, on this ground, were very good indeed.

Meanwhile Assange, electronically tagged like a pheasant on the shooting estate in Norfolk, used the first six months of his freedom in 2011 to complete his 'Cablegate' work, dispatching information to ninety different countries about the corruption of their political elites, as detailed by US diplomats. He also signed a book contract for an autobiography, and found a friendly ghost (the writer Andrew O'Hagan) with whom he completed fifty hours of taped interviews. I thought this exercise important to humanise him, tell his interesting and often amusing Australian story, state his philosophy as unpedantically as possible and give his side of the Swedish story, since the allegations against him were being promoted extensively by those with whom he had fallen out, and would soon feature in hostile books and films.

To the frustration of his supporters, he did not much care about bad publicity, or if he did he would ascribe it to a world that did not understand him. He fell out with Mark Stephens,

his devoted solicitor, not over the quality of his representation but over its costs. Here, he had a point, because English
solicitors are the most expensive in the world, but he became
obsessed with the notion that he was producing an autobiography in order to pay his solicitor's fees. He received a first draft
of the book and then announced to his long-suffering publishers Canongate that 'all memoir is prostitution' – which in some
sense it is, but not in the commercial sense under which he had
been contracted. They published nonetheless, under the oxymo-
ronic title *Julian Assange – the unauthorised autobiography.*

He urged his supporters not to buy it – another pity, because the
early chapters give an insightful as well as entertaining account of
his peripatetic childhood, his time as a hacker and his autodidac-
tic learning curve. The contractual kerfuffle meant that the book
was not available for purchase by Steven Spielberg or others who
wanted to make films about him: they had to work from unsym-
pathetic books by *Guardian* journalists and a malicious German
sidekick whom Assange had fired from WikiLeaks.

I have read a copy of the original script of the film *The
Fifth Estate*, leaked to Assange before the movie even started
shooting, which Spielberg ended up basing on these two books.
Assange is played by Benedict Cumberbatch (and played well,
I am sure – he is a fine actor). But the script is crafted by the
writer of *Buffy the Vampire Slayer*. The 'Cablegate' story turns
out to be that of Woodward and Bernstein-style journalists, and
of one noble WikiLeaker (Assange's sacked sidekick) as they
struggle to control the megalomaniac Australian 'information
anarchist', intent upon 'outing' a crucial and courageous spy.

As Assange metamorphoses from charming hacker into
metadata monster, we are led to believe that WikiLeaks imperils
the world by helping nasty regimes identify and kill those who
would inform on their evil purposes. The message of the original
script was the message of the Pentagon – whistleblowers cannot
be tolerated because they put lives at stake.

Some invention is allowable in movies. I was so impressed
by the Oscar-winning *Argo* that I bought the book, only to

discover that the last half-hour of the film never happened. The nerve-racking interrogation at the airport, the Revolutionary Guards chasing the plane – all Hollywood invention. It might well have happened, however, and so was to this extent ethically acceptable. *The Fifth Estate* scenario could never have happened as a result of 'Cablegate', for reasons explained in the previous chapter: Manning did not have access to 'top' or 'ultra' secret sources – only to material that had been classified below those categories on the basis that it would not put lives at risk. *The Fifth Estate* will be propaganda if it propagates the lie that Assange has blood on his hands, and that Bradley Manning (who does not appear in the movie, although if 'Cablegate' has a hero, it is he) deserved the severe punishment (thirty-five years in prison) that he received. It may, of course, have been rewritten or edited to take into account the Pentagon admission that no lives were lost: if not, it should do more damage to Spielberg's reputation than to Assange, whose portrayal by an actor as good as Cumberbatch will make him more memorable than the movie.

~

The Assange appeal against extradition to Sweden was heading for the Divisional Court in London in July 2011 and then – if that court gave permission – to the Supreme Court in 2012. I had settled the appeal grounds and was quietly confident that Supreme Court judges schooled in the open justice tradition could not order him out of the country to face a secret trial.

This was the point, however, at which Julian Assange sacked his (and my) solicitor Mark Stephens, and I was surprised to read (in a left-wing Bay area newspaper in San Francisco, of all places) that his legal strategy had changed – he would no longer be making any criticism of Sweden or its legal system.

That meant he would no longer have much chance of resisting extradition, because the 'open justice' argument, allied with the politically appointed judges and the lack of bail, was far and away his best shot. But sure enough, these grounds were all withdrawn and his appeal went to the Divisional Court clothed only in technical points and the 'judicial authority' argument – the only point he was given leave to take to the Supreme Court after the Divisional Court turned him down.

Media reports said that his strategy changed in the hope that the Swedish government and the two complainants might be mollified and would drop the extradition request. This seemed unduly hopeful, for a man famous for declaring 'Sweden is the Saudi Arabia of feminism', and who had taken every opportunity to condemn, quite rightly, the country's justice system.

It was also reported that overtures were made on his behalf to the two complainants after this radical change of tack, but they and their state-funded lawyer (always available when the media wanted someone to attack Assange) proved unwilling to budge.

I haven't asked Julian why he threw away the best legal card in his hand, although people under pressure do have moments when the seeming impossibility of their position does produce a sudden collapse of confidence. At one point, for example, Salman Rushdie sought to escape the *fatwa* by reconverting as a Muslim – the worst decision he ever made, he would later admit. At any event, I was not party to this change of strategy – I had written an appeal brief for him on the open justice point and I thought it would succeed.

The attempt to curry favour with the Swedes extended to a *mea culpa* of sorts – his counsel at the Divisional Court described his behaviour to the women as 'discourteous and disrespectful' (although consensual and lawful), but this concession fortified his detractors in describing him as a 'sex pest' and an 'Australian sleazeball'. He also had to contend with the absurd theory, solemnly investigated by the Swedish police, that he was some sort of cult leader in Sweden on a mission to father as many children as possible, to be brought up on the generous child allowance provided by the state.

More seriously, withdrawal of the human rights appeal grounds deprived him of the best answer to the question 'Why don't you go to Sweden – you will get a fair trial there?' His counsel at the Divisional Court and another counsel at the Supreme Court argued the 'judicial authority' point well, but his final appeal was rejected. He was given seven days to pack before he would have to surrender to police, be placed in handcuffs, and be taken as a prisoner to Gothenburg.

A few days before the deadline, I met him and his rather gloomy Swedish lawyers at a farewell party thrown by Baroness Helena Kennedy. He did his best to be upbeat, giving a little speech of thanks, but his heart was not in it. I thought I detected fear in his eyes, the sort of fear I had seen in the faces of men as I had farewelled them on death row, although that might have been my imagination. He was not off to the gallows but to Sweden, and his loss of freedom would not be eternal – at worst it would last a year or so. His work at WikiLeaks had been completed while he was on bail – perhaps he could use the time to work on an *authorised* biography.

But if there *was* fear in his eyes at that party, it was certainly not fear of Sweden. It was fear of ending his life in an American 'supermax' prison.

Julian Assange has always believed that Sweden would be his gateway to America. The WikiLeaks cables fed this belief: in them, US diplomats boasted that behind its pretence of neutrality, the right-wing Swedish government was strongly pro-American. At the time of his arrest on the EAW, it was being advised by none other than Karl Rove – 'turd blossom' as George W. Bush so familiarly described his election guru.

In 2006, Sweden had been caught illegally 'rendering' terrorist suspects to the CIA without allowing them any court process, and had been condemned by the European parliament for so doing. Might America not prevail on this country to 'render' Assange as well? A grand jury had been sitting on his case since 'Cablegate' (November 2010) and it had subpoenaed the records of some of his associates. At Bradley (now Chelsea) Manning's trial, the prosecution suggested that Manning had made personal contact with Assange, the latter using the internet name 'pressassociation'. Since the grand jury continued to sit (and still does at the time of writing) an indictment could be delivered from the US, and an extradition request made to Sweden, at any time after he arrived.

Although no evidence had emerged to support the initial claims by some supporters that the rape accusation was a CIA 'honeytrap' – it seemed a case of cock-up rather than conspiracy – there was good reason to think that the Swedes would be happy to comply with any request from the US Justice Department. Any onward extradition would, under EAW law, require the consent of the British government, but that consent would certainly be forthcoming (although there might be a slim possibility of challenging it). Assange, in other words, had a not unreasonable fear that, once acquitted or else having served his sentence in Sweden, he would be re-arrested, and held for extradition to the US. He would not be a free man for many years.

~

I don't think that Assange pre-planned his walk into the embassy of Ecuador the day before he had to surrender. He had struck up a good relationship with President Correa when he had interviewed the president for a TV show the previous week, and he was doubtless aware of the possibility of asylum in an embassy protected by diplomatic immunity. Maybe he simply could not face entering that dark tunnel that had formed in his mind, down which he would go – to America and permanent loss of liberty.

Assange's arrival pleased the Ecuadorians, keen to flex a political muscle in Latin America, where everyone thought they had acted to defy the Yankees – and the US could not take reprisals or put on economic pressure because that would be an admission that they really did want Assange. It even pleased Correa's opposition: his new friendship with media freedom meant he might stop persecuting the local press.

The British government fumed and at one point wrote an ill-advised legal letter suggesting they were entitled to invade the embassy – nothing so united Latin American states in fury than this threat to violate Ecuador's inviolability and demean its dignity. The foreign secretary retracted, but kept the police, unnecessarily and expensively, on patrol outside the embassy. There was a large van parked illegally (but never troubled by parking wardens) that was probably scooping up conversations inside: it departed whenever Australians came to discuss policy formulation for the WikiLeaks party. (There are some secrets that even MI6 does not want to know.)

What seemed at first merely a gamble to delay the inevitable soon took on a life of its own. By June 2013, Assange was celebrating his first anniversary as whistleblower-in-residence, singlemindedly suffering the loss of his freedom of movement in return for retaining his freedom of speech. The UK and Sweden remained intransigent, the US was silent and the Swedish complainants showed no sign of retreating from their position that Assange 'needed to be taught a lesson'. (It did not seem to occur to them that putting a man in semi-captivity for nearly three years might be regarded as teaching him no end of a lesson, certainly about complying with any stated wish by sexual partners to use condoms.) However, they were entitled to bring Assange to trial, and the question now was how to bring Assange to the trial. Or at least to justice in Sweden that could be seen to be done.

~

Has Australia done enough to help? Assange, in his asylum application, maintained that his own country had abandoned him, but this was not the full story. Certainly its prime minister had declared him guilty under the *Crimes Act* when she should have known that he was innocent under the *Crimes Act*, but her mistake was pointed out and she did not repeat it. The consular help to Assange, after a slow start, was good, from the embassies in Stockholm and in London. But response at a governmental level left much to be desired. At one point I had a message from Bob Carr, via the high commissioner, to ask whether there was anything they could do to assist Assange. I reeled off some diplomatic initiatives, and added that I thought his chronic chest infection needed a specialist. The message came back from Canberra that they would be very happy to pay for a specialist, but would do nothing more. Assange declined this offer, thinking that the government would trumpet its humanitarian concern as an excuse for its lack of diplomatic initiative. So I arranged for my own specialist to see him, and fortunately he did not need treatment in hospital – his ambulance would have been chased through the London streets in a denouement that even Hollywood would not dare invent.

Should the Australian government be doing more to cut the Gordian knot that keeps Assange in Ecuador indefinitely? It has a duty to help its nationals in difficulty, without necessarily supporting the conduct that has led them into that difficulty. The failure of the Howard government, over five years, to utter a squeak about the unfairness of the proceedings against David Hicks was deplorable and although the two cases are different, the failure for almost three years to seek a fair trial for Assange in Sweden does begin to look like indifference. Our foreign minister should summon the Swedish ambassador and make four requests:

1. That on Assange's return to Sweden, arrangements should be made that would leave him at liberty (in the Australian embassy if necessary) until any custodial sentence imposed at the end of his trial.

2. That his trial must be held in open court.

3. That he should be tried by judge alone, or at least without 'lay judges' recruited from political parties.

4. That when found 'not guilty', or at the end of any prison sentence served on conviction, he should be permitted to leave Sweden and return directly to Australia irrespective of any extradition request from any other state.

This would remove the prospect that Assange would receive an unfair trial and would give Ecuador no basis for continuing its protection – so long as the US was prepared to stay its hand (e.g. by not having him arrested in Dubai or Singapore, the Qantas stops on his way back home). That would require a foreign minister with the gumption to ask our great ally to put up or shut up.

The US grand jury has been sitting since October 2010: the prosecutors should either discharge it, or else bring down an indictment. If they do want to put this Australian on trial, will they please wait until he returns to Australia and then make their extradition request, so that Australian courts can consider whether to extradite an Australian?

This would be an entirely appropriate way for an independent country to act in relation to one of its nationals accused by prosecutors in a friendly nation of spilling its secrets. As well as consular assistance, it can and should express concern when his treatment falls short of the minimum values that Australia itself promotes, certainly when they are in any case universal minimum standards: open trial, impartial judges and the opportunity for bail in the case of Sweden; due process and freedom of information in the case of the United States. Just as the Howard government should have spoken out for Hicks when his detention at Guantanamo became indefinite, so an Abbott government should be capable of asking the US to decide whether it wants to prosecute Assange as a spy, and, if so, produce its evidence to an Australian court once he returns home. Only if that evidence proves that he incited Chelsea Manning (or Edward Snowden) to make disclosures they would not otherwise have volunteered, and that harm done by those disclosures outweighs their public benefit, should the extradition to the US from Australia be contemplated. The High Court would then decide the threshold question of whether a US claim to haul Assange into its courts for conduct committed outside its jurisdiction is disproportionate and exorbitant.

Meanwhile Julian Assange cools his heels at the embassy, a prisoner of his own conscience. He suffers the slings and arrows of outrageous libels – enemies know that he has no money to sue for defamation and could not turn up in court if he did. But he still receives accolades, the highest of which was the decision of the editors of *The Simpsons* to make him – and not Mandela or Madonna – the honoured guest on the 500th episode of the programme. Kathy Lette was asked to contribute dialogue, so when Assange cooks a barbecue for Homer and Marge and they ask the recipe for his delicious marinade, he replies, 'I'm sorry, but I never reveal my sauces.'

If the Australian government fails to negotiate a solution then his pursuers may have to await a change of government in Ecuador, in 2018 at the earliest, before flushing him out. For now, he has plenty of visitors who leave their bicycles leaning on the embassy railings (it's the only place in London where you don't need to chain your bike) and take treats from the Harrods food hall to add to his menu. Although deathly white from lack of sun, there is little chance that this maverick Australian will pale into insignificance.

~

Postscript

Edward Snowden is in some respects more important than Chelsea Manning as a whistleblower – critics insist on the term 'leaker', although a whistleblower is just a leaker with something of public importance to leak. Snowden had some-thing of great importance, and he had none of the personal problems that beset Manning. He was a straight-talking and straight-thinking twenty-nine-year-old American, so straight that the only unusual fact that the media could dig up was that his ballet-dancing girlfriend had once pole-danced.

He was not in the military, and so could not even be court-martialled. He was employed by a 'contractor' – one of those large corporations that make large profits from secret work for the US government. He exposed the fact that PRISM and other programs run for the National Security Agency (NSA), in conjunction with Britain's GCHQ, had become a monitoring octopus circumventing privacy protection every-where. Any electronic communication could without let or hindrance be scooped up, and was if it contained one of 70,000 'key words'.

Snowden revealed a secret court where judges chosen by the US chief justice rewrote and restricted constitutional protections to allow spying on Americans as well as foreigners – a court that had only rejected ten of 20,909 NSA applications since 2001.

President Obama conceded that the revelations exposed a system that called for public debate, but Dick Cheney and John Kerry called Snowden a 'traitor' and the attorney-general laid charges against him under the *Espionage Act*.

But how to get hold of him, once WikiLeaks had taken him under its wing? He had quickly decamped from Hong Kong to an airside hotel in Moscow to consider his asylum options. Putin was prepared to allow him to stay, provided he did not antagonise America (which meant he could not open his mouth); Venezuela was happy to host him if he *did* antagonise America, but how could he get there? He booked an Aeroflot flight to Cuba (which as a consequence was packed with journalists) but at the last moment was well advised not to take it in case it was forced down in Florida. The journalists were left to take pictures of his empty seat and enjoy themselves in Havana.

The problem, of course, is America's view that international law, which emphatically asserts freedom to traverse international airspace, is binding on every state except America (and Israel). When the *Achille Lauro* hostage-takers did a deal with the Egyptian government under which they were allowed to take an EgyptAir flight to Tunis, the US had no compunction in intercepting it over international airspace and forcing it down in Italy. When America snaps its fingers, its NATO partners scramble in obedience. At one point the president of Bolivia's private jet was thought to contain Snowden – France and Portugal closed their airspace and forced it to land in Austria, where to the president's injured dignity it was searched by police. This too infuriated Latin American states, and more made asylum offers.

The Snowden saga brought Assange back as a force to be

reckoned with. Even holed up in the Ecuadorian embassy, he can still inspire confidence in the consciences of otherwise unremarkable people – to risk reprisals, loss of employment, criminal prosecutions and even exile, to get out a truth that they believe to matter. That is a good thing, so long as there are objective or at least measurable grounds for their belief, and a public interest defence to any prosecution brought against them. A public interest defence for whistleblowers is wholly lacking in the *US Espionage Act* and the *UK Official Secrets Act.*

It is remarkable how since 9/11 we have lost any sense of an 'Orwellian nightmare' about state invasion of privacy – only in Germany (with memories of the Gestapo and the Stasi) were there any serious public protests following Snowden's revelations. Much as I am in favour of looking for terrorist needles in data haystacks, I cringed at the British government's response to Snowden – its foreign secretary intoned that 'law-abiding citizens have nothing to fear'.

It is precisely law-abiding citizens who have had careers ended and characters besmirched by dissemination of secret state surveillance. Until there is real control over the collection, distribution and keeping of intercepted data – and not by patsy politicians or secret judges – law-abiding citizens will be at risk. Ironically, an early victim of NSA's metadata search machine was General Petraeus, the CIA director himself, found to be guilty – if only in American eyes – of adultery. How many others, in less exalted positions, do the secret spies now have the opportunity to ruin?

That, of course, is the evil that it is most important to prevent. The hitherto intractable problem is that no 'oversight' system has yet been devised that has held the secret state to account, because the overseers sit in secret and have security clearance at a level that precludes any critical thought about those who accorded it to them. Politicians, army generals and anonymous judges in secret courts provide no reassurance that data collected on law-abiding but inconvenient individuals, accessed under the excuse of looking for terrorists, will not be used to discredit or destroy their careers.

Americans do get testy about being spied upon without cause, but care nothing about surveillance on Europeans – accomplished in any event with the help of a member of the European Union, namely the UK through GCHQ, and DSD in Australia (remember Pine Gap). European treaties that are supposed to regulate data protection are in consequence useless, and anyone who really wants privacy should forswear every form of communication and go back to writing letters (in the hope that the authorities may have lost the knack of steaming them open).

The real irony of Snowden's revelations is that they have exposed a system under which state officials inevitably have access to vast amounts of personal information on individuals who by no stretch of the imagination can be described as terrorist suspects, and the only way to deter its misuse is to punish those who leak it either to the media (always avid for sensation) or to allied agencies of the state that might be interested in perusing it to the detriment of that individual.

Snowden has revealed that for all the legal pretensions of domestic and international law to upholding privacy as a human right, there is no hiding place. Our thoughts, whenever electronically transmitted, may be scooped up by the state and used however its guardians – its heavily vetted loyalists – determine. The *quis custodiet ipsos custodes* question – 'Who guards the guardians?' – comes back with the post-Snowden answer *nemo*: nobody.

QUIZINE ANSWERS

Round 1 – Australian History

1. Matthew Flinders. Trim the cat sailed with him
2. Lizard Island – see Preface, 'The View from Lizard Island'
3. Bathampton – see Chapter 2, 'Losing the Plot'
4. Windjana Gorge in the Kimberleys – see Preface, 'The View from Lizard Island'
5. A trick question: for all possible answers, see Chapter 6, 'Independence Day?'
6. Thomas Curnow – see Chapter 3, 'As Game as Tom Curnow'
7. Saxe-Coburg Gotha – see Chapter 28, 'The Queen and I'. Hence the only joke known to have been made by the Kaiser – 'Do they still perform *The Merry Wives of Saxe-Coburg* at Windsor?'
8. Yorkshire – see Chapter 21, 'Teach the Children Well'
9. 'Doc' Evatt – see Chapter 4, 'Doc Evatt and the Tolpuddle Martyrs'
10. Ezra Norton

Round 2 – Flora, Fauna and Fora

1. Neither can walk backwards
2. The wombat
3. The hippopotamus
4. The elephant

5. Shot by hunters
6. Ratites
7. Diarrhoea
8. The Order of the Thistle
9. Mt Macedon
10. Glenelg

Round 3 – Business

1. *Australian Financial Review.* Bonus point: 9
2. Newcastle, 1915
3. Tjuringa
4. Amsterdam, 1602
5. James McCartney Anderson. Bonus point: Juanita Neilsen
6. Pakistani
7. Honduras
8. The black box – see Chapter 7, 'In a Tasmanian Ferry, on the Thames'. Bonus point: David Warren
9. Architect
10. 'Never Mind the Bollocks, Here's the Sex Pistols'

Round 4 – Art and Music

1. 'Shearing at Newstead'
2. Frederick McCubbin
3. a. William Dobell; b. Joshua Smith; c. Garfield Barwick
4. c. Helen Porter Mitchell
5. d. Brett Whiteley
6. Blood
7. Rosaleen Norton. The 'magic' that restored power to the famous conductor's baton was fellatio
8. Sat-a-gee
9. b. Fire her
10. Beneath our radiant Southern Cross
    We'll toil with hearts and hands;
    To make this Commonwealth of ours
    Renowned of all the lands;
    For those who've come across the seas

We've boundless plains to share;
With courage let us all combine
To Advance Australia Fair.
In joyful strains then let us sing,
Advance Australia Fair.

Round 5 – Sport

1. Sir Donald Bradman's test batting average
2. Ken Rosewall
3. Scotland
4. Jack Gibson
5. The hop, step and jump, now called the triple jump
6. South Melbourne
7. Bold Personality
8. John Landy
10. Margaret Whitlam, née Dovey, in swimming

Round 6 – Literature/Film

1. Gregory Peck and Ava Gardner
2. Dirty But Clean
3. b. Sidney Nolan
4. Ethel Florence Lindesay Richardson
5. Tom Collins
6. Princess Anne
7. 42
8. Peter Kocan, who tried to kill Arthur Calwell
9. Barry Humphries
10. Mark Twain
11. Because it's fucking close to water

NOTES

Chapter 1
Beyond the Bicentennial
An oration delivered at Launceston Town Hall on 26 January 1988.

Chapter 2
Losing the Plot
This article was published in the now sadly defunct *Bulletin*, 1 May 2007. The *60 Minutes* program on Channel 9 aired in the same month.

Chapter 3
As Game as Tom Curnow
This appeared in a book edited by Peter Cochrane, *Australian Greats* (William Heinemann, 2008).

Chapter 4
Doc Evatt and the Tolpuddle Martyrs
Introduction to H. V. Evatt, *The Tolpuddle Martyrs: Injustice within the Law* (Sydney University Press, 2009 edition). The current historiography was reviewed by Tim Leonard, 'The Sacrifice of the Tolpuddle Martyrs', (*New Statesman*, 16 July 2009). Evatt's role in promoting the Genocide Convention is described by Samantha Power in her book *A Problem from Hell: America in the Age of Genocide* (HarperCollins, 2003) pp 59–60. Its progenitor, Raphael Lemkin, was obsessive about

his idea for a convention against genocide and Evatt was one of the few who recognised the need for such a law and then used his presidency of the General Assembly to achieve it. The case of *Chester v Waverley Municipal Council* is reported at (1939) 62 Commonwealth Law Reports, p 1.

Chapter 5
1901
This article was published in the Federation Centenary issue of the *Bulletin*, January 2001.

Chapter 6
Independence Day?
Extracted from *The Statute of Liberty: How Australians Can Take Back Their Rights* (Vintage, 2009) pp 51–6.

Chapter 7
In a Tasmanian Ferry, on the Thames
Speech delivered in 1996 to launch the 'New Images' campaign for the Australian government.

Chapter 8
Bringing Back the Bones
This is an extract from written submissions made on behalf of the TAC to the mediation that followed the court proceedings against the National History Museum in 2009. The (then non-binding) *United Nations Declaration on the Rights of Indigenous Peoples* has now been endorsed by both the UK and Australia (after Australia originally opposed its adoption). Article 12 maintains the specific right to repatriation of human remains, and holds that states adopting the Declaration should effectuate it through fair, transparent and effective mechanisms developed in conjunction with the indigenous peoples concerned. Article 11 upholds the right to restitution with respect to cultural, intellectual, religious and spiritual property taken without the free, prior and informed consent of indigenous people. The High Court decision in *Mabo* is reported in the 1992 Commonwealth Law Reports at page 1; Claude Lévi-Strauss is quoted from

his book *Race and History* (UNESCO, Paris 1968). Benjamin Madley's article 'Patterns of Frontier Genocide, 1803–1910: the Aboriginal Tasmanians, the Yuki of California, and the Herero of Namibia' was published in 2004, Volume 6, Number 2 of the *Journal of Genocide Studies* at page 167.

Chapter 9
Rabbit-Proof Fence and the Great Socialist Shame
This article was published in the *New Statesman,* 11 November 2002. *Broken Circles – Fragmenting Indigenous Families 1800–2000* by Anna Haebich was published by Freemantle Arts Centre (2000). There is an excellent critique of the eugenics movement by David Bradshaw in *A Concise Companion to Modernism* (Blackwell, 2003).

Chapter 10
The Trials of Nancy Young
A longer version of this article, which was co-authored with John Carrick, was published in the *Australian Quarterly,* June 1970, p 34 et seq, the original having appeared in G. Robertson & J. Carrick (eds), *Blackacre '68* (Sydney University Law School, 1968), which also contains a seminal essay by Jim Spigelman, 'Legal Services in the War on Poverty' (p 15). The *Australian Quarterly* article is fully footnoted in respect of the transcript of the trial in Roma. The *This Day Tonight* program was transmitted by the ABC on 18 April 1969 (reporter Frank Bennett); the ABC *Four Corners* program was transmitted on 30 July 1969; the second Court of Appeal decision, *R v Young* (No. 2) is reported in 1969 QLD Reports 566. The ABC's refusal to sell the *Four Corners* film to the BBC was reported by the *Australian,* 12 November 1969. On 10 January 1970 that paper reported the attacks by racist vigilantes on Nancy's newly assigned home. The best account of the trials of Rupert Max Stuart is to be found in K. S. Inglis, *The Stuart Case* (Melbourne University Press, 1961).

Chapter 11
Give Adelaide Back (Grotius on the Torrens)
Originally published as the Foreword to Shaun Berg (ed) *Coming to Terms – Aboriginal Title in South Australia* (Wakefield Press, 2010). The *Gove Land Rights Case* is reported as *Milirrpum v Nabalco Pty Ltd* [1971] 17 FLR 141 (Justice Blackburn). The statement of Rev. John Dunmore Lang, from a letter he had written in 1834, is printed in the Minutes of Evidence of the select Committee on Aborigines (British Settlements) 1837, at pp 682–4. Their quoted conclusion is at p 79 of the Select Committee Report to the House of Commons.

Chapter 12
For a Tumut Schoolteacher, Blown Up at Bapaume
This speech was delivered at Bapaume on 26 March 2011, at the unveiling of the memorial to Australian victims of the Hotel de Ville bombing. The Leon Gellert poem is titled 'These Men', from *Songs of a Campaign*, G. Hassell & Co., 1917, and was composed in the trenches in July 1915.

Chapter 13
You've Got to be Carefully Taught: Our South Pacific
'Our South Pacific' was written as a program note for the Australian Opera production, and was also published by the *Age* and the *Sydney Morning Herald* on 21 July 2012. James Michener's *Tales of the South Pacific* is still in print.

Chapter 14
44 Days
The television documentary that I wrote and narrated was directed by David Salter and researched by Lesley Holden. It was transmitted by the ABC on Anzac Day 1992 with a repeat at the same time the following year. Osmar White's recollections, *Green Armour*, were published by Penguin in 1992, and John Jackson's war diaries were self-published by his daughter Patricia (*A Lot to Fight For*) in 2001. The story of 'Australia's epic battle for the skies of New Guinea' is the subject of *Storm*

over Kokoda by Peter Ewer (Murdoch Books, 2011). The poem 'High Flight' is by John Gillespie Magee Jr, a Canadian airman who met his death shortly after writing it.

Chapter 15
Hicks in Guantanamo
This extract from the 2006 Kenneth Myer lecture, at the National Library of Australia in Canberra, was published by the *Age* on 17 August 2006. The *Hamdi* case, *Hamdi v Rumsfeld* is reported in 542 US 507 (2004) and *Hamdan v Rumsfeld* is at 548 US 557 (2006).

Chapter 16
Send in the Drones
This essay was published under the heading 'Drone attacks go against every human rights principle in the book', in the *New Statesman*, 13 June 2012. A fuller treatment of the subject of targeted killings is to be found in *Crimes Against Humanity – the Struggle for Global Justice'* (Penguin 2012) at p 640 et seq. The case in the European Court relating to the assassination of suspected IRA terrorists is *McCann v United Kingdom* (1995) 21 EHRR 97. Harold Koh's justification for drone killings was from his speech to the American Society of International Law, 'The Obama Administration and International Law', 25 March 2010. The Israeli Supreme Court ruling was made in the case of the *Public Committee against Torture in Israel v Government of Israel*, HCJ 769/02, 13 December 2006.

Chapter 17
The Right to Know
This lecture was delivered at the Wentworth Hotel, Sydney, at a dinner in August 2007 to inaugurate the 'Right to Know' campaign. Partly as a result of its work, which achieved some reforms, Australia had by 2013 climbed to twenty-third in 'World Press Freedom' rankings, although it remained below most European countries. The great US Supreme Court case of *New York Times v Sullivan* is reported at 376 US 254 (1964).

The Australian High Court discovered an 'implication' of free speech, in a constitution that does not mention it, in *Nationwide News Pty Ltd v Wills* (1992) 177 CLR 1 and created a 'responsible journalism' defence in *Lange v ABC* (1997) 189 CLR 520. The case that established a broad public interest defence for 'responsible journalism' in the UK is *Jameel v Wall Street Journal Europe* (2007) 1 AC 359. The European Court of Human Rights determined to protect journalistic sources in the case of *Goodwin v UK* 22 EHRR 123 – the quote is from para 39. Jeremy Bentham's justification for the open justice principle comes from his 'Draught of a New Plan for the Organisation of the Judicial Establishment in France' – see *The Works of Jeremy Bentham, Vol IV* (Tait, 1843), p 316. The privacy case concerning CCTV is *Peck v United Kingdom* (2003) 36 EHRR 41.

Chapter 18
Rupert the Bare
This polemic was published by the *Daily Beast* on 18 July 2011, under the title 'Questions for Rupert'. He was asked few of them when he appeared before the Parliamentary Committee the next day, although MPs did draw blood with the inquiry about whether the paper was still paying the legal fees of the hacker Mulcaire. Was News International still paying them? Rupert and James shamefacedly admitted that they had only just discovered that indeed it was. The next day the company announced that it was stopping payment, but Mulcaire took them to court and established that his extremely generous employment contract required it to underwrite his defence (*Mulcaire v News Group Newspapers Ltd* [2011] EWHC 3469 (Ch)).

Chapter 19
Lady Chatterley at Fifty
This essay, entitled 'The Gamekeeper had a wife also . . .' was published by Penguin Books in the 50th anniversary edition of *Lady Chatterley's Lover* (Penguin Group, 2010, p 303). The Larkin lines are from 'Annus Mirabilis' in *High Windows* (Faber & Faber, 1974).

Chapter 20
We Name the Guilty Men
This program was recorded at the studios of Channel 9, Sydney, on Friday 27 April 1984. The transcript was made overnight, but then the tapes mysteriously disappeared and the program was never edited or put to air.

Chapter 21
Teach the Children Well
This address was delivered to a conference of state school-teachers in Canberra on 28 March 2009. The head-teacher's letter is taken from Richard Pring, *Personal and Social Education in the Curriculum: Concepts and Content* (Hodder & Stoughton, 1984). Tony Vinson's report was 'Dropping off the Edge: The Distribution of Disadvantage in Australia' (2007).

Chapter 22
Tosca and the Ticking Time Bomb
This essay formed the introduction to the Australian edition of *Torture*, a book edited by Kenneth Roth and Minky Worden and published by Human Rights Watch in 2005. The cases from the European Court of Human Rights are *Ireland v UK* (1978) ECHR 1 (18 January 1978); *The Greek Case* (1969 11 Ybk of the ECHR 501) and *Selmouni v France* (1999) 7 BHRC 1. The Privy Council case that ruled lengthy incarceration on death row to amount to torture, requiring commutation of the death sentence is *Pratt & Morgan v Attorney-General of Jamaica* (1993) All ER 769. A more detailed analysis of the Torture Convention will be found in *Crimes Against Humanity: The Struggle for Global Justice* (Penguin, 2012), at p 330 et seq.

Chapter 23
Dr Haneef
This is my introduction to *Haneef: A Question of Character* (Halstead Press, 2009) by Jacqui Ewart. Judge Clarke's report

– the 'Clarke Inquiry' – was presented to the government on 21 November 2008.

Chapter 24
Under a Borrowed Mortar Board
Oration delivered at Sydney University on the occasion of the graduation for education and social work students, April 2006.

Chapter 25
The Great Charter Debate
1) Father Frank's Caravanserai

This article was published by *The Monthly*, issue 51, November 2009. The Brennan Report is available at http://www.ag.gov.au/ RightsAndProtections/HumanRights/TreatyBodyReporting/ Pages/HumanRightsconsultationreport.aspx

2) Statute of Australian Liberty

This is based upon the charter devised for *The Statute of Liberty: How Australians Can Take Back Their Rights,* Vintage, 2009. Chapter 8 explains the provisions and adds the rules and procedures necessary for its implementation.

Chapter 26
Creativity: the Tonic for a Nation
This is an edited version of my speech at an Australia Council/ UBS forum on philanthropy and the creative arts. It was published in the *Australian* on 23 December 2004. Richard Florida's book *The Rise of the Creative Class* was published by Perseus Book Group in 2002.

Chapter 27
All the Global Atheists
The Christopher Hitchens Memorial Lecture, delivered at the 'Celebration of Reason', the Global Convention of Atheists, Melbourne Convention Centre, 14 April 2013. Further commentary on child molestation by priests can be found in *The Case of the Pope – Vatican Accountability for Human Rights Abuse* (Penguin, 2010). Iran's human rights record and

prospects for its acquisition of nuclear weapons are the subjects of *Mullahs Without Mercy – Human Rights and Nuclear Weapons* (Random House, 2012). The ruling of the Human Rights Committee protecting atheists is *General Comment 22: The Right to Freedom of Thought, Conscience and Religion*, CCPR/C/REV 1/Add 4. The European Court of Human Rights case of *Sahin v Turkey* is reported at (2007) 44 EHRR 5. An internet posting of this lecture is at http://www.youtube.com/watch?v=OHJGhWeNSeA/.

Chapter 28
The Queen and I
This article was published in the *Independent* on 26 April 2011. The case that insisted on free speech for republicans was *R (Rusbrigder & Toynbee) v Attorney General* (2003) UKHL 38. David Cameron announced the UK's intention to change the royal primogeniture law shortly before the marriage and the New Zealand government stepped forward to co-ordinate support from the Commonwealth for changing national laws relating to Head of State succession. In the UK, the *Succession of Crown Act 2013* abolished male preference primogeniture and the ban on marrying Catholics, but the rule that the monarch must be Protestant remains, ridiculously, in place.

Chapter 29
Mea Maxima Culpa
The first of these articles was written for the *Independent* (11 February 2013) and the second for the *Daily Beast* (12 March 2013). They touch on arguments developed in more detail in *The Case of the Pope: Vatican Accountability for Human Rights Abuses* (Penguin 2010).

Chapter 30
The Law of the Rings
This essay was written as a program note for Opera Australia's production of Wagner's *The Ring Cycle*, November and December 2013.

Chapter 31
Farewell, Rumpole
This obituary of Sir John Mortimer was published by the *Guardian*, 17 January 2009. John is a presence in the early chapters of my memoir *The Justice Game* (Vintage, 1998). His authorised biography is by Valerie Grove, *A Voyage Around John Mortimer* (Penguin Viking, 2007).

Chapter 32
Václav Havel, and All That Jazz
This obituary was published in the *Daily Beast* for 22 December 2011 and the *Australian* (24 December 2011). A fuller account of our time in Prague is contained in *The Justice Game*, Chapter 10 ('Show Trials').

Chapter 33
Singapore's Lion
Obituary published by the *Guardian* on 7 October 2008. See also Chris Lydgate, *'Lees Law – How Singapore Crushes Dissent'* (Scribe Publishing, 2004).

Chapter 34
Michael Kirby at Seventy
Published as 'Your Honour', an introduction to *Appealing to the Future: Michael Kirby and his Legacy* edited by Ian Freckleton and Hugh Selby. The case in which I appeared before the High Court is *Gutnik v Dow Jones* [2002] HCA 56. Its result has been disapproved in America: *Young v New Haven Advocate*, 315 F3d 256 (4th Circuit, 2002) and its effect has been reversed by the 2013 *Defamation Act* in the UK. 'My life in the Lower Court' was published in *Blackacre '68* (Sydney University Law Society, 1968). Michael Kirby was recently appointed by the Human Rights Council to conduct a special investigation into human rights abuses in North Korea.

Chapter 34
The Case for WikiLeaks
This speech was delivered in the course of a public debate over

WikiLeaks with Philip Ruddock and Michael Kirby in 2011, and has been updated to take into account Bradley Manning's trial and sentencing proceedings.

Chapter 36
Assange in Ecuador
This hitherto unpublished reflection on Julian Assange and his current predicament was written in August 2013 for this book.

INDEX